P9-DWA-316

33
3
94

149560

N.L. TERTELING LIBRARY
ALBERTSON COLLEGE
CALDWELL, IDAHO

PURCHASED WITH NEH
ENDOWMENT FUNDS

Staging Howells

Staging Howells

Howells

PLAYS AND

CORRESPONDENCE

WITH LAWRENCE BARRETT

EDITED BY

George Arms,
Mary Bess Whidden,
and Gary Scharnhorst

University of New Mexico Press / Albuquerque

PS2033
A43
1994

Library of Congress Cataloging in Publication Data

Howells, William Dean. 1837–1920.
Staging Howells: plays and correspondence with Lawrence Barrett /
edited by George Arms, Mary Bess Whidden, and Gary Scharnhorst.—1st ed.
p.   cm.
Contains the complete correspondence between Howells and Barrett, in
addition to the original version of Howell' Counterfeit presentment, the
earliest version of his A New play, and a manuscript fragment of his Civil
death.
Includes bibliographical references (p.   ) and index.
ISBN 0-8162-1487-1.
1. Howells, William Dean, 1837–1920—Correspondence.
2. Dramatists, American—19th century—Correspondence.
3. Howells, William Dean, 1837–1920—Stage history.
5. Barrett, Lawrence, 1830–1891—Correspondence.
6. Theatrical producers and directors—United States-Correspondence.
7. Theater—United States—History—19th century.
I. Barrett, Lawrence, 1830–1891.
II. Arms, George Warren, 1912–
III. Whidden, Mary Bess, 1936–
IV. Scharnhorst, Gary.
V. Howells, William Dean, 1837–1920. Counterfeit presentment. 1994.
VI. Howells, William Dean, 1837-1920. New play. 1994.
VII. Howells, William Dean, 1837–1920. Civil death. Selections. 1994.
VIII. Title.
PS2033.A43 1994
818'.409—dc20   98–8856
[B]   CIP

© 1994 by the University of New Mexico Press
All rights reserved.
First edition

149560

To V. B. Price,
in sincere appreciation
for his unrelenting generosity,
and to Elizabeth, Angela, and Sandy

N. L. TERTELING LIBRARY
ALBERTSON COLLEGE OF IDAHO
CALDWELL, ID 83605

Contents

Acknowledgments

Howells' plays have been more neglected than studied in the past, perhaps understandably so given the importance of his fiction. Still, we are indebted to the pioneering scholarship of Walter Meserve, whose edition of *The Complete Plays of W. D. Howells* (1960) set a standard for our own work. The present volume, with its focus on the period 1877–1880, supplements Meserve's book; certainly it does not supersede it. As the notes to our introduction may suggest, we also profited from the chapter on Howells' plays in Arthur Hobson Quinn's *History of the American Drama from the Civil War to the Present Day* (1936) and the chapter entitled "The Literary Realists as Playwrights" in Brenda Murphy's *American Realism and the American Drama, 1880–1940* (1987). Both Quinn and Murphy discuss the texts of Howells' plays in fairly general terms. We were also spared considerable biographical and bibliographical spadework by the only two doctoral dissertations written about Barrett to date: Mark Bailey's "Lawrence Barrett, 1836–1891" (Michigan, 1952) and James R. Miller's "Lawrence Barrett on the New York Stage" (Tufts, 1972).

Officials at several libraries have granted us permission to publish the relevant letters in their collections: Raymond Wemmlinger, Curator and Librarian, Hampden-Booth Theatre Library, New York City; Jean Preston, Curator of Manuscripts, Princeton University Library; Roger Stoddard, Associate Director, Houghton Library, Harvard University; Thomas J. Culbertson, Archivist, Rutherford B. Hayes Library, Fremont, Ohio; and Jeanne T. Newlin, Curator, Harvard Theatre Collection, Harvard College Library. Literary rights to all previously unpublished material were granted by William White Howells, whose special permission extends only to this book, and V. B. Price. We owe special thanks to Wesley T. Mott, Michael Milliken, Lynn DelMargo, Margaret Shinn, Bruce F. Jaffe, and our friends at Scalo, where much of the business of this book was transacted. We are also indebted to Richard Peck, President of

the University of New Mexico; B. Hobson Wildenthal, former Dean
of the College of Arts and Sciences; Robert Fleming, Associate
Dean of the College of Arts and Sciences; and Lee Bartlett, former
chair of the Department of English, the University of New Mexico,
for their unwavering support. Thanks, too, to Connie and Jim
Thorson for their discussions of this project during the regular Fri-
day afternoon English department seminar; Carolyn and Joe
Osborn for their hospitality and interest; Sally Leach of the Human-
ities Resource Center, University of Texas at Austin; John W.
Crowley of Syracuse University and David Nordloh of Indiana Uni-
versity for their suggestions; Alfred Rodriguez; Beth Hadas and
Barbara Guth of the UNM Press; and Kate, Laurie, Fran, and David
McPherson for their spirited reading of *Yorick's Love* in the Jemez
Mountains.

M. B. W.
G. S.

1 November 1992

Abbreviations

Bailey   Mark Bailey, "Lawrence Barrett, 1838–1891" (Ph.D. diss., University of Michigan, 1952)

Harvard   Howells Collection, Houghton Library, Harvard University

Hay-Howells Letters
             John Hay–Howells Letters, ed. George Monteiro and Brenda Murphy (Boston: Twayne, 1980)

LB   Lawrence Barrett

LinL   *Life in Letters of William Dean Howells,* ed. Mildred Howells (Garden City, N.Y.: Doubleday, Doran, 1928), 2 vols.

Mark Twain–Howells Letters
             Mark Twain–Howells Letters, ed. Henry Nash Smith and William M. Gibson (Cambridge, Mass.: Belknap, 1960), 2 vols.

Meserve   *The Complete Plays of W. D. Howells,* ed. Walter J. Meserve (New York: New York University Press, 1960)

Miller   James R. Miller, "Lawrence Barrett on the New York Stage" (Ph.D. diss., Tufts University, 1972)

Price   V. B. Price Collection, Albuquerque, New Mexico

Princeton   Princeton University Library

SL   *Selected Letters of W. D. Howells,* ed. George Arms et al. (Boston: Twayne, 1979–1983), 6 vols.

WDH   William D. Howells

Introduction

Like many other critical clichés, the notion persists that the American dramatic tradition originated with Eugene O'Neill. The facts belie the assertion, of course. Clyde Fitch, Bronson Howard, Augustus Thomas, William Gillette, David Belasco, Steele Mackaye, and James A. Herne were famed playwrights in the late nineteenth century, as celebrated in their day as film directors are in ours. N. P. Willis, Thomas Bailey Aldrich, Kate Field, Bayard Taylor, Joseph Kirkland, and Joaquin Miller each tried to write popular drama, albeit with mixed success, and the theatrical impresarios Dion Boucicault and Augustin Daly wrote and produced dozens of new plays. W. D. Howells, Henry James, Mark Twain, and Bret Harte, the leading American writers of fiction, took time from their other literary labors to compose over sixty plays among them.[1] In 1912, four years before the Provincetown Playhouse staged O'Neill's *Bound East for Cardiff,* Howells announced that "now already we have a drama which has touched our life at many characteristic points, which has dealt with our moral and material problems and penetrated the psychological regions which it seemed impossible an art so objective should reach."[2] With the recent recovery of Howells' letters to the actor Lawrence Barrett and other primary documents long since presumed to have been lost—documents in the possession of Barrett's great-grandson V. B. Price and published here for the first time—a missing chapter in Howells' career as a dramatist may finally be written.

To be sure, the plays of W. D. Howells (1837–1920) constitute but a slender part of his oeuvre. More native than Henry James, more mannered than Mark Twain, Howells was the central figure and lifelong patron of a coterie of American writers, James and Twain foremost among them, who emerged after the Civil War. He joined the staff of the *Atlantic Monthly* in 1866 and assumed the editorship in July 1871 at the age of only thirty-four. Over the next decade he was a remarkably productive man of letters. While occupying the most influential editorial post in the country, Howells wrote such promising novels of manners as *A Chance Acquaintance* (1873), *A Foregone Conclusion* (1875), *The Lady of the Aroostook* (1879), *The Undiscovered Country* (1880), and *A Fearful Responsibility* (1881). During these years, too, he published some of his first plays in the pages of the *Atlantic*. After resigning his editorial duties in 1881, he earned a reputation as the preeminent American novelist, author of such works as *A Modern Instance* (1882), *The Rise of Silas Lapham* (1885), and *A Hazard of New Fortunes* (1890). Yet even in his heyday, Howells wrote dramatic literature, including comic opera, blank-verse dialogues, and one-act farces and drawing-room comedies with such titles as *The Mouse Trap* and *The Sleeping Car*. Nor was he merely an occasional or avocational playwright; in all, he wrote over thirty plays during his career. As Booth Tarkington later reminisced, these plays "began to be acted everywhere within a week or two" of their appearance, "and a college boy of the late eighties and 'golden nineties' came home at Christmas to be either in the audience at a Howells farce or in the cast that gave it."[3]

In the late 1870s, while still editor of the *Atlantic,* Howells wrote plays not for collegians on holiday but for Lawrence Barrett (1838–1891), one of the stars of the nineteenth-century American stage. A professional actor from the age of eighteen, Barrett founded a repertory company and toured the country, mostly performing Shakespearean drama, in the early and mid 1870s. Much as the ever-vigilant Howells later promoted the careers of such figures as Stephen Crane, Hamlin Garland, and Frank Norris, Barrett became a patron of the American dramatic arts. To enlarge his company's repertoire, he commissioned a number of plays by American writers—e.g., James Schonberg's *True as Steel* (1870); William Young's *Jonquil* (1871), *Pendragon* (1881), and *Ganelon* (1889); and George H. Boker's *Francesca da Rimini* (1882). Howells, too, seemed just the sort of playwright who might prosper under the right conditions. Barrett first contacted the *Atlantic* editor, as his letters attest, on 9 June 1875 to inquire whether Howells might be interested in scripting a play for him. Over the ensuing months, especially after Howells serialized *A Counterfeit Presentment* in the *Atlantic* late in 1877, the two men entered into a delicate literary and business partnership.

As both dramatist and drama critic, Howells acted as a catalyst in the development of the American theater. In his most sanguine moments, especially late in his life, the so-called Dean of American Letters could confidently declare that "the drama is distinctly a literary form; in fact, it is the supreme form" and that the "primal purpose of the play is to illustrate life or to reproduce it."[4] Such oracular pronouncements, reminiscent of Howells' defense of realism in *Criticism and Fiction* (1891), should not obscure another fundamental truth, however: Howells wrote plays for much the same reason that such actors as Barrett, Edwin Booth, and Joseph Jefferson staged them—in hopes of reaping commercial success. "For all their explicit hostility to marketplace valuation of literary work," Daniel H. Borus has concluded, "realists found it difficult to segregate art from the intrusions of economic life."[5] The man of letters was also a man of business. A popular play often earned greater royalties than did a typical novel or collection of tales, moreover. Harte once calculated, for example, that scripting a successful play was his "only hope of getting some relief to this perpetual grinding out of literary copy."[6] Twain congratulated Howells on the news that Barrett was to produce *A Counterfeit Presentment:* "I hope you get good terms out of him, & have drawn your contract from the standpoint that he is the blackest-livered scoundrel on earth."[7] Twain had received a thousand dollars a week for a stage adaptation of *The Gilded Age.* Barrett urged much the same mercenary motive on Howells the very day of the premiere performance of *A Counterfeit Presentment:* "Score a success my dear Howells, and try again—the next time for big *money*" with "a broader theme," a "bevy of characters," and a "stage full of incident" (letter 17). He echoed the point two weeks later: "Hurry up the Spanish play, and let me make you rich in Royalties" (letter 29). Howells heeded the advice in his adaptation of *Un drama nuevo* by Manuel Tamayo y Baus (who wrote under the pseudonym Joaquin Estébanez), which Barrett added to his repertoire under the titles *A New Play* and *Yorick's Love.* The melodrama was Howells' "greatest stage success" and earned him thousands of dollars, as Walter Meserve allows, but it was withal "a feeble and late remnant of the extravagant poetic drama that reached its height in mid-nineteenth-century America."[8] When William Seymour, an actor in Barrett's company, reread the script in 1916—"how the lines and business came back to me"—he insisted that "It *is* a splendid play—tho' a bit old fashioned."[9] Paradoxically, Howells—the foremost American realist, the champion of Zola, Tolstoy, and Ibsen—collaborated with Barrett in the production of romantic, sentimental, and even sensational drama.

The present volume, especially the extant letters Howells exchanged with Barrett, silhouettes the circumstances of this collaboration. All but three of their letters are published here for the first time. The chain of correspondence opens with Barrett's solicitous letter of 9 June 1875 and closes with Howells' note of condolence to Barrett's widow on the occasion of the actor's death in March 1891. The volume also contains the original version of Howells' *A Counterfeit Presentment* as it was serialized in the *Atlantic Monthly* and performed by Barrett late in 1877; the earliest version of *A New Play,* a complete and partially revised manuscript in Howells' handwriting in the V. B. Price Collection; a later acting version of the first part of *Yorick's Love* with corrections and revisions by Howells, also in the Price Collection; and a manuscript fragment in Howells' hand of *Civil Death,* his translation of Paolo Giacometti's *La morte civile,* submitted to Barrett in 1880 but never produced. This fragment, also found among Barrett's papers, is all that apparently survives of a play Howells scholars had presumed lost in its entirety.[10] That is, this project recovers all of one and part of another hitherto lost dramatic text.

More important, these documents also detail the frustrations associated with the collaborative process and establish the context in which both writer and actor attempted to accommodate the imperatives of the theatrical market. As a character in Howells' roman à clef *The Story of a Play* (1898) remarks, "Who would ever have dreamt . . . that simply writing a play would involve any one in all these exasperating business details."[11] Barrett continually worried, as his letters reveal, that local elections or Lent or other entertainments would distract or draw away his audience. On at least two occasions, he was compelled to retract or apologize to Howells for statements attributed to him in print. Whereas Howells decried the gossip, Barrett coveted the publicity. When the *Nation* editorialized in July 1877 that "one of Mr. Howells's comedies" ought to be produced and that *A Counterfeit Presentment* in particular seemed "to have been written with reference to a stage and a general audience,"[12] Barrett rather than the playwright hastened to announce publicly that a "carefully prepared version" of the play would be "acted during the coming season, and I shall have the honor of appearing as the hero—having purchased the drama of Mr. Howells."[13] The play opened to mixed reviews in Cincinnati on 11 October 1877. Two months later, in an interview with the *St. Louis Globe-Democrat,* Barrett related a self-serving account of the events preceding his "purchase" of the play: "One of the purposes of my career," he explained,

> one of the delights of my life, one of the cherished aims of my ambition, has been to bring to the stage the best writers of our country. And with that view I paid a visit to Mr. Howells two years ago, and invited him, as the rising American writer, to turn his attention to the stage, and to give us an American comedy. He doubted his ability, and I quitted him with the fear that I had not been successful. Two years later he brought me the manuscript of 'A Counterfeit Presentment,' and told me if I would act it he would give it to the stage, but doubted then its capacity, its acting quality. Although I was doubtful of its success dramatically, thought it too delicate for representation, I accepted it in the hope that it might produce better things.[14]

To publicize the play, Barrett here emphasized his own role as patron at the expense of the playwright. Twenty years later, in *The Story of a Play,* Howells would respond by satirizing a similar interview with a histrionic tragedian printed in a midwestern newspaper.[15]

In his comments on the play's genesis, too, Barrett exaggerated his initial doubts about the commercial viability of *A Counterfeit Presentment.* Like the actor Godolphin in *The Story of a Play,* he in fact waxed and waned for months over the prospects for success the play might enjoy on the boards. Sometimes he expressed his satisfaction with the script, while he othertimes feared it was too highbrow for any but the most cultured audiences and too brief to "fill out . . . a grand evening's entertainment" (letter 19). He also occasionally quibbled over the title, thinking it too long for a marquee and "*above* the crowd" in its allusion to *Hamlet* (letter 13). He repeatedly tinkered with Howells' script, adding characters and assigning the best lines to the roles he acted, proposing bits of dialogue and stage business he expected Howells to incorporate into the script, sacrificing Howells' suggestions about casting and staging for reasons of economy or to his own ideas of theatricality. He once complained privately of his "sense of being Father, Son, and

Holy Ghost" to the play.[16] In a letter to Howells on 5 October 1877, he brusquely dismissed a series of changes the playwright had proposed because he did "not think the situation in the last Act would be improved." A month later, he responded to another set of Howells' revisions in similar terms: "I don't like what you send me" (letter 32). In the end, Barrett staged *A Counterfeit Presentment* fewer than thirty times and paid Howells barely five hundred dollars for his trouble.

On his part, Howells went to extraordinary lengths to mollify the actor. He apologized for seeming to object to minor alterations in his scripts and repeatedly acceded to requests for major revisions. Not to put too fine a point on it, he was accommodating to a fault. Despite Barrett's reservations, he contrived a new act to be interpolated into *A Counterfeit Presentment* to prolong its playing time and hence increase its theatrical appeal. "[Y]ou will find me willing to create to the extent of my powers in making the play what you wish," he wrote Barrett on 9 November 1877. "[M]y design" will be "to co-operate with you" in making all desired changes, he insisted again three days later (letter 38). Ironically, the playwright-protagonist of *The Story of a Play* reflects bitterly upon the many revisions in his play Godolphin had required: ". . . everything he ever got me to do to it . . . was false and wrong." Tailoring a script for the stage, as Howells' character Brice Maxwell comes to realize, is

> a compromise all the way through—a cursed spite from beginning to end. Your own words don't represent your ideas, and the more conscience you put into the work the further you get from what you thought it would be. Then comes the actor with the infernal chemistry of his personality. He imagines the thing perfectly, not as you imagined it, but as you wrote it, and then he is no more able to play it as he imagined it than you were to write it as you imagined it. What the public finally gets is something three times removed from the truth that was first in the dramatist's mind.[17]

Nevertheless, when Barrett staged *A Counterfeit Presentment* before a distinguished audience at the Boston Museum on 1 April 1878, it was hailed as "the best American play yet written" and Howells was called to the stage from his seat in the audience before the final act "and greeted with cheers."[18] As the playwright wrote his father, "I never had my popularity at arm's length before, and it was very pleasant."[19] The Harvard philosopher William

James, who attended the performance, commended it in a letter to his brother Henry, the novelist, who agreed the dialogue "was certainly charming."[20] Howells thought well enough of the script to publish it as a book that remained in print well into the next century. As Brenda Murphy fairly concludes, the play "was about forty years ahead of its time."[21]

For better or worse, the same cannot be said of Howells' translation of *Un drama nuevo,* the next project he undertook on Barrett's behalf. In effect, Howells learned to pander to the demands of the temperamental actor. He promised "to supply any deficiencies you find" in the script (letter 81), "to make the play quite what you want it" (letter 96), yet even this generous offer failed to satisfy the actor. Howells strenuously objected to Barrett's unauthorized revisions in the play on 14 October 1878 in the sternest of all his letters to the actor. "[I]f you make changes in the plot or dialogue not submitted to or approved by me," he declared, "I cannot consent to your announcing it as my adaptation. . . . I refuse to father the work of any one else" (letter 86). Howells wrote his friend John Hay, who attended the premiere performance of *A New Play* in Cleveland on 25 October 1878, to inquire exactly what had been staged: "I haven't the least idea how far Barrett has let my work alone. . . . Is there a second part of the last act in which Yorick loses himself in the character of Count Octavio? And does the play close with a speech of Yorick's?"[22] As their letters and the partial manuscript of Act I in the Price Collection indicate, Howells was instrumental in the evolution of the text long after he first translated the play. In an interview in January 1880, in fact, Barrett praised Howells for inventing "the domestic scene between *Mistress Alice* and the *Manager,* which now opens the play. It is one of the strongest in the whole piece, and more than that it strengthens by the natural effect of light and shade, the tragic scenes which follow."[23] Still, the version of *Yorick's Love* (as the actor eventually called the play) produced in Philadelphia in January 1880 was advertised as "adapted by Mr. Howells and revised by Mr. Barrett from the Spanish of Joaquin Estebanez."[24]

Characteristically, Howells would claim little credit for the popularity of *Yorick's Love,* preferring to credit the pseudonymous author of the original Spanish tragedy. When the drama critic for the Philadelphia *Press,* in his review of its first performance in the city, wondered "How much of the play is Mr. Howells['],"[25] the author

replied with a letter to the editor of the paper, hitherto unknown to
Howells scholarship, that details his debt and merits republication
in its entirety:[26]

To the Editor of The Press:

DEAR SIR:

I believe Estebanez is a pseudonym, and I do not know his real
name. The play was got for me from Spain by Count Premio-
Real, consul general for Spain at Quebec, and I translated it with
such changes and additions as Mr. Barrett and I agreed upon.
But the conception and structure of the piece are so very essentially the Spaniard's that I always feel free to speak of his noble
and impassioned tragedy as it deserves.

It seems to me one of the finest I know, and I particularly like
the delicacy with which the intrigue is managed. The lovers are
innocent in everything but having confessed their love to each
other. This forms the strength and unique quality of the drama;
and the situation is treated with Northern conscience and
Southern passion. Hawthorne or George Eliot could not have
managed the plot more profoundly, while no one that I can
think of could have touched it with such force and fire as this
Spaniard. Beside his work in the play my own is not worthy to
be spoken of. If you should mention it again I wish you would
say that I have not palliated the intrigue between *Alice* and
Edmund at all.

Estebanez had the genius to imagine it as it stands, and thus
to distinguish it from all the vulgar intrigues of that kind in
which the crime abounds.

                                        Yours very truly,

                                        W. D. HOWELLS.

                                        Boston, January 8, 1880.

A year later, Howells again protested privately that "the play is *not
mine,* as many suppose, but is merely my translation and modification. Above all, it is the Spaniard's idea."[27] As late as 1916, Howells
insisted that "*Yorick's Love* is not my play, though I tampered with

a masterpiece in making some slight additions to it. . . . I translated it for Lawrence Barrett, who, against my entreaties, called it mine in his advertisements."[28] He remembered, "I somewhat disgustedly and disgustingly" adapted it, though "where I did not tamper" with the original Spanish text "the play is fine."[29] For all that, Barrett performed the play forty-nine times in 1878–79, its first season, one hundred and ten times the next year,[30] and he kept *Yorick's Love* in his repertoire until his death, last performing it in New York in February 1891.[31] The actor Louis Morrison revived the play in the mid 1890s,[32] and Seymour vainly tried to interest a theatrical or motion picture company in the play as late as 1917.[33]

However vexed he may have been in his earlier negotiations with the actor, Howells wrote two more plays for Barrett and outlined three others in his letters between August 1879 and February 1884. As before, the actor admonished him to "Be *commercial* now and think of the 'gate money'" (letter 114), in order to earn "Money and fame" with "a play of alternate tears and laughter" (letter 135). First Howells composed a four-act comedy entitled *Priscilla* based on Henry Wadsworth Longfellow's "The Courtship of Miles Standish," a project complicated by a published report (which no doubt originated with Barrett though perhaps a distortion of his remarks) that the novelist was collaborating with the poet on a play for the actor. Next Howells translated Giacometti's *La morte civile* for Barrett, who for several months in 1880 considered producing the play before finally deciding against it. Though unpolished, Howells' script—or at least the fragment of it that survives—is vastly superior to the anonymous English translation first published in 1873 in conjunction with a New York production of *Civil Death* starring Tommaso Salvini. Howells' version is more idiomatic than this somewhat awkward and literal translation. In his letters to Barrett, Howells subsequently sketched dramatic plots based on William Kirby's historical novel *The Golden Dog* and José Echegaray's drama *Conflicto entre dos deberes* and prepared a scenario of a play to be entitled *The Puritan*. In the end, none of these plots satisfied Barrett's requirements for a "*money* play." Barrett thought *Civil Death* too depressing and would "have no more horrors in [his] repertoire" (letter 132), for example, and *The Golden Dog* lacked in his opinion "the ruling passion of Love to make it what we want" (letter 135).

Collaborators and business partners, Howells and Barrett were usually on friendly terms, but they were never intimate friends. Their correspondence closed in August 1890, in fact, on something of a sour note, with Howells defending James Russell Lowell from Barrett's subtle accusation of snobbery. A quarter-century later, Howells reminisced that the actor had been of "an heroic nature, and ridiculous as well as sublime."[34] At Barrett's death in March 1891, however, he had pronounced a more suitable benediction: "No American actor desired so strongly as he to bring the stage and literature together," Howells recalled. "He loved them both, and he would have made any sacrifice to bring about the consummation of this, his chief ambition."[35] It was a consummation devoutly to be wished by each man. As their letters reveal, their marriage of the stage and literature was occasionally strained if only because neither of them regarded it as a marriage of convenience.

Although not all of the Howells-Barrett correspondence survives, 169 of their letters, telegrams, and postcards have been recovered. Of Howells' 67 manuscript letters to Barrett, 1 is in the Rutherford B. Hayes Library in Fremont, Ohio (#71), 1 is in the Hampden-Booth Theater Library in New York (#149), and 10 others are in the Princeton University Library (#39, 46, 55, 77, 78, 87, 101, 129, 136, and 152). Of the letters at Princeton, 3 have been published in their entirety in the second volume of the *Selected Letters of W. D. Howells,* edited by William M. Gibson and Christoph K. Lohmann (1983). These letters have been entirely re-edited for the present volume. The other 55 Howells letters are owned by Barrett's great-grandson, V. B. Price of Albuquerque, New Mexico. Some of these letters are damaged, either by tears or through disintegration of the paper. The editors have silently restored words and parts of words whenever they can be inferred from the context and have indicated where such elisions cannot be reconstructed. All 102 of Barrett's extant letters, telegrams, and postcards to Howells are located in the Howells Collection at the Houghton Library, Harvard University. Although these letters are all intact, we were occasionally puzzled by words in Barrett's crabbed or hurried handwriting. Nor were we alone in our puzzlement: Mollie Barrett once needed an expert to decipher one of her husband's letters,[36] George H. Boker joked about his "hieroglyphics,"[37] and the actor himself apologized to Howells for his scrawl in his letter of 13

October 1877. Still, we have transcribed Barrett's letters as accurately and as completely as possible. We have retained the original punctuation, spelling, and abbreviations of all letters, and our occasional insertions in the texts appear in brackets.

We have opted to reprint in this volume the original three-act version of *A Counterfeit Presentment* from the August–October 1877 issues of the *Atlantic Monthly* for two reasons. It is the first of Howells' plays that Barrett performed on stage, and it is less accessible to modern readers than the revised, four-act version that Howells published in book form, which is reprinted in Walter Meserve's edition of *The Complete Plays of W. D. Howells* (1960).

The script of *A New Play* printed here for the first time is Howells' original translation of *Un drama nuevo* by Manuel Tamayo y Baus, which he mailed to Barrett act by act in September 1878. Written on the recto sides of folded sheets embossed with a figure of the U.S. Capitol and the legend "Congress"—sheets no doubt obtained through Elinor Mead Howells' cousin Rutherford B. Hayes—the play consists of 138 holograph pages numbered consecutively and 12 loose pages interpolated into the text. Arthur Hobson Quinn reported the existence of this manuscript in 1925.[38] Meserve, who published in his edition of Howells' plays a handwritten script of *Yorick's Love* that Barrett had submitted to the Lord Chamberlain's Office in London in 1884, readily allowed that "a version copied in Howells' hand would have been preferable to Barrett's copy, admittedly a slipshod job," but added that he had been unable to locate such a version.[39] In editing the Howells manuscript for publication, we have endeavored to establish the text of the play Howells originally sent the actor, uncorrupted by subsequent revisions that appear on the pages in a variety of hands, including Howells'. We have been aided in this task by a copy of the play Lawrence and Mollie Barrett transcribed from Howells' original manuscript. This copy, in the Harvard Library (MS Thr 137.1), includes diagrams of the settings and Barrett's detailed stage directions and is complete in all respects save that in its final pages Yorick's speeches are pruned to his cue phrases. It enabled us to distinguish between the many corrections in Howells' hand in the text as it was originally submitted to Barrett and those changes (mostly deletions) made by Howells, Barrett, and perhaps others who tinkered with it later. To be sure, this text is not a polished version such as Howells would have published. He wrote Barrett as late as 22 April 1879, after interminable changes in his early script, that his dialogue "is not yet as I should *print* it."

We also include in the present volume another version of the first part of *A New Play* preserved in the Price Collection. According to a penciled headnote by William Seymour, "This is the act that I wrote for Mr Barrett in Sacramento Cal. July - 1879." This partial script contains numerous revisions in Howells' hand and familiar blue ink, as well as ten pages of interpolations, no doubt the changes that Howells submitted to Barrett in August 1879, to which both playwright and actor referred in their letters at the time. Howells' revisions to Seymour's acting text, a version at least two removes from Howells' original translation, basically finished the script Barrett would perform to the end of his career. Similar in most respects to the text published by Meserve, it is nevertheless a much different play from the one Howells originally translated, and we print in bold type those passages he wrote for it. Students of the American theater thus may now compare three distinct versions of the play dating from 1878, 1879, and 1884.

Howells' manuscript fragment of *Civil Death* in the Price Collection—a revised draft on half-sheets numbered 1–12, 35–44, 57–81, and 83–92—adapts about half of the Italian play on which it is based. After agreeing to terms with Barrett, Howells began to translate the drama in early August 1880 and completed the manuscript three weeks later, as he wrote Charles Eliot Norton.[40] Though Barrett paid Howells five hundred dollars for his work, Barrett's interest in the project apparently flagged when he learned that Tommaso Salvini was reviving the original play at Booth's Theater in New York in December 1880.[41] Howells was known to have completed the manuscript, but Barrett retained all rights to it and chose not to exercise them. Howells' play was thus literally buried in Barrett's theatrical trunk.

There it remained until recently. Like the vast majority of Howells' letters to Barrett, the manuscripts of *A New Play* and the fragment of *Civil Death* have finally seen the light of day after a series of serendipitous discoveries. One day in 1989, as a result of a chance remark, V. B. Price brought to our attention—and to lunch at a local restaurant—the holograph letters Howells had written Barrett between 1875 and 1890, the one he mailed Barrett's widow when the actor died in 1891, and the manuscript fragment of *Civil Death*. These documents lay naked on the table, without folder or envelope, through the meal, as we discussed our pets and the state of the world. Mr. Price invited Mary Bess Whidden to look around the storage room where he had located the letters. There she found a trunk lined with burgundy velvet and filled with letters, memoirs, prompt books, play parts, clippings, and photographs, which she spread on a table in the winter sun under a giant cottonwood, almost within sight of the Rio Grande. Several days later, Mr. Price brought us a plastic bag filled with another batch of documents and photographs from a stray box he had found in a shed. The very week we planned to complete this project, Mr. Price called to report that, in cleaning out this shed, he had opened a box he thought was full of crockery and found yet another cache of scripts that had belonged to his great-grandfather. At the very bottom of this box lay the manuscript of *A New Play* that had been rumored to exist—the original adaptation in Howells' hand. It was—both the material and the moment—the stuff of biographers' dreams. Suffice it to note that all of these fragile documents are now safely under lock and key.

A final note: George Arms, Professor Emeritus of English at the University of New Mexico and the most distinguished Howellsian of his generation, withdrew from this project in its final stages for reasons of illness. Professor Arms collaborated with Mary Bess Whidden on this book during the last two years of his life, and we inherited from him a box full of detailed notes and memos, including one dated only three weeks before he was hospitalized that listed the twelve footnotes that remained to be written. This book quite literally could not have been completed without his advice and assistance even in its final stages. We have tried to honor his wishes and his memory by seeing it through to publication.

Notes

1. Brenda Murphy, *American Realism and American Drama, 1880–1940* (Cambridge: Cambridge University Press, 1987), p. 51.

2. "Reminiscences of an Evening with Howells," *North American Review* 212 (July 1920): 12–13.

3. Booth Tarkington, "Mr. Howells," *Harper's Monthly* 141 (August 1920): 348. See also Brander Matthews, "Bret Harte and Mr. Howells as Dramatists," *Library Table,* 13 September 1877, pp. 174–75.

4. W. D. Howells, "The Recent Dramatic Season," *North American Review* 172 (March 1901): 478; and "The Plays of Eugène Brieux," *North American Review* 201 (March 1915): 407.

5. Daniel H. Borus, *Writing Realism: Howells, James, and Norris in the Mass Market* (Chapel Hill and London: University of North Carolina Press, 1989), p. 62.

6. Bret Harte to Anna Harte, 17 September 1889 (Bancroft Library, University of California, Berkeley); cited in Gary Scharnhorst, *Bret Harte* (New York: Twayne, 1992), p. 86.

7. *Mark Twain–Howells Letters,* ed. Henry Nash Smith and William M. Gibson (Cambridge, Mass.: Belknap, 1960), 1:180.

8. Walter Meserve, *The Complete Plays of W. D. Howells* (New York: New York University Press, 1960), p. xxv. Meserve echoed the point later in *An Outline History of American Drama* (Totowa, N.J.: Littlefield, Adams, 1965), p. 193: "Howells, the Father of Realism[,] . . . occasionally slipped from his throne of realism and cavorted with the romantics." Obviously, Barrett gradually corrupted Howells' original text in performing the play over the years, as a cursory comparison of the earliest version of *A New Play* with the latest *Yorick's Love* will reveal. Still, Meserve's comment applies even to the earliest text of the play.

9. Seymour to Milly Barrett, 21 March 1916 (Price Collection, Albuquerque, N.M.).

10. Meserve, p. xxiii.

11. W. D. Howells, *The Story of a Play* (New York and London: Harper and Bros., 1898), p. 148. In a subsequent preface to the novel, Howells acknowledged that it "was founded . . . upon several experiences of my own. . . . I had written one piece and adapted another [for theatrical production], and from the joint fate of these I evolved the story" (George Arms, "Howells's Unpublished Prefaces," *New England Quarterly* 17 [December 1944]: 588).

12. "Notes," *Nation,* 26 July 1877, p. 56.

13. "Correspondence," *Nation,* 2 August 1877, p. 70.

14. "The Stage," *St. Louis Globe-Democrat,* 9 December 1877, 3:4.

15. Howells, *The Story of a Play,* pp. 116–18.

16. Barrett to James R. Osgood, 13 December 1877; quoted in Meserve, p. 70.

17. Howells, *The Story of a Play,* p. 78. George H. Boker lodged a similar complaint in a letter to Barrett on 10 November 1886, as he was writing the play *Calaynos:* "For God's sake do not propose any rewriting of what I have already done at present! Your last note threw a cold, wet blanket over me,

from which I can hardly recover. Your proposed changes take away my heart to go on. . . . I cannot turn these dramatic somersaults, at a moment's notice, and you must not expect it of me" (Price Collection).

18. "Music and the Drama," *Boston Advertiser,* 2 April 1878, 1:9. See also "Mr. Howells's New Play," *Boston Transcript,* 2 April 1878, 4:3; *The Letters of Henry Wadsworth Longfellow,* ed. Andrew Hilen (Cambridge and London: Belknap, 1982), 6:348–49; "Boston Correspondence,"*Hartford Courant,* 6 April 1878, 1:5–6; "Boston Correspondence," *Hartford Courant,* 6 April 1878, 1:5-6; and note 2 to letter 94, this volume.

19. *Life in Letters of William Dean Howells,* ed. Mildred Howells (Garden City, N.Y.: Doubleday, Doran, 1928), 1:250–51.

20. *The Letters of Henry James,* ed. Percy Lubbock (New York: Scribner's, 1920), 1:60.

21. Murphy, p. 76.

22. *Life in Letters of William Dean Howells,* 1:259.

23. "Yorick's Love," Philadelphia *Press,* 16 January 1880, 5:1.

24. "Dramatic and Musical," Philadelphia *Press,* 1 January 1880, 4:4. The drama critic of the *Press* noted two days later that the script had been "worked over by Mr. Barrett and the author" (3 January 1880, 2:1); and in an interview published in the *Press* shortly before the end of his engagement in the city Barrett claimed that "a number of the situations were altered by Mr. Howells and myself conjointly" (16 January 1880, 5:2).

25. "Music and the Drama," Philadelphia *Press,* 6 January 1880, 8:3.

26. "A Letter from the Adapter," Philadelphia *Press,* 16 January 1880, 5:2. The letter was also excerpted in "Theatrical Notes," *New York Times,* 18 January 1880, 7:3. See also "Topics of the Day," New Orleans *Daily Picayune* (afternoon edition), 9 June 1880, 1:5. Howells echoed this letter fifteen years later in his column for *Harper's Weekly,* again observing that the play "united to one powerful effect the motives of Northern conscience and Southern passion" (20 July 1895, p. 677).

27. *Life in Letters of William Dean Howells,* 1:291.

28. Quoted in Arthur Hobson Quinn, *A History of the American Drama from the Civil War to the Present Day* (New York: Appleton-Century-Crofts, 1936), p. 70. See also note 2 to letter 127, this volume. At a curtain call during his London engagement in 1884, Barrett also thanked the audience for "your reception of Mr. Howells' play" (*New York Herald,* 5 July 1884, p. 9).

29. *Selected Letters of W. D. Howells,* ed. William M. Gibson and Christoph K. Lohmann (Boston: Twayne, 1983), 6:100.

30. James R. Miller, "Lawrence Barrett on the New York Stage" (Ph.D. dissertation, Tufts University, 1972), p. 156.

31. Meserve, p. 114. Regarding Barrett's New York productions of *Yorick's Love* in the 1880s, see also the *New York Times,* 13 October 1881, 5:3; 13 February 1885, 5:3; 27 February 1886, 5:2; and 31 October 1886, 4:6; William Winter's review in the *New York Tribune,* 3 August 1886, rpt. in *Edwin Booth and His Contemporaries,* ed. Brander Matthews and Lawrence Hutton (Boston: Page and Co., 1890), pp. 52–53; Mark Bailey, "Lawrence Barrett, 1836–1891" (Ph.D. dissertation, University of Michigan, 1952), pp. 182, 394; and Miller, pp. 159–63, 194, 200, 203–4, 225, 232, 239, 260, 277–78, 289.

32. Meserve, p. 114.

33. Seymour to Milly Barrett, 21 March 1916, 18 February 1917 (Price Collection). Among those Seymour contacted about reviving the play was the actor James O'Neill, father of the playwright Eugene O'Neill. Barrett had predicted in 1880 that, while he did not regard *Yorick's Love* as "the greatest play ever written," it would "live long after I am dead" (Philadelphia *Press,* 16 January 1880, 5:1).

34. *Selected Letters of Howells,* 6:100.

35. "Boston Letter," *Critic,* 4 April 1891, p. 184.

36. Mary [Mamie] Barrett to ?, 8 March 1927 (Price Collection).

37. George H. Boker to Lawrence Barrett, 25 May 1885 (Price Collection).

38. Arthur Hobson Quinn, "Tracking Down Two Lost Manuscripts," *New York Post Literary Review,* 10 October 1925.

39. Meserve, *The Complete Plays of W. D. Howells,* p. 112.

40. *Selected Letters of Howells,* 2:265–66.

41. *New York Times,* 19 December 1880, 7:2. The play remained in Salvini's repertoire under the title *The Outlaw* for the next several years (cf. the *New York Times,* 17 April 1883, 4:7).

Illustrations

Publicity still of Lawrence Barrett as Yorick, *ca*.
1880.

Steelcut of Barrett as Yorick from a studio photograph by Sarony of New York. Reproduced from the cover of *Harper's Weekly,* 30 January 1886.

W. D. Howells from a portrait by F. P. Vinton in 1881, engraved for *Century Magazine,* March 1882.

Marie Villa, Barrett's home in Cohasset, Massachusetts.

Barrett in his library at Marie Villa.

STAR THEATRE,

BROADWAY AND 13th STREET.

Doors open at 7.30,   ·   ·   Performances commence at 8.
Saturday Matinees at 2.

OPENING OF THE REGULAR SEASON.

Week of August 30, 1886.

MR. LAWRENCE

BARRETT

SUPPORTED BY

HIS EXCELLENT COMPANY.

Under the direction of Mr. ARTHUR B. CHASE.

Monday, Tuesday and Wednesday Nights and Saturday Matinee,
Aug. 30 and 31, and Sept. 1 and 4.

Mr. W. D. Howell's adaptation from the Spanish, in Three Acts, entitled

YORICK'S LOVE

CAST OF CHARACT 1S:

MASTER YORICK..........MR. LAWRENCE BARRETT.	
Comedian of the Globe Theatre.	
MASTER HEYWOOD, Manager of the Globe Theatre.Mr. NEWTON GOTTHOLD	
MASTER WALTON, Leading Actor of the Globe Theatre..Mr. S. E. SPRINGER	
MASTER EDMUND, Protege of Yorick...............Mr. CHARLES WELLES	
MASTER WOODFORD, Author of a new play........Mr. CHAS. M. COLLINS	
GREGORY, an old servant of Yorick....................Mr. BEN G. ROGERS	
THOMAS, Prompter of the Globe Theatre...............Mr. J. M. STURGEON	
PHILIP.... ⎰ Servants of Warrener, ⎰ ....Mr. J. L. FINNEY	
TOBIAS.... ⎱ the Painter, ⎱ ....Mr. KENDALL WESTON	
MISTRESS ALICE, Wife of Yorick....................Miss MINNA K. GALE	
MISTRESS DOROTHY, Maid to Alice..................Miss MIRIAM O'LEARY	

CHANGE OF CHARACTERS IN ACT THIRD.

COUNT OCTAVIO (Yorick)..Mr. LAWRENCE BARRETT
MANFREDO (Edmund)............................Mr. CHARLES WELLES
LANDOLPHO (Walton)...............................Mr. S. E. SPRINGER
BEATRICE (Alice)......................................Miss MINNA K. GALE

STAGE DIRECTOR .. ....(For Mr. Barrett).........Mr. LEON J. VINCENT

SYNOPSIS OF SCENES:

ACT L...Yorick's Home
ACT II...Yorick's Garden
ACT III.—Scenes 1 and 2..Green Room and Stage of Old Globe Theatre

BUSINESS MANAGER FOR MR. BARRETT..........MR. THEODORE BROMLEY
GENERAL BUSINESS AGENT FOR MR. BARRETT............MR. JOSEPH LEVY

The Orchestra, under the direction of Mr. HERMANN BRODE, will perform the
following selections :

OVERTURE....................." La Gazza Ladra,".......................Rossini
SELECTIONS............" The Maid of Belleville " (first time)........Millöcker
PIÈCE DE SALON.... ...."La Tourturelle,"....................Eilenberg

THURSDAY EVENING, SEPT. 2—**RICHELIEU.**
FRIDAY EVENING, SEPT. 3—**HAMLET.**
SATURDAY MATINEE, SEPT. 4—**YORICK'S LOVE.**
SATURDAY EVENING, SEPT. 4—**JULIUS CÆSAR.**

During this engagement Mr. Barrett will produce a revival of

RIENZI, the Last of the Tribunes.

LADIES' PARLOR ON SECOND FLOOR.

BUSINESS MANAGER.....(For Star Theatre).....Mr. CHARLES BURNHAM

The Pianos used in this theatre are from the establishment of MR. ALBERT WEBER,
108 Fifth Ave.

LAWRENCE BARRETT— RIENZI.

In tragedy the leadership of the American stage rests with two actors, Edwin Booth and Lawrence Barrett, and this season these two leaders have, in a manner, joined forces and will work together. Each will lead a distinct company and each will travel on a separate track. But Mr. Barrett will manage both of these expeditions, and it is the ambitious, incessant, indomitable spirit of this actor which having brought about this combination, will urge onward the complex and momentous enterprise it involves. Certainly there is no worker in the cause of the stage, as an intellectual profession, who excels Lawrence Barrett in high purpose, determined zeal and practical capacity for the noble tasks he has undertaken. He is the standard-bearer and he will bear it to victory.

Lawrence Barrett will come to the Star Theatre on the 30th of August and will remain there four weeks. His engagement ends on September 26. He will begin with *Yorick*— a characteristic performance and a part in which he stands alone. He will then present in succession *Cassius*, *Hamlet* and *Richelieu*, and so fill out the first week. The romantic tragedies of "Francesca da Rimini" and "Hernani" will occupy his second week. On or about September 14 he will effect a revival of Miss Mitford's tragedy of "Rienzi," and this, doubtless, will run till the end of his engagement. The old piece has been considerably altered and improved, and it will be garnished with fine scenery. "Rienzi" has not been acted in New York since the days of Wallack's old theatre, at Broome street and Broadway, where it was presented in 1857 with the elder Wallack as *Rienzi*, Mrs. Buckland as *Lady Colonna* and Mrs. Hoey as *Claudia*. The version then used was one that Mr. Wallack himself had provided.

Mary Russell Mitford's tragedy of "Rienzi" preceded Bulwer's novel on that subject and is not an adaptation of the more widely known story. It was written in 1825, although not brought forward on the British stage until October 4, 1828, when it was acted at Drury Lane, with Charles Young as *Rienzi*. A MS. copy of it was brought to America by Macready in 1826. The first presentation of Miss Mitford's play in New York occurred in January, 1829, at the old Park Theatre, when the elder Wallack enacted *Rienzi*, Barry and Peter Richings were in the cast, and *Claudia* was impersonated by Mrs. Hilson. The play was brilliantly successful at that time. "You will be glad to hear," wrote Miss Mitford—May 29, 1829, to her friend, Sir William Elford—"that 'Rienzi' has been received rapturously all over America. No play, I am told, has ever produced such an effect there. I gain nothing by this, but one likes that sort of rebound of reputation—that traveling along with the language." The phrase "all over America," to describe a bit of our Atlantic sea-board is comical; but English ideas of America have generally been mistaken and often are so still. Bulwer's novel of "Rienzi" appeared in 1835, and in the preface to the first edition of that work the author states that his novel bears no resemblance to Miss Mitford's tragedy, except in so far as both works relate to a love-intrigue between one of *Rienzi's* relatives and one of the antagonist party. A

play by Miss Ma Bulwer's novel, old Bowery TI splendor of scene 1836, when *Rie* Hamblin. At s spring of 1886 Bulwer's novel, Jonas B. Phillip old Franklin TI with John R. Se Alexina Fisher, in that cast. I revived at the P as *Rienzi* and N Fisher) as the I tractive. Miss of fine scenic di of Mr. Barrett t brilliant featur His sagacity as knowledge of h have been exer vious essays in tl and there is go prosperous resu Later in the se Mr. Barrett wil "Mercedes," by piece is publis its popular aut acted. Mr Be "Mercedes" wi Garrick." — 1,.

Playbill for *Yorrick's Love* during Barrett's New York engagement in 1886.

*En chd Ave. Opera House
Cleveland this. Oct 25th.*

... ... Drama in 2 acts entitled

A NEW PLAY

Translated from the Spanish, by D. W. Howells, Esq., for Lawrence Barrett.

...RICK, a Comedian in Shakespere's Theatre..LAWRENCE BARRETT

...st. John Heywood, Manager Globe Theatre, with Mast. Shakespere, 1603......J. B. Curran

...ster Edmund, Actor of Young Heroes, at the Globe Theatre....................Frank Weston

...ster Walton, Leading Actor at the Globe Theatre.......................................H. S. Duffield

...ster Woodford, Author of the "New Play,"...........................Charles M. Collins

...mas, Prompter of Globe Theatre...................................Charles Hawthorne

...m, an old servant of Yorick................. ....R. C. Hudson

...e, Wife of Yorick, and Actress at the Globe Theatre..........................Emma Maddern

Original Cast.

Playbill for the premiere of *A New Play* in Cleveland, October 25, 1878.

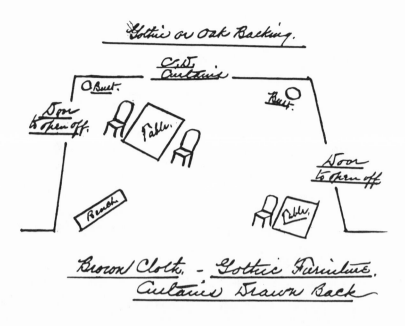

Stage settings for *A New Play,* Act I (above), and Act II (below).

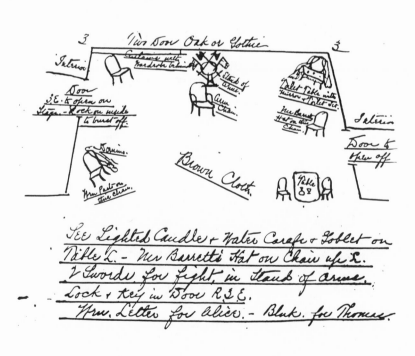

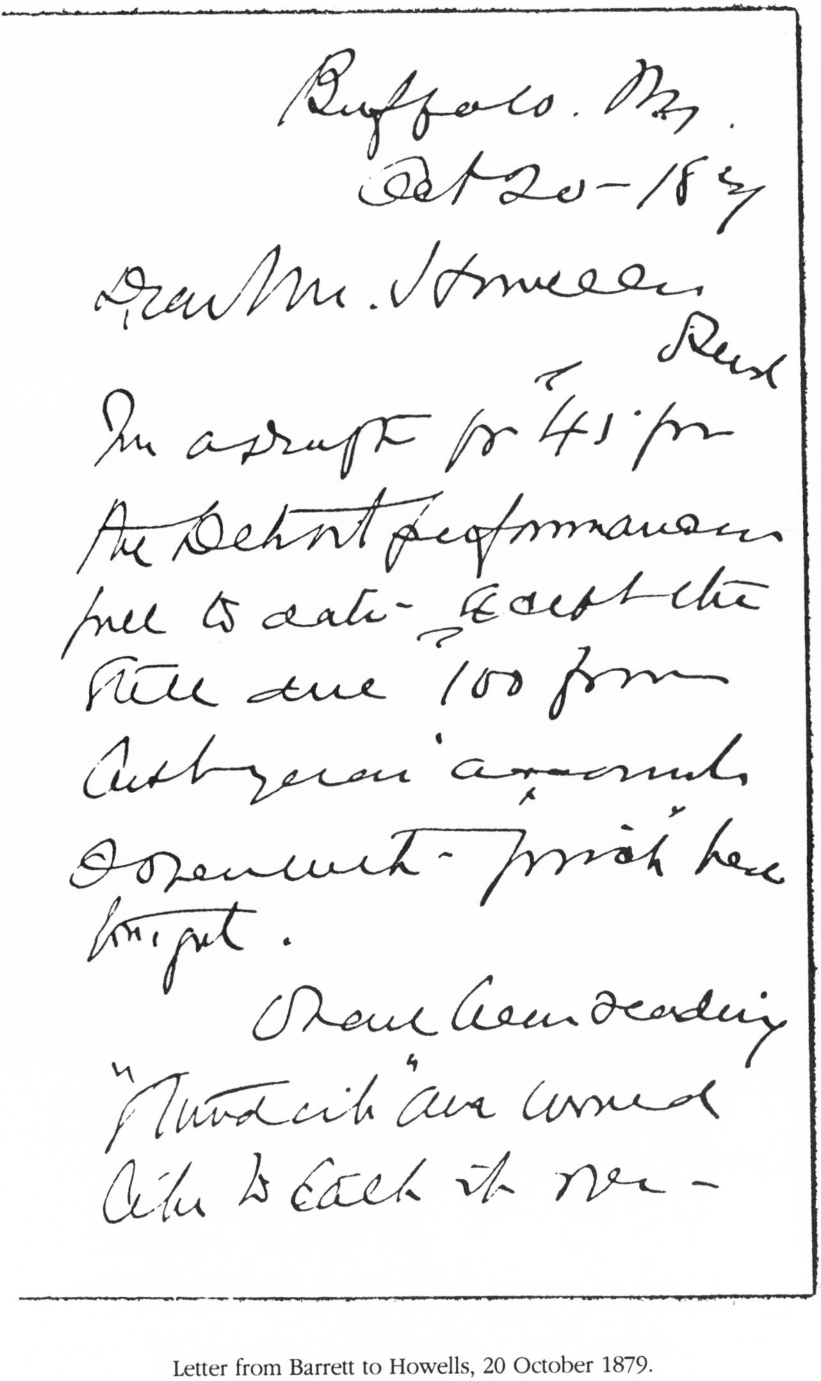
Buffalo. N.Y.
Oct 20–1879

Dear Mr. Howells

[illegible] a draft for $41 for
the Detroit performances
up to date— except the
still due $100 from
last year's accounts
[illegible]— which I have
forgot.

[illegible]
"Yorick" are coming
[illegible]

Letter from Barrett to Howells, 20 October 1879.

Belmont, Oct. 31, 1879.

Dear Mr. Barrett:

I am sorry to bring this
inclosed paragraph to your notice, for
I suppose you have already been
annoyed by it; but I wish to ask
you for a line of some sort which
I may send to Mr. Longfellow from
you. I can easily see how an
interviewer could torture your statement
that Mr. Longfellow had said he
would like to work over the poem with
me into an announcement that we
were writing a play together; but I
am not sure that he can, and
I am unwilling to seem to have exploited myself at his expense. The
play, of course, was never mentioned
between us except as something that I
was solely concerned in. This printed
gossip embarrasses me with him.

I have your letter from Cleveland inclosing check for $30, and tell-

[handwritten] ...ing on of the play's good luck there. I wish I had been there to see it.

Yours sincerely

W. D. Howells

1879

Letter from Howells to Barret, 31 October 1879.

Staging Howells

Letters and Correspondence

1. BARRETT TO HOWELLS, 9 JUNE 1875, MS.
(HARVARD, 2 PP.)

Cohasset Mass

June 9th 1875.

W. D. Howells. Esq.

Dear Sir,

I have the honor to enclose a line of introduction to you from my Friend, Mr. Fields—in obedience to my request—the object of which, I will briefly explain, in the hope that it may lead to an interview at your leisure, when I may more fully unfold my idea.[1]

I have long cherished an idea that the genuine *American comedy* has not yet been given to the public—and I think I have got the outlines in my head, out of which that Comedy may be wrought, through the genius of an American Writer. Familiarity with your writings has led me to think that you can do this work, and I would like to lay *My Material* before you and get your views of the subject—I need not tell you how valuable such a work, if successful, would become pecuniarily and otherwise, and I earnestly hope that you may find time and inclination to discuss the matter.[2]

If you please to appoint time and place to suit your engagements I will do myself the honor to wait upon you.

In the meantime, I have the happiness to subscribe myself.

Your Sincere Admirer,

Lawrence Barrett

1. Fields' letter of introduction (8 June 1875, Harvard) describes LB as a friend "whose high rank on the stage you are no doubt aware of" and ends "if

3

you can[']t write a play you are not the man I take you to be." James T. Fields (1817–1881) edited the *Atlantic Monthly* from 1861 to 1871; he had appointed WDH assistant editor in 1866 and was succeeded by him upon retirement.

2. WDH later recalled that LB had visited Cambridge to ask him to write a comedy with a Harvard student as the leading character ("Boston Letter," *Critic,* 4 April 1891, p. 184).

2. HOWELLS TO BARRETT, 17 JUNE 1875, MS.
(PRICE, 2 PP.)

. . . The Atlantic Monthly.

. . . *Cambridge, Mass.* June 17, 1875.

My dear Sir:

I have the plot of a comedy in mind which I believe will be just what you desire, if it is a cultivated American as a hero that you mainly desire.[1] The subject that you suggested has not recommended itself more strongly than at first, but I haven't dismissed it. —I wish very much that I had seen you play; for I could then work at the character with an eye to you as well as the person of the drama. It may be that I can soon show you the sketch of my plot; and yet it may be a good while. But please think of me as at work on something for you.

Very truly yours
W. D. Howells.

Mr. Barrett

1. The play may well be *A Counterfeit Presentment,* which appeared in the *Atlantic* between August and October 1877 and as a book on 5 October 1877. However, *Out of the Question* preceded it in publication (*Atlantic,* February–April 1877, and book publication on 25 April 1877); though never produced, WDH had finished it in September 1876, when Augustin Daly (1838–1899), the producer and playwright, was considering it (*SL,* 2:129). Still a third possibility is *The Parlor Car* (*Atlantic,* September 1876, and book publication 4 December 1876), also considered by Daly.

3. BARRETT TO HOWELLS, 24 JUNE 1875, MS.
(Harvard, 3 pp.)

Cohasset, Mass.

June 24, 1875.

My Dear Sir,

Your favor of the 17th has been set aside for reflection, and I now take it up for reply—. If one interview achieved the result of leading you into the field of Dramatic Writing, I shall feel satisfied, even if I am not regarded worthy of being your interpreter. I hope you will not fetter yourself by my suggestion, but select your own hero.— Place him in a good stage frame and I will engage to furnish the Actor. The hero of an American Play will not be difficult for presentation—my fears are not many on that point. A character containing mixed good and ill,—a combination of Comedy and Pathos, set in an American frame, written in such language as I know you will give it, is certain of success. I have not yet made up my promised plan of scene and character,—and perhaps, I had better not do so—it might only confuse you since you have[,] as you say, hit upon a plan of your own. If you see fit to submit your scheme to me I will gladly say the truth of it—and aid you in any way possible. I want to see an American hero before I leave the stage, and I feel that *you* can make him—I think you will not disappoint my expectations. Cherishing a pleasant memory of our recent interview, I beg to call to mind your promise to see me here some day—we can talk over the Comedy, and perhaps take a cod at the same time—certainly it will give me pleasure to offer you such slender entertainment as can be had at a plain home on the sea shore—till then, I am, My dear Mr Howells

Very Truly Yours
Lawrence Barrett

W. D. Howells, Esq.

Bret Harte has been with us a couple of days—left yesterday.[1]

1. Bret Harte returned to Cohasset later in the summer, taking a house there with his family (letter to LB, 22 September 1875, Knox College). According to

an article in the *Chicago Tribune* (4 July 1876, 7:1–2), Harte was under considerable pressure from Stuart Robson (1836–1903), a popular comic actor, and from LB to complete *Two Men of Sandy Bar,* which was to have its premiere at Hooley's Theatre in Chicago on 18 July 1876. Robson had paid Harte $3,000 in advance, with $3,000 more to be paid in royalties.

4. BARRETT TO HOWELLS, 13 MAY 1877, MS.
(HARVARD, 1 P.)

Marie Villa.

Cohasset.

May 13, 1877.

Dear Mr. Howells,

I am happy to hear that you have written a Comedy, and I "dare swear" it is a good one.[1] It will give me great pleasure to read it. Will you send the "precious treasure" here or bring it—or shall I go to you, or what? Awaiting your reply.

Yours Very Sincerely,

Lawrence Barrett

W. D. Howells Esq.

1. Probably LB had heard the news from James R. Osgood, who played a part in the collaboration. Osgood (1836–1892), who became WDH's publisher in 1872 with *Their Wedding Journey,* frequently advised WDH on his literary productions and subsequently issued *A Counterfeit Presentment* as a book. Though his reply is missing, as frequently happens with the 1877 letters before mid-October, WDH chose to go to Cohasset, as is clear from LB's next letter.

5. BARRETT TO HOWELLS, 17 MAY 1877, MS.
(HARVARD, 1 P.)

Marie Villa.

Cohasset.

May 17, 1877.

Dear Mr. Howells,

If the weather is fair on Tuesday next I will expect you—

take the Old Colony train at 7-something in the morning and eat your breakfast here.— Then we can have a Comedy—any of it—and you *can* return at 4 P.M. Will this do?— I wish to take you on the water if the day be fair.— Answer if this will serve.

Yours Very Truly,

Lawrence Barrett

6. BARRETT TO HOWELLS, 14 JUNE 1877, MS.
(HARVARD, 2 PP.)

Marie Villa.

Cohasset.

June 14, [18]77

Dear Mr. Howells,

The sheets came to hand this day. I have read the Play over this evening, and I like it as well as ever,—perhaps a little better. It will not make a deep sensation, possibly, but it will strike the cultivated people and do well, if I can only make myself into dear crusty Bartlett. Keep at the title question— "Sport of Chance" is pretty near it.[1] So is "For His Own Sake," but we shall do still better.

I shall make an acting copy and send it to you to read, with such theatrical suggestions as come to me, all within the next few weeks.[2]

Should you drop this way, you will find Osgood on my porch smoking his Havana, at almost any hour of the day, to my great pleasure. Join us there.

I hope you will have a pleasant vacation.

Very Sincerely Yours,

Lawrence Barrett

1. Since the first installment of the play did not appear until the July issue of the *Atlantic,* published in mid-June, the sheets sent by WDH were surely proofs—and not only for this installment but for the whole play. As will become evident, LB's dislike of the title persisted as long as he presented the play.

2. Though WDH's printed plays lack technical stage directions, they con-

tain frequent observations on scenes and characters. As he wrote John Hay on 22 February 1877 when *Out of the Question* was appearing in the *Atlantic,* "The play . . . seems to me to prove that there is a middle form between narrative and drama, which may be developed into something very pleasant to the reader, and convenient to the fictionist" (*Hay-Howells Letters,* p. 24). Meserve comments that WDH "foreshadowed Shaw and Barrie with his literary stage directions and took considerable pride in this part of his playwriting" (p. 34).

7. BARRETT TO HOWELLS, 1 JULY 1877, MS.
(HARVARD, 2 PP.)

Marie Villa.

Cohasset.

July 1, 1877

My Dear Mr. Howells

I have so far progressed with the nameless Comedy that I am ready for an interview with the Author.— Whenever your other affairs call you towards Boston—please take a night for this place—be my guest and "let me wring your heart"—by showing you how cruelly an Actor can "slash out" lovely scenes of composition.

I can house you at any time—so take your own time.

Very Sincerely Yours

Lawrence Barrett

W. D. Howells Esq

P.S. I have written something upon the life of "Edwin Forrest" apropos of Alger's Biography. May I send it to you?

8. BARRETT TO HOWELLS, 5 JULY 1877, MS.
(HARVARD, 3 PP.)

Marie Villa.

Cohasset.

July 5, [1877]

My Dear Mr. Howells,

I send you my article on "Edwin Forrest," which was drawn from me after reading Alger's "Life." I have *some* fame to lose and prefer to have the truth from your pen than from the Press generally, after publication. If you think it unworthy of the "Atlantic" (as I know it must be) then tell me if it will injure me to place it in the "Galaxy."[1] You can alter or amend as you choose, but be candid and don't spare me. I can stand a good deal of punishment, be assured. I think you will see why I wrote it. It seemed very good to me at first, but now I am out of concert with it and had not Osgood encouraged me you would never have seen it. I am satisfied there are places where I am attitudinizing—cut all that out if you please—or send it back if you please—only don't flatter me as if I were aiming at authorship and were oversensitive. I can't afford to be ridiculous, but if it will do, I should be delighted to have it in an early number of the "Atlantic." Do you see what I am aiming at? Come as soon as you can conveniently; as I want a long business talk with you on the play—and the sooner you are at the amendments the sooner I can begin to study the part of Bartlett.

Mr. Aldrich is here at the Anthony's.[2] We are becoming a poetic neighborhood, are we not? I met Msrs Longfellow, Emerson and Holmes at the Hayes dinner as you saw, perhaps, and am just enchanted.[3] I am not yet *auteur genius*, but I am

Very Truly Yours,

Lawrence Barrett

1. LB's article entitled "Edwin Forrest, an Actor's Estimate" appeared several months later in *Galaxy* (vol. 24 [October 1877]: 526–34). For a description of the composition and approach of Alger's *Life of Edwin Forrest,* a "pulpit point of view" in contrast with LB's "actor's estimate," see Gary Scharnhorst, *A Literary Biography of William Rounseville Alger* (Lewiston, N.Y.: Mellen, 1990), pp. 114–21. LB may have met Alger (1822–1905) before writing the review or at least heard him preach; he attended Alger's Church of the Messiah in Denver at least once in 1879.

2. Thomas Bailey Aldrich (1836–1907), poet and novelist, became a friend
of LB's as he already was of WDH's. At one time, Barrett considered producing
a play by Aldrich. Andrew V. S. Anthony (1835–1906) also was associated with
Boston publishing circles as a wood engraver and book designer.

3. Rutherford B. Hayes (1822–1893), the president of the United States,
received an LL.D. from Harvard on 27 June 1877, which he had attended as a
law student. He was also the guest of honor at a banquet in Boston on June
26.

9. BARRETT TO HOWELLS, 17 JULY 1877, MS.
(HARVARD, 3 PP.)

Marie Villa.

Cohasset.

July 17 — [1877]

Dear Mr. Howells,

I send you the additions you requested for the Forrest
article. If they are worthy, you will place them wherever they
will best appear, and any finish or alteration you may deem
necessary—pray make, and don't fear to wound me—

The thoughtful present to my little daughter was very
graceful in you.[1] It gave her great satisfaction and a second
Birthday. The "Napoleon" is taking shape in my imagination,
and you need not be surprised if I submit shortly a pretty
synopsis.[2] If you adapt the character and can give time to the
work I am certain it will be a grand thing. In taking the *youth*
of the man we are allowed to invent any fine interest we
please, and he will fit almost any romantic garment,—so long
as it does not violate the history or interfere with the
Josephine affair—pray keep it in your mind—and if not that,
then let your brain dwell upon some other story.

You left behind you here your night-gown. It will be forwarded by Express— Our first thought was to keep it, and
make it a good excuse for another visit, but we fear you
would count the sacrifice too great—so it must go by Express—

My wife joins me in kind remembrances. So do the children—upon whom you made a deep impression— The

Anthonys and Osgood are well, suffer[ing] only with the heat, and I am, dear Sir,

Very Sincerely Yours,

Lawrence Barrett

1. LB's youngest daughter was Milly, born in 1869. At this time the Howells family was summering on Conanicut Island in Narragansett Bay just west of Newport, but WDH often returned to Cambridge and vicinity.

2. As LB notes in a letter a few months later, he had a "Napoleon mania," though as far as is known it never resulted in a play written by or for him. See also his postcard to WDH of 28 July 1877.

10. BARRETT TO HOWELLS, 19 JULY 1877, MS.
(HARVARD, 4 PP.)

Marie Villa.

Cohasset.

July 19 — [1877]

My Dear Mr. Howells,

I have yours of Yesterday. I rely upon a copy of the "Atlantic" for your "business" of the play.[1] I shall find it there *in full*—and can give it the *stage* features in the blank leaves.

Your letter has confirmed a thought which has haunted me of late—making me "all over prickles" when it is upon me. I need not "refer to Osgood"—I am convinced that the "dear dailies" would say just what you think they would say—and I am resolved to avoid it.[2] I never hoped for more than your opinion as to the propriety of printing my article—and as you have said it will do—I am content—but it must not appear in the "Atlantic"— If you will kindly touch it where needed and return [it] to me, it can go into the "Galaxy," and the Play can stand, as it has always stood, upon its merits. I shall sleep in peace and still be deeply indebted to you. There! a great load is off my mind, and we have defeated the journalists of every class— I am anxious to see what you have done to the play. Don't forget the music for the Serenade, have it "catchy"—but not too difficult— I sing—but not professionally above criticism—and I want to be at the learning [of] it.[3]

The little Book is a great success. Milly will have it by heart
in a week— All join me in kind regards, and I am,

Very Sincerely Yours,

Lawrence Barrett

P.S. I have already a Lady for Constance, in my regular Company.[4]

1. Here LB distinguishes between WDH's descriptions in his plays and the
practicalities of staging.

2. LB evidently refers to a letter from WDH that anticipated criticism of the
editor of the *Atlantic* publishing a review by the actor who was to produce a
play by him. Although *Atlantic* reviews and a few articles were unsigned, their
authorship was usually an open secret, with frequent identifications in news-
papers.

3. The song, entitled "Romance," appears in the final act. No identification
of the composer of the music has been made.

4. Ellen Cummins (sometimes Cummens) appeared in a half-dozen plays in
New York and Brooklyn between 1878 and 1883 and once in 1887; she was a
member of LB's regular company in New York and Brooklyn in April–May
1878 and was with the company in its 1877–78 tour, playing the part of
Constance in *A Counterfeit Presentment*. She played the part of Alice in the
same play with LB at the Park Theatre in Brooklyn in April 1880 and at the
Park Theatre's one-month presentation of *Yorick's Love* in New York between
20 December 1880 and 15 January 1881.

WDH had evidently written LB that he was uneasy about the casting of the
female lead in the play. As he wrote Charles Eliot Norton on 13 August 1877,
"You have seen perhaps that my new comedy is to be played. The actor
professes great faith in its success; but I profess to wait and see. If some
actress of intuition and sympathy could be found for Constance I should feel
safer about it" (quoted in Meserve, p. 69).

11. BARRETT TO HOWELLS, 25 JULY 1877,[1]
MS. (HARVARD, POSTCARD)

Cohasset

W. D. Howells—Esq.

P.O. Box 160

Newport R.I.

Package received—both those of Thursday last and yesterday— The work will now stand— Don't fail to return my
Forrest when you have touched it for me.

L.B.

1. This card is dated by the postmark of the stamp.

12. BARRETT TO HOWELLS, 28 JULY 1877,[1]
MS. (Harvard, postcard)

Cohasset

W. D. Howells,

P.O. Box 160

Newport R.I.

Package received— If I publish I will ask you to look over
proofs—have accepted all your amendments. Send sketch of
your idea for play—I am thinking of the Bonaparte— Amendments to play excellent— Don't forget the title.

L.B.

1. This card is dated by the postmark of the stamp.

13. BARRETT TO HOWELLS, 3 AUGUST 1877,
MS. (Harvard, 3 pp.)

Marie Villa.

Cohasset.

Aug 3 — [1877]

Dear Mr. Howells,

The Play is now in the Binder's hands—three volumes—and
I am beginning to "put on" Bartlett— I hope he will fit me— I
ask you to send me a diagram of the Parlor at Ponkwasset—
with the openings merely—and where you thought of placing
the furniture— That will not be arbitrary—of course, as I may
be obliged to invent new openings or abolish old ones—when
the characters begin to move before me—but I want your idea
to start with.[1]

You may also give me your idea of the dress of Bartlett—
and of Cummings—the rest can manage alone— I have sent
for Photographs of several of our Celebrated Painters—to
select a head from. I fancy it will be "Weeks" from all I hear of
him, if I can get up a mask to resemble his handsome one.
The head you describe may not suit my frame or style—and I
must look like an artist if I can. I entreat you to send me a
"catchy" air for the Serenade, and something that a poor
uninstructed-uninspired fellow can get on with—Even though
I am "unseen."

I dreadfully fear the audience will apply the title of your
story to my representation of the Hero.— I am not so sure of
myself as I am of *you*—but *nil desperandum*— I am at it as if
I were to succeed—

The title distresses me—but I fear it must be "A Counterfeit
Presentment."—a dreadfully *long* title—and *above* the crowd—
How would "Up at the Hill" do?—or "As Good as Gold"—or
"Down in our Village"—or "Bartlett's Love"—or "The Painter's
Love"—or "Two Pictures"—or "Only a Flower"—or "Color-
Blind"—or "On Vacation"—or "A Counterfeit Presentment"—
Now go on if you can and help me out.[2]

Ever yours

Lawrence Barrett

1. As WDH may have replied, *Out of the Question,* which also takes place
at the Ponkwasset Hotel, describes the furnishings of the parlor: two haircloth
sofas, two haircloth easy chairs, a cane-seated chair of divers patterns, a piano,
a marble-topped table supporting a state lamp of kerosene—"a perfume by
day, a flame by night." Although WDH does not describe the dress of the men
in *A Counterfeit Presentment,* he portrays their features and bearing in some
detail.

2. The nine titles proposed by LB along with the two in his letter of June 14
amusingly parallel WDH's own alternatives for titles of his novels throughout
his career. Best known are the twenty he once listed for *The Son of Royal
Langbrith* in 1903; see David Burrows, "Introduction" to *The Son of Royal
Langbrith* (Bloomington: Indiana University Press, 1969), p. xiv.

14. BARRETT TO HOWELLS, 20 AUGUST 1877, MS. (HARVARD, 3 PP.)

Marie Villa.

Cohasset.

Aug 20—1877.

Dear Mr. Howells,

Mr. Boucicault has been with me several days— He has carefully read the Play—and made [a] few suggestions,— generally commending its originality and freshness.[1] The changes which he suggests strike me favorably—I offer them for your consideration. The opening Scene should be the entrance of the Father, Mother and Daughter to the Hotel, embracing a brief outline of the Daughter's delicate health— and they then go to the rooms which the Landlady announces as ready. This character briefly explains that there are only two other guests—an Artist and a Clergyman. The General tears the party away from the articles which have been dropped upon the sofa.

The audience is now interested in the girl—and curious to see the men— When Bartlett examines the garments later on, the audience see the truth of the picture—and the comic side. This story is perfect. So much for the opening—The recognition takes place as follows—The girl and her Mother enter the Parlor *first*—they have a word with Cummings—then Bartlett advances— They recognize him. Then enter the General, and the Scene goes on as before. The solemnity of the situation is perfect—for they know the parties from previous acquaintance (the audience I mean) and this will lessen fear of laughter when Wyatt raises his cane on Bartlett. Do you see all this? or am I in my usual muddle[?] If you see fit to make these changes, put them in short-line dialogue and in brief speeches.

I will put them in their places—

Yours Very Truly,

Barrett

1. Dion Boucicault (1820–1890), dramatist and actor, began his career in

the United States in 1853, where he produced more than a hundred plays of his own writing. As LB's next letter suggests, WDH may have experimented with the major revision proposed—opening the play with the Wyatts rather than with the two young men. Since the General enters early in the version of the first act printed in Meserve, when "the Scene goes on as before," the change would probably have extended the play somewhat.

15. BARRETT TO HOWELLS, 27 AUGUST 1877, MS. (HARVARD, 3 PP.)

Marie Villa.

Cohasset.

Aug 27 — [1877]

Dear Mr. Howells—

The package with your alterations has arrived. They are good, and what you have now written will stand as the opening of the Comedy, without further change. The suggested alteration later will [make] the act begin, at "It's the only thing that makes conversation." Now let the Mother and Daughter enter to sit on the balcony, while "the other rooms" are being prepared. They meet Cummings—he could advance to aid Entrance in some slight way. Then let Bartlett turn—be recognized by Constance and the Mother. The former faints—and as soon as this has been fully worked out—let the General enter at sound of his wife's voice—see Bartlett—raise his cane—thus going on in original—ending with the General's assurance that he will return to explain his conduct. You will then make the whole scene more dramatic as Mr. Boucicault suggested.[1]

I leave on Saturday, and if not ready by that time you can forward to one of my places of rest. I am at "Hooley's Opera House, Chicago" from Sept 10th— Send to me there.[2]

Thanks for your good offices about the "New Drama"—[3]

Sincerely Yours,

Lawrence Barrett

I give you my places for next week in case you wish to find me— They are "flying visits"—Monday, Tuesday, Wednesday, Toronto Canada—Thursday, Port Huron, Mich. Friday—Bay City Mich—Saturday East Saginaw—Mich.

1. In this paragraph LB appears to offer a further revision of Boucicault's proposal. It would seem to differ in that Constance faints before the General appears, rather than after, perhaps again with the effect of prolonging the opening and delaying the confrontation of the General and Bartlett.

2. For Hooley's Opera House, see an earlier reference to it in the note to letter 3.

3. LB likely uses the phrase "New Drama" to refer to *Un drama nuevo*, which ultimately became *Yorick's Love*. In an 1880 interview, LB recalled that WDH had tried to locate a copy of the Spanish play in "the stock of every publishing house in New York and Boston. All these exertions were made, you must understand, on the stimulus of hearsay, for neither Mr. Howells nor myself had seen the play we were both striving so hard to obtain. . . . Through Count Premio Real, the Spanish consul to Quebec, who curiously enough is a distant relative of Mr. Howells, he obtained the original Spanish play" (Philadelphia *Press,* 16 January 1880, 5:1). On 4 August 1877 WDH had asked his father to remind Count Premio Real, José Antonio de Lavelle y Romero, about *Un drama nuevo* (*SL,* 2:170–71), but only shortly before 12 October 1877 did he telegraph LB that he had finally received a copy of the "Spanish play." A copy of the fifth edition of *Un drama nuevo* in the Howells Collection at Harvard is inscribed "To W^m D Howells Esqre with the Count de Premio Real's compliments."

16. BARRETT TO HOWELLS, 5 OCTOBER 1877, MS. (HARVARD, 2 PP.)

Burnet House,
Cincinnati, O[hio].

Oct 5 — [18]77

Dear Mr. Howells,

Your letter of the 23^d ult. directed to Chicago was sent to Detroit, and has just reached me. I do not think the situation in the last Act would be improved by what you suggest so I will not adopt it. We have already rehearsed the Play—and the performance is deferred until the 11*th* inst. on account of the Election here on Tuesday which would divide public interest.[1]

The papers have done nobly—in Editorial and slip matter— and I hope for the best. The play rehearses slowly—but I think the interest will hold the audience, and everything will be done for it that I can think of. The actors are anxious—and by Friday next I can tell you the fate of your *first* play —

In a former letter I assumed a liberty in asking you to favor a writer who had composed some lines to me which he had submitted to you[.] I ask your pardon for doing so and withdraw my request. I had no right to make it, and have *no* interest whatever in its publication.[2] The thought was an impulse unconsidered.

Very Truly Yours

Lawrence Barrett

1. *A Counterfeit Presentment* opened on the day anticipated by LB. A complete list of performances follows, reproducing the enclosure of LB's letter of 15 June 1878. The bracketed dates are those of Miller's list (pp. 153–54), based on "Lawrence Barrett's Account Book," then in the collection of Mrs. David Williams, LB's granddaughter-in-law. These dates also conform with those given from time to time in LB's letters. No payment appears in LB's accounting for the six New England performances, since, as LB explains in his letter of 15 June 1878, WDH had requested LB to "strike out" the royalties at those places; in the same letter LB also explains the $25 charge for copying "the Ms & parts." As WDH remarked in a letter to James Russell Lowell of 22 June 1879 (*SL*, 2:231), "My comedy was played some thirty times, but is now in abeyance—not to use a harsher expression."

PERFORMANCES OF A COUNTERFEIT PRESENTMENT

Cincinnati —	2 —	[11, 13 Oct.]	$50.
Cleveland —	2	[25, 27 Oct.]	50.
Pittsburgh —	1	[8 Nov.]	25.
Indianapolis	2	[23, 24 Nov.]	50.
Detroit —	2	[27 Nov., 1 Dec.]	50
St Louis —	1	[14 Dec.]	25
Buffalo —	1	[21 Dec.]	25.
Worcester —	1	[26 Dec.]	
Springfield	1	[31 Dec.]	
Providence	1	[28 Dec.]	
Hartford	1	[2 Jan.]	
New Haven	1	[3 Jan.]	
Waterbury	1	[4 Jan.]	
Washington	1 —	[10 Jan.]	25
Savannah	1	[26 Jan.]	25

New Orleans —	1	[13 Feb.]	25
Philadelphia —	3	[15, 16, 17 Apr.]	75
Boston —	3	[1, 2, 3 Apr.]	75
San Francisco	1	[27 May]	<u>25</u>
		27 —	$525.00
Cash —	$200		
[Ms +] parts	<u>25</u>		<u>225.</u>
	225		300.00

2. The poem on LB did not appear in the *Atlantic* or elsewhere, as far as is known. For the same poem or another on him, see letter 82.

17. BARRETT TO HOWELLS, 11 OCTOBER 1877, MS. (HARVARD, 3 PP.)

Burnet House,

Cincinnati, O[hio].

Oct 11 — [18]77

Dear Mr. Howells,

When I went to the theatre this evening, my heart was heavy. The many rehearsals of the Comedy had failed to give me confidence of its success.— I feared it would be slow for want of action—and I was also fearful of myself. The house was poor—but very select—the setting only so[-]so—the acting excellent—and the Comedy made a hit— At the end of the first act there was a very tempest of applause—and I was twice before the curtain—the second act was a little slower— but the end was good. I can elaborate the scene with the girl by performance—so that it will go still better—the last act closed the mat[t]er well, and the whole play I may say honestly to you was a genuine success,—the audience sat it out with interest and applause. I shall play it again for the Matinée,— and hereafter, once at least in all my cities, during the season— The defects in it are lack of action—and the small number of characters—which places the dialogue in so few hands that it lacks variety— The clearing up at the end is too abrupt—the change in Constance too sudden for dramatic effect and the cause not strongly apparent.— [T]hat I fancy cannot be changed, it is so much a part of the story.—but I assure you the dialogue is as sparkling and bright as possible—and the audience laughed "right out in meetin".— I congratulate you—and now I want to see you go to work in earnest to write a play for representation— When *that* is in my hands I will return you this Comedy—till then I will play Bartlett, with pleasure.

I don't know what the papers will say tomorrow and I don't care— As Kean said of Lord Essex—"d—n Essex—Mary—the pit rose at me"—the public have judged its merits—that's *my jury*—.[1] Score a success my dear Howells, and try again—the next time for big *money*—with a broader theme—and a bevy of characters—a stage full of incident—and a series of pictures— With sincere delight I remain.

Yours very faithfully

Lawrence Barrett

1. There are several versions of the story, of which that in Raymund Fitzsimmons' *Edmund Kean: Fire from Heaven* (1976) serves as a good example: "When he reached home after his first performance [as Sir Giles Overreach in Philip Massinger's *A New Way to Pay Old Debts*] and Mary asked him what Lord Essex had thought of it, he replied, 'Damn Lord Essex, *the pit ROSE at me*.'"

18. BARRETT TO HOWELLS, 12 OCTOBER 1877, MS. (HARVARD, 3 PP.)

Burnet House,

Cincinnati, O[hio].

Oct 12—[1877]

Dear Mr. Howells—

Your telegram has arrived telling me that you have received the Spanish Play—I may ask you still further to favor me by employing some one to translate it into good English—that I may see what it is like.[1] Is there not some scholar in Cambridge who can do this at no very great expense? Or am I putting you to too much trouble?—

The papers endorse all I said last night— The only fault is

the *length* of the Comedy.[2] Could you introduce another character or two?— Say an old Doctor who imagines he is curing the girl by medicine—a hard headed old fellow—out of whom some fun could be got— The present characters have already enough to say for themselves. A mistress and love scenes for Cummin[g]s might also be created.— Making the play about an hour longer—but even as it is—it will do you no wrong—and I shall fill up Bartlett's scenes with new business very rapidly— The girl made a hit—quite unexpectedly to me—the *character* is very dramatic.

Let me know at Cleveland about the translation of the Play—if you can have it done—when—and how much— I will attend to the seats for Mr. Howells at Cleveland.

Yours Very Truly,

Lawrence Barrett

W D Howells, Esq

P.S. The enclosed "Times" notice is the "other side."[3]

1. The "Spanish Play" was doubtless *Un drama nuevo* by the pseudonymous Estébanez (Manuel Tamayo y Baus [1829–1898]), which WDH eventually adapted in *Yorick's Love*. First presented in Madrid in 1867, Estébanez' play had been a great success, though a literal translation by José Goday had failed when staged by Augustin Daly at his New Fifth Avenue Theatre on 5 December 1874.

2. The most notable Cincinnati reviews were those in the *Commercial* and the *Gazette*. In the former, WDH's friend John J. Piatt (1835–1917) commended the "pretty, quiet comedy of real life," while lamenting that "there was not enough of it" and that it gave "the appearance of being played against time" (12 October 1877, 8:2–3). In the latter, Samuel R. Reed (1820?–1889), WDH's former colleague on the staff of the *Ohio State Journal,* praised the "elegant comedy," which he thought was "remarkably well constructed for acting. Its characters bec[a]me living and natural." Reed predicted that the play would "keep the stage" and prompt WDH "to continue in this line of literature" (12 October 1877, 4:4). The play was also favorably reviewed in the *Cincinnati Enquirer* as a "quiet success . . . admirably rendered" and "enthusiastically received." The critic noted, however, that the "little drama" was "over by a quarter of ten o'clock . . . leaving room for both author and actors to fill out and mellow their work" (12 October 1877, 8:4).

3. The *Cincinnati Daily Times* excoriated the play on the fourth page of its

12 October 1877 issue: "It is too nice in its literary embellishment for an average audience to become enthusiastic over it. It is too sketchy to excite more than that quiet attention which often makes the virtue of approval a necessity. Its wit is too refined to convulse the careless or vulgar, and its incidents too stale as well as meagre to enchain the interest of the cultivated."

19. BARRETT TO HOWELLS, 13 OCTOBER 1877, MS. (HARVARD, 8 PP.)

Burnet House

Cincinnati, O[hio].

Oct 13 — 1877

Dear Mr. Howells,

The second performance of the New Comedy took place today, and confirmed the success of the first— I am now satisfied that I have got a *character* which can be made a strong one—and very attractive.—but I have also to speak more fully of the Comedy in which the character moves. It is too short for an evening's entertainment—and yet no more dialogue can be introduced into the mouths of the actors as the play now stands.[1] It does not so much need lengthening as broadening if I can be understood. The story will bear more *dramatis personae*. I take the liberty of offering some ideas suggested by the two performances. It is so much easier to pad out a good body than to create another that it is worth some labor, and I know we have got a story which can be worked up to a great popular success. I go at once to my story—You will see that I am only offering an outline of suggestions.

Open the Play with the entrance of an old-fashioned New England Doctor—who comes with the Landlord—(a Yankee of very pronounced type)— The Doctor is a friend of Wyatt's—summoned by telegraph to meet the General—at this House—from another Hotel near—where himself and niece are stopping for his vacation.[2] He has left his niece to take a look at the mountain from the Porch— The Landlord is loquacious and we learn all about the House—and all about its occupants from this interview— The Landlord has been notified of the

coming of the General's party—but no name has been given—
the girl enters—a breezy-healthy downright New England
girl—the very opposite of Constance, her friend—and the
friend of Miss Harlan also— The Doctor tells her that the
Parson is here—but forbids any fresh tenderness on her part
for him or on his for her—he will not let Poverty and religion
enter his family—a Doctor for her husband or nothing—he is
very proud of his professional skill—Knows nothing else—is
always quoting it. She is delighted at the coming of Constance
whom she has not seen since she went abroad—wonders
what ails her—has heard of her broken engagement—and is
curious to know her secret. Indifferent about her own love for
the Parson, she takes a deep interest in the care of
Constance—and chuckles over what she knows of Bartlett's
heartbreak—which she knows all about. The Landlord has a
word here and there in this scene and goes to meet the sick
party when all is ready for their entrance. A scene of recognition—awkwardness—gushing on the part of the niece—tender
on Constance['s] part.—she is glad to meet her— The Old
Doctor will cure her—nothing can resist his skill. The General
does not tell him her trouble—and the humor lies in his belief
that he is the instrument by which she can be saved. The
party goes off—the Doctor and Niece last—he charges her to
follow—and to be distant to the Parson—she goes back to
[the] door roguishly to have a look at her old bashful lover—
has a wicked fling at him and runs off after her father—
unseen by the young men who now enter—then go on as
before—up to the recognition—which is a double one—that
of Bartlett as a Counterfeit and the Niece by the Parson—
surprise of all except the family—The Old Doctor seeing the
assault upon Bartlett, imagines the old General to be mad—
and the daughter to inherit the mania, a nice complication.
Then as before between Bartlett and Cummings— At his exit
(B['ls)—the niece could steal in to the Parson to try to worm
the secret out of him—Wheedles and bullies—while he tries to
send her politely away, anticipating B's return—she goes off in
a pout—surprised by Bartlett who asks the Parson if that is the
way he gets the explanation. End act as before—except that
the Parson will also stay, on the niece's account.—and to the
Doctor's disgust.—*Act 1ˢᵗ Ends*—³

Open Second Act with scene between Niece and Bartlett—
two excitable creatures—she, laughing at him about Miss
Harlan—and he fearful that she will suspect his love for
Constance.—a scene of equivoque—ending by the Doctor's
entrance who sends the girl to Constance—and mysteriously
tells Bartlett that his presence is preventing the recovery of the
girl—that she is not in her right mind—and his medicines have
not their full efficacy while his influence exists so near her—
The Doctor who fears his niece will fall in love with the
Painter—this scene could be made very strong by the bewilderment of Bartlett and the stupid dulness of the Doctor,
whose belief in Homoeopathy is supreme. He (B) is warned
to avoid her sight, and as he hears her coming down he
comes away—meeting the Parson whom he throws into the
Doctor's arms—to the disgust of the latter.— On comes
Constance led by her Mother & her Father—and the Niece—
while Mary carries the pillows—she is placed in the chair—
and the stage is full of people—the General and Doctor are
speaking aside while the Niece is speaking to Constance, and
trying to get her secret—the Parson speaking to the Mother—
then the group can change—leaving the Doctor to prescribe
for the girl—but with his eye always upon the General whom
he thinks out of his head still— Now, into the midst of this
group enter Bartlett—(he need not go off when the others
come on—the Parson stops him) searching for the brush—
thinking the room empty—a conversation scene—he always
trying to escape her sight—Yet being caught with it—whenever he gets away,—the old Lady talks to him of pictures and
high Art—the niece of Love—slyly hinting at the Harlan
affair—Constance of his habits—the Doctor of his health—a
give and take dialogue— On the height of this—let the General propose a ride on the Lake—in the moonlight—all go off
to this except the Mother and Bartlett—after a moment Mary
calls the Mother away and then the scene between the two as
in the original— The substance of the scene between
Constance and her Mother at opening of Act can be introduced quietly in the above dialogue—the Mother trying to
keep Constance amused, the other morbidly dwelling on the
past—putting in fragments before the audience [of] what is
now done in a long dialogue— In the Scene between B &

Constance alone—he could make up the dose which the
Doctor has prescribed—a large glass of water, a small powder,
and a spoonful more in twenty four hours— Now let the Artist
go off—the Mother come in—then the scene as at present—
enter the General for wraps for the party—it has grown cool—
Cannot Constance come with them—she can see the boat
from the porch in the moonlight— That is Bartlett's cigar she
sees now alight—she will not go—is cool to her father—he
goes off to meet his party returning—then as before only it is
the niece who runs in to tell of the accident—the stage running over the General— She speaks of Bartlett's gallantry, then
enter Bartlett—then enter all—a line for the Doctor about his
medicines—for the Parson—who is full of his friend's gallantry—then after Constance speaks—the Niece says "I know
the secret now—She loves him"—*End of Act.* (In the foregoing
act we learn that the Parson goes away in the morning to be
absent at a conference for some weeks.)

Act 3^d six weeks later—as before—Bartlett at work— Enter
mysteriously the niece—who tries to console B.—he thinks
she means Miss Harlan still when she says "he is loved"—and
a scene of much confusion ensues—ending in her leaving him
abruptly—with entrance of the Doctor—she says "You have
mistaken my meaning"— The *Doctor* still urges him to go
away—before his niece has fallen in love with him—and he is
hindering the recovery of his Patient— Bartlett is in despair—
and after no cues of cross purposes the Doctor goes out
saying "You are mistaken"—then comes the Mother with a few
lines—ending in the same way—then the General—same
ending—a day of "mistakes"—at last comes the Parson—he
only exited awhile ago—has been dressing and saw Constance
for a moment— The scene as before—only that Bartlett goes
out at the end and leaves the Parson—who then has a scene
with the niece—in which they combine to unite the other
couples if possible, she not listening to the Parson's own suit.
Constance comes to the niece—the Parson goes off to find
Bartlett. Then after some dialogue between the girls—
Constance is left alone—Romance. This scene as before—
interrupted by entrance of General and the Doctor. The
General's explanation—the Doctor says he was not informed
of *that* symptom— Enter the Niece and Parson—End—Parson

makes his own suit favorable—

N.B. The Doctor has removed to the Ponkwasset Hotel to be near his Patients.

If you can read my writing you will see what I propose is extensive—but it will fill out the present play into a grand evening's entertainment.

Don't regard this an impertinence—I can act the Comedy as it is with much pleasure—but if altered it would run in Boston some weeks—and in N.Y. a hundred nights—I will be in your neighborhood late in December—

Yours Hastily

Lawrence Barrett

1. In remarking that the play was too short, LB anticipates his attempt to mitigate this situation in Cleveland, where he added a shortened version of *The Inconstant* by George Farquhar (1678–1707) to the program. But as the *Cleveland Herald* complained in its review of 24 October 1877, "It was an unfortunate programme for the later piece, for it was rather tedious and dull after the fresher, purer humor of 'A Counterfeit Presentment.'"

2. WDH apparently refused to consider introducing the Doctor and his niece, whose presence would have produced a second love affair in the play. For the proposed landlord he substituted a landlady, Mrs. Ransom, who appears in some of the playbills as a member of the cast.

3. Early in the paragraph LB provides a link between the doctor's niece and Bartlett's earlier love, Miss Harlan, not named in the published text, however, until the fourth act (Meserve, p. 100). We may presume that at the end of the paragraph LB has the parson stay to prepare for his success in winning the niece, though somewhat inconsistently he lets him leave for six weeks at the end of the second act, as did WDH. One may also guess that LB has the niece report the General's accident rather than Mary, the maid, to keep her in the foreground, for the play, as LB ends it, emphasizes the niece-parson suit as much as, if not more than, that of Bartlett and Constance.

20. HOWELLS TO BARRETT, 17 OCTOBER 1877, MS. (Price, 1 p.)

. . . *The Atlantic Monthly.*

. . . *Cambridge, Mass.* Oct. 17, 1877.

Dear Mr. Barrett:

I'm driving along on Act IV, with two new people, new situations, and new scenes. I think you'll be pleased. The closing scene is in a summer cottage—Dr. Harlan's—at Cohasset.[1]

Do your best with what you have for a while, yet, and believe in

Yours ever

W. D. Howells.

P. S. Let me know your cities *and theatres* and dates.

1. Presumably WDH had received LB's letter, which in effect asks him to rewrite the play, on the 14th or 15th and replied on the 16th (see letters 21–22). One wishes LB had saved that letter as well as the present one. Still, the mention of Dr. Harlan's cottage at Cohasset may discreetly refer to the unnamed doctor and to the prominence given to Miss Harlan in LB's proposal. Actually, WDH was not writing a fourth act but inserting a third—the amusing painting lesson given Constance by Bartlett, chaperoned by the sleepy General.

21. BARRETT TO HOWELLS, 18 OCTOBER 1877, MS. (HARVARD, 2 PP.)

Opera House

Cleveland

Oct 18 — [18]77

Dear Sir,

I have your favor of the 16th.[1] In reply, I have only to state, that as the Landlady was a Yankee, I selected a Yankee name for her—that I used two men to bring on the wounded General, who had to be named. I will remove those names from the bills on Tuesday next.

I do not agree with you that the Play requires another act or any prolongation of the present interest. It will not bear it. Some such padding as I suggested might be done with profit to the play. Mr. Osgood has written me that I ought now to

produce it in Boston where the feeling is well worked up to
witness it. I recal[l] to you the motive I had in taking your
Comedy—namely:—the bringing you to the stage: that is
accomplished—and I now can safely offer you the opportunity
of reclaiming a good thing, and making a better market elsewhere than I can afford you for it[.] You are at liberty to
present your work to a Boston manager and disregard me in
the matter—as I could not think of producing the Comedy in
its present shape as a night's entertainment to an eastern
audience. This will fulfill your own desires and not in any way
interfere with me. Regarding the Spanish play—I have only to
say that I prefer an arrangement of the following character
should be made. I will pay you whatever you deem just for a
translation of the Play—then I will read it—and, as it will need
free adaptation[,] if you consent to make such alterations as I
will suggest I will cheerfully pay you the royalty or hand you
back the MSS. for your own use elsewhere. Please inform me
if this meets your views.

I will send the tickets to Mrs. Howells, as you request

Yours Truly

Lawrence Barrett

W. D. Howells. Esq

1. Though WDH's letter of the 16th is not extant, much of this letter seems
to reply to that of the 17th.

22. BARRETT TO HOWELLS, 18 OCTOBER 1877, MS. (HARVARD, 2 PP).

Opera House

Cleveland, O[hio].

Oct 18 — [1877]

Dear Mr. Howells:

Your letter of the 16th came before your letter of the 14th
(which has just arrived).—that will explain a character of mine
to you— I was a little hurt—but it is past—and don't let it
weigh for a moment as you hint.

I do the "Parlor Car" on Tuesday—and if it goes as I expect[,] the result will be perfect—and you need not touch the C[ounterfeit] P[resentment]—but the double bill will be all I want— I have read D'Abrantes and that's where I got my Napolean [*sic*] mania.[1] Will write again on Sunday.—

Yours Always Sincerely

L. Barrett

1. Laure Junot, duchesse d'Abrantés (1784–1838) was encouraged by Honoré de Balzac to write her *Memoir at the Court of Napoleon,* a lively if not altogether reliable account of her relationship with the emperor, members of his family, and associates. Published between 1831 and 1835, the work was immediately translated into English and was widely distributed.

23. HOWELLS TO BARRETT, 19 OCTOBER 1877, MS. (Price, 3 pp.)

. . . The Atlantic Monthly.

. . . Cambridge, Mass.

Oct. 19, 1877.

My dear Barrett:

Your letter of the 18th makes me afraid that I may have annoyed you by what I carelessly and casually said of those characters added in the play-bills.[1] Nothing was farther from my intention. I know how much the play must have owed not only to your delicate and sympathetic acting, but to your skilful management in every way[,] and I fully appreciated your self-sacrifice in foregoing [*sic*] your favorite parts for the purpose of representing [them].[2]

As for its [half line missing] [I] am not at all impatient, and have not been. In fact I should be sorry to have it played in Boston till I had done my best to amplify and strengthen it. After writing sixty pages on the additional act, I have thrown that aside, and shall adopt your idea of filling up and interpolating. I have already imagined some episodes, giving business to the minor characters, and introducing a principal scene for Bartlett which shall fill out the intention of the drama while taking from it much of its present *hurry.*

I will write you again about the Spanish play. Your proposal

is entirely satisfactory but I should be willing to stand in you[r]
[one word missing] getting the transla[tion] [rest of line missing
plus a word at start of new page] done by another hand, and
my copy is freely and heartily yours already. If I need this
version it would be for you alone (as I have made, and think
of making all changes in my own play,) and I should not think
of offering it to any one else, if you didn't like it. Perhaps we
can both look it over together when you come on in December.

Yours ever

W. D. Howells.

1. Apparently WDH is answering letter 21 but has not yet received letter 22,
though LB had written both the day before.

2. The bracketed words and omissions result from the disintegration of the
lower corners of the first two folded pages and the upper corner of the first
page, the verso side of which had been written upon. A rough draft of this
letter located in the Howells Collection at Harvard (bMS Am 1784.1[1]) does
not, unfortunately, supply the omissions.

24. HOWELLS TO BARRETT, 20 OCTOBER
1877, MS. (PRICE, 2 PP.)

. . . *The Atlantic Monthly.*

. . . *Cambridge, Mass.*

Oct. 20, 1877.

My dear Barrett:

I knew that I had somehow vexed you, and I answered
your first letter of the 18th in the right spirit—as I hope you
will think. Your second letter came this morning, to my great
relief, for I was most sincerely sorry that I had unwittingly
wounded you. Do, my dear friend, believe me once for all
incapable of ungrateful or ungracious feeling toward you;
revile me to the handiest by-stander if I *seem* to say any thing
you don't like,—and give me twenty-four hours' grace.

I'm proud and glad that you're going to do the Parlor Car,
but all the same I'm going to improve A C[ounterfeit]
P[resentment]—make it three quarters of an hour longer, and
indefinitely delightfuller.

I wish I could be in Cleveland when you bring out the two plays, but it is too pleasant a thing to be possible. I get up at six o'clock every morning, and my work hounds me along till bed-time. Just now the Atlantic for December is closing up, and I can't leave. Give my love and thanks to all those kind friends who telegraphed Osgood.

Yours ever

W. D. Howells.

25. HOWELLS TO BARRETT, 21 OCTOBER 1877, MS. (Price, 2 pp.)

. . . *The Atlantic Monthly.*

. . . *Cambridge, Mass.*

Oct. 21, 1877.

Dear Barrett:

I send a letter from a New York man containing some words I thought you'd like to see; for written words let us more into the heart of things than printed ones. Mr. Whelpley of Cin., writes me that the man who wrote the adverse Times criticism had not seen the play![1] This seems amazing.

Will you kindly have this enclosed letter conveyed to my brother Joe, if you know where he sits in the audience Tuesday night?[2] If you don't, no matter: tear it up. I've given him a card of introduction to you which he will present if all goes well, and he isn't too shy.

Yours sincerely

W. D. Howells.

1. With letter 18, LB had enclosed the *Cincinnati Daily Times* review as showing the "other side." Starting on 11 October 1877, A. W. Whelpley (1831–1900), then a printer and later a librarian of the Cincinnati Public Library, had written WDH several times about his play (letters at Harvard). On October 17, Whelpley remarked that "I have ascertained through my reporter friends, on comparing notes, that the article was penned without the play being witnessed— He never *saw* it, & I am confident never *read* it" (*SL,* 2:175).

2. This was Joseph A. Howells (1832–1912), of the *Ashtabula Sentinel,* the family newspaper edited in Jefferson, Ohio. The newspaper was still edited by

William Cooper Howells (1807–1894), the father, though he had been U.S. consul at Quebec since 1874. Joe filled nearly a column in the issue of November 1, though all except a short introductory paragraph consists of a review in the *Cleveland Herald* for October 24. The first paragraph begins "Quite a number of our citizens went to Cleveland last week" to see the comedy and observes that those who were there "seem all to have pronounced the comedy a success."

26. BARRETT TO HOWELLS, 21 OCTOBER 1877, MS. (HARVARD, 2 PP.)

Sunday Oct 21st [18]77

Kennard House

Cleveland[,] O[hio]

Dear Mr Howells,

When we came to work out the *scene* for the "Parlor Car"— it was found that no chairs could be had in the city, and we had to abandon the idea. It was a pity[,] for the idea is a very ludicrous one and would *act* well— Put it into a long Comedy—as an episode—and the scene can then be put expensively on the Stage— Shall be anxious to see the new act—I am sorry you could not come here. That telegram came out of a Lunch party at the club[1]— My next stationary point is Pittsburgh Nov 5ᵗʰ[.] *[H]ere* another week[,] then on the road—then Pitts—

Ever yours Truly,

Lawrence Barrett

1. The telegram is not extant. Probably it was the "dispatch insisting on your coming out next week" referred to by John Hay to WDH in a letter of October 19 (*Hay-Howells Letters,* p. 28).

27. BARRETT TO HOWELLS, 23 OCTOBER 1877, MS. (HARVARD, 3 PP.)

Cleveland[,] O[hio].

Oct 23—[18]77

Dear Mr. Howells,

I have *two* letters from you today.— Bury my last mullygrub letter deeper than ever plummet &c.— I am glad you are broadening the Comedy—that is all it will need to make it a *strong* success. I hope you will go at the Spanish Play as soon as possible— We can not quarell [*sic*] about the terms.— Make a literal—or (free translation) to suit yourself, then if it requires adapting we can talk it over. We hunted for the Pullmans Chairs, or a substitute, every where but could find nothing,— so hard to abandon the Parlor Car— It would not pay to produce it meanly— I shall do it in Detroit surely[1]— Make a "Howell's Night" of it— There was much regret that you could not break away for tonight, but all see the force of your excuse— We will think of you—there is to be a fine house, I send you Mason's Editorial—which is strong.[2]

Hammer away at the Spanish Play when you are able to do so—and let me have that and the new additions as soon as you please—

Ever yours faithfully

Lawrence Barrett

P.S. Let us mildly objurgate the "Times" man—he represents the average "critic"—but we appeal only to the *extra*-average.

1. Evidently, the staging of *The Parlor Car* in Detroit was abandoned, for no mention of it appears in the telegram LB sent WDH on December 1 or in his letter of December 3.

2. Frank Holcomb Mason (1840–1916) served on the staff of the Cleveland *Leader* between 1865 and 1880; after that he was a consul or consul general in several European cities.

28. BARRETT TO HOWELLS, 24 OCTOBER 1877 (HARVARD, TELEGRAM)

THE WESTERN UNION TELEGRAPH COMPANY. . . . Cleveland, O[hio]. 1877 . . .

Oct. 24. . . . *To* W. D. Howells

Success greater than before Am quite convinced of its enduring qualities

Barrett

29. BARRETT TO HOWELLS, 24 OCTOBER
1877, MS. (Harvard, 4 pp.)

Oct 24th, [18]77

Wednesday

My Dear Howells

I could not get hold of a bit of paper last evening after the play—or you should have had a midnight letter from me— I can now tell you that the occasion was a brilliant one—the audience just such as you would have desired—and they accepted all as charmingly as possible. The applause was continuous, only disturbed by the laughter.[1] You will believe Col Hay sooner than an interested party—and I am sure he must have written in a eulogistic vein.[2] I beg that you will finish the play as soon as possible—for I am *now* anxious to try Boston— Bartlett *fits* me well—they say—and I like the part.

Please say no more about my momentary vexation— I can never feel other than kind towards one whose character and genius I so much admire—

I shall play A C[ounterfeit] P[resentment] again on Saturday—and on Monday I shall gladly send [a] check for $100—for four performances— Hurry up the Spanish Play, and let me make you rich in Royalties— To the old Boy with the [price tag?]!— You are now the great American Dramatist—one of Shakespeare[']s guild—and you must obey your inspiration—

Ever yours faithfully

Lawrence Barrett

1. The *Cleveland Plain Dealer* reported that the audience testified to its amusement with "continuous applause and hearty laughter." The reviewer also complained, however, that the play was "scarcely long enough" (24 October 1877, 4:4). The Cleveland *Leader* added that the "extraordinary" audience had "accorded to the play the heartiest approval—laughed at its humor" and "sympathised with its pathos" (24 October 1877, 8:4). The *Cleveland Herald* also noted that the play "gave complete satisfaction and great pleasure" (24 October 1877; rpt. in *Ashtabula Sentinel,* 1 November 1877).

2. As one of Lincoln's secretaries, John Hay (1838–1905) had been instru-

mental in securing WDH's appointment as U.S. consul in Venice in 1861. The two had since kept in touch. Hay had attended the performance of *A Counterfeit Presentment* in Cleveland on October 23 and reported to the playwright that it

> was a most delightful affair—a full house, of the people who rarely go to the play—a good performance, close attention and interest in the house, and the most unequivocal signs of pleasure as well as approval. It seemed to me almost too good to act—but I see my mistake now—it is an admirable acting piece, and it must be a new sensation to the actors to have good lines written for them—as delightful as it is to the audience to *hear* conversation on the stage worth listening to. The pleasure of the audience in the play was what made me glad—first, of course, on your account, and next because it is a good sign to see people liking a pure comedy. You will write other plays now—and they will bring you gold and remonetized silver—and they will do good to our degraded stage (*Hay-Howells Letters*, p. 29).

30. HOWELLS TO BARRETT, 24 OCTOBER 1877, MS. (PRICE, 2 PP.)

. . . The Atlantic Monthly.

. . . Cambridge, Mass.

Oct. 24, 1877.

Dear Mr. Barrett:

I received with joy your telegram of to-day, telling me of the success of the play in Cleveland, and affirming your confidence in it—which is more important than present success, though I want that, too. I believe, now, that I am on the right track in enlarging the play; the whole thing is clear in my mind, and if I have luck, you shall have the changes in print by the time you reach Pittsburgh.[1] Pray let me know how to address you there.

I was sorry[,] of course, you couldn't do the Parlor Car; but you must be the judge of its possibilities. If you think again of trying it, let me suggest that a few pivotal library-chairs could, with a little drapery, be made to represent those of a Pullman car well enough. It seems to me that it would have a good effect on the stage.

I send a scrap from the Tribune—by Bayard Taylor, I suppose.[2]

Yours sincerely

W. D. Howells.

1. The principal change from the original edition of *A Counterfeit Present-ment* is the addition of a new third act entitled "Dissolving Views." The action in it largely consists of Bartlett's problem in teaching Constance (hardly an apt pupil) to paint, verging toward courtship and then ending in a quarrel. WDH apparently had the act set in type to ease the task of editing it.

2. Unidentified. See also note 1 to letter 31.

31. BARRETT TO HOWELLS, 27 OCTOBER 1877, MS. (HARVARD, 3 PP.)

Cleveland, O[hio].

Oct 27 — [18]77

Dear Mr. Howells.

My address in Pittsburg[h] will be "Library Hall",—I am rejoiced to learn that I may expect the "filling" of the Comedy there. I shall then put the new matter in rehearsals and if it suits—will do it in Detroit.— I am anxious that it may be broadened to make an evening's work for I want to do it in real "Bostony"—for a run of some weeks. The "Tribune" article seems a little so-so-ish.— Do you think B. T. did it?[1] I shall get even with him when his Don Carlos appears.[2] I have a pleasant letter from your Brother who did not see me on Tuesday Eve. I hope he said to *you* as much as he said to *me*— You will then get an idea of what my performance of Bartlett is like— If I don't play the part 100 times this season it will be because your new matter is not equal to the old.

I am thinking of what Hay and wife will say to you next week—they saw the Comedy and can tell you the effect. I hope the verdict will be favorable to

Yours Ever Sincerely,

Lawrence Barrett

1. LB's question whether Bayard Taylor was the author of the unlocated "scrap" may be due to the fact that William Winter was the regular drama critic of the *New York Tribune* from 1865 to 1909.

2. According to Frederick W. C. Lieder, who had access to Barrett family papers, LB prepared an outline for Taylor's adaptation and translation of Schiller's *Don Carlos,* eventuating in a manuscript dated 14 January 1878. Though LB never presented the play, Lieder regarded the adaptation as superior to Richard Mansfield's version, which was performed in 1905–06 (*Journal of English and Germanic Philology,* January 1917). Soon after submission of the manuscript to LB, Bayard Taylor (1825–1878), a popular travel writer, poet, and novelist, was appointed U.S. minister to Germany. After Taylor's death on December 19 of that year, WDH wrote John Hay that "I have it on my soul to tell you that Barrett has paid Taylor's estate the remaining $1000, and that I judged him hastily from the delay" (*Hay-Howells Letters,* 2 May 1879).

32. BARRETT TO HOWELLS, 4 NOVEMBER 1877, MS. (Harvard, 4 pp.)

Monongahela House,

Pittsburg[h].

Nov 4th [1877]

Dear Mr. Howells—

Arriving here this morning after a week in the oil regions, I find your letters of the 29th & 31st *ult* with enclosures.[1] I would like so much to *talk* with you of the Play—as I cannot *write* what I wish to say, so that it may be persuasive. I will try to explain, however, and I only ask that what I say[,] if it seem rude to you, I may be excused on account of the anxiety I feel that what has been so well commended should not be marred. Briefly, then, I don't like what you send me—because I don't think it at all necessary. Four lines will explain the situation to the audience of the girl's sudden change— Cut out the line "I love him still"—and repeat the argument much later of her faith to the absent so long as he is not proved false to her— and the situation is dramatically covered.[2] But don[']t draw out the interest so fully that the audience grow weary of it. Bartlett's absence from the scene is forced—and ineffective— he is too long silent as it *now* stands—but this change would make his last act secondary to the girl in importance—whereas the whole plot demands that he should remain central. You tell me that you intend introducing a new act also—Well!—you

may be right—but I fear!— What the play wants is not a new
act in which the present characters should be extended, but
new incident and new characters in the present acts—³ The
second act as it now stands lacks movement—and is the only
tedious part of the Play—as it is dangerous for two people to
occupy the stage *relating* as Constance and her mother do—
for so long a time. I am timid in offering my suggestions—but
refer again to my ideas written out so hastily in Cincinnati,—of
new characters introduced—and the play thus *broadened*—
not lengthened or spun out. The idea did not seem to strike
You—as you did not refer to it—but I think I am right. The
Dramatis personae is not complete for a long comedy—Now,
my dear Mr. Howells, I offer my opinions modestly, and I may
be in error— The Comedy has thus far had an excellent
hearing—before friends—and with audiences where I am a
personal favorite. But the truth remains that for a great and
enduring success, much remains to be done,—that is—to
make it valuable to *me*. Until the changes are made which I
deem of absolute necessity, I cannot think of asking Boston's
attention to it, with myself as the hero, but I repeat in all
kindness my willingness to step aside and let some one else
try it there if you think I am in error about what is necessary
in the alterations. This is my answer about Worcester. I had
already arranged to play the Comedy in Providence, but
cannot consent that any unusual attention should be called to
it in Boston, until the changes are made.⁴ I can play it in its
present shape there (at P.) and you can come quietly and see
it. Then you can judge for yourself if I am right or wrong. To
make a great success—much work must yet be done—but the
"game is worth the candle" and I hope you will start properly
about it. But neither you nor I can afford to push a Boston or
New York verdict—which would forever prevent its recovery,
even if thereafter altered. Don't think me pig headed[,] My
Dear Sir[,] but reflection here only convinced me that my
original impression was the right one—the introduction of
new characters—attached to the plot—the Comedy to remain
in three acts—the scenes between Constance and the Mother
shortened and relieved by action and the movement of the
new characters—let [the] *denouement* alone—it will stand—

(one hour's talk between us—and ten minutes with the actors will fix *that* difficulty)— Thus broadened and fattened—the Play will challenge attention and enduring success—which is what you will only be contented with—of course, You probably reject my suggested characters—but I am certain they would be dramatic—and as this treatment would be your own there could be no claim to joint-authorship on my part, if that is in your mind. I am an Actor—I want a Play—and am content with my calling— *You* can furnish it, and I know it. Then, do it and let us dine somewhere over the "100*th* consecutive performance"— I remain here this week, and shall play the piece in its present shape on Thursday—also in Detroit and Indianapolis and St Louis.— I shall be in Providence Dec 27–28–29—

Always Yours

Lawrence Barrett

W. D. Howells, Esq.

When may I expect the translation of "The New Play"?— Did you get $100 from my agent for royalties due?—

1. WDH's letters of 29 and 31 October 1877 have apparently not survived.

2. The line referred to appears, slightly different in its wording, in the printed text (Meserve, p. 106).

3. LB wrote Osgood this same day that he attributed the success of the play to the "friendly and cultured audiences" where he had performed it and that "it must now please the popular taste which will not accept fine writing and pretty dialogue in a thin plot. He [WDH] talks of adding a new act—that would be fatal. I want him to add new characters and revamp his dramatic personae and add new incidents—not more fine talk" (quoted in Meserve, p. 70).

4. LB offered *A Counterfeit Presentment* in Worcester on 26 December 1877, in Providence on 28 December 1877 (which performance WDH attended), and in Boston on 1, 2, and 3 April 1878.

33. HOWELLS TO BARRETT, 9 NOVEMBER 1877, MS. (PRICE, 2 PP.)

. . . *The Atlantic Monthly.*

. . . *Cambridge, Mass.* Nov. 9, 1877.

Dear Mr. Barrett:

The printers have been extremely slow with the fruits of the new act. But I'm to have it all to-morrow night, and then I'll revise it at once and send it to you. I have no idea how you'll like it, but you will say, and then I'll work out the possibilities. I'm as loath as yourself to cut our goose open, and you will find me willing to create to the extent of my powers in making the play what you wish.

Mr. Emerson has sent me a check for $100, as you kindly directed.[1]

Very truly yours

W. D. Howells.

I'll send the new matter to you at Wheeling.

I hope you know that I agree with you entirely about that wretched stuff I sent you for the last act.

I'll work at the Spanish play as I have time.

1. Warren Emerson acted as LB's agent for several years and sent WDH checks for LB's performances, including the one mentioned here on 6 November 1877.

34. BARRETT TO HOWELLS, 9 NOVEMBER 1877, MS. (HARVARD, 3 PP.)

Monongahela House,

Nov 9 — 1877.

Dear Mr. Howells,

The Comedy made a fresh hit here last night. Capturing these iron-mongers as it did the coaldealers of Cleveland and the Pork-fanciers of Cincinnati, its attractiveness is unmistakable, and I shall be glad when you have made Bartlett so consequential that I need play nothing else for a season of 250 nights and keep sending you checks accordingly— You can do this and I expect no less from you. I am anxiously waiting for the new act,—and hopeful that it will serve— I shall do the Comedy in Worcester and in Providence—and perhaps in

Springfield next month, but Providence will be the place for you to see it, as the setting will be better there. I have jogged my Agent's memory about the check—he had *overlooked* that part of my instructions. I may repeat the Comedy for the Matinee tomorrow here. I want to talk with you about the Comedy—And can scarcely wait for December—as I think I could get fifty nights for it in N.Y. if properly changed—before the present season is over—but I can run no risk in such [a] place—Where failure would be fatal—[1]

Ever Yours Sincerely,

Lawrence Barrett

[(]Give me the Spanish Drama as soon as you can)

1. Though the play was rumored to be headed for New York a year later ("Notes," *Nation,* 9 January 1879, p. 34), it was never produced there.

35. BARRETT TO HOWELLS, 9 NOVEMBER 1877, MS. (HARVARD, 1 P.)

Monongahela House

Nov 9, [18]77

Dear Mr. Howells,

I sent you the morning papers containing notices of the Play, and enclose one from the Evening Chronicle. This gives you a fair idea of the effect of the play upon the average auditor, and in that sense is as good a notice as the play has had.[1]

Yours Very Sincerely,

Lawrence Barrett

1. The *Pittsburgh Commercial Gazette* reported that the performance at Library Hall "was remarkably successful. . . . [E]very point of Howells' charming comedy was brought out" (9 November 1877, 4:5). The *Pittsburgh Evening Chronicle* noted that the comedy was "a welcome relief from the class of plays" that are "so surcharged with action and incident as to render reflection absolutely impossible" but asserted that its "defects of construction are apparent. The play does not lack movement, but at times the action drags. This is especially noticeable in the beginning of the second act, and in the last act." In

all, the critic wrote, "Howells has given us a society play in the true sense of the words, but one which, while it commands instant admiration of the literary capabilities of the author, reveals [his] inexperience as a playwright" (9 November 1877, 3:2).

36. BARRETT TO HOWELLS, 11 NOVEMBER 1877, MS. (HARVARD, 2 PP.)

Monongahela House

Pittsburg[h].

Nov 11ᵗʰ [18]77.

Dear Mr. Howells,

I have not yet had the new act,—and as I leave tomorrow, I wish to give you my itinerary for some weeks ahead

Nov 19ᵗʰ	Indianapolis—one week (*C.P.*)
Nov 26—	Detroit— " " (*C.P.*)
Dec 3 } " 10	(*C.P.*) St. Louis (Olympic Theatre) two weeks
" 17.	London, Canada.
" 18.	Hamilton "
" 19.	St. Catherines
" 20 " 21 " 22	Buffalo. N.Y. (C.P.)
" 24.	Seneca Falls, N.Y.
" 25.	Syracuse "
" 26.	Worcester—Mass. (C.P.)
" 27 " 28 " 29 " 31	Providence, R.I. (C.P.)

I mark the places where I do the Comedy— If I find the new act at Wheeling tomorrow, and I hope I may—I will be able to try it at Indianapolis.— This will give ample time for rehearsals—

I have been laid up all the past week with a painful knee—but have crawled out at night for my work— I am better today, but overworked as most of us are who work at all in this country.

Very Truly Yours,

Lawrence Barrett

37. BARRETT TO HOWELLS, 12 NOVEMBER 1877,[1] MS. (HARVARD, 4 PP.)

Monongahela House.

Monday.

Dear Mr. Howells,

I have read and again read the new matter sent me, and I am today better convinced than yesterday that it would be hurtful to send Bartlett from the scene. The difficulty with the Scene seems to be that the girl expresses too much when she says "Hold. I love him still"[2]— You can explain this away in an Essay, but words go for their full value when spoken by the actor— She does not mean that, surely—, for she unconsciously loves Bartlett,—she adheres to the other until satisfied that he is worthless.—Then her heart is free and can follow its instincts—to Bartlett.— Now, if she were to say, "Hold—he loves me still"—would not that express more clearly to the audience her position? Then let her say in reply to his "it is still your dream"—"Until I know that he is worthless I must still be true to him"— This makes the complication, and what follows should unravel the web. Your idea in the new matter is to show how she is trying to reconcile her past conduct with the new feeling which she, at last, allows to take possession of her. Cannot this be done as well with Bartlett present as absent?— To send him away is an apparent trick—the audience knows he will be recalled. He could aid her in making up her mind—show her how to do it—and thus the most interesting character of the Comedy would amuse, while he satisfied the auditor. Now, mind, I am not one of the critics who complain of the present situation—that is to say—I only ask that the idea I offer of a change of words in the present text be accepted— I shall then be able to show you, when you see the Play, how the actors can fill up a chasm which the

story seems to necessarily create. So much for the last act—
which is one of the best of the play—perhaps the very best—
I wrote yesterday that I did not approve of another act, but of
course I am prepared to defer to you in case you see no other
way of working—but I must respectfully maintain my right to
decline in case I am not satisfied with the change.[3] This holds
you free from obligation on your own part to leave the play in
my hands—as I am resolved to please you in any way I can—
provided I cannot please myself in the first place—or rather,
provided we cannot be mutually pleased. I know it is easier to
write a new work than to alter an old one— It is very dangerous to touch the *sunshine* of this Comedy—it is good as it
stands—it only wants fixing up. The progress of the action is
as it should be—no halt—no delay—but not too rapid—now a
new act must affect either the speed or the breadth of the
movement—if I am understood—and there lies the danger.
The fault will be in giving the present characters new lines—
when they have already enough— Through three acts your
well written dialogue sustains a perfect interest,—but it is
doubtful if it will bear more—at no time are there more than
two persons on the stage together—thus the eye is not fed by
variety of movement and action—as it might be, a closer
knitting of the work (in its present frame) would accomplish
this—and do more than I fear can be done by the addition of
an entire new Act. *You* created Bartlett. I have stood in his
shoes—I have moved with him—and I now know just where
he and those who move around him stand in need of support.
But I labor under a great disadvantage in trying to explain
myself,—because you have not seen your work. My advice is,
my dear Sir, to suspend all work upon the Comedy till you see
it in Providence as it is—thus I *know* you will adopt my
theory, and you can work more knowingly. It is well worth
waiting for—and I am not hurrying you to spoil a good thing.
Turn your mind for a time to the translation of the Spanish
Play—let me be paying you a royalty for that also, and by
Xmas you will have made up your mind by seeing the play,
just what it wants.

                                        Very Truly Yours,

                                        Lawrence Barrett

1. Almost certainly the letter was written on this date. LB stayed in Pittsburgh on two Mondays, 5 and 12 November 1877. Letters of the 5th, 9th, and 11th clearly precede this one, presumably written before LB left on the same day for Wheeling.

2. A line almost exactly the same as this appears in the printed text (Meserve, p. 106) when Constance cries out to Bartlett, "Oh, wait! I—I love him yet," to which after an intervening speech in which Constance suggests the false fiancé still loves her, Bartlett replies, "Why, this is still your dream." From this it appears that the "new matter," sent to LB before the new act, as WDH implies in letter 30, had revisions no longer extant, including Bartlett's temporary absence from the stage in this act, noted by LB in this letter.

3. In the letters from LB that WDH saved, probably all to this juncture, LB had not objected to the new act openly since October 18; in his haste to leave Pittsburgh on the day he wrote this letter, he apparently forgot what he had said in his letter of November 11—any enthusiasm for a new act is notably lacking in what he wrote between mid-October and mid-November.

38. HOWELLS TO BARRETT, 12 NOVEMBER 1877, MS. (PRICE, 4 PP.)

. . . *The Atlantic Monthly.*

. . . *Cambridge, Mass.*

November 12, 1877.

My dear Barrett:

I have your two welcome notes from Pittsburgh, and the newspaper notices. You will understand my joy when I tell you that Pittsburgh has been a crucial point in my mind, and I had expected the play to *flat* there. I am almost too glad to write coherently about it. Certainly you as actor, and I as author, have every reason to ha[ve been] deeply gratified by the [one word missing] and recurring appre[ciation] that has followed our efforts to produce a good, self-respectful drama, without dodges or tricks or any sort, and as severe in structure as a classic play. I know very well that we must not task the auditorial imagination too far, however, and my design will be, when we must, to co-operate with you for the introduction of all possible relief to that severity. I dep[end] upon you to suggest points and situations, which must have occurred to

you in acting. Do make a note of them. I have the proof of
the new act in my hands, but I want to mull it over two or
three days, and you will not get it before you reach Indianapolis at the end of this week. If you change your course,
please telegraph me on getting this letter, and please send a
line anyway to say you *have* got it.

I read Osgood the new act last night, and he fully
appro[ved,] as he will tell you. I thought him a good test, for
though he is my friend he is "not a damned[1] fool," as the man
said about being a spiritualist.

I shall work with good spirit and in the impulse of your
recent notes.

Yours truly ever

W. D. Howells.

1. WDH has drawn a line through "amne" of "damned."

39. HOWELLS TO BARRETT, 14 NOVEMBER
1877, MS. (Princeton, 8 pp.)

. . . *The Atlantic Monthly.*

. . . *Cambridge, Mass.* Nov. 14, 1877

Dear Mr. Barrett:

I mail you herewith the new act. I need not lecture upon it.
You will see what it is. Understand that I don't hold you
bound to like it, and above all that I don't expect you, or
desire you to accept it if you don't like it.

I have worked with the idea of telling the story more fully
and of developing Bartlett's character by certain situations in
which I leave almost everything to your acting. You will see
what I mean when you come to the love-making which must
be made love-making, as concerns the audience, and kept
from seeming love-making, to Constance. I think that in these
scenes you have the opportunity for some of the finest effects
in the play.

Of course I want all the suggestions and criticisms you can
give.

We had a lovely visit from the Hays, and much more talk
about the comedy in Cleveland than I can report. They spoke

with unqualified praise of your acting, which they said interpreted the most delicate shades of character, while it gave the
broad effects with force and vigor. They spoke of uncommon
quality in the audiences *drawn* by the comedy and yet of the
capability the play has of pleasing the popular element.— Mrs.
Hay says the applause often started from the galleries. I asked
particularly about the song, and Hay said you did it charmingly, and with the prettiest effect.[1]— In a letter recently
received from Miss Constance Fennimore [*sic*] Woolson (the
writer,) she says: "Letters from Cleveland speak of your play
with enthusiasm: it was greatly admired by the best people
they have out there. 'I don't know when I've seen anything
better or brighter,' writes a lady whom I consider an excellent
and fastidious judge."[2]

—What pleases me about all the praise the play gets, both
on your account and my own[,] is that people seem honestly
glad of an American comedy that makes its way without
farcical or melodramatic effects. Does n't this indicate a great
field before us? You have your finger on the patient's pulse
and can tell how much of his joy is real & how much is
affected.

The Hays were full of kind words about you, and after
listening to them, I almost felt that I had seen you act. They
had not a word of adverse criticism. I have broken ground on
the Spanish play.

—I infer from all the notices that the play succeeds as a
comedy of *character.* In this direction I have worked in the
new act.

Can you do me the favor to send me a play bill from each
place? I want to make a collection. I shouldn't care for them
with a second play.

Yours truly

W. D. Howells.

Sorry for your lame knee. Hope it's all right now.

Postscript.

The canvas on which Constance proposes to paint must be
portentously large—say three or four feet by five. In drawing
she must use a mahl-stick in her left hand to support her right.

The easel should stand so as to bring the canvas almost edge-wise to the audience, and interpose it like a screen between her and Bartlett, where they stand before it, and General Wyatt where he sits beside her small table. This is mere suggestion—the way I imagined the scene.

I feel anxious about the General's *snore*. Pray have it a snore of the utmost possible refinement. If a sufficiently comical effect could be produced by his simply being discovered asleep when his paper drops, the snore might be omitted.[3] I may think of some better device to make Bartlett laugh and Constance angry if the act pleases you otherwise.

1. "Romance," a three-stanza song, is sung by Bartlett in the final act, unaware that Constance overhears it.

2. Constance Fenimore Woolson (1840–1894) lived in Cleveland for most of her girlhood.

3. In the new act the snore had been described as "a loud, prolonged, and very stertorous respiration."

40. BARRETT TO HOWELLS, 15 NOVEMBER 1877 (HARVARD, TELEGRAM)

THE WESTERN UNION TELEGRAPH COMPANY . . . Youngstown Ohio 1877 . . . Nov. 15. . . . *To* W. D. Howells
Let Act meet me Monday Indianapolis will try there Friday
Lawrence Barrett

41. BARRETT TO HOWELLS, 19 NOVEMBER 1877 (HARVARD, TELEGRAM)

THE WESTERN UNION TELEGRAPH COMPANY . . . Indianapolis Ind 1877 . . .Nov. 19. . . . *To* W. D. Howells
New matter read and with delight on Saturday I will tell you what public think of it My hopes are high
Lawrence Barrett

42. HOWELLS TO BARRETT, 21 NOVEMBER
1877, MS. (PRICE, 3 PP.)

. . . The Atlantic Monthly.

. . . Cambridge, Mass. Nov. 21, 1877.

Dear Mr. Barrett:

I have to thank you for your thoughtful kindness in tele-
graphing me your good opinion of the new act, and I hope
with all my heart that it will justify your liking. It seemed to
me good, and done on the right theory, but I am never over-
confident about what I've done; and I waited your judgment
with great anxiety. If this new act, on experiment[,] has the
s[ame] success you desire, if it gi[ves] you the sort of scope
that I think it will, I believe we can add several fine effects to
differing parts of the play. I wish that to this end you would
make a note of any contrivable situation that occurs to you,
and we will talk it over when you come east and we meet at
Providence. It seems to me that Bartlett can be made a part
that the public will like always to see you in, and nothing shall
be wanting in me to do this.

I shall be glad to hear from you on Saturday. —I often think
what a worried and excited life you must lead, and wonder
that you can stand it. Anything exciting uses me up at once
and an actor's life is all excitement. I suppose there isn't a
moment of the winter when you don't long for the summer in
Cohasset. Adieu and good luck.

Yours sincerely

W. D. Howells.

43. BARRETT TO HOWELLS, 22 NOVEMBER
1877 (HARVARD, TELEGRAM)

THE WESTERN UNION TELEGRAPH COMPANY . . . Indianapolis
Ind *1877 . . .*Nov. 22. . . . *To* W. D. Howells
Try new matter in Detroit cannot get ready sooner
Barrett

44. BARRETT TO HOWELLS, 1 DECEMBER
1877 (HARVARD, TELEGRAM)

THE WESTERN UNION TELEGRAPH COMPANY . . . Detroit Mich
1877 . . .Dec 1 . . . *To* W. D. Howells
New act went well score another success & write me down no
prophet God bless you[1]

Lawrence Barrett

1. LB wrote Osgood the next day that he had been "Sold again!—the new
act made a good impression and by many who saw it I am told that it is now
nearly complete as a play[,] which fills me with joy" (quoted in Meserve, p.
70).

45. BARRETT TO HOWELLS, 3 DECEMBER
1877, MS. (HARVARD, 3 PP.)

Lindell Hotel [St. Louis]

Dec 3 — 1877

Dear Mr. Howells,

I have only to repeat what I said in my telegram about the
new act. It was a success, and a good addition to the play—in
spite of my fears. I took the liberty of making one or two
changes, which I think you will approve—cutting the scene
between Mrs Ransom and Mary—and keeping Bartlett on the
stage, at the end, instead of sending him off as you did.[1] I play
it here next week with a new Cast—which will be a trial for
the play—the actors will scarcely have a chance to get into the
work but that will be a test of the Comedy. You will make
some other changes after you have seen it and by the time we
are ready for Boston—we shall be ready *indeed*[.]

I once more congratulate you—and have requested my
agent to forward you a check for the second hundred due in
Detroit—

Very Truly Yours

Lawrence Barrett

1. In the new act as printed, Mrs. Ransom, the landlady, does not appear,
nor does Mary, a servant; and Bartlett remains on stage. But as Meserve indicates (p. 90), the prompt copy at Harvard has cue parts for Mrs. Ransom and

Mary. Also, the cast as reported in the *Detroit Free Press* for 28 November 1877 includes "Landlord of the Hotel" and "George, a Villager" as well as the landlady and Mary, though this review is of the first performance, still based on the original three-act text, since the four-act version was introduced at the matinee of December 1.

46. HOWELLS TO BARRETT, 7 DECEMBER 1877, MS. (PRINCETON, 2 PP.)

Cambridge, *Dec. 7, 1877.*

Dear Mr. Barrett:

I received the dispatch you were kind enough to send me from Detroit, and was extremely glad to know that the new act has not failed. I hope you will find it what you want, in the way of an enlargement of the play, and that the public will like it too. I confess I am getting curious myself to see the performance.

Your agent has this day sent me a check for $100, for which many thanks.

I send this letter to St Louis, where I suppose you are, and where I hope the play will have a good fate.

At what odd moments I have I work on Yorick.

Yours cordially

W. D. Howells.

Do you know that you owe me three or four letters[?][1]

1. This remark is puzzling in light of WDH's earlier remarks in the letter. LB had written him on December 3 and telegraphed him on November 22 and December 1.

47. BARRETT TO HOWELLS, 10 DECEMBER 1877, MS. (HARVARD, 2 PP.)

Lindell Hotel [St. Louis]

Dec 10th, 1877

Dear Sir,

I have read over for the first time the Detroit interview,[1] and

52 LETTERS AND

I write to say that I never made use of such trash as is there printed about yourself and your Comedy— It is made out of the whole cloth by the Reporter— The paper was marked and sent by my Agent[.] Pray do acquit me of complicity in such maudlin conversation, and believe me

Yours Truly,

Lawrence Barrett

We do the whole Comedy here on Sunday next. Please acknowledge receipt of $100—in full of claim to Nov 30th leaving Matinée of Dec 1st still due—

1. The so-called interview almost certainly refers to the second paragraph of the review of the play that appeared on page one of the *Detroit Free Press* for 28 November 1877. While it hardly qualifies as trash, as WDH's diplomatic reply implies, LB could easily have thought it portrayed him as overshadowing the author. That he suggests not having seen it until he wrote this letter nearly two weeks later verges on the unbelievable, for LB followed reviews of his performances closely and only by chance would have missed this enthusiastic and lengthy piece on *A Counterfeit Presentment*. The offending paragraph reads:

> This delicious comedy is the result of a brief conversation between Mr. Howells and Mr. Barrett. The latter had read with great satisfaction "A Chance Acquaintance" and other works of a similar character by the brilliant editor of the Atlantic, and he suggested to him the desirability of writing a comedy for stage presentation, promising to play it himself. "A Counterfeit Presentment" soon afterward appeared in the Atlantic. Barrett saw it was precisely what he wanted to round out his repertoire, studied the role of "Bartlett," and brought the play out in Cincinnati a few weeks ago. Its first representation proved the correctness of Mr. Barrett's judgment, for it captivated the public at the outset.

The review goes on to mention the "exceptionally cultured and critical" audience, one of the "largest seen at that theater this season," and does not neglect the principal actor, who "seems to fairly revel in the opportunities [the play] offers for exhibiting his admirable powers in quite a new light." The *Free Press* had indeed hailed LB from start to finish, beginning with an anticipation of "That prime favorite and truly eminent tragedian" in its November 25 preview of the coming week and closing with a December 2 retrospective review of the eight performances, which, with their receipts exceeding $4,000, the largest of the season, showed "conclusively enough that Lawrence Barrett has that quality of 'draw,' so dear to the managerial heart." In both the earlier and later summaries *A Counterfeit Presentment* received more emphasis than any of the other plays, though each of them also drew favorable though less ecstatic reviews.

48. BARRETT TO HOWELLS, 13 DECEMBER 1877, MS. (HARVARD, 1 P.)

Lindell Hotel,

St. Louis.

Dec 13 — [1877]

My Dear Sir,

As Mr. Osgood informs me [that] you have opposed the plan of a Special train to Worcester, I wish to advise that you see the Play first on Friday the 28th at Providence—where your presence may be unobserved and unknown—to audience and actors.

Yours Very Truly—

Lawrence Barrett

49. HOWELLS TO BARRETT, 16 DECEMBER 1877, MS. (PRICE, 2 PP.)

. . . *The Atlantic Monthly.*

. . . *Cambridge, Mass.* Dec. 16, 1877.

Dear Mr. Barrett:

I have just received your note of the 13th; that of the 10th I found at home on my return from a visit at Hartford.[1] I did not know where to send a reply, and I now enclose this to Osgood, asking that he will "back" it to you.

Of course I saw how the Detroit interview had distorted and misunderstood you, and after a moment's vexation I dismissed the subject from my mind. I can conceive [that] you were far more annoyed than I was. The St. Louis interview is very interesting, as a statement of your ideas in regard to the drama, and will do you credit with all who read it.[2]

We shall both, I think, find it best not to try the excursion scheme to Worcester; I don't believe the play could be properly criticized by the Boston papers at that distance, and halfway work would hurt its future chances. I shall be on hand at Providence.[3]

I return the account with my signature.

Yours sincerely

W. D. Howells.

1. WDH visited the Clemenses in Hartford with his daughter Winifred between December 11 and 15 and gave two lectures there.

2. WDH refers here to a lengthy interview with LB conducted by Thomas Betterton and printed in the *St. Louis Globe-Democrat* (9 December 1877, 3:3–5).

3. WDH's reluctance to go to Worcester may have resulted from the publicity involved in a special train for that event.

50. BARRETT TO HOWELLS, 16 DECEMBER 1877, MS. (HARVARD, 2 PP.)

Lindell Hotel

St. Louis, Dec 16 1877.

My Dear Sir,

The notice in the "Republican" was written by Mr. Thomas Garrett, one of the Chief Editors, and is, I think, one of the best ever written of the Comedy.[1] Would you think it unworthy of yourself to drop me a line which I might send to him? It would aid the play when done here again, and reward him for a piece of work which will certainly help your comedy in St Louis. You may either address me or him. I can hear from you at Buffalo at the end of the coming week—at the Academy of Music.

Hastily Yours

Lawrence Barrett

1. Garrett, in the *Missouri Republican* (16 December 1877, 8:5), noted: "It is purely American" in "subject and treatment, without the least scrap of sensational padding, or the least trace of French scum. . . . The naturalness and

simplicity of the action of the play are a substitute for the plot, and the interest never flags. Its true character drawing is a dramatic treasure, and an original American comedy has been written." For the record, the play had also been favorably reviewed in the *St. Louis Globe-Democrat* (15 December 1877, 3:6).

51. HOWELLS TO BARRETT, 20 DECEMBER 1877, MS. (PRICE, 1 P.)

Cambridge, Dec. 20, 1877.

Dear Mr. Barrett:

In your note of the 16th, you speak of a notice in the St. Louis Republican. I suppose you sent me, or ordered to be sent me, a copy of that paper containing a review of your performance of the comedy at St Louis. I should have been glad to see it, and no doubt to do what you asked in regard to it; but it must have miscarried, for it has never reached me. Promising myself the pleasure of seeing you next week,

Yours sincerely

W. D. Howells.

52. BARRETT TO HOWELLS, 1 JANUARY 1878, MS. (HARVARD, 1 P.)

Haynes Hotel

Springfield, Mass

Jan 1st *1878*.

My Dear Sir,

Your kind favor of Books reached me last night—also your letter and the changes. I will look the latter over, at my leisure. Many thanks for the Biographies—[1]

We closed the year with the Comedy disasterously [*sic*], our house was $120—the smallest I have played to in the year—while Shylock tonight promises $600—do they read in New England?[2] A Happy New Year to you.

Yours Sincerely

Lawrence Barrett

1. Presumably the five autobiographies (including one by Carlo Goldoni, the Italian playwright), for which WDH had written introductions, published by James R. Osgood and Company.

2. Ironically, the Providence *Evening Bulletin* had hailed the play three nights earlier as "a genuine comedy in the pure sense. . . . It is a picture from the American society of to-day as perfect in tone and spirit as can be" (quoted in Meserve, p. 70). Still, WDH wrote Osgood on 5 January 1878 that he felt "awfully discouraged about the thing" (Harvard).

53. BARRETT TO HOWELLS, 8 JANUARY 1878, MS. (Harvard, 3 pp.)

Arlington House

Washington, [D.C.].

Jan 8 — 1878

Dear Mr. Howells,

Your thoughtful favor met me here. Many thanks for the letters. General Garfield was an acquaintance a good many years ago—but it will revive it strongly to have such a good endorsement. I will try to muster up courage to call upon the President. I may be able to correct that bias in his training which keeps him from the Theatre.[1] Don't worry about the comedy, or its unpopularity. I made an overestimate of New England forgetting that the population of its large towns is not entirely made of readers or thinkers. The Dime novel and the soul-stirring record of the "Mill Girl's Perils"[2] are the current literature in that region—and only the few know Howells and good taste. The boundless West can teach them culture—if it can be learned. The Comedy will take care of itself and of them, too, by and bye—

I will tell you what they think of the Comedy here on Friday.

Very Truly Yours

Lawrence Barrett.

I may send you something in the Dramatic Way during the Winter—with "Garrick" as the title—but I don't know whether it will be good for your purposes.[3] You can only reject it—and no harm will be done.

1. James A. Garfield (1831–1881), close family friend of the Howellses, at this time was a congressman from Ohio. Rutherford B. Hayes, the president, also a cousin of WDH's wife and the subject of a campaign life by WDH in 1876, had less bias against the theatre than LB may have thought. Though his printed diary records his attending only a few plays, he was usually enthusiastic, as when he noted in 1883 that *Othello* (with LB as Iago) was a "noble spectacle."

2. Apparently a title of LB's invention but a common theme in novels and serials.

3. As far as is known, LB's essay on Garrick, if written, was not published. However, about this time LB either was playing or getting ready to play *David Garrick,* a comedy by Thomas W. Robertson (1829–1871), which was made famous in England and the United States by E. H. Sothern (1826–1881). Sothern had always presented it as a separate play, but in his revival of it LB almost invariably combined it with a shortened form of *The Merchant of Venice* and occasionally, though much later, in combination with a cut version of *Yorick's Love.* Whether LB also abbreviated *David Garrick* in these combined performances is not known, but its acting time was less than two hours and the complications of the comedy would not allow much abridgement.

54. HOWELLS TO BARRETT, 14 MARCH 1878, MS. (PRICE, 1 P.)

. . . The Atlantic Monthly.

. . . Cambridge, Mass. March 14, 1878.

My dear Barrett:

Don't worry about the money on my account.[1] I'm not pressed for it, and should be very sorry if you inconvenienced yourself under a contrary impression.

Write me a line to say when I can see you about the comedy for half an hour, and let it be in the afternoon if possible.

Yours sincerely

W. D. Howells.

1. WDH is apparently replying to a letter from LB that does not survive.

55. HOWELLS TO BARRETT, 19 MARCH 1878,
MS. (PRINCETON, 3 PP.)

. . . The Atlantic Monthly.

. . . Cambridge, Mass. March 19, 1878.

Dear Mr. Barrett:

Since seeing you, I have thought over the cast for the comedy, and I very much wish that you could get Mrs. Vincent to take the landlady's part, and give Mrs. Wyatt's part say to the lady who played Duchatelet's mother last Saturday afternoon in The Marble Heart.[1] Mrs. Vincent has so much of the *vis comica* that I don't see how she is to restrain herself within the bounds of the somewhat subdued anxiety of Mr[s]. Wyatt. That is a part which might be acted neutrally, colorlessly and no harm done; but people are so used to laughing at everything Mrs. Vincent does, that I'm afraid that with the best ideas of what it should be, she would find it taken in a comic sense. I owe her too much gratitude for pleasure in times past to say anything that should seem to slight her powers; I know what a delightful artist she is, and if she would only take the landlady's part, she would really add another character to the play, and contribute vastly to its success. We could restore much that we cut out of the opening scenes of the new act, and the part would not be so slight as it now is.

Madame Duchatelet (I don't remember her name) would make a good enough Mrs. Wyatt. If you think fit, please show this letter to Mr Field.[2]

I forgot to ask who does the general. Mr. Clannin?[3]

Yours sincerely

W. D. Howells.

1. Mrs. J. R. Vincent, née Mary Ann Farley (1818–1887), was born in England, where she first acted. She came to the United States in 1846 and joined the Boston Museum company in 1852. Among her celebrated roles were Mrs. Malaprop in Richard Sheridan's *The Rivals* and Mrs. Hardcastle in Oliver Goldsmith's *She Stoops to Conquer.* Laura Phillips, who was to play the part of Mrs. Ransom the landlady, had been Duchatelet's mother in *The Marble Heart,* a popular play translated from Theodore Barrière's *Les Filles de Marbre* (1853), which LB often presented.

2. R. M. Field (1833–1902), born in Boston and a graduate of the Latin School, was managing producer of the Boston Museum company from 1864 until it closed in 1893. The author of an obituary claimed he was "perhaps the best liked theatrical man in the United States." He has been sometimes confused with Roswell Martin Field (1851–1919), a midwestern journalist who wrote music and drama articles.

3. Robert F. McClannin (1832–1899) was another permanent member of the Museum company, which he had joined after the Civil War.

56. BARRETT TO HOWELLS, 21 MARCH 1878,[1] MS.
(Harvard, 2 pp.)

Thursday.

Dear Mr. Howells—

Yours received. It would be fatal to put the Lady you speak of in Mrs. Vincent's part. The audience will accept the latter Lady in any part, however misfitted she may be.

Miss Clarke is cast for Constance.[2] We can get Miss Cummins— If you write to Mr Field and say she is your preference it can be managed and I may escape a professional annoyance which could not touch you. It would be for the good of the play—and I hope you will consider it. Please do it at once as time is precious, and refer Mr. F. to *me*. I will then endorse your requests. What shall I say to the Taylor Committee[?][3] Would you mind framing a few lines for a poor creature whose head is confused by rehearsals and performances?

Ever yours

Lawrence Barrett

1. The letter is dated as a response to WDH's letter of 19 March 1878 (Tuesday).

2. Annie M. Clarke, who did play the part of Constance, had become a permanent member of the Museum company in 1861 and later the leading actress until her retirement in the late 1880s. During LB's April engagement she appeared in seven of the nine plays he presented.

3. Neither the identity of the Taylor Committee nor the nature of the few lines LB requested has been ascertained.

57. BARRETT TO HOWELLS, 16 APRIL 1878, MS. (HARVARD,
2 pp.)

Continental Hotel. [Philadelphia.]

April 16th [18]78

My Dear Mr. Howells,

We played the Comedy last night to a wretched house—but
with its usual success—and I send you the morning notices
with more to follow.[1]

I want you now to do me a friendly act. I wrote to Aldrich
last week declining to play the Comedy at Ponkapog—on
account of a sneering notice of the fact, which a paltry scrib-
bler had seized upon to wound me.[2] Was wrong to notice it—
wrong to make it an excuse for violating a promise— I have
so written to Aldrich—and have, moreover, asked that he
would allow it to pass as if it had never happened and let the
performance take place, thus allowing me to regain my self
respect which I have somehow forfeited by my horrid temper— If he does not allow this—I shall feel that I have
wounded him beyond repair—and that will be a severer
punishment than I deserve— Pray aid me with your good
offices in the matter if you can—and let the Comedy be acted.[3]
I play it here four times this week—but of course it will not
draw now that it has opened so badly—but it will leave a
mark which will not be forgotten.

Heartily Yours

Lawrence Barrett

1. According to the Philadelphia *Public Ledger,* the play "abounds in scenes
of a serio-comic, as well as laughable character" (16 April 1878, 3:6). The
Philadelphia Inquirer averred, however, that "it is not a good acting play, and
cannot be made so," because "it has no plot worth mentioning" (16 April 1878,
4:5); and the Philadelphia *Press* also carped that it lacked a plot and its denouement was "simply puerile," that WDH "had no practical idea of the requirements of the stage" (16 April 1878, 8:3–4). The Philadelphia *North American* praised the "easy and graceful style" of the play and dismissed as "a
superficial view" the complaint that "there is not enough of a story for the time
that is occupied in the telling. . . . A bright, clean and pure play like this can

never be a failure, and the more we have of such plays the better for the stage and for the public morals" (16 April 1878, 1:2). The *Philadelphia Evening Bulletin* also allowed that the "witty, refined" comedy was "composed of slight material" but pronounced it "the best American piece produced on the stage for many a day" (16 April 1878, 2:4).

2. Thomas Bailey Aldrich (1836–1907) was the author of *The Story of a Bad Boy* (1870) and succeeded WDH as editor of the *Atlantic Monthly* from 1881 to 1890. LB apparently was chagrined by a critique of his acting by a small-town Massachusetts journalist (unlocated).

3. WDH complied with LB's request and wrote Aldrich the next day to urge him to accept the apology (Harvard). Aldrich then wrote LB on 13 May 1878 "to tell you that I shall not take the advantage of your good nature. Indeed, I have not enough interest in the Ponkapog theatre to let you carry out your generous idea, for it was very generous to offer to play there after you had winter's work and your California campaign" (Price).

58. HOWELLS TO BARRETT, 18 MAY 1878, MS.
(PRICE, 1 P.)

Cambridge, May 18, 1878

Dear Mr. Barrett:

I heard from Mr. Osgood, the other day[,] that you were in town last week, and I regretted not to have seen you, for I had hoped to speak with you of a conversation [I][1] have had with Mr. Field about a comedy for the Museum.[2] I explained to Mr Field at that interview that I regarded it as a preliminary to a talk with you; and I suppose I need not say that nothing has been concluded or intended in prejudice of any known plans of yours in regard to myself.

Yours truly

W. D. Howells.

1. The word *I* has faded completely from the manuscript, though to judge by other semifaded letters in this part of the original, as well as a rough draft of this letter in the Houghton Library at Harvard (bMS Am 1784.1 [43]), it once existed.

2. Aware of LB's increasing uneasiness with *A Counterfeit Presentment,* WDH had approached R. M. Field offering an earlier comedy, *Out of the Question* (see the note to letter 2). On 3 May 1878, Field wrote WDH acknowledg-

ing his letter of May 2 (not extant) and approved of his work as "the ground-work for an excellent play." On 29 August 1878 he asked WDH if he would "dispose of *Counterfeit Presentment* for production at the Museum," and in a letter of September 24 he told WDH that *A Counterfeit Presentment* had been cast and would be produced. However, on 4 November 1878 Field reported to WDH that his revision still required "further invention and elaboration," though it would at length be produced at the Museum on 15 and 16 January 1879. For more on those performances, see the note to letter 76. All of Field's letters to WDH cited in this note are in the Howells Collection at Harvard.

59. BARRETT TO HOWELLS, 29 MAY 1878, MS.
(Harvard, 3 pp.)

Occidental Hotel

San Francisco, May 29 *1878.*

Dear Mr. Howells

I was glad to receive your letter of the 19th.—[1] Mr. Field had spoken to me of his plan, and I expected you would speak of it to me also. I think you will do wisely to let the Museum have some of your works and I have also concluded that I can be of no further service to you with the "Counterfeit Present-ment." Mr. Field will gladly play the piece a week or longer next season with his stock company, to your profit, and then aid you better than I could in placing it elsewhere. The public will not come to see me in genteel comedy—as is proved by your beautiful Play. If you think I have done any good in advertizing the Play—and can see justice in the further pay-ment of $100 on my part to make your reward for the year $300—I will be much thankful—and will hand you that amount and a release from all obligations to me on account of the actors rights. I think what I have done will help your profit when it is reproduced at the Museum— But I simply suggest this as a sort of settlement in surrender of the right I hold—holding myself at your command for the complete fulfilment of my obligation.

The Play was too far above their heads here and failed utterly the first night—I took it off at once. The difference in audiences is surprising. The notices of the play are unworthy of your perusal.[2]

My engagement has been an excellent one—and I return in a few days— I can find your reply at Cohasset—from whence I can send you my marked copy—[3]

Yours very Truly

Lawrence Barrett

1. In view of what LB says of it, the letter that he acknowledges is WDH's of May 18, not May 19.

2. The *Alta California,* for example, dismissed it as "pleasantly written but rather lightly constructed." The critic complained particularly that much of the dialogue in the final two acts seemed to have been "inserted as padding" to prolong the play (28 May 1878, 1:4). Similarly, the *San Francisco Bulletin* panned the production: "It is mere talk, sometimes clever, but with a sameness to its cleverness" (28 May 1878, 3:1).

3. Surrendering of the marked copy, presumably the printed book with four acts, indicates beyond any doubt that LB considered the San Francisco performance his farewell to the play. When he impulsively offered to play it again in Boston in letter 122, dated 7 December 1879, he asked for "the book and parts" to be sent to him, and WDH responded in letter 123 that he was sending the "books of the comedy" through the actor William Seymour, though on this occasion LB did not offer the play. However, he did give a one-time performance at the Park Theatre in Boston on 5 February 1881, presumably using the copies of the book and parts that had been returned to him in December 1879.

60. BARRETT TO HOWELLS, 15 JUNE 1878, MS. (HARVARD, 2 PP.)

Cohasset, Mass.

June 15th—1878

My Dear Sir,

I have been ill since my return, and only now find time to attend to your request. I send the Ms & parts by Express.[1] They cost me about $25 to copy, so I charge you with that amount. I will assume the *more* of the royalties, saving only those places in New England which you requested me to strike out when I last saw you—I will be obliged to delay the final payment until my fall season commences—say Oct. 1st, when I will send you $300 as per list enclosed.[2] With best wishes permit me to subscribe myself,

Sincerely Yours,

Lawrence Barrett

W. D. Howells, Esq.

1. Here LB's "Ms & parts" differs from his letter of 7 December 1879 when he asks for "the book and parts" to be sent to him. While LB tends to be somewhat loose in his designation of the medium of what is written, the $25 copying charge points to an actual manuscript, though in both cases the "parts" may refer to a prompt- or parts-document.

2. The list is that of "Performances of Counterfeit Presentment," which is printed at the end of note 1 to letter 16.

61. BARRETT TO HOWELLS, 14 JULY 1878, MS.
(HARVARD, 3 PP.)

Cohasset

July 14 [1878]

My Dear Sir.

I have at last obtained the version of "A New Play" which was given originally in New York, and have read the Drama for the first time. I am now confident that it can be made highly successful—and I write to ask that you will[,] as soon as possible, complete a translation, with a purpose to make, then, a free adaptation for my use. I am prepared to make any reasonable money advance to reward you for your giving up any other employment during your work upon the Play and I trust you will be able to state in reply that you can cooperate with me in the matter. I will meet you generously, and I am certain I can assure you a handsome return. I will make it the staple of my season and do it in N.Y. in November. I prefer doing this to presenting any other version, as I am confident you can best do it. I must buy all rights from the authors of this version. I now have to secure the title, which is better than the original.[1] Please let me hear from you soon—and believe me,

Very Truly Yours

Lawrence Barrett

P.S. If you like, I will make an offer for the translation, and a price for the performances. Pray keep this in confidence, whether you assent or no.

W. D. Howells, Esq.

1. As noted in note 1 to letter 18, the Daly presentation of *A New Play* under the title *Yorick* in 1874 had not succeeded. In an interview later, LB recalled that Daly "sent me over the play in manuscript" and that, although he had been "delighted with the story and dramatic plot," he "finally came to the conclusion that I could do nothing with it." LB then asked Daly "what he would take for the title alone. He replied that I might use it for $2,000 the first year, and after that we would make terms. I sent back the manuscript, leaving the offer open" (Philadelphia *Press*, 16 January 1880, 5:1). See also the note to letter 87.

62. BARRETT TO HOWELLS, 17 JULY 1878, MS.
(HARVARD, 2 PP.)

Cohasset, Mass.

July 17 — 1878

My Dear Sir.

Yours received. I will send up the version of the play I now have that you may read before we meet. That will simplify our talk. I have no doubt we can arrange the terms, if you see the alterations clearly— I will do myself the honor of calling either on Friday afternoon at the office, or at Belmont on Saturday.

Sincerely Yours

Lawrence Barrett

P.S. Of course that which I send is merely to show what *has been* done as a suggestion of how much better is possible. My servant will deliver this.

63. BARRETT TO HOWELLS, 20 JULY 1878, MS.
(HARVARD, 2 PP.)

Tremont House.

Boston.

July 20 *th* 1878.

W. D. Howells.

My Dear Sir.

I will accept your offer to translate the Spanish Play "The New Play" and to make such alterations and additions as we spoke of for $500. The original copy of the play will also then be mine, and you agree to make no copy of the same, for another's use or for your own. I will agree to pay this $500 Aug 1st 1878 when you will begin the translation and you will deliver the work to me before the 1st of September 1878.

Should we then decide to make any elaborate adaptation of the play, we can, as you say, arrange the terms for the same, later.

The only change I have made in your offer is to change the date of my commencement of the work to accommodate some financial matters which will be easier Aug 1st than now. I hope this will not be disagreeable to you.

Please confirm my understanding of the contract by an early reply.

Yours truly

Lawrence Barrett

64. BARRETT TO HOWELLS, 23 JULY 1878,[1]
MS. (HARVARD, POSTCARD)

Cohasset

W. D. Howells Esq

Belmont, Mass.

Letter received. Will see you, or you will hear from me during the week on the subject of "Y[orick]." Please defer the matter till then.

Yours,

L.B.

1. This card is dated by the postmark of the stamp.

65. BARRETT TO HOWELLS, 24 JULY 1878, MS.
(HARVARD, 2 PP.)

Cohasset Mass.

July 24 — [1878]

My Dear Sir.

I think we both mean the same, and I here put what I think a fair interpretation upon paper of our understanding. I will pay you $500 for your advance upon the play which you will translate and adapt—and $15 for every performance until you have received $2000—when the play becomes my property. If this is your understanding, please say as much, and I will be ready Aug 1st with the $500—I would like to produce it first in Detroit during the week of September 16th and if it goes well, it can afterwards be given in my other regular engagements. I think Dick Burbage will be better than Shakespeare—and I wish you to think on a title, as we cannot use "Yorick[.]" I put down some that occur to me.

"Poor Yorick."

"A poor Player."

"A New Play."

Awaiting your reply

Very truly yours

Lawrence Barrett

66. HOWELLS TO BARRETT, 26 JULY 1878, MS.
(PRICE, 2 PP.)

. . . *The Atlantic Monthly.*

. . . *Boston.* July 26, 1878.

Dear Mr. Barrett:

I have your letter of the 24th, proposing to pay me $500 in advance for translating the *Drama nuevo*, and thereafter for changes or adaptation, $15 a night for each performance till the royalties amount to $2000 when the play becomes yours. This is satisfactory, and I agree to it.

—I wish if you have any account of the stage, or the actors of Shakespear's time, and can easily lay your hand on it, you would send it [to] me, or give me the title of it. The character of Shakespear in the play is so nobly and gravely imagined and the relation he has to bear to Alice and Edmund is so serious, that I do not see how we could give his character to such an actor as Burbage.[1] What I am thinking of is some other actor, like Dekker, who was also a poet and dramatist and whom the language put in Shakespear's mouth would fit.

I have thought how to write a preliminary scene, and some other points, but I shall first make a translation.

Yours sincerely

W. D. Howells.

P.S. A New Play seems rather tame for a title. I'll try what I can do.

1. Before rejecting the idea, WDH had penciled a note on the first page of the manuscript of *A New Play* in the Price Collection to "Substitute Burbage for Shakespear," as LB had proposed in his previous letter. Richard Burbage (1567?–1619), the most popular actor of his time, was widely desired for the chief parts by William Shakespeare, Ben Jonson, and the collaborative dramatists Francis Beaumont and John Fletcher. He is definitely established as having played in *Hamlet, Othello,* and *Richard III.* Thomas Dekker (1570?–1632) wrote plays prolifically both alone and in collaboration, including *The Shoemaker's Holiday, The Honest Whore,* and *Old Fortunatus.* WDH made a mistake in referring to him as "some other actor," as LB observes at the beginning of letter 68.

67. BARRETT TO HOWELLS, 27 [?] JULY 1878,[1]
MS. (Harvard, 2 pp.)

S. D. Warren & Co.

Cathedral Building,

Boston.

Saturday. A.M.

My Dear Sir,

"I have slept" upon our talk— I can *now* speak. What do you say to *this?*[2]

I will pay you $250 August 1ˢ and $250 Sept 10ᵗʰ for the translation of the Play—and afterwards allow you $15 per night royalty until payments have passed 100 performances, when I am to possess *all* rights upon payment of $500 more. The payments of the first $500 I have made easier than you wished (for myself) and I hope you can accept— A "Yes" or "No" by bearer will be final.

Yours in haste,

Lawrence Barrett

W D Howells Esq

1. The letter is tentatively dated from the circumstances outlined in the two preceding letters. Since LB writes from Boston and WDH's letter of July 26 was most likely addressed to him at Cohasset, LB almost certainly had not yet received WDH's letter.

2. In this letter LB sweetens the terms offered in letter 65. Though it splits the first $500 into two parts, it requires only 100 performances, upon which a bonus of $500 is offered, as against 133 performances in the earlier letter. The total amount is $2,500 in both letters.

68. BARRETT TO HOWELLS, 30 JULY 1878, MS. (HARVARD, 4 PP.)

Cohasset

July 30 — [1878]

Dear Mr. Howells,

Yours of the 26 received. I cannot find that Dekker was either Actor or Manager—"Galts Lives" would be useful—but I have not a copy—"Doran's Annals" give you a good view of the Theatre of the time—also the 1ˢ Vol of Ulrici[1]—Burbage was actor and manager—so was Alleyne—but not authors. Peele, Lodge, Marlowe, Jonson, Shakespeare, Heywood were actors.

I quote from Taine:—"Many (authors) are roysters, who give themselves up to every passion—undermine their health, and mar their glory." "Such are Nash, Dekker, Greene." "Dekker passed three years in King's Bench Prison."[2]

I think he will hardly fill the space which the Spanish

author here allotted to Shakespeare in this play. Can we not *imagine* Dick Burbage an Author? I would like to rescue his honorable name from oblivion. I feel certain you will hit upon a good name for the character before you are done. How would Marlowe do? In the translation you can use the old name, and when you are adapting the change can be made. I will send you the $500 during the week.

Yours Very Sincerely,

Lawrence Barrett

Taine's 1^s volume gives a good idea of the theatre in those days. I will lend you mine if you have no copy.

1. John Galt, *The Lives of the Players* (1831); John Doran, *Annals of the English Stage* (1864); Hermann Ulrici, *Shakespeare's Dramatic Art* (in two volumes, first translated into English from German in 1876).

2. LB follows fairly closely H. Van Laun's translation of Hippolyte-Adolphe Taine's *History of English Literature* (1863), book 2, chapter 2: "Many are roysterers, sad roysterers of the same sort, such as Musset and Murger, who give themselves up to every passion, and 'drown their sorrows in the bowl'; capable of the purest and most poetic dreams, of the most delicate and touching tenderness, and who yet can only undermine their health and mar their fame. Such are Nash, Decker, and Greene. . . . Decker, who passed three years in the King's Bench Prison. . ."

69. BARRETT TO HOWELLS, 30 JULY 1878, MS.
(HARVARD, 3 PP.)

Cohasset,

July 30 — [1878]

Dear Mr. Howells.

I have just had a disappointment which will affect our agreement. I was promised $500 (due me some time since) positively on the 1^s August and confidently expected it. I am apprised tonight that it will not be paid, and I must ask you to defer the work for five or six weeks, till I am at work again when I will forward the money. I hope you will be able to go on with it at that time, and that I may not suffer a second disappointment. The delay is a serious annoyance to me as I had hoped to play the Drama in September, and it cannot now be done till late in the season. I hope I am not also causing *you* a disappointment. I write at once on receipt of the news, so unfavorable to my hopes. My wish is that you will be able to go on with the translation by Sept 10*th* when I can surely send the money. I shall miss the *personal* interview after this translation which could so much advance the adaptation, but I must *pay* for my confidence in my friends.

Please let me know that I have not given you annoyance by this failure,—and let me know if you can make the new arrangement.

Yours Sincerely

Lawrence Barrett

70. HOWELLS TO BARRETT, 1 AUGUST 1878,
MS. (PRICE, 2 PP.)

. . . *The Atlantic Monthly.*

. . . *Boston*. Belmont,

Aug. 1, 1878.

Dear Mr. Barrett:

I have your letters of Tuesday,[1] and am sorry for your disappointment about the money. My chief inducement to the translation, as I explained to you, was the hope of a certain sum immediately in hand for present use.

I had already turned some nine pages of the play into English, and I feel inclined to proceed with the version, for ther[e] seem to me numerous possibilities in the plot. For example, what an effect by simply turning Yorick's first soliloquy into dialogue with Edmund, and preparing [for the] impressions of the next scene, and the climax at the end of the act! The play should open with a scene between the dramatist (to be substituted for Shakespeare) and a servant in Yorick's house, which would possess the spectator of the situation in outline.[2]

Your notification of inability to make the advance payment
came in good time to have saved me any work if I had delayed till the time appointed for beginning.

Yours sincerely

W. D. Howells.

1. Letters 68–69.

2. Mostly WDH wished to substitute someone else for Shakespeare in the
play, though sometimes he wavered from this position. LB tended to favor
retention of Shakespeare but finally agreed to the substitution.

71. HOWELLS TO BARRETT, 11 AUGUST 1878, MS. (RUTHERFORD B. HAYES LIBRARY, FREMONT, OHIO, 2 PP.)

. . . *The Atlantic Monthly.*

. . . *Boston.* Belmont,

Aug. 11, 1878.

Dear Mr. Barrett:

I have been going on with the version of the play, and have
now almost finished the first act. It seemed to me that you
ought to open the season with it, and I hope to show you the
complete translation by the 1st of September. The better I
know the play the more I like it, and the less I like what I can
remember of the version you showed me. I think you will be
able to make even a greater hit in Yorick than in the Man of
Airlie.[1]

Please let me know just when you start out on your fall
campaign.

Yours sincerely

W. D. Howells.

1. *Man o'Airlie,* by W. G. Wills (1828–1891), was first presented by LB in
the summer of 1871 and became one of his standard productions; many paid
tribute to his portrayal of James Harebell, the Scotch poet and hero of this
popular drama. See Bailey, pp. 116–24.

72. BARRETT TO HOWELLS, 13 AUGUST 1878,
MS. (HARVARD, 2 PP.)

Cohasset

Aug 13 — [1878]

Dear Mr. Howells.

Mr. Emerson has given me the result of his interview with you.[1] I had supposed you gave up the work. I now authorize you to go on—and by the 10th Sept I will be ready with the $500.— Can you not submit the translation before I leave on the 29th? We can then talk over the alterations you propose. I am happy to hear that you will go on with the work and I will abandon what I was preparing else where.

Hastily yours

L Barrett

1. LB had apparently not received letter 71, WDH's note of August 11, when he wrote this one, though he seems to have heard something to the same effect from Emerson.

73. HOWELLS TO BARRETT, 20 AUGUST 1878,
MS. (PRICE, 1 P.)

Belmont, Aug. 20, 1878

Dear Mr. Barrett:

I wrote you last week proposing to meet you at the Tremont House on Monday the 26th at 2 p.m. Please let me know whether you will come. I shall have the version almost finished by that time, and we ought to spend several hours in going over it together.—I'm afraid that I couldn't meet you later in the week on account of engagements.

Yours sincerely

W. D. Howells.

74. BARRETT TO HOWELLS, 21 AUGUST 1878,
MS. (HARVARD, 1 P.)

Cohasset

Aug 21 — [18]78

Dear Mr. Howells—

My engagements take me away on Thursday next when my
(too short) vacation ends. I will meet you on Monday at the
Tremont House—but it would favor me if you could name an
earlier hour that I may return here by the 330 p.m. train. I
have had frequent "thinks" about the alterations, and I presume you have also had many and better ones than mine— I
will lay my ideas before you on Monday—till then,

Very truly yours

Lawrence Barrett

75. HOWELLS TO BARRETT, AFTER 26 AUGUST 1878,[1] MS. (PRICE, 4 PP. FRAGMENT)

[. . .] include that material in a new scene. Here, for example,
would it do to drop the idea of a *public* representation of the
mimic scene, and have the denouement, with Edmund's death
and Yorick's suicide[,] take place *in the last rehearsal* [?] This
would get over all awkwardness about having to face two
audiences; the place where the mimic scene begins could be
boldly indicated and all those good lines of the mimic scene
kept for you.[2] I could then address and fire up all the parts; I
could have what people I liked on the stage, and all the
coming and going, natural and easy. I think this is a good
idea. It occurred to me when I was translating. If adopted, it
would save all the picturesqueness of the original; it would be
novel; and there would be no break in the act from beginning
to end.

III. Without recapitulating your points, I will say in general
that I will include them all in the new version unless something better occurs to me. If you don't like my changes from
them then I will restore your points. This shall be a matter of
mutual agreement. I will do the work as rapidly as possible.
Send me *my* MS., which I could work from best.

Now, as to terms. When this new version is done, I will

relinquish all claim to future royalties from the play, and I will work at the version in minor particulars till it is perfect, after you have tried it. But before I *begin* upon it you must pay me one thousand dollars.

I make this condition because I cannot afford to do so much work, and have you possibly reject it, or shelve the play before my royalties come to enough to pay my trouble. If the play were my own, I would take all chances with you. My proposition will give me a certainty, and it will put the adapted play in your hands for $1000 less than you have offered me in royalties.

—If you prefer to have some [one] else do the work, I will not stand in your way. But in that case, I merely stipulate that my name shall not be connected with it.

Yours sincerely

W. D. Howells.

1. The surviving portion of this letter probably was written after the meeting at the Tremont House in Boston on Monday, August 26. The stationery is the standard letterhead, "*Atlantic . . . Boston.*"

2. WDH refers to the final scene of the third act. The mimic scene was a point of some difference between WDH and LB, whose views shifted.

76. HOWELLS TO BARRETT, 3 SEPTEMBER 1878, MS. (PRICE, 3 PP.)

. . . *The Atlantic Monthly.*

. . . *Boston.* Sept. 3, 1878.

Dear Mr. Barrett:

I send you by express today the first Act of *A New Play*, and I hope you will like the additions and emendations. I have made them very carefully, and in the exact line of our talk. They strike me, I will own, as good, and I am going to ask you to telegraph me when the MS. comes to your hand that you have received it, and to add a word of satisfaction if you can. I shall let you have the next two acts very soon.

—I have seen Mr. Field (who wrote me after you called) and he will give the comedy sometime in October.[1] He assents to my wish to place it afterwards with some actor but I will ask you not to act for me, as you kindly proposed, until I have offered the play to Miss Morris.² I shall perhaps refer her to you for an opinion on its acting qualities;* if I do, I shall expect perfect frankness from you: that is I sh'd not send her to you for praise, merely.

—A *New Play* fills me more and more with admiration. I think you are destined to make a great hit with it. I wish I had written it! In my changes, I have kept humbly to the author's spirit.

Yours ever truly

W. D. Howells.

'I have concluded not to do so, for I think I have no right. I decidedly think that *A New Play* should be the name.

1. As noted in regard to letter 58, Field produced *A Counterfeit Presentment* at the Museum, not in October but for three performances on Wednesday (afternoon and evening) and Thursday, 15 and 16 January 1879, each performance followed by the "glorious farce" *Seeing Warren.* Sandwiched between performances of *H. M. S. Pinafore,* which was finishing its eight-week run, it received no more than a minor notice in the *Boston Transcript,* though Field ran advertisements from January 7 to 15. WDH's play evidently failed to attract audiences on this occasion, for on 22 January 1879 Field wrote somewhat apologetically that the box receipts (total amounts, not WDH's royalty) had come to $197.70, $226.95, and $164.00.

2. Clara Morris (1848–1925) did not act in the play or produce it. She had appeared in New York between 1870 and 1873 with Daly's company, and until her retirement in the 1890s she was well known for the emotional force of her performances. Just as unsuccessful were WDH's efforts to interest the more famous actors Joseph Jefferson in January 1880 and William Gillette in February 1881; see Meserve, p. 71, for references to these overtures.

77. HOWELLS TO BARRETT, 6 SEPTEMBER
1878, MS. (PRINCETON, 1 P.)

. . . The Atlantic Monthly.

. . . Boston. Sept. 6, 1878

Dear Mr. Barrett:

I will send you the 2d act of the play on Monday, and I

now enclose a comforting letter with reference to the copy-right.[1] You will see that you cannot copyright it as *Yorick*. As *A New Play*, my version of the play is perfectly intangible, I should think.

I hope that the first act has reached you in safety. Do you write me about it.

Yours sincerely

W. D. Howells.

P.S. Please return Mr. Spofford's letter.

1. The "comforting letter" is one of 4 September 1878 (Harvard) from Ainsworth R. Spofford (1825–1908), who became chief assistant to the Librarian of Congress in 1861 and was Librarian-in-Chief between 1864 and 1897. WDH interprets the letter correctly: Spofford comments that a new translation of a work in another language does not infringe upon copyright unless the translation is plagiarized from a version duly protected and then adds that a play *Yorick* was entered in 1874 in "this Office." Though Daly's name is not mentioned, this obviously is his version.

78. HOWELLS TO BARRETT, 9 SEPTEMBER 1878, MS. (PRINCETON, 2 PP.)

Belmont, Sept. 9, 1878

My dear Mr. Barrett:

I send you by express Act II, which I have gone over very carefully. The longer speeches of Yorick I have let run into blank verse, which they did naturally; but I have kept the prose, so that you have two lists to choose from.[1] I have bracketed [ ] the passages duplicated in verse, using pencil. I shall push on Act III, and send it to you at Detroit by the end of the week.

Yours sincerely

W. D. Howells.

1. As true as his word, WDH had literally pasted the speeches in blank verse over the corresponding prose in the manuscript he mailed. As LB indicates in letter 80, he preferred the blank verse. He also copied the verse rather than the prose in his "stage version" of *A New Play* at Harvard.

79. BARRETT TO HOWELLS, 12 SEPTEMBER 1878, MS. (HARVARD, 2 PP.)

Plankinton House . . .

Milwaukee, Sept 12, *1878*

Dear Mr. Howells,

I have your favors of the 3^d and 6th. Also the first act of the "New Play"—(its title.) I am hard at work on the copying and stage managing it,—and like what you have done immensely; I will report any error I find, of which there seem but few— like the silent exit of the Author—who must have some good plan of escape at Shakespeare's entrance. I will club all I find and send in a body. Your first scene is in the exact spirit of the original, and I promise you much glory for your work. It is no *mere* translation—as a comparison with the Daly version shows.[1]

I shall take the liberty of writing to Miss Morris about the comedy—as you seem timid about making use of me and telling her what I *know.* I will write more when I have closed up the first act[.] I *intend* to try for Chicago as its birthplace.

Very Sincerely Yours

Lawrence Barrett

1. As noted in note 1 to letter 18, the Daly translation opened for a short run in New York on 5 December 1874.

80. BARRETT TO HOWELLS, 17 SEPTEMBER 1878, MS. (HARVARD, 2 PP.)

Detroit.

Sept 17—1878

Dear Mr. Howells,

The second act came duly, and I like it as well as the first. I am hard at work upon it, doing all the copying myself.[1] The blank verse is very much stronger than the prose—and your own additions are excellent. I shall yet have as good a play from your own brain as this. I have every hope.

I shall do it in Chicago if the other act comes this week or even next.[2]—as we will be ready w[ith] what we have very soon now. I will send you $500, on Saturday or Monday, and I have to roll up the royalties quite satisfactorily. My season opens brilliantly with good houses well concerned.

In haste,

Very Sincerely Yours

Lawrence Barrett

1. The Harvard College Library holds a manuscript "stage version" of *A New Play* with acts I–II in LB's hand and act III transcribed by Mollie Barrett (MS Thr 137.1). In the first two acts, the figure of the playwright is named Shakespear, as in WDH's manuscript. Soon after WDH finished the play, however, he convinced LB to change the name of the character to Heywood, and the third act of the Harvard ms. reflects this change. This version of the play is the one LB's company produced in the fall of 1878.

2. Though at this point LB planned to open *A New Play* in Chicago, which would have been on October 8, its premiere finally took place in Cleveland on October 25.

In view of the imminent production of the play, it may be convenient to place here an accounting by LB of its performances during the 1878–79 season. Though undated (and obviously written sometime after 26 July 1879), as with the list for *A Counterfeit Presentment* it provides a schedule at the beginning of the season. Since the list is among the WDH letters from LB at Harvard and is in LB's hand, it constitutes LB's financial report to WDH; the $15 performance fee agrees with that stated in letters 65 and 67.

		Night	Mat.
Cleveland	Oct. 25	1	
Pittsburg[h]	Nov. 12	1	
Louisville	Dec 6	1	
Boston	Feby 3.4.5.	3.	1.
Washington	" 12. 15.	2.	
Baltimore	" 19. 22.	2.	
Springfield Ill.	Mar 7	1.	
St Louis	" 11. 13. 15.	2.	1.
Cincinnati	April 7.8.9.12.	3.	1.
Bloomington Ill	" 14.	1.	
Quincy "	" 15	1	

St Joseph Mo	" 16	1	
Kansas City.	" 17	1	
Leavenworth	" 18	1	
Council Bluffs	" 19	1	
Omaha	" 21	1	
Virginia City	May 9	1.	
Sacramento	" 16	1.	
San Francisco	June 9th & week	6.	1.
Portland	" 24	1.	
Oakland	" 30	1.	
San Jose	July 2	1	
Stockton	" 3	1	
Sacramento	" 5		1.
Salt Lake	" 10	1.	
Denver	" 16. 19	2.	
Pueblo	" 21	1	
Col Springs	" 22	1	
Central City	" 24	1	
Georgetown	25	1	
Cheyenne	26	1.	
		43.	5

48.
15.
240
48
$720

81. HOWELLS TO BARRETT, 19 SEPTEMBER 1878, MS. (Price, 5 pp.)

. . . *The Atlantic Monthly.*

. . . *Boston.* Sept. 19, 1878.

Dear Mr. Barrett:

I have your letters of the 12th and 17th, & am glad that you find the play so much to your mind. I shall not only be willing but anxious to supply any deficiencies you find in it. I am particularly pleased that you like the speeches in blank verse. I shall have the last act ready in a few days.

The check will be very welcome when it comes, and I hope you will be able to send it without fail on Saturday.

Yours sincerely

W. D. Howells.

82. BARRETT TO HOWELLS, 20 SEPTEMBER 1878, MS. (HARVARD, 1 P.)

Palmer House [Chicago]

Sept 20 — [1878]

My dear Mr Howells—

We go [to] the public with our Play on the 8^{tb} of Oct— It will then be ready— The act is pretty good, not great and I hope for a Success and will strive to secure it—*You* have done *your* part—I will now do *mine*. My engagement here is very great—against Booth—a perfect match—[1] Mr Wilson has sent me a few rhymes upon my poor self.— Which he says he has submitted to you for publication.[2] If they do not disgrace your poetical column—they will do my reputation service when published.

I am very Sincerely Yours

Lawrence Barrett

W. D. Howells, Esq.

1. LB and Edwin Booth, who were at the time on less than friendly terms, were both playing in Chicago at different theaters in *Hamlet* and *Richard III*. According to Bailey (p. 258), notices on the whole were favorable to both.

2. Francis Wilson (1854–1935), who acted occasionally with LB and met WDH at least a few times, published *Francis Wilson's Life of Himself* in 1924. Though he wrote other books and essays, no poems by him are known to be extant.

83. HOWELLS TO BARRETT, 23 SEPTEMBER 1878, MS. (PRICE, 3 PP.)

. . . *The Atlantic Monthly.*

. . . *Boston.* September 23, 1878.

Dear Mr. Barrett:

Yesterday I finished the play, and I have now only to give it my revision. In this act I make what I consider my great addition to the drama: a final speech for Yorick, in which I sum up and express all the meaning and beauty of this character, and conclude the action in the only possible way. The speech is rugged and simple: if it effects [sic] your hearers as it did the author, the curtain will go down upon their tears. But perhaps a man who pays his money will not cry so easily! Nevertheless I count on *your* enthusiasm for that speech, and I should like immensely to hear you speak it. It is broken with dialogue and action, and is some sixty lines of blank verse. It gives you a great chance to clinch the effect of the drama.

Here is a letter from Count Premio-Real. Please note his request, and in some newspaper notice, have stated what he asks. It won[']t hurt us, and will gratify an amiable man. Let me have his letter again.[1]

I want you to telegraph me, on receipt of this, your Chicago address. I put your profession on the envelope of this to make sure it reaches you.

Very truly yours

W. D. Howells.

1. Of the letters from Premio Real to WDH, only one survives at Harvard; dated 14 February 1879, it mentions the play, though it is obviously not the letter WDH forwarded to LB.

84. HOWELLS TO BARRETT, 30 SEPTEMBER
1878, MS. (PRICE, 4 PP.)

. . . *The Atlantic Monthly.*

. . . *Boston.* Sept. 30, 1878.

Dear Mr. Barrett:

I sent you the first half of the last act by the American Express on Saturday, and to-morrow the rest will go to you by the same carrier. I have marked both packages, *To be called for,* as I did not know your local address in Chicago. I found the $500 at the express office on Saturday, and hereby acknowledge the receipt of it with many thanks.

I have taken particular pains with the closing speech which I have written for Yorick. This, with the accompanying action, terminates the play as I think it should end, and I believe it will have a good effect. It gives Yorick the final prominence. I have fancied the speech spoken with a wearied, distraught manner, dashed with freaks of gayety; then tender passages or bursts of wild affection. The simplicity of certain parts of the material is of course intended.

—I can't let the thing go from me without telling you what was said to me by a friend who saw the play given in New York: "Oh—I'll tell you what killed that play." We had spoken of it before. *"It was bringing Shakespear on the stage."* My friend is a great theatre-goer, a man of taste but not hypercritical. I confess that I still feel great misgiving about keeping Shakespear's name. I strongly suggest Heywood, who like Shakespear, was both dramatist and actor, and an admirable man.[1] A few strokes of your pen will effect the substitution, which I'm greatly inclined to urge upon you. The text might stand almost exactly as it is, with Heywood's name for Shakespear's.

Yours sincerely

W. D. Howells

<You can have Shakespear as manager of the theatre in which Heywood and Yorick are both[2]>

You can easily make the change to Heywood. My fear is that the mere association with Shakespear's name in the mind of the spectator will dwarf Yorick's character. I want you to have that character untrammeled by any such presence on the stage.— If I had the MS. I could change it to Heywood in ten minutes.

1. Thomas Heywood (1574?–1641) is best known for his plays *A Woman Killed with Kindness*, *The Fair Maid of the West*, and *The English Traveler*. His *Apology for Actors* (1612) is well regarded as a traditional defense of the stage.

2. This line was canceled by WDH. This passage and all that follows appear on the fourth page of the letter, as a postscript.

85. BARRETT TO HOWELLS, 9 OCTOBER 1878,
MS. (HARVARD, 7 PP.)

Chicago

Oct 9 — [1878]

Dear Mr. Howells,

The packages met me here on Monday. I had worked very
hard upon the other acts, and after much trial, with the aid of
the Actors, and by repeated rehearsals, had got them into
shape changing the endings of the acts—and shortening many
of the speeches— But the last act has reached me at so late an
hour, and the rehearsals have so exhibited its defects that I
fear I must withdraw the announcements, and take it into my
work room[1] for a couple of weeks more. As there were no
directions in your Mss for the disposition of characters in any
scene or on exits or on entrance[s], I was put to great trouble
in making all those things out, and I shall have much more
trouble yet in completing the work.[2] I now come to the
compensation, and I hope you will agree with me that some
modification should be made in the terms, in view of the fact
that you have only done what you agreed to do in one of
your letters:—namely, "translate the Mss—and make such
alterations as you went along as were convenient and not
difficult"—and that you have not "made a radical and extensive adaptation involving much labor[.]"[3] For the first of these
duties you would receive $500 cash, but for the latter you
were to have a royalty.

Now, I write before I have *tried* the play and I ask whether
you will not part with *that last* clause of your contract either
for a fixed compensation or upon a modified scale—in justice
to both parties.— I am, of course, prepared to carry out to the
letter my promise, but I feel bound to tell you just how I feel
about the work as *you* would not hesitate to do with *me*, in a
like case. It will probably be given first in Cleveland now, in
case I withdraw it here. I will speak frankly about it. I like the
translation of the whole very much but I object entirely to the
speech at the end—as being too long, in the first place and as
putting the other characters in such a "waiting" attitude as

would cool off the whole of our previous labor. Frankly, it seems to me that your whole work has been translation, and that adaptation must be now done by me—and I will show you what I mean. I regard the mimic representation, involved in the change of scene at the end, to the stage of the theatre, as unnecessary on our boards—the whole matter may be more effectively given to our audience by a bringing of the characters back to the dressing room of Alice—and there and then completing the *denouement.* This really involves careful adaptation, and much ingenuity—but in its present shape—it will be hard to make it clear where the "New Play" text leaves off—and the *real* text begins. The machinery of the Prompter's Box could be laughed at by our public—as they know nothing of such a contrivance. I have, also, completely rearranged the end of the Second Act[,] finding by rehearsals, that the old way was weak and ineffective, the involving of Shakespeare in the jealousy entirely unnecessary. Since writing the foregoing, I have consulted with the actors who are already perfect in their parts, and they all advise a withdrawal of the Play—until a different arrangement of the last Act can be made—and I have substituted Othello in its place for Friday—very much to my own annoyance, and dislike to disappoint the public. I prefer to avoid the worry of last season when so many changes had to be made in the Comedy *after* its production. They shall be in advance in *this* case if I can make them[;] if not, I shall shelve the Mss.

I close by hoping that you will agree with me pleasantly that what you have furnished is a *translation* not an *adaptation* of the "Spanish Play."[4]

Yours Very Sincerely

Lawrence Barrett

1. WDH was so nonplussed by this comment that he quoted it disparagingly in a letter to John Hay three weeks later (*Hay-Howells Letters,* p. 35).

2. Though WDH marked some entrances and exits in his script, LB's copy at Harvard is heavily marked with blocking directions and includes diagrams of the set at the beginning of acts I and III.

3. LB apparently cites here the unrecovered letter WDH sent him in mid July 1878 specifying the terms under which he would translate the play.

4. No further letters from LB to WDH appear until 19 January 1879. But

letters from WDH indicate that LB continued to write. On 29 October 1878
WDH wrote John Hay, "Since then [three weeks ago] I have not heard from
him" (*Hay-Howells Letters*, p. 35), though WDH's letter of November 2 acknowledges an LB letter of October 31.

86. HOWELLS TO BARRETT, 14 OCTOBER
1878, MS. (Price, 9 pp.)

. . . *The Atlantic Monthly.*

. . . *Boston.* Oct. 14, 1878.

My dear Barrett:

I am glad that you have written me so frankly about the
play, and I am sorry the work on it strikes you as badly done.
I have tried to think it over in your interest as well as mine,
and I wish to say without offence that it seems to me you are
in a panic about it, and I beg you to consider what I have to
say about it before you give yourself the useless labor of
attempting any structural changes. I would not urge my
impressions if I were ignorant of the drama, or if I had not—
according to your own admission—some instinctive percep-
tions of the exigencies of the stage.

I. I feel sure that if you drop the mimic representation from
the third act you will throw away the very hinge on which the
play turns.[1] I too had thought of rejecting that because of the
difficulty of making seen the joint between the mimic and the
real play; but this would, I now feel, be as evident as the
separation between the mimic and the real play in Hamlet.
You can substitute nothing that would not mar the dramatic
symmetry of the piece and defeat the author's intention. If the
short *aside* which I wrote for Yorick at the point where he
makes the mimic passion his own, does not more than indicate his double part, then a few more lines will. I am sure that
the play as it stands will be as effective as it is noble. You
ought to remember that you are not dealing with raw material,
but with a tragedy which has already achieved a splendid
success in Spain. (The copy from which I translated was of the
fifth edition!)

II. It is wholly immaterial whether the prompter stands
under a half-shell (as I have often seen him in opera in

America,) or in the wings, or wherever you commonly hide him.

III. As to the speech at the end: it sums up the character of Yorick, and restores him to the spectator's sympathy after his killing of Edmund. I expected you to cut the speech to your liking, but I don't think that, if you spoke it and acted it as you can, any one would notice that the other actors were waiting, though you spoke the whole of it: the attention of the spectators being now concentrated on him with tenfold intensity.

IV. What you say of my not marking exits and entrances simply confounds me. I cannot assert that I did, in the face of what you say, but if I did not put in everything of the kind which the original contained it was through the most extraordinary oversight. As to *placing* the actors, properties, etc., I supposed that to be stage-manager's work, and did not attempt it.

VI.[2] As to the whole thing being a translation or adaptation, what you wrote me from Detroit—"it is *no mere translation*, as comparison with the Daly version shows"[3]—is just. It is quite as much an adaptation as that version; and it is often a paraphrase rather than a rendering of the Spanish. I am loath to assert myself in regard to any work[4] I have done, and I will not now.

I will receive in good part the offer of a sum in cash for my further claims on the play, and I will do my best to meet you as to terms.

I wish to say distinctly, however, that if you make changes in the plot or dialogue not submitted to or approved by me, I cannot consent to your announcing it as my adaptation. There are many highly successful plays on the stage with which I would not connect my name. If you have ideas which you want put in form I will attempt the work, though I would far rather take a sum outright for what I have done and leave the whole thing to you; but I refuse to father the work of any one else.

Yours sincerely

W. D. Howells.

1. Though WDH insists on this occasion on the importance of "the mimic representation," in letters 88 and 89 he qualifies the point.

2. WDH obviously misnumbers his points, going from IV to VI.

3. See letter 79.

4. At this point, the pages as numbered by WDH go from "6" to "8." Since the sequence both grammatically and contextually suggests no missing page, however, it seems virtually certain that the letter is complete.

87. HOWELLS TO BARRETT, 18 OCTOBER 1878, MS. (Princeton, 1 p.)

. . . The Atlantic Monthly.

. . . Boston. Oct. 18, 1878.

Dear Mr. Barrett:

I have just received a note from Mr. Daly declaring his copyright in the title of "Yorick," and I have written him that when I last saw you, it was your intention to call my version "A New Play," and that the paragraph which he had seen "in one or two papers" describing it as "Yorick"—was probably an interviewing fragment, and not your authorized announcement.[1]

Yours truly,

W. D. Howells.

P.S. I have not myself seen any announcement of the play in any quarter.

1. In an undated fragment to WDH (Harvard), Daly complains that LB had requested and received a copy of his *Yorick* and then returned it without acknowledgment, and that he has now read a paragraph in which the indication is that LB now uses the title *Yorick* rather than *A New Play*. WDH's answer of October 18 to Daly (Folger Shakespeare Library, Washington, D.C.), which dates Daly's letter as "the 4th instant," replies in almost the same words as he reports here to LB. A draft of WDH's letter to Daly is also extant at Harvard, suggesting WDH's legal concern in the matter.

88. HOWELLS TO BARRETT, 2 NOVEMBER 1878, MS. (PRICE, 2 PP.)

. . . *The Atlantic Monthly.*

. . . *Boston.* Nov. 2, 1878.

Dear Mr. Barrett:

The only change, of those you suggest, (in yours of Oct 31,)[1] which I cannot make, is the change in the dénouement. The play is a tragedy,[2] as Othello is, and starts from a totally different motive from that of a melodrama. Desdemona was guiltless, yet Othello killed her—as Yorick kills Edmund. In both cases it is jealousy at work, and jealousy needs no cause. A "good ending" would make Yorick's previous anguish ridiculous.

I think your other suggestions in the right directions. I would even change the 3d Act so as to get rid of the mimic scene; but if you send me the MS. for revision it is with the understanding that the catastrophe remains as it now is.

—Suppose Othello were stopped with the pillow in his hand, and made to embrace Desdemona on Emilia's proving her innocent?

Yours sincerely

W. D. Howells.

1. This letter from LB apparently does not survive.

2. WDH's insistence on the tragic elements of his play may have been prompted in part by a letter he received from John Hay, who saw it performed in Cleveland on October 25: "I went home last night moved and shaken to the core by your play, and I woke up this morning with that vague sense of calamity, with which a sorrow of the night before tinges the morning. . . . I am sure I never saw Barrett play so well, with such sustained agony of passion. . . . It was a great tragedy, nobly played, in short, and it had last night an honest and legitimate success. . . . I am sure I never left a theatre feeling such a sense of *tragedy* as last night." Hay continued "with the hateful candor of a friend," however, to warn WDH that "I do not believe that as the play stands it will ever have great runs, or make you much money. The plot is so simple, the story so sombre and heart breaking, that after the play becomes known, few people will go to see it except those who enjoy the very best things in writing

and in acting. It is too concentrated, too intense. The five people in it are in such a prolonged agony that an ordinary audience would grow nervous" (*Hay-Howells Letters,* pp. 33–34).

89. HOWELLS TO BARRETT, 8 NOVEMBER 1878, MS. (PRICE, 4 PP.)

. . . *The Atlantic Monthly.*

. . . *Boston.* November 8, 1878.

Dear Mr. Barrett:

I have your express package from Wheeling.

Your suggestions, except those that relate to the change of dénouement, and which we are both now agreed to drop, are excellent. I believe that I could act upon them successfully, but they would involve a great deal of delicate work, at a time when I am in the most difficult part of the story, now printing in The Atlantic.[1] I will, however, see you through the affair, if you will meet me as to terms.

I. I will work up the character of Woodford, so as to give the tragedy comic relief. This it has been in my own mind to do.

II. I will follow your suggestions in regard to Heywood, whose attitude toward the plot must be modified to suit the change from Shakespear.

III. I will do away with the mimic scene in the third act, and somehow[2]

1. The second installment of *The Lady of the Aroostook,* chapters 7 through 10, was about to appear in the December *Atlantic,* normally published on the 15th of the preceding month. Probably the "most difficult part" would have begun with the arrival of Lydia Blood, the heroine, at Trieste, her meeting with her aunt in Venice, and her ensuing courtship there with Staniford. The arrival in Trieste occurs at the end of the February installment and is followed by the final installment in March.

2. The letter breaks off here at the end of the second page of a folded leaf. Though the few surviving words of paragraph "III" may appear to surrender the mimic representation, it remained in the play.

90. BARRETT TO HOWELLS, 19 JANUARY 1879, MS. (HARVARD, 2 PP.)

The Brunswick,

Boston, Jan 19 1879

My dear Sir,

It is my purpose to produce "A New Play" two weeks from tomorrow at the Museum, and I write to ask if you will not reconsider your determination, some time ago expressed, to make the necessary adaptations for a fixed sum.[1] That which ought to be done *can* be got through with in a week, I think, and I hope you will consent to return to the terms of the agreement, and give me a chance to make the coming performance something more than a success for the Spaniard, and receive a royalty for yourself which will exceed the $1000 you demanded.

If you refuse, I must then go back to the *translation* cutting out all the *opening* words and request that you will give me the last scene as the Spaniard has it.— But I trust you will desire to score another great hit—and I will aid you in every way possible— Pray let me have your ultimatum at once—as I am going to work immediately with the company.

Yours Truly,

Lawrence Barrett

W. D. Howells, Esq.

P.S. I would like to have a dispatch tomorrow if possible— "Yes" or "No"—as time is precious.

1. LB may refer to letter 86, WDH's note of 14 October 1878, which replied to LB's surprising charge that WDH had done only a translation and not an adaptation of the play and then went on to stipulate that LB must not alter the play without WDH's approval and still use his name. Still, LB had made the proposal in his letter of October 9 for a fixed sum considerably less than the $2500 in installments formerly agreed upon. Thus, unless the missing letters LB sent WDH between October 9 and the present one explain WDH's "determination" to revise the play only for a fixed sum, the rest of this letter must have come as a surprise.

WDH would have been well aware of LB's forthcoming engagement at the Boston Museum because of his own involvement in the staging of *A Counterfeit Presentment* in mid-January. The *Boston Transcript* had also announced LB's engagement in Boston between January 20 and February 8, during which time he would mount WDH's play "translated from the Spanish for Mr. Barrett."

In its review of the play, the *Boston Post* commended the "charming three-act tragedy" and summarized its plot (4 February 1879, 3:7). However, the *Transcript* exhibited little enthusiasm for WDH's play on page four of its issue for February 4. The reviewer complained that WDH's "recast of the not very successful drama from the Spanish" omits the character of Shakespeare. After conceding that "the merry Yorick" standing "in the dubious plight of the wronged husband" has an element of artisticality, the critic opined that "Here are the makings, certainly, of a powerful drama." As if to repudiate the review and perhaps disavow any suspicion of his own authorship, E. P. Whipple (1819–1886), a highly esteemed critic, sent WDH a note on February 8 (Harvard). After regretting his inability to do a proposed *Atlantic* review, Whipple continued: "I congratulate you upon your glory as a tragic dramatist. For *affectiveness* the play cannot be exceeded. The close of the second Act, especially, is effective beyond anything I have witnessed for a long time on the stage."

91. HOWELLS TO BARRETT, 2 FEBRUARY 1879, MS. (PRICE, 2 PP.)

Belmont, Feb. 2, 1879.

My dear Barrett:

Since seeing the rehearsal the other day, I have thought with intense interest of the play, the greatness of which impresses me more than ever.[1] I never saw such *texture* as the plot displays, and I think my threads in the web don't coarsen or weaken it. I am so glad you think well of the close as I planned it, and now I will try to give you my theory of the final spirit and situation (you will decid[e] upon its practicability.)

Alice's cry "A sea of blood that I am drowning in!" when the crowd about you opens, and she is seen being borne off,[2] and you are discovered crouching over Edmund's body, I imagine a perfect silence, and you begin your speech in a low, *absent* voice—as if you were thinking it aloud—as low as you can make heard. The climax has been reached before, and now the spectators are to be made to pity Yorick. Everything therefore should be as simple, and tender, and appealing as possible. Y[orick]'s mood is that of bewilderment, which reaches its height when he asks Heywood, "Canst thou imagine how I could *kill* my boy?" You still proceed in a dreamy tone, but you snatch his sword, as he shrinks back, in a fury! When he cries "He's mad!" your answer "O no, *was* mad!" must be solemn, not maniacal; let your laugh arise when you speak of that blackmoor of Venice. Then you fall *absent* again in your final lamentation over Edmund. At the words, "Here, Heywood, take my sword,—it tempts me"— drive it into your breast *and pull it out* and fling it across the stage with a *clang*. This bursts the quiet, and as you fall on the body, Heywood crowns expectance with Shakespear's words, "Alas, poor Yorick!"[3]

Forgive my prolixity, and consider whether this is all right.

Yours ever

W. D. Howells

I may drop in at the [rehearsal?] tomorrow afternoon[.]

1. The play opened at the Boston Museum on February 3, the fourth performance after one each in Cleveland, Pittsburgh, and Louisville between October 25 and December 6. For excerpts of the reviews in Cleveland, see Meserve, p. 112. For favorable reviews of the Louisville performance, see the *Louisville Commercial,* 7 December 1878, 4:2; and the *Louisville Courier-Journal,* 7 December 1878, 4:2–3.

2. The quotations and action are close to those of the Meserve text of the play (pp. 138–39).

3. In letter 92, of which only a fragment survives, WDH modified this proposed action with the sword.

92. HOWELLS TO BARRETT, 7 FEBRUARY 1879, MS. (PRICE, 2 PP.)

Belmont, Feb. 7, 1879.

Dear Mr. Barrett:

I have put the last speech together again, and I think in
better fashion. It seemed to me that you had better not make a
spectacle of Yorick's death, but fall straightway on Edmund's
body after[1][. . .]

[. . .] wanted something different there—something that
clicked more.

Can you send me my MS of that part?

Good luck go with you.

Yours sincerely

W. D. Howells.

Consider everything I say as suggestion merely.

1. Both pages of the manuscript are torn away just below the middle, but
what follows on the second page (beginning with "wanted") appears to end
the letter.

93. HOWELLS TO BARRETT, 16 FEBRUARY 1879, MS. (PRICE, 3 PP.)

Belmont, Feb. 16, 1879.

Dear Mr. Barrett:

I have made you a bit to get over that awkwardness of
Walton's offering himself a chair;[1] and I've thought of a possible ending for Act I. See the page of MS. Couldn't you after
Walton's saying "A very singular mischance!" go first to
Edmund, put your hands on his shoulders, and after staring at
him, repeat the action with Walton, and then turn to Alice with
a cry, or moan? And would that convey to the audience the
fact of your dawning suspicion?

I don't think the end of Act II can be bettered unless possibly you let Walton say, rising to one knee from where you
throw him, "Thou shalt weep tears of blood for what thou hast
done." I'm not sure it would help.[2]

I've not yet thought how to joint the mimic and the real

play, but I can mend that, and as I find time I'll rewrite the character of Woodford.[3]

When Yorick says to Walton "an old lover <u>with whom she had often</u>,["] please leave off the words underscored; they seemed a little too explicit on the stage.[4]

I hope you did well at Washington, but your not sending me notices makes me doubt.

When shall you be in this vicinity again?

Yours truly

W. D. Howells.

1. See act I, scene III, where Walton with apparent irony offers himself a chair. LB did not apparently approve of WDH's suggestion, for the passage in the original manuscript appears virtually unchanged in the 1884 version of the play (Meserve, p. 122).

2. Evidently LB agreed that this speech would not help, for it is not in any known version of the play.

3. See the note for letter 86 about the mimic play.

4. LB spurned this advice, too, for the 1884 version of the play in the Meserve edition (p. 131) includes the phrase "was an old lover, with whom she had often sinned."

94. BARRETT TO HOWELLS, 19 FEBRUARY
1879, MS. (HARVARD, 3 PP.)

Barnum's City Hotel

Baltimore, Feb. 19 *1879.*

My dear Mr. Howells,

Your favor of the 16th is at hand with enclosures. They will help the places where we are weak. The newspaper notices in Washington give you no idea of the hit of the Play—it was announced for one performance only—and so great was the success that I removed Richard 3d from the bill—and repeated it to a large house on Saturday, and we shall do it twice here, although my business does not warrant it—as the Opera is drawing the town away from me.[1] But the "New Play" is a standard hereafter. I am in hopes of taking it into New York next season for a run— There is no question about the play—

I encourage you to keep doing such work upon it as you have leisure for to the end that by the summer it may be as nearly perfect as you could wish. I will send notices from this place if they are worth it, but you have had proof in Boston of how much value such things are in determining the success or failure of a play.[2] We could have continued the piece in Boston longer to a rising business, but it will go again, and will be on the bills for "a many a year." You will see. The next performances will be given in St Louis, where the notices will be worth reading. I am paying an obligation which drains me for a couple of weeks. If not inconvenient to you I will defer settlement of past performances until about March 15th

Next week Walnut St. Theatre Philadelphia.

Sincerely Yours

Lawrence Barrett

W. D. Howells, Esq.

1. As the performance list in the notes for letter 80 indicates, LB gave the play two nights in Washington and two nights in Baltimore. The reviewer for the *Washington Post* observed, for example, that if WDH "will write as good plays for us as this one that he has translated from the Spanish, we shall be more easily reconciled to sparing our most charming story writer" (13 February 1879, 4:2). Although the *Baltimore American* also noted that *A New Play* was "warmly commended in Washington" (19 February 1879, 4:5), its reviewer subsequently complained that the plot "seems capable of better development. . . . The greater part of the first act is decidedly prosy and tiresome, and through the entire piece an impression prevails that something is needed to bring out the full intensity of the narrative" (20 February 1879, 4:5).

2. On the one hand, *A Counterfeit Presentment* had been staged to popular acclaim in Boston in early April 1878—so much so that WDH had been called to the stage to receive the applause of the audience. On the other hand, other reviews in the Boston papers of *A New Play* were evidently as restrained in their approval as that of the *Boston Post* and *Boston Transcript* cited in the notes for letter 90. Still, LB had scheduled his Boston Museum engagement so that he did not offer *A New Play* until the first three days of the third week, and as far as that goes played his popular *Man o'Airlie* on the final three nights.

95. BARRETT TO HOWELLS, 16 MARCH 1879, MS. (HARVARD, 4 PP.)

Lindell Hotel. . . .

St. Louis, March 16 *1879.*

Dear Mr. Howells,

I send you some slips from the Sunday paper here—The "New Play" was given three times last week, and although the houses were poor—the enthusiasm was great.[1] I am working into the character firmly—and by the time it is done in New York—it will be much better than when you saw it.

I call your attention to a suggestion in the Republican which is pertinent. The great fault of the Play is the abruptness of the Story—and the lack of any domestic interest before the tragedy begins.[2] Could not an Act be introduced in opening—giving a home scene something like that in Harebell? Full of lightness and frolic and playfulness—and a tender devotion to Alice—Unsuspecting but anxious? The Poet might be introduced seeking to have his Play accepted. Heywood could be on—and Edmund. The situation of the lovers only hinted at—no interview between them. Just a home view—so that when the second act opens the play could begin almost as the original stands. Think of this. I have fixed the Play in my repertoire and I want to keep it there a long time. I shall play it in Cincinnati on the 7th of April for a run of several nights, and I play it seven nights in the Mid West—in towns like Bloomington—Kansas City—St Jo—Omaha &c. I play it also in Virginia City—Nevada next month and I shall begin my engagement with it in San Francisco May 26th[.][3] Now that is the place where I would like to produce it with the final touches, and if you see fit to make the new Act, pray let me have it for that place. I shall begin my full season in Chicago with it, and it will be given at Booth's Theatre, N.Y.[,] during the fall if you alter it to suit me.

The Jealous act (now the 2nd) could be given in Yorick Garden—to make a change in the scenic part, and then the new act would be in the interior as well as the (now) 1st act.[4] I have devised a scene for the last which can easily be done and without much expense. It makes clear to the audience what they are looking at. I will be in Boston on Monday the 25th and will see you at Osgood[']s during the forenoon if you please. Send me a line to the Brunswick naming a convenient hour—early—as I play in New Bedford that night. If you make the change in the new act I shall be glad to make it an object to you beyond your royalty. I will pay you your balance when we meet.

Ever yours,

Lawrence Barrett

1. The article in the Sunday *Missouri Republican* for 16 March 1879 (9:1–2) begins by noting the "lull in theatrical business" during the previous week and that LB "did not draw the people" to his performances. Still, *A New Play* "received the unqualified approval of the audiences."

2. LB refers here to the critic's complaint that "there seems to be a lack of something in the first act. . . . It would, doubtless, increase the reality and interest of the subsequent movement if [Yorick and Alice] had a connubial scene wherein Yorick could portray the depth and quality of his love for his wife, with misgivings as to the reciprocal quality of her love for him on account of difference in ages." Such a scene "would fill a blank" and explain "Yorick's sudden suspicion" later.

3. As noted earlier, the schedule follows the final report on the tour, except that the Virginia City performance was on May 9 and the San Francisco ones during the week of June 9.

4. The new act LB urged WDH to write became an additional scene incorporated into act I. All known versions of the play are three acts in length, and the settings of each act remained unchanged.

96. HOWELLS TO BARRETT, 19 MARCH 1879, MS. (PRICE, 1 P.)

. . . *The Atlantic Monthly.*

. . . *Boston*. March 19, 1879.

Dear Mr. Barrett:

I have your letter from St Louis. Your idea of a preliminary act strikes me as good, and after we have talked the matter over, if we can make the thing the clear[1] to each other, I will attempt it. *I shall want nothing for the change beyond my royalty;* but if you can conveniently anticipate a part of that, I shall be glad.

I am anxious to make the play quite what you want it.

Yours sincerely,

W. D. Howells.

P.S. I will meet you at Osgood[']s at 10:30 Tuesday, a.m. March 25.

1. WDH wrote "the thing the clear"—an unusual form of dittography.

97. BARRETT TO HOWELLS, 30 MARCH 1879, MS. (Harvard, 7 pp.)

Hotel Brunswick

Boston. March 30. [18]79

Dear Mr. Howells,

Yours received. I hope you will make as little of Gregory as possible unless he becomes a humorous fellow, and *entirely out* of the secret. I can make nothing of him in acting, and I hope the first act will be purely domestic—having none of the *story* in it—let that come as the Spaniard has it—in its present form. If Heywood speaks of the history of the lovers in connection with the 'New Play['] it injures the revelation which is made later by the parties themselves. How would this do?[1]

Heywood looking at a painting of Alice done by some great artist—the painting being shown to him by Gregory—Heywood describes her glowingly—feels towards her like a Father or Brother[—] alludes to a shadow upon her brow of future sorrow—vows to shield her from harm if it ever approaches her—then Woodford seeking the manager to get his Drama accepted—relates the argument amidst the laughing retorts of Heywood, who has already perused the play—and is half inclined to accept it. Here a good narration of the plot might be given in the two men running over the characters and casting them—Heywood need say nothing of the similarity of false and real characters—I never thought that neces-

sary—the audience only need to know the plot of the Drama
clearly to see at once when the actors unfold their purposes in
the *real* drama what is meant. There is too much stress laid on
this at present. In naming the characters Walton's *real* nature
may be declared, and his unfriendliness towards Yorick for
some unknown cause and the tragedy of his life made known
to the audience incidentally. The author might express his
sorrow that he could not have Yorick in his play—who is
known only as a comedian— Heywood can *now* consent to
give the Play—and before Woodford leaves the scene Alice
might enter. Then a joyful declaration of the author's delight
that his play is to have such a heroine, and he can go out,
promising to bring the Mss in an hour— Alice has come in to
see the picture—a present from Yorick: a proof of his tenderness for her. Heywood tries to draw from her the cause of her
depression—she declares she has no sorrow—tries to smile
and becomes quite cheerful under Heywood[']s joyful manner,
who betrays nothing to the audience of his suspicions—*her
manner* alone being suspicious—and just as she begins to
laugh at some quip of Heywood[']s, and they are at the top of
their mirth[,] let Yorick and Edmund come in—Yorick dragging
Edmund who holds back from the playful urgency of Yorick—
then a lively rally of them all by Yorick—of Edmund for his
absence so long from Yorick's home—of Heywood who has
become very dignified since he has become the Manager—
and of Alice who now forces her manner and is disturbed. A
scene of cross purposes—of tenderness by Yorick—of suppressed annoyance by Edmund and of distress by Alice—
relieved by the return of Woodford, who has the parts in the
New Play—they are given to each—by Heywood who is
lightly interrupted by Woodford,—and at last Yorick demands
to know why he has been forgotten—a part of the Disloyal
Wife for Alice—of faithless friend for Edmund—and nothing
for me! 'Alas poor Yorick'—

I do not see how the act is to end—but I think such a plan
as I have roughly drawn out could be successfully made an
opening to the Drama—and prepare the audience for the
Second Act where Heywood comes in to see Yorick—and the
latter demands the part of the jealous husband. I hope you
can make a scene where all are talking together. It gives more

chance for action—and relieves the eye—as well as the ear—a long scene between two persons is unwieldy— If I have your work at "Omaha" on the 21st of next month it will be in time. I hope you will give it your best work—for I am anxious that this should be the finishing touch to a great play.

I enclose you a check on R. M. Field at the Museum— It will be honored on presentation. I will send you another hundred from Cincinnati April 14th—and a couple of hundred in ten days after that.

Very Truly Yours

Lawrence Barrett

1. In the main, the outline proposed here is an elaboration of what LB wrote in letter 95.

98. BARRETT TO HOWELLS, 8 APRIL 1879, MS.
(HARVARD, 3 PP.)

Burnet House

Cincinnati, April 8th *1879.*

Dear Mr. Howells,

I began here last night in "Yorick"—and in spite of election and Lent—it made its usual impression. The paper will notice it tomorrow. We tried the new scenic effect at the end—a complete success. I play it three times more here—and seven times on the road after leaving here and before reaching San Francisco. So you see I am earning money for you while you sleep—

Have you read the "Hilt of the Sword"? Please give me an idea of the plot. I like the title and I may see myself in the part. I hope the new act will be a complete success—and trust to find it here before I leave on Sunday next. If not, it may reach me at Bloomington on Monday—Quincy on Tuesday— St. Joseph on Wednesday—Kansas City Thursday— Leavenworth Friday—Council Bluffs on Saturday of the following week or at Omaha on the 21st inst. If you are as late as that with it—you may send it to the Brunswick to my wife who joins me at Omaha, and can bring the precious Mss with her. Let me have an outline of the "Sword[']s hilt" as soon as possible—[1]

I cannot tell you how I liked the "Lady of the Aroostook[.]" I regard it as your very best novel and the girl your best female character—and everybody seems to be of that opinion.—[2] The American Lady will bless you, and so do I,—for your characters are possible human beings—and say and do pretty much what the Lord has created them to say and do—they are consistent creatures. That's only a thousandth part of what I would like to say to my ["]Great Dramatist."

Ever yours Sincerely

Lawrence Barrett

1. *The Hilt of the Sword* or *Sword's Hilt* has not been identified.

2. *The Lady of the Aroostook* had been published by Houghton, Osgood and Co. on 27 February 1879.

99. BARRETT TO HOWELLS, 12 APRIL 1879
(Harvard, telegram)

THE WESTERN UNION TELEGRAPH COMPANY . . . Cincinnati O Apr[l] 12 1879 . . . *To* W. D. Howells/Belmont Ms. . . .

Cannot await mail to say how beautifully new work is done—Manuscript returned to day—Thanks heartily—

Lawrence Barrett.

100. BARRETT TO HOWELLS, 12 APRIL 1879,
MS. (Harvard, 5 pp.)

Burnet House

Cincinnati, April 12 — *1879*.

Dear Mr. Howells,

Your package came out of the Post this morning. I have read it twice, and I wish only I were near you that I might *say* what [I] cannot write. You have done your work in the most perfect way, and at last we have an opening which will secure the success of the Drama beyond question. Nothing sweeter or lovelier was ever written than this act from the beginning to the end, I think—I thank you from my very utmost soul.

Don[']t think that too strong.[1] I mean a great deal more, and
now I am almost ashamed to make a suggestion, but I feel
that you will consider what I say frankly. My first objection is
the opening. Could you open with Gregory superintending the
bringing the portrait in by a couple of servants, whom he
orders to place it in its position, such and such a spot, to be
careful, and then he orders them away—to him enter
Heywood—and then a few lines about the picture.— By this
the audience are at attention. Now the scene between
Heywood & Alice—and oh! dear Howells, put these thoughts
about the first suggestions of the portrait now in Gregory's
mouth as a description into the mouths of Alice & Yorick as
dialogue.[2] It would be a playful scene of broken lines—and
seems too good for such a character as Gregory— All the act
is perfect, (of course subject to the failings which you note as
necessary at the margins) until you come to the finale of the
Act—and here I venture to offer a suggestion, which may
bring a better climax[.] Instead of Yorick's exit, let him be
impatiently urging his friends into the dinner &c, while
Woodford insists upon explaining the plot to Alice &
Edmund—broken lines all—Yorick calling—Heywood laughing—Alice and Edmund in terror—a scene of bustle and haste
on one side[,] of anxiety and dismay on the other—closing by
a burst of fun from Yorick—of this manner—"Behold the cast
of the [']New Play[']"—a Villain for Walton—a disloyal wife for
my dear Alice, an ungrateful son for Edmund, and nothing for
the Comedian—Alas! Poor Yorick." Can you not bring the
curtain down upon some such busy tableau? I hope you will
not quit this act till you have finished it to your own satisfaction, as I am sure it will be a perfect success. During the
summer I shall ask you to go over the language of the whole
play—and next fall I shall play it one hundred nights in N.Y.[,]
the greatest success we know—mark my words—

I send you my route—Omaha—21st—Virginia City, Nevada,
April 28th—for two weeks—Opera House—May 12th Sacramento one week. If I do not get it till May 1st, at Virginia it will do,
as I shall do it the old way there—and the *new* way at Sacramento[3]— I *open* my Engagement with it at San Francisco,
where it will be given with new scenery,—and if you have
any changes for the other acts, of a trifling nature, send them,

and I will use them there. I repeat the Play by request here tonight.

Many, many thanks. I shall send you $100 next week[.]

Sincerely Yours

Lawrence Barrett

I hold myself bound to make Extra compensation for *this* work[.]

1. LB wrote his wife Mollie the same day that WDH's new act "was wonderfully fine—the best thing he ever did and is just the thing" (quoted in Meserve, p. 110).

2. As WDH responds in letter 101, in revising the opening scenes he could not change Gregory's description to an Alice-Yorick dialogue.

3. The route is the same as that actually taken (see the note to letter 80), but after Omaha on April 21 the final dates are up to a week later than LB anticipated here.

101. HOWELLS TO BARRETT, 22 APRIL 1879, MS. (PRINCETON, 3 PP.)

. . . *The Atlantic Monthly.*

. . . *Boston.* April 22, 1879.

Dear Mr. Barrett:

Here is the new act amended, as nearly as I could mend it after your wishes. I *could not* put that talk of Gregory's into dialogue for Yorick and Alice, and that is the only point at which I have wholly failed. I give you here seventeen pages of fresh matter, and I have got you several new turns that work out Yorick as a humorist.[1] There is also *click* at the close of the act, which it wanted before. I now suggest that the second act (old first,) begin with the enclosed lines spoken in soliloquy by Heywood while he briefly waites [*sic*] Yorick's entry.[2]

—Of course, the diction of the act is not yet as I should *print* it; but its very roughness is a merit, in some respects. I want you in acting to make note of any little turns that will improve it, and we will fight over them in the summer.

You are kind enough to say that you feel bound to make

me extra payment for this new work. *I shall not receive it.* If you can on receipt of this MS. send me $300—making up the $500 royalties which you were to have paid by the 21st—I shall be glad indeed. But I want finally no more, all told, than the $2000 royalties originally agreed on.[3] That is enough. And I mean to make this play just what you want it if I can.

Yours sincerely

W. D. Howells

1. WDH indicated on the manuscript of his original translation of the play in the Price Collection where these seventeen pages were to be inserted into the text. Three of these pages survive with this letter at Princeton and consist of a brief dialogue between Heywood and Gregory in act I, scene I; and four other loose pages in the Price Collection constitute part of act II, scene I, in which Gregory, Walton, and Dorothy appear.

2. The Heywood soliloquy no longer appears at this point or elsewhere in the text.

3. Though WDH accurately observes that the royalties were set at $2000, he neglects to include the $500 payment before royalties. Thus, the total, as stated in letters 63 and 67, remains $2500.

102. BARRETT TO HOWELLS, 8 MAY 1879, MS.
(Harvard, 2 pp.)

International Hotel . . .

Virginia, Nev. May 8 — 1879

Dear Mr. Howells,

The MSS arrived in due time. I like much of what you have done, after a more careful reading, but I am afraid it will not do to use it as an Act by itself. I am trying to work it so that it may take the place of the present opening of the Play—and if I fail to do so I shall leave it until we meet, when I think you can readily put it in form—I am afraid to risk any thing in San Francisco. I have thought of some other title[s]—and here offer them for your approval or rejection.

"Yorick's Love"
"Yorick's Wife"
"Her Majesty's Servants"

If you like either or neither of these say so by telegraph—that I can use or reject in San Francisco—where I open May 26th—

I will order Mr. Emerson to send you $200 June 1st which will make up the $300 you ask for—as he has already had orders to send you $100 which I hope he has done.

My business is very large—we play Yorick tomorrow.

Heartily Yours

Lawrence Barrett

W. D. Howells Esq

103. BARRETT TO HOWELLS, 10 JUNE 1879, MS. (HARVARD, 3 PP.)

Palace Hotel.

San Francisco, June 10, *1879.*

Dear Mr. Howells.

I send you the first notices of the "New Play." It was a triumphant success, the greatest it has yet made, I regard it now as perfect.[1] The management here declined to allow me to begin with it, but they ruined my whole term by their obstinacy. I go out in a blaze of glory—instead of being ushered in by one—or rather, *we* do—for I gladly yield you your due in the mutual glory— I will send you all that is said hereafter and will "top off" by a talk when we meet[.] I wrote you from Virginia about a change of title and acknowledged what you sent of new matter.[2] No answer. I presume you did not receive my letter.

I wrote also to my Agent to send you $200 June 1st— He does not acknowledge receipt of first letter so I fancy both letters went awry— I jog his memory today, and he will send you $200 at once.

Again I thank you— You have given me a great vehicle by which to advance my fame and fortune, and I only hope I can reciprocate in what I do for you— I shall be home late in July—but you will hear of nothing but Yorick from New York next year[.] We continue the play through the week.[3]

CORRESPONDENCE

You will see that I have a "Dorothy" who comes on to take away her mistress in the opening scene—

Thankfully Yours

Lawrence Barrett

1. The *Alta California,* for example, hailed the "powerful tragedy, full of very strong situations" with its "charm of quaintness." LB "has no part in his *repertoire* in which he is greater than 'Yorick'" (10 June 1879, 1:2). The San Francisco *Chronicle* declared it "a brilliant work" that was "very strong in sensational effect, combining noble sentiments, bright humor and intense pathos, clothed in language of force[,] elegance and refinement" (10 June 1879, 3:4). The next day, the San Francisco *Morning Call* asserted that the play "has all the strength and flexibility of Shakespeare in the text, and greater dramatic force in the action" (11 June 1879, 1:8); and the San Francisco *Bulletin* described it as "a great play," compared it favorably to *Othello,* and concluded it "is almost invulnerable to criticism" (11 June 1879, 2:3).

2. Of the three titles proposed by LB in letter 102, he chose *Yorick's Love* and continued to use it.

3. The play was acted at the California Theatre in San Francisco each night from June 9 through June 13 to increasingly larger audiences.

104. HOWELLS TO BARRETT, 13 JUNE 1879, MS. (PRICE, 2 PP.)

. . . *The Atlantic Monthly.*

. . . *Boston.* June 13, 1879.

Dear Mr. Barrett:

I have just received your letter of May 8, dated at Virginia, Nevada, and I have no doubt you have fully shared "my pain and my surprise" at the long interval in which we have not heard from each other. I had, as usual, renounced you, and what you had done in regard to me I shudder to think. What has that letter been doing for the last six weeks?

If it is not quite too late to be of any use, let me say that if you change the name of the play, Her Majesty's Servants seems to me the best title. Is there some technical phrase in English for the first night of a play, like première in French? If there is, why not that?

I hope you have had luck in adapting the new act; but if not, I hold myself ready, and I feel myself able, to make it what you want, if we can have ten words together.

Yours ever

W. D. Howells.

105. HOWELLS TO BARRETT, 19 [?] JUNE 1879, MS. (Price, 2 pp.)

. . . The Atlantic Monthly.

. . . Boston. June 19,[1] 1879.

Dear Mr. Barrett:

I have yours of the 10th, with the enclosed notices, and am vastly delighted. I hope the play ran successfully through the week, and I shall be eager to hear more from you about it. When you come back with it we must neither of us spare any pains to perfect it in the highest degree. I hope to have finished my story by the end of July, and to be quite at leisure to talk drama with you.[2]

—I wrote you about a week ago, on receipt of your 8th of May Virginia letter, which had been wandering round ever since.

I have not yet heard from Mr. Emerson, but suppose I shall do so today.

Yours sincerely

W. D. Howells.

1. A "9" appears to be written over an "8." The date of June 19 also conforms with WDH's answer of June 13, noted as "about a week ago" in the second paragraph.

2. WDH had "nearly finished" *The Undiscovered Country* by June 22, but he still had "the very last chapter to write" the following December 14 (*SL,* 2:231, 241). Apparently WDH did not realize that LB was to stay in the West, where he presented the season's final performance of *Yorick's Love* in Cheyenne, Wyoming, on July 26.

106. BARRETT TO HOWELLS, 4 AUGUST 1879, MS. (HARVARD, 1 P.)

Cohasset Mass

Aug 4 — 1879.

My dear Mr. Howells,

Please let me know how I may have a few hours' chat with you about a new play—and next season's work. If it could be had *here* it would be a great relief to one nearly broken down—and trying to snatch from every breeze a little recuperation.

Hastily Yours,

Lawrence Barrett

107. HOWELLS TO BARRETT, 8 AUGUST 1879, MS. (PRICE, 1 P.)

Belmont, *Aug. 8, 1879.*

My dear Mr. Barrett:

Suppose we say the 11 A.M. train, Saturday of next week,[1] which will bring me to Cohasset about 12. That will give you time to breathe, and to turn the points over in your mind.

Yours sincerely

W. D. Howells.

1. Writing on Friday the 8th, WDH is proposing to visit on Saturday the 16th.

108. BARRETT TO HOWELLS, 19 AUGUST 1879, MS. (HARVARD, 1 P.)

Cohasset

Aug 19 — 1879.

My dear Mr. Howells,

I send you a check for $120— This leaves a balance of $100 still due—which I will send you Sept 1ˢ, ten days hence. The old MSS goes by this mail. I hope the new work will give you but little trouble.

Heartily Yours,

Lawrence Barrett.

109. HOWELLS TO BARRETT, 21 AUGUST 1879, MS. (Price, 1 p.)

Belmont, Aug. 21, 1879.

Dear Mr. Barrett:

Many thanks for the check for $120. The old MS. has also come to hand, and I shall let you have the revision by the 1st, I hope.

Yours sincerely

W. D. Howells.

110. BARRETT TO HOWELLS, 22 AUGUST 1879, MS. (Harvard, 1 p.)

Cohasset

Aug 22 — 1879.

Dear Mr. Howells,

Your favor at hand.

Please favor me by giving me the perfected Mss as early next week as possible. I set out in so short a time that I must get out the parts and have the actors at work—and every moment is important to us— I hope you can find time to help me at once—

Ever heartily yours

Lawrence Barrett

111. HOWELLS TO BARRETT, 25 AUGUST 1879, MS. (Price, 1 p.)

Belmont, Aug. 25, 1879.

Dear Mr. Barrett:

I send you the first act with emendations by express to-day, and I hope you will like them.[1] Please go over the whole, and see where I have corrected some misreadings.

It has been tough work. I will send the opening passages to act second before the week is out.

Yours sincerely

W. D. Howells.

1. The revision that now begins with WDH's sending the first act evidently results from their story-conference of August 16. This revised first part of act I is reproduced in the present volume with WDH's changes in bold type.

112. BARRETT TO HOWELLS, 27 AUGUST 1879, MS. (Harvard, 1 p.)

Cohasset. Mass.

Aug 27 — [18]79

Dear Mr Howells.

I have the corrected Mss. I have put it in its place and it will be just the thing. I like it very much. The first act is now perfect,—and shall not be touched again.

Now for the second, and then for Toronto and home— I know it is "tough"—but I can see you grow. Every time you touch the pen for dramatic work—

Heartily Yours

Lawrence Barrett

I have got a perfect Cast for this Play.

113. HOWELLS TO BARRETT, 29 AUGUST
1879, MS. (Price, 2 pp.)

. . . *The Atlantic Monthly.*

. . . *Boston.* Aug. 29, 1879.

Dear Mr. Barrett:

I'm delighted that you like my emendations. It seems to me that I have hit your purpose also in the part I send this morning. I could not let the servants even seem to make light of the language of the play, but I have kept the situation as you planned it.

—I saw Mr. Longfellow, the other day, and he most cordially consents to our using Miles Standish.[1] He said [. . .][2]

1. The play, *Priscilla: A Comedy,* was not produced and first appeared in print in Meserve, pp. 140–204. As Meserve notes in his introduction, LB seemed to have lost interest in it, a view reinforced by the letters WDH sent the actor. Meserve's text derives from a manuscript, perhaps the copy offered to Aldrich for the *Atlantic* and evidently declined; WDH's letter 163 to LB mentions a partly typewritten copy, but it has not been found.

2. The second page is mostly torn off vertically. From the remaining words on the left edge (usually single words), five lines of letter text have been lost and at least three lines of a postscript.

114. BARRETT TO HOWELLS, 28 SEPTEMBER
1879, MS. (Harvard, 3 pp.)

St. Louis

Sept 28th — [1879]

Dear Mr. Howells,

The Mss by White came yesterday. I like it— When it is in type, will ask you to overlook it again. He has promised and then again retracted the Mss till I was surprised at its arrival—I send him the $100 tomorrow.[1]

I send you $60 for the four performances in Toronto— I was sorry not to have seen your Father again, but was rehearsing all the time when I was not asleep or acting, and he had sickness at home. We do the New Play here tomorrow and for three performances at least. I still owe you $100 on last season's acct. Will send it with next simultaneous.

Hastily Yours,

Lawrence Barrett

Will you not send for Mr. Seymour of the Boston Museum and talk with him of the great "Colonial Drama" which is to make our fortunes?[2] He has all my ideas, and better ones of his own— Be *commercial* now, and think of the "gate money," for awhile.

L. B.

Detroit on the 6th Oct for one week

1. On 24 August 1879, not long after his story-conference with LB, WDH had written Richard Grant White (1821–1885), a frequent *Atlantic* contributor, offering $100 from LB for a five-page account of the Globe Theatre, the setting of the final scene of *Yorick's Love* (New York Historical Society). White asked for more details in a letter to LB dated 12 September 1879: "Mr Howells has told me nothing but that the play is a translation from the Spanish, & that its scene is the Globe theatre in the time of Shakespeare" (Price).

2. William Seymour (1855–1933) played parts in New York and Boston companies during most of his career and was also a stage manager. In the 1870s he toured with LB; he also had a summer home near him in South Duxbury.

115. BARRETT TO HOWELLS, 7 OCTOBER 1879, MS. (HARVARD, 3 PP.)

Russell House

Detroit. Oct 7—*1879*

Dear Mr Howells,

I send you the Detroit notices of "Yorick's Love."[1] I hope you will like the title. The old one was confusing—and at last I decided to change it. We had a successful beginning here last night. The play will be repeated on Friday. We did not play it last week, my second in St. Louis.

I like Yorick better and better every day, and will soon learn to play it well.

I rehearsed Don Carlos—and am now satisfied that I paid poor Bayard Taylor 2000 too much for it—I shall never play it.[2] It is badly translated and the adaptation is still worse. But *all* Dramas are turgid after "Yorick['s] Love"—

What are you doing in *my* way? I have looked for something of the "Standish" matter ere this.

I will write again on Monday, next sending you the royalties for this week—and the extra $100 due on last season. I have published White's article in the Free Press here and it will now go into a pamphlet—I think it reads very well.[3]

Hastily Yours

Lawrence Barrett

I would not charge you anything, if you were to publish the White article in the Atlantic—pardon the business-impertinence of the suggestion.[4]

LB

1. The Detroit *Evening News* declared the play "is a grand one, and it was finely set and well presented" (7 October 1879, 4:4). Similarly, the *Free Press* asserted that the production deserved "unstinted praise" and that "No stronger play of modern origin has come to light on the American stage in many years" (7 October 1879, 6:2–3). The *Free Press* had also printed a synopsis of the play on October 3 (1:4) and concluded in a subsequent notice that it was "the most emphatic success" produced on "the American stage in many years" (12 October 1879, 6:3).

2. On Taylor's play, see letter 31 and accompanying note 2.

3. Richard Grant White's "The Globe Theatre" appeared in the Detroit *Free Press* on 5 October 1879 (11:2–4).

4. As with all of LB's suggestions for publication in the *Atlantic,* nothing came of the present proposal.

116. BARRETT TO HOWELLS, 8 OCTOBER 1879, MS. (HARVARD, 3 PP.)

Russell House.

Detroit, Oct 8—*1879*

Dear Mr. Howells,

I open in Boston at the "Park" Jan 19-1880, for a three weeks' engagement. I purpose doing "Yorick's Love" as one of the attractions, and will open the season there with your Miles Standish, if you can have it ready and approved by Dec 1st as I wish to try it for a few performances elsewhere before facing Boston.

If you see fit to go on with it and will show your work to Seymour as it progresses he will perhaps be of assistance in solving stage difficulties, and thus prevent trouble after it comes to me. Have you the time and the inclination to undertake this? I am ready to play the Drama if it comes to me in acting form. Regarding terms. I will give a royalty of 20 per night and 10 for each afternoon performance for a 4 act play—and continue this until you receive $2000 for the work.

I cannot afford to give a bonus in advance, and I hope you will not exact it.

The royalties of Yorick will be going on now regularly, and I have no doubt by New Years' I could advance something for the future in case I accepted the "Standish."

The play ought to resemble "Dora" by Charles Reade.[1] Have you seen it? Seymour can get it for you to read. The very perfection of a Domestic Drama. One scene to an act exterior and interior, a series of pictures. I hope you can bring Standish forward stronger than Longfellow does where Alden is so strong. Think of this—and let me hear from you at your earliest— If I am to have it this season it must be in my hands December 1st

Yours ever sincerely

Lawrence Barrett

I append[:] write —

Detroit—Whitney's Opera House till Oct 17—

Buffalo Theatre, Oct 20 to 25—

Cleveland—Oct 27—to Nov 1—

1. *Dora,* a sentimental play glorifying self-sacrifice based on the poem of the same title by Alfred, Lord Tennyson, was by Charles Reade (1814–1884), a

friend of Charles Dickens. Less than successful in its first London production, starring Kate Terry in 1867, its first New York presentation ran for only a week, with a few sporadic revivals in subsequent years. Reade's pamphlet *Dora: The History of a Play* may have brought it to LB's attention about this time.

117. BARRETT TO HOWELLS, 20 OCTOBER 1879, MS. (HARVARD, 3 PP.)

Buffalo, N.Y.

Oct 20—1879

Dear Mr. Howells,

I send you a draft for $45 for the Detroit performances full to date—except the still due $100 from last years' accounts. I open with "Yorick" here tonight.

I have been reading "Standish" and would like to talk it over—[1] It can only be the framework of a play, an episode— The Drama should be in four acts—a picture of Pilgrim life.[2] First act in Europe ending with embarkation of the Pilgrims. Second act in Plymouth—Early life there. Third act—Declaration of Alden[.] Last act[,] return of Standish and Wedding—I have lots of things to offer when we meet.

Ever yours heartily

Lawrence Barrett

1. WDH would write Henry Wadsworth Longfellow on 22 October 1879, in apparent response to this letter from LB, that "Mr. Barrett continues urgent for the drama of *Miles Standish,* and with your kind leave I am coming soon to look over the poem with you" (*LinL,* 1:277).

2. As printed, *Priscilla: A Comedy* is in four acts, but they do not reflect LB's proposal of the first two as background for the famous scene between Priscilla and John Alden. As in the Longfellow poem, Alden proposes on behalf of Miles Standish early in the action—at the end of act I—and Priscilla counters with "Why don't you speak for yourself, John?" In the main, other events follow Longfellow, including Standish's reported death and reappearance, though with many more complications and characters (fourteen in all).

118. BARRETT TO HOWELLS, 28 OCTOBER 1879, MS. (Harvard, 1 p.)

Euclid Avenue Opera House,

Cleveland, O. Oct 28—*1879*

Dear Mr Howells,

Another great hit for Yorick here. It is grounding itself firmly—[1] I have postponed the New York opening until another fall, when I can get everything in our favor.

I send $30 for the two performance[s] last week.

Hastily Yours

Lawrence Barrett

1. The *Cleveland Plain Dealer* had hailed the play earlier that day as a "grand production" that deserved "high praise" and alluded to "the perfect harmony" of its plot (4:3). The paper reviewed a performance of the play two days later (30 October 1879, 1:6) in similar terms.

119. HOWELLS TO BARRETT, 31 OCTOBER 1879, MS. (Price, 2 pp.)

Belmont, Oct. 31, 1879.

Dear Mr. Barrett:

I am sorry to bring the enclosed paragraph to your notice, for I suppose you have already been annoyed by it; but I wish to ask you for a line of some sort which I may send to Mr. Longfellow from you. I can easily see how an interviewer could torture your statement that Mr. Longfellow has said he would like to talk over the poem with us into an announcement that we were writing a play together; but I am not sure that *he* can, and I am unwilling to seem to have exploited myself at his expense. The play, of course, was never mentioned between us except as something that I was solely concerned in. This printed gossip embarrasses me with him.[1]

I have your letter from Cleveland enclosing [a] check for $30, and telling me of the play's good luck there. I wish I had been there to see it.

Yours sincerely

W. D. Howells.

1. The *Boston Advertiser* for 28 October 1879 had reported that "Mr. Longfellow and Mr. Howells . . . are writing together for Mr. Lawrence Barrett a play [based] upon the story of Captain Miles Standish." WDH had immediately written Longfellow to express his dismay: "I have never given anyone the slightest ground for making this extraordinarily foolish statement" (*LinL,* 1:278). WDH's sensitivity about the item was set at rest by a brief note from Longfellow dated 8 November 1879: "Pray do not be troubled by that newspaper paragraph. It has not given me the slightest annoyance" (*The Letters of Henry Wadsworth Longfellow,* ed. Andrew Hilen [Cambridge: Belknap, 1982], 6:532). Once published, however, the story acquired a life of its own, and it was even printed in the Leipzig *Literarische Correspondenz* for 15 November 1879 (*Literary World,* 17 January 1880, p. 29).

For the record, George H. Boker complained to LB of a similar leak to the press a few years later. Boker clipped a brief notice from a Philadelphia paper that he "had finished another play for Mr. Lawrence Barrett" based on Edward Bulwer-Lytton's *Last Days of Pompeii* and sent it to the actor on 25 May 1885 with this query: "Who has been letting the cat out of the bag? I have not said a word to anyone regarding the proposed play" (Price).

120. BARRETT TO HOWELLS, 4 NOVEMBER 1879, MS. (HARVARD, 1 P.)

Nov 4 — 1879.

Dear Mr. Howells,

No words of mine could or should have been so tortured as the paragraph reads.

The man who interviewed me did so covertly, and with no declaration of saying publicly anything I said. Except of the changes in Yorick—I may have said that you would dramatize Standish—with Mr. Longfellow's permission—but no more—and that was not for publication.

Can I say more?

Yours Truly

Lawrence Barrett

121. HOWELLS TO BARRETT, 12 NOVEMBER 1879, MS. (Price, 1 p.)

. . . The Atlantic Monthly.

. . . Boston. Nov. 12, 1879.

Dear Mr. Barrett:

I have had a very pleasant note from Mr. Longfellow; so that affair is all right.[1]

Many thanks for your prompt and satisfactory letter.

Yours sincerely

W. D. Howells.

1. See the note to letter 119.

122. BARRETT TO HOWELLS, 7 DECEMBER 1879, MS. (Harvard, 3 pp.)

Plankinton House. . .

Milwaukee, Dec 7, 1879

Dear Howells,

I send you a Draft for $100 on account. The last payment covered the Cincinnati performance to the date of Nov 17th. I played the Drama ten times in Chicago and three times here— so my next draft will cover [the] balance due to date. (always excepting that last season's $100.)

The Play is making its way—and another season will be a furore. I am wise in keeping it out of New York this season[.] It will command a grand opening next year. It is a great work and you will be delighted with our cast in Boston.[1] It will there be beautifully mounted—and I shall not take it off the bills while it draws expenses—ditto Philadelphia.

I will do your "Counterfeit Presentment" at Boston if you like.[2] Can't you change the title?

I am preparing to do Boker's Francesca da Rimini, and if Yorick permits[,] Boker shall see the crooked Lanciotto.[3] I may also do Delavione's Louis XI[4] and Mr. W. W. Young has nearly completed his play for me after three year's labor.[5]— I have

seen them who have heard it read and I am certain it will be
fine. Do you not think the Drama is looking up? You are our
foremost Dramatist—pray remember that—and the Stage looks
to you that every Dramatist "shall do his duty." I wish I could
have looked in upon you at the Holmes Anniversary.[6] It must
have been a delightful affair.

I may hear from you at Pittsburg[h] Xmas week.

Ever yours very sincerely

Lawrence Barrett

Please acknowledge $90 sent by my treasurer and the Enclosed.

1. LB played *Yorick's Love* at the Park Theatre with his own company between January 19 and 29 (eleven performances in all).

2. Though WDH sent LB books of his comedy through Seymour, as his next
letter notes, in view of the disappointment with the reception of the comedy at
the Museum in January 1879, he may have wondered at the wisdom of another performance a year later. None was given, but in January 1881 LB played
it once after a short run of *Yorick's Love.*

3. On LB's production of George H. Boker's *Francesca da Rimini,* see note
2 to letter 152.

4. As far as is known, LB did not produce *Louis XI* (1832), often regarded as
the best tragedy of Casimir Delavigne (1793–1843) and adapted by Dion
Boucicault in 1855. Boucicault had recently played it in his own version (11
October 1879) at Booth's Theatre in New York, but it lasted only a week,
according to its detractors because Boucicault's marked Irish brogue had been
imitated by most of the cast, producing an odd effect in view of the French
setting.

5. William Young (1847–1920), eventually author of a half-dozen plays including *Ben Hur* (1899), had his first play *Pendragon* produced by LB in 1881
(cf. Bailey, pp. 185–90). Several of Young's poems had been published in the
Atlantic by the time of this letter and were collected with others in an 1885
volume.

6. The Holmes breakfast on 3 December 1879, a celebration of Oliver
Wendell Holmes' seventieth birthday, received a twenty-four-page report in a
supplement to the February 1880 *Atlantic.* As toastmaster, WDH introduced
speakers and poets, among whom were Aldrich, Clemens, Osgood, and Winter.

123. HOWELLS TO BARRETT, 19 DECEMBER 1879, MS. (PRICE, 2 PP.)

. . . The Atlantic Monthly.

. . . Boston. Dec. 19, 1879.

Dear Barrett:

I wish to acknowledge the two checks: one from your manager at St. Louis for $90; and one from you at Milwaukee for $100, and I thank you very much, and am most heartily glad the play is going so well.[1] I long to see it again with the additions and changes, and I am impatient for the 20th of January.[2] I've no doubt but you're right in keeping it from New York till next year.

Mr. Seymour will have sent you the books of the comedy, which I hope have reached you safely. If you think any change of name will help it, how will it do to call it, *Beside Himself?* But I should say to keep the old name, which I will cordially yield to your judgment.

I am curious to know of how you find Mr. Young's play. He has written some very striking poems for the Atlantic.

I have some months['] work between me and the Miles Standish, but if I live and flourish, [you] shall have it to—reject next fall. At any rate, it shall be ready.

Yours ever

W. D. Howells.

1. Probably the letter from the manager at St. Louis is that from Theo. T. Bromley dated 24 November 1879 (Harvard), though it is datelined Chicago. LB had requested an acknowledgement in letter 122.

2. WDH writes "20th of January," but the play opened on Monday, January 19, as LB's next letter reminds him.

124. BARRETT TO HOWELLS, 12 JANUARY 1880, MS. (HARVARD, 2 PP.)

The Continental . . .

Philadelphia.

Jan 12, 1880.

Dear Mr Howells,

Of course you will see the opening on Monday at the "Park"—and help to give us a send off for the week. Please notify Mr. J. D. Murphy my Agent how many seats you will want, and he will forward them to you.[1] I hope you will make your party 25 at least. I will ask Osgood to aid us also in the same way.[2]

I am acting the Play here for two weeks to a present loss but it will be all right in a future time.[3] George Boker has seen it twice and pronounces it the "greatest work of our time"—[4] Please do not fail to drop a line to Mr. M. giving the number of seats you want. We want a "boom"—

Heartily Yours

Lawrence Barrett

P.S. Address Mr. M. Park Theatre.

1. While Bromley in the letter of December 19 is called LB's manager, J. D. Murphy is here designated his agent and also appears to have a close connection with the Park Theatre in Boston. Neither man has been otherwise identified.

2. LB is arranging to "paper the house" with complimentary tickets.

3. The *Philadelphia Evening Bulletin* noted that the opening of the play in the city on 5 January 1880 had "provoked much applause from the audience" and predicted the play "will be received with equal favor whenever it is repeated in this city" (6 January 1880, 5:3). The *Philadelphia Inquirer* thought the play "remarkably strong in every essential of the highest dramatic art"; that is, it contains "thrilling passages and startling scenes" in abundance (6 January 1880, 8:2). The Philadelphia *Press* averred that "as a literary work it is as perfect as Shakspeare," that its structure "is almost as simple as a Greek play," but that LB "is probably used to acting before a larger audience" than attended the opening in the city (6 January 1880, 8:3; cf. also 10 January 1880, 6:1). Though the *Philadelphia North American* believed the script "impressive in its simplicity and forcible in its directness" (6 January 1880, 1:4), the critic also conceded that LB "has not drawn crowded houses" (9 January 1880, 1:6) and that *Yorick's Love* "will with difficulty be made a popular play" (13 January 1880, 1:6). The *New York Clipper* reported in its 17 January 1880 issue that the play did only "moderate business" in Philadelphia (p. 342).

4. According to the *Philadelphia North American* for 9 January 1880, "Mr. George H. Boker congratulated Mr. Barrett upon his performance" on

Wednesday, January 7, "and Miss Anna Dickinson was among the delighted auditors on the same night" (1:6). LB subsequently revived Boker's play *Francesca da Rimini* (see note 2 to letter 152).

125. BARRETT TO HOWELLS, 17 JANUARY 1880,[1] MS. (HARVARD, 1 P.)

Saturday.

Dear Mr. Howells,

I send you the tickets for Monday Evening. No's 21-22-23-24 are for yourself and family. The balance is the row out of which you can make your dispositions for invited guests. They run in numerical order from 190—to 210.[2]

Hoping to share in a grand victory on Monday, remain—

Very cordially yours

Lawrence Barrett

1. With the play opening on the 19th, this date has been selected as the most likely Saturday preceding the opening.

2. WDH sent tickets to Horace Scudder (1838–1902), his close friend and later editor of the *Atlantic,* and to Holmes and Longfellow, who expressed regret at their inability to attend but retained tickets for family use (Harvard).

126. HOWELLS TO BARRETT, 21 JANUARY 1880,[1] MS. (PRICE, 1 P.)

My dear Barrett:

Great anxiety reigns here in regard to the *box* for to-morrow night, of which we knew nothing. If it is not wholly convenient to let me have it, don't bother. I'm only too glad of the seats.

Yours ever

W. D. Howells.

Wednesday evening.

1. *Yorick's Love* had opened in Boston the evening of January 19. Howells had evidently attended the opening night but had left before the play was finished. See letter 127 below.

127. HOWELLS TO BARRETT, 22 JANUARY
1880, MS. (PRICE, 2 PP.)

. . . The Atlantic Monthly.

. . . Boston. Jan. 22, 1880.

My dear Barrett:

I send some letters for your private view which you may
like to see. Please return them at your convenience.

—I had to come away at the end of act second; but the play
had thrilled and moved me as much as if I had never seen it
till then.[1] I wanted to lay hold of you in that great pass with
Walton, and cry in Shakespeare's words, *Go slow!* Otherwise,
even *I* could not have improved you—which is a great deal
for a critic to say! The support, all but Woodford, was of
wonderful adequacy. Miss Cummins was out of key only in
the scene where she talks of her love with Edmund. There she
was too loud and furious. She ought to have been quietly
intense. Their antiphonal confession to Heywood was simply
perfect.

I don[']t know when I shall get to see you—possibly Saturday. Mrs. Howells is better, but we have other sickness in the
family, and I am working against wind and tide.

Yours ever

W. D. Howells

P.S. The Spaniards behaved very badly to the inhabitants of this conti-
nent; but *ought* I to rob poor Estebanez of the honor of his play? Please
temper Mr. Murphy's announcements. Have him say "H.'s play from
the Spanish of E." or something like it.[2] I can't be turned plagiarist at
my age.

1. WDH's reference in a subsequent paragraph of this letter to the illnesses
in his family may explain why he had to leave at the end of the second act the
night the retitled and revised version of *Yorick's Love* opened in Boston.

2. The first advertisements (presumably "Mr. Murphy's announcements") in
the *Boston Transcript* for January 14 through 17 give all the credit to Estébanez
that WDH could wish: "Mr. Lawrence Barrett will begin a limited engagement
at the Park Theatre, supported by his own company, in the powerful drama,

adapted by Mr. W. D. Howells, editor of the Atlantic Monthly, from the Spanish of Joaquin Estebanez, and entitled YORICK'S LOVE, which has drawn crowded houses wherever presented." On January 19, shorter advertisements appeared that referred only to "Mr. Howells's great play, YORICK'S LOVE." These continued through January 24, when "great play" became "great tragedy," as it remained through the end of the run. Why Murphy made the change of the 24th without more attention to WDH's request remains a puzzle.

128. BARRETT TO HOWELLS, 23 JANUARY 1880, MS. (HARVARD, 1 P.)

Jan 23 — 1880.

My dear Howells,

I return the letters[.] They are all good but the Box Office tells a still better story.[1] I hope to see you tomorrow and to hear that Mrs Howells is better, and the shadow of trouble gone past your household.

I will try my hand at Murphy—and I think Estebanez small potatoes to W.D.H.

Faithfully Yours

Lawrence Barrett

1. *Yorick's Love* was reviewed in the *Boston Transcript* for January 20 (1:4–5), perhaps by Whipple, certainly by a different reviewer than the one who had panned the Boston Museum performance the year before (see the note to letter 90). The notice merits brief quotation:

It does not seem to have been greatly changed [from its "moderate *success d'estime* here"] except in the reduction of the length of the speeches. A uniform condensing pressure has been applied all through, apparently, and yet the distinction of the literary style has not been 'estroyed. On the contrary, the rare elegance and grace of the dialogue are decidedly more effective for being less conscious and conspicuous. . . . Stripped down to this "business portion" of the play, Mr. Howells's adaptation proves to have tremendous vitality and "go"; its success with the upper tiers of the house was most marked last evening. The acting of it by Mr. Barrett's troupe is in accordance with this altered artistic motive. The presentation is not so fine or artistic as the performance at the Museum, but it is far more effective.

The *Boston Post* made much the same point in its review: the play "has been vastly improved upon since its production at the Museum something less than a year ago" (20 January 1880, 3:3). An anonymous correspondent familiar with the details of LB's career noted in the *Boston Transcript* (26 January 1880, 6:1–2) that *Yorick's Love* "has been gradually moulded and made compact during its travels in the West" until it "is a joint honor to Mr. Howells and to its chief interpreter."

129. HOWELLS TO BARRETT, 25 JANUARY 1880, MS. (PRINCETON, 1 P.)

. . . *The Atlantic Monthly.*

. . . *Boston.* Jan. 25, 1880.

My dear Barrett:

A Harvard tutor,[1] who has been twice to our Yorick and is going again to-morrow, has told his class of students to go to it as the best illustration they could have of what he had been saying to them about Greek tragedy.

I expect to call at your house sometime between 3 and 4 p.m. to-morrow (Monday.)[.]

Yours ever

W. D. Howells.

1. Louis Dyer (1851–1908) graduated from Harvard in 1874, where he met WDH, and after three years at Oxford returned to Harvard to teach Greek until 1887. After that he lived mostly at Oxford, with various teaching appointments there and also in the United States.

130. HOWELLS TO BARRETT, 4 FEBRUARY 1880, MS. (PRICE, 1 P.)

. . . *The Atlantic Monthly.*

. . . *Boston.* Feb. 4, 1880.

Dear Mr. Barrett:

Here is the play I mentioned, today.[1] You can tell from the present version whether it will serve your purpose. It was Salvini's strongest piece, and magnificently effective.

Yours ever

W. D. Howells.

P.S. I acknowledge the $100 you handed me.

1. The play is almost certainly Paolo Giacometti's *La morte civile*, widely recognized as Tommaso Salvini's best modern production. For WDH's relationship with Salvini and his play, see the note to letter 145 as well as subsequent correspondence.

131. HOWELLS TO BARRETT, 22 FEBRUARY 1880, MS. (PRICE, 2 PP.)

. . . The Atlantic Monthly.

. . . Boston. Feb. 22, 1880.

My dear Barrett:

I send in the book again, and I have just read your suggestions for a first act. Oddly enough, I had been thinking of a marine *locale* for the play.[1] But I had thought of Venice, which has not been put upon the stage for a long time, and in which something wonderfully picturesque could be done. I will keep your memoranda carefully, and when I read the play, I have no doubt they will come into the work admirably.

Yours sincerely

W. D. Howells.

1. WDH sent the play in a book first published for Salvini's U.S. tour in 1873 and reissued in later editions (see the note to letter 145). Though *La morte civile* was set in the vicinity of Naples, WDH had served as a consul in Venice during the Civil War and often wrote about the city. Still, the possible change of locale was not mentioned again.

132. BARRETT TO HOWELLS, 21 MARCH 1880, MS. (HARVARD, 1 P.)

Rathbun House, . . .

Elmira, N.Y. March 21 — *1880*

Dear Mr. Howells,

I have pondered over and studied the Civil Death—until I have resolved that it will not do.[1] The subject cannot be made lighter—and I will have no more horrors in my repertoire. It was my dream. I shall stick to what I have until you give me something better at your leisure—adding *only* a few of the assured plays of the past.

I return the volume by Express—and a draft for $100 on account.

Sincerely Yours,

Lawrence Barrett

W.D. Howells, Esq

1. The decision against *Civil Death* turned out to be far from final, for beginning in August and continuing at least until October LB was again eager to produce it.

133. BARRETT TO HOWELLS, 7 APRIL 1880, MS. (HARVARD, 3 PP.)

WILLARD'S HOTEL . . .

Washington, D. C.

April 7, 1880.

My dear Howells,

I gave my Sister an order to send you a check for $100 some days ago—I spur her up by this mail[1]— The Book of Civil Death is at home—I will send it to you when I go on week after next.

I play Yorick in New York December 20—make a note, and arrange to be present, if you can.[2]

I shall be in Boston on Sunday, the 18th, and go away early Monday—the 19. but I fear I cannot get to Belmont to see you—and there will be no chance after that, till I return from England. I shall, therefore, ask you to write me about your plans for a new play— I shall do "Arthur Pendragon" by W. W. Young next year—but I will always be glad to welcome anything from your pen— How about the colonial play?[3]

Mrs. President Hayes saw Yorick tonight—and I hope she was pleased.[4] She certainly made a grand figure in the Box—and filled my idea of an American Queen—all dignity, grace, and courteous bearing. What she thought of the play—you will doubtless hear—

I hope you will not think me too urgent in repeating my request for any letters you may see fit to entrust me with—to England. John Hay gave me a note to Mr Hoppin[5]—and other friends have been equally generous— I want to meet the writers and men of letters generally—and I shall try not to prove unworthy of any letters you may give or obtain for me. I can hear from you at the Victoria Hotel, New York—

Sincerely Yours

Lawrence Barrett

W D Howells Esq.

1. This sister was Kate Barrett Tisdale, whose husband Frank had died in about 1873. LB contributed to her support and sent her son Archibald to St. Mark's School and Harvard.

2. WDH finally decided not to go to New York to see *Yorick's Love*. As he wrote Osgood on 15 December 1880, "I feel about it just as I did at first: that being present at the play in that way would be assuming an unwarrantable and untenable relation to it; and the notion grows more and more distasteful to me" (Harvard).

3. The "colonial play" is *Priscilla*. See note 1 to letter 135.

4. Neither a diary entry by her husband nor any biography of Lucy Webb Hayes provides details of this occasion.

5. William Jones Hoppin (1813–1895) served as secretary of the U.S. Embassy in London from 1876 to 1886.

134. HOWELLS TO BARRETT, 11 APRIL 1880,
MS. (PRICE, 5 PP.)

. . . *The Atlantic Monthly.*

. . . *Boston.* April 11, 1880.

My dear Barrett:

I send you letters to Lowell, James and Conway; and I am sure they will all be glad to be of use to you in any possible way. They are the only people I know in London, except Mr Leslie Stephen, and as I have failed on my story for him—that is, given up writing it—I am not sure that I have a right at his hands to the sort of consideration I should like to ask for you.[1]— Conway is no end of a good fellow: Huxleyan in religion, Virginian by birth, and ex-Cincinnatian. You will like each other.

—I am not sure that I shall get to see you next Sunday, and I'm awfully sorry. I keep pegging away in my mind at the colonial play. My other subject was the *Chien d'Or* of Quebec: the legend of which is that in the time of the last French intendant[,] the owner of the house, a merchant named Philibert[,] was killed by De Repentigny, an officer who was billeted upon him.[2] De R. fled, but returned to Quebec with the king's pardon and remained there for 12 years. The widow Philibert not opposing this registration of his letters of indemnity. Meantime Philibert's son Pierre Nicholas grew to early manhood, aware, obedient, and always brooding on his father's murder. At 23 he left Quebec by demand[ing] a commission in the army. Ten months later he wrote home from India that he had killed De R. in a duel at Pondicherry. Costumes of Louis XV's time. Scene, Quebec, Paris and Pondicherry.

Act I. The quarrel between Philibert and De R. [Then] P.'s murder, which his son witnesses, vowing vengeance. (Suppose the quarrel to have sprung from De R's insolence to Mme P.)

II. De R's return to Quebec with his pardon. The widow's helpless acquiescence. Pierre challenges him, and is contemned as a boy and a plebeian.

III. Pierre embarks for France to gain rank as a soldier, and thus equalizes himself with De R. By chance *they both embark on the same vessel.*

IV. In Paris De R. uses his influence against Pierre with the king. But P. gets his commission, and act closes with his triumphant interview with De R. in Louis's presence.

V. They meet, both officers of the king, at P[ondicherry], and De R. falls. (I think I should have him killed by a stray English bullet at the siege, just when he and Pierre have met, so as not to leave his blood on the young man's hand.)

Here you have something immensely picturesque in locale, and with plenty of work for your carpenter; a strong motive; a good character for you in Pierre, and a vivid and rapid action. Tell me what you think.

—I'm glad you had Mrs. Hayes at the play; but she never writes letters, and we shall have to wait till we see her.

Yours ever

W. D. Howells.

Mrs. Mayer sent me the $100.[3] Awfully glad you're to take Yorick to New York.

1. At this time James Russell Lowell had just become the U.S. minister to the Court of St. James; and Henry James, though in Florence during the spring, was about to return to London. Moncure D. Conway (1831–1907) was a Unitarian minister and writer. Leslie Stephen (1832–1904) edited the *Cornhill Magazine* from 1871 to 1882 when he became founding editor of the *Dictionary of National Biography;* he accepted WDH's novel *Dr. Breen's Practice* but withdrew his offer when WDH could not meet his deadline.

2. The proposed play derives from William Kirby's *The Golden Dog (Le Chien d'Or): A Legend of Quebec* (1877). This historical novel, immensely popular in its day and still reprinted in one form or another, reflects the antagonism between the bourgeoisie and the aristocracy in mid-eighteenth-century Quebec.

3. Mrs. Philip J. Mayer was the mother of LB's wife.

135. BARRETT TO HOWELLS, 15 APRIL 1880, MS. (HARVARD, 6 PP.)

"The Victoria".

New York City.

April 15 — 1880.

My dear Howells,

I thank you with all my heart for the letters you have given me. I will try to justify your confidence. They will be of great value.

I wish I could see a play in the plot you sent me. It lacks the ruling passion of Love to make it what we want—a Comedy-drama—not a Tragedy.— Turn again to the Colonial play—and give the world a picture of good society in that day—with a love story such as your brain will readily furnish.[1] Money and fame lie there, in a play of alternate tears and laughter.— Have you read the "Waggoner"?[2] That may offer you some hint. The ideas you gave me long ago of a plot—the dinner party—the intrigue and so on—would come in as well in Colonial times as now—and the quaint dresses would give a charming color to it. I shall not go to Boston on Sunday—so I will not ask you to bear with me as I feared you would be called upon to do—but I will see you before I sail.

I have a note from Mr W. W. Young—whom you know in a literary way. I have accepted and will act next season—a tragedy by him—called Arthur Pendragon—I think a great play with original ideas of construction. He writes me that he has an Article Embodying his theories in shape and writes me to ask favor in the publication of it in the "Atlantic" as an Essay thinking it will not only be of interest to your readers in itself, but will aid in calling attention to the play as an Example of his rules.[3] If I am not too bold I make the request—qualified by the assurance that you will only consent upon the merits of the article—and not as a favor to me. I dare say I need not say as much—for it is a question of business, with you as Editor. He says it will only occupy ten pages of the Atlantic.

To conclude, let me say that I can at any time make room for the Colonial or any other good play by you—and will hold myself at your command in any way you please to use me.

Let me hear again from you while I am here next week.

I shall certainly see you before sailing in June.

Sincerely Your Friend

Lawrence Barrett

P.S. I find that Mr. Young is anxious that the Essay should appear not later than August (*this* by reference to his letter).

1. By the "Colonial play" of this letter LB doubtless refers to *Priscilla*. Though it is uncertain how much of the play WDH had written at this time, LB had proposed a four-act drama in letter 117. Since WDH usually replied promptly to LB's suggestions, and since he did write within eleven days about the mention of the play attributed to LB in an interview (see letter 119) and followed it up with an acknowledgment of LB's reply of November 4, it seems likely that a direct response to LB's letter of October 20 has been lost. The next mention of *Priscilla,* which LB usually called "Standish," occurs in letter 148, dated 3 February 1881, which declines it. Still, in a letter to Osgood dated 1 October 1882 (Harvard) WDH inquires whether LB might present the play that fall.

2. No record of a play entitled *Waggoner* has been found. LB may refer to Wordsworth's 855-line poem *The Waggoner* (1819), an amusing story of a mail driver who unsuccessfully tries to hide his less-than-sober state while journeying through the Lakeland hills, a situation that could have been adapted for the stage.

3. The essay did not appear in the *Atlantic* and has not been found elsewhere. On 16 January 1880, WDH wrote a Mr. Young (Middlebury) to reject an essay on drama but to suggest the possibility of anonymous publication of a "greatly reduced" version of it in the "Contributor's Club" section of the *Atlantic*.

136. HOWELLS TO BARRETT, 23 MAY 1880, MS. (PRINCETON, 2 PP.)

. . . The Atlantic Monthly.

. . . Boston. May 23, 1880.

Dear Barrett:

The paper on Burbage is too sketchy. If you find time to make a study of the actors of his time,—or if you would like to review a book, lately published, The Lights of the Old English Stage—I sh'd be extremely glad to have you do so.[1] Perhaps the review would be the most convenient form for saying what you wish, and I should like much to have your name in the Atlantic.

I am glad you're to be at Cohasset this summer. Really, I think we can do something together.

Yours ever

W. D. Howells.

1. *Lights of the Old English Stage* was published in New York by Appleton in 1878 and was reissued under the title-page date of 1881. Its first chapter is entitled "Richard Burbage and Other Originals of Shakespeare's Characters," which may explain WDH's remark to LB that a review of the volume "would be the most convenient form for saying what you wish" even as he rejected LB's essay on Burbage for publication. Nevertheless, the *Atlantic* published no review of the book by LB or anyone else.

137. BARRETT TO HOWELLS, ca. 15 JUNE 1880, MS. (Harvard, 1 p.)

Wednesday

Dear Mr. Howells,

I expected to have sent you $200 yesterday, but am compelled to put you off for about ten days— These are trying times for us all—and I am struggling for a gleam of sunshine in the business heaven.

I hope you will not be inconvenienced by this delay—

Yours Very Truly,

Lawrence Barrett

138. HOWELLS TO BARRETT, 25 JUNE 1880, MS. (Price, 1 p.)

. . . *The Atlantic Monthly.*

. . . *Boston.* June 25, 1880.

Dear Barrett:

I wish to acknowledge the check for $200 which you sent me. Thanks.

—What a most amusing time we had yesterday! We all stopped at St. Bottle's in town,[1] where Warner[2] recollected that we had not drunk Osgood's health. So they drank it, in lemonade and soda. We wondered how and when you got home.

Yours ever

W. D. Howells

1. St. Botolph was a club on Newbury Street in Boston.

2. Charles Dudley Warner (1829–1900), editor of the *Hartford Courant,* is best-known today as Mark Twain's collaborator on the novel *The Gilded Age* (1873).

139. BARRETT TO HOWELLS, 3 JULY 1880, MS.
(HARVARD, 2 PP.)

Cohasset. Mass.

July 3—1880.

My dear Howells,

Two or three points only:— Let me have the statement I
sent during the winter of Yorick accounts. I wish to compare
with mine which I fear is wrong— *Yours* is right.

What will you charge me for performances of C[ounterfeit]
P[resentment] next season?

Please return my pages on Burbage—hastily written and
wisely rejected.

Always Sincerely Yours

Lawrence Barrett

140. HOWELLS TO BARRETT, 5 JULY 1880, MS.
(PRICE, 2 PP.)

Belmont, July 5, 1880.

My dear Barrett:

I enclose the last account you gave me, from which it
appears that there are now $510 due, for Yorick.

As for A C[ounterfeit] P[resentment], if you make nothing on
it, I certainly want nothing: that is, I don't want you to give me
so much a night, succeed or fail. Could you arrange some sort
of equitable percentage on the receipts after expenses were
paid? Or is that too troublesome?[1]

I feel pretty sure that I returned your Burbage paper when I
wrote you. How did my letter reach you? I believe I sent both
to Cohasset, finding that I was too late to hit you at Detroit.
Will you kindly overhaul your papers? I don't lay my hand on
the MS. here.

Yours sincerely

W. D. Howells.

1. Nothing came of this suggestion except that LB offered *A Counterfeit*

Presentment on 5 April 1881 at the Park Theatre in Boston. See also note 2 to letter 148. For some other efforts by WDH to revive the play, see note 1 to letter 76.

141. HOWELLS TO BARRETT, 15 JULY 1880, MS. (PRICE, 2 PP.)

Belmont, July 15, 1880.

My dear Barrett:

I have made [a] thorough search for your MS., and I can't find it. I have only the fact that I never lost a MS. before to stay me in the strong belief that I sent it to Cohasset when I wrote to you about it. When and where did you get my letter? My poor, helpless recollection is that I sent the letter and the MS. in the same large envelope.

I am very sorry indeed that it should have been lost. If there is anything I can do in reparation I shall be extremely glad to do it.

I expect to read that play, which I've received, to-day, and I will report upon it to you at once.[1]

Yours ever

W. D. Howells.

1. Since WDH's promised report on "that play" is not extant, it is uncertain what play he mentions. But in view of LB's next two letters in early August, *Civil Death* is the most likely candidate.

142. BARRETT TO HOWELLS, 1 AUGUST 1880, MS. (HARVARD, 3 PP.)

Cohasset. Aug 1—1880

My dear Howells.

Enclosed find check for $310 leaving just $200 balance due on Yorick—please let that rest for thirty days.

Now will you put "Civil Death" in good English for me? I have decided to play the piece if you will try it. But I want it at once. The only change needed at first is that the Priest should be made a magistrate or local town officer of some

kind, and I would like to have the period of the play set back
a hundred years so that I can get into a picturesque costume
and avoid trowsers. I wish to try it as it is, and if it needs great
alterations to learn that from the audience. I will work with
you as usual, that is, I will tell you how it rehearses and you
can change [it] as you deem advisable. Now how will you do
this? I mean in the way of compensation. Please ponder it and
give me an early reply— I would like to have the work by
Sept. 1st. I can then give it in Chicago—in October. Could you
not run down here some day and talk it over? We can do so
much with just a little gossip—

Always sincerely yours

Lawrence Barrett

W. D. Howells Esq

143. BARRETT TO HOWELLS, 5 AUGUST 1880, MS. (Harvard, 2 pp.)

Cohasset, Mass.

Aug 5 — 1880.

My dear Howells,

I sent you the "Civil Death" yesterday. I now write to ask
you whether you cannot find it in your heart to modify the
price for the translation, making it the same as for Yorick $500.
There will be changes, and structural ones, and I will then
make new terms with you for those services satisfactory to
yourself.

Now for the *time* of payment. In September I begin my
season— In September I am using a great deal of money—
family going abroad &c. &c.— Will it not serve you if I send
you $500 October 1st?— It will be a relief to me, as I will have
to send you the remaining $200 for "Yorick" by Sept 1st— Let
me have your decision on these points, and believe me

Always yours

Lawrence Barrett

144. HOWELLS TO BARRETT, 6 AUGUST 1880,
MS. (PRICE, 2 PP.)

. . . *The Atlantic Monthly.*

. . . *Boston.* Aug. 6, 1880

(*Mrs. Calvin Winsor's, Duxbury.*)[1]

Dear Barrett:

I have read the Civil Death, and it seems to me greater than ever—very touching; and most thrilling; I couldn't read or see that last scene without tears. You will be immense as Corrado.

I will agree to translate the play for $500, and as you wish, wait till Oct. 1st for the money. But I shall make character and other changes that occur to me as I go; and I shall trust to you to account to me for them. I expect to begin work to-morrow. The monsignore can be easily turned into a magistrate, or perhaps a meddling old advocate.[2]

I shall do the work with pleasant [*sic*], and hope to your profit.

Yours ever

W. D. Howells.

1. Mrs. Calvin Winsor was related by marriage to Justin Winsor (1831–1897), a historian who had become librarian at Harvard in 1877 and who rented the house at 37 Concord Avenue built by the Howellses in 1872–73.

2. In the portion of WDH's adaptation that survives, Don Gioacchino is twice described as a syndic and once as a magistrate.

145. BARRETT TO HOWELLS, 8 AUGUST 1880,
MS. (HARVARD, 3 PP.)

Cohasset, Mass.

Aug 8, 1880.

My dear Howells,

I am rejoiced to read your hopeful lines about the play. I will aid you in making it successful, only give me such a version of the original as you only *can* give, and I will answer for the rest. I want to talk with you about the *acting.* You

have seen Salvini—the Master—and may remember such
things as may be used by me in my own poor way.[1] Could
you spare me a day here during your vacation? Or I will go to
you— Let me have your Mss act by act for copying and study.

Give me a head of Conrad if you can do so in a sketch.

I will do the play *in* Chicago—and by the time I reach
Boston I will not disgrace you— Thanks for the concession
about terms. I think you may rely upon me to deal fairly—
Can you aid me in finding a picturesque costume for the part?
You have been in Italy and have seen the pictures of the
people of different Eras.

So little time is ours that I am groping in all ways for light
on the play—

Heartily yours

Lawrence Barrett

1. Presumably WDH had not only seen Tommaso Salvini (1829–1916) during his first U.S. appearance but had also seen him in *La morte civile,* as the
request for a sketch of the head of Conrad (or Corrado) implies. Very likely the
occasion occurred in Boston, where Salvini presented the play on 28 November 1873 in its first Boston performance (*Boston Transcript,* 29 November
1873, 1:4). Though there is no direct evidence that WDH attended this production, his interest in Italian literature and his dining with Salvini at Longfellow's
home on December 3 increase the probability. As with other plays in Salvini's
repertoire, the entire company delivered their lines in Italian; and all the plays
were available in Italian with English translations on facing pages. *La morte
civile,* "expressly written for Sig. Salvini by Paolo Giacometti," was first printed
in New York in 1873 and was reissued in 1880 and 1881 with variant title
pages. The translation is literal and undistinguished.

146. HOWELLS TO BARRETT, 14 SEPTEMBER
1880, MS. (Price, 2 pp.)

Belmont, Sept. 14, 1880

My dear Barrett:

I am glad to have seen this, for it satisfies me that we have
by far the best version of the play.[1] It is a great stroke to have
changed the Abate to a magistrate, and *not*[2] to have Corrado
poison himself is immense. By that poisoning, all the Italian

dramatist's high and noble intention would be lost, and all your chance of showing Corrado's physical break-up, which can be made so touching, lost with it.

As to re-dating the piece, we can have it just after the fall of the Parthenop[p]oean Republic, under the Directory, when Nelson brought the Bourbons back.[3] In that case, just strike out Fernando's references to Garibaldi in the first scene with the old Agatha, and have her[4] object concerning Dr. Palmieri that he is "imbued with French ideas and principles." If you don't think you can manage the change satisfactorily, please send me the pages, and I will do it, and return immediately.

But if you can keep the date modern, I should greatly prefer it, for the feeling and morality of the piece are intensely and wholly modern. The costumes should be:

Corrado, Roman peasant's dress.

Agatha,   "   "   ".

Don Gioacchino, black knee breeches, 18th century coat.

Don Fernando, hussar's dress.

Dr. Palmieri, gentleman's frock, (or Directory costume, if you wish that date.)

Rosalia and Emma, picturesque lady's dress.

Gaetano, livery.

—You'll see that by keeping it modern, you lose only one picturesque costume: Palmieri's.

—I acknowledge with thanks your check for $200, in full payment for Yorick.[5]

Yours ever

W. D. Howells.

1. WDH has apparently compared his version to an earlier treatment of Giacometti's play prepared by LB, perhaps with the help of Seymour, as well as the English translation prepared for Salvini's audiences in the United States.

2. Above "and *not*" LB has written in pencil the words "(thanks to you)" and in the next line he has underlined "immense."

3. In WDH's manuscript the action takes place shortly after 1860, when Garibaldi dismissed his volunteer army and recommended its enrollment in that of King Victor Emmanuel. Yet in his next letter LB requested changing the date of the play. The Parthenoppoean Republic, not mentioned in the Italian original, had been briefly established in the first half of 1799 and then suppressed by the combined forces of Horatio Nelson and the Bourbon monarchists.

4. The word *her* is inserted in pencil, as are the quotation marks that follow, probably by LB.

5. The full payment for *Yorick's Love* came to $2,500, as offered by LB in letters 65 and 67 and as confirmed by WDH's report to Samuel Clemens on 1 October 1880 that LB "has paid up in full the $2500 promised me for Yorick" (*Mark Twain–Howells Letters,* 1:329).

147. BARRETT TO HOWELLS, 1 OCTOBER 1880, MS. (Harvard, 2 pp.)

Indianapolis Oct 1—1880

My Dear Howells,

I have to ask the favor of a delay in payment of a part of the amount due you on "Corrado." I have been using a good deal of money lately in transporting my people to Germany— and I hope I shall not inconvenience you if I ask that for the remainder of your account I delay until about January 1st—I may be earlier.[1] I enclose my check for $200— This will be a favor to me. Let me hear your reply at Grand Pacific, Chicago[,] next week if you please—and send me the lines you spoke of in changing the date of the play— I read it yesterday to the company—it seemed to read dramatically.

Sincerely Yours

Lawrence Barrett

W. D. Howells

1. At about this time LB had begun to go to Germany to "take the baths" at health resorts, and his family often joined him.

148. BARRETT TO HOWELLS, 3 FEBRUARY 1881, MS. (Harvard, 1 p.)

Hotel Vendome. [Boston]

Feb. 3 — 1881.

My Dear Howells,

I have re-read the "Standish"—and reflected upon it since we talked together.[1] I think you can do better with it elsewhere than with me, as it would be kept back somewhat by the fulness of my present repertoire, and thus delay your income from it. I return the Mss. with many thanks and of course a thousand wishes for its success when produced.

I enclose the ten tickets for Saturday[']s.[2]

Always Yours

Lawrence Barrett

1. LB seemed to have forgotten the "Standish," his term for *Priscilla,* since at least 11 April 1880. Though LB dismissed the script at this point, it occasionally resurfaced in the correspondence, though it was never produced.

2. LB played *Yorick's Love* in Boston at the Park Theatre from 17 to 22 January 1881, and over the next two weeks he presented other plays in his repertoire, ending the engagement with a performance of *A Counterfeit Presentment* on Saturday night, February 5 (the performance for which he sent the tickets). The *Boston Transcript* ran the usual LB advertisements but no reviews. LB had been playing *Yorick's Love* for a solid four weeks in New York until January 15 (see George E. Montgomery's reviews in the *New York Times* for 21 December 1880, 4:7–5:1; and 26 December 1880, 5:1–2) and returned there for other plays from March 14 to 26, as well as for a brief appearance in Brooklyn from March 29 to April 2 that seemed to have included performances of *Yorick's Love.*

149. HOWELLS TO BARRETT, 25 OCTOBER 1881, MS. (HAMPDEN-BOOTH THEATRE LIBRARY, NEW YORK, 3 PP.)

Belmont, Oct. 25, 1881.

My dear Barrett:

I shall be very glad indeed to come to the breakfast. But we have no train from Belmont that will get me there exactly on time, and I shall ask you to keep the other fellows from eating my napkin, if I'm half an hour late. (The only man I really fear is Osgood.)[1]

I was meaning yesterday to call upon you, but I was forewarned of your invitation, and so postponed myself. I wanted to tell you how thoroughly interesting, just, sensible, and manly I thought your life of Forrest. It was a difficult task performed most successfully.[2]

Yours ever

W. D. Howells.

1. WDH attended a breakfast in Boston on 1 November 1881 to which Osgood and others were invited (*SL* 2:300). He had resigned as editor of the *Atlantic* earlier in the year.

2. Osgood had published LB's brief biography *Edwin Forrest* in the "American actor series" some two weeks before WDH wrote this letter.

150. BARRETT TO HOWELLS, 16 JANUARY 1882, MS. (Harvard, 3 pp.)

Washington, D.C.

Jan'y 16 — 1882

My Dear Howells,

I have waited until I heard the good news of your convalescence, before saying the word which came up from my heart when I knew you were ill; and, with joy, I now congratulate you upon your escape from the sick room.[1] From Henry James I learn how ill you have been, and how much you suffered, and, although it is all past and gone, I may still say how sorry I am to know that you were compelled to undergo it all.[2]

Have you not while convalescing, my dear Friend, had time to reflect that you have gone a pretty rapid pace in the workshop these late years, and were earning your breakup by over work? If this illness has given you the pause which hard-stepping men require, it will not have been entirely an evil, although I hope it will leave no other reminder in your body or memory. Among the many who will rejoice at your happy recovery, there will be none more sincere than myself, nor anyone who would sorrow over any serious trial of any kind to you or yours.

I shall hope to see you during my forthcoming New England Engagements. Till then believe me to be, my dear Howells,

Your Sincere Friend,

Lawrence Barrett

W. D. Howells

1. WDH's breakdown of 1881–82 began shortly before Elinor Mead Howells wrote his father about his illness on 17 November 1881, and it continued well into the first two months of the next year. As he wrote Clemens on January 20, "I'm *not* myself, by any means. I'm five years older than I was two months ago. I may young up again, but that is the present fact. The worst of it is I work feebly and ineffectually" (*Mark Twain–Howells Letters,* 1:385). Though he had to leave his Belmont house, he soon recovered, continued his writing at full scale, and went with his family on a European visit from July 1882 until July 1883. For details see *If Not Literature: Letters of Elinor Mead Howells,* ed. Ginette de B. Merrill and George Arms (Columbus: Ohio State University Press, 1988), pp. 239–42; and John W. Crowley, *The Black Heart's Truth: The Early Career of W. D. Howells* (Chapel Hill: University of North Carolina Press, 1985), pp. 116–23.

2. Henry James, who returned to the United States for a visit in October, was in frequent touch with the Howellses, especially during WDH's illness.

151. BARRETT TO HOWELLS, 5 [?] MARCH 1882, MS. (HARVARD, 2 PP.)

5 — Ave. Hotel. N.Y.

Mar — 5 [?]—1882.[1]

My Dear Howells,

When you have the Mss of "Standish" ready—please send it to me—I would like to be at work upon it in my "hours of Idleness." If all is lucky I will hope to produce it at the "Park" in Boston next September.

I am in Philadelphia next week and the one after—let me hear from you there at the Chestnut St Theatre.[2]

Pendragon pleased the "good"—and did not displease the thoughtless—it was nearly three weeks—

I hope your health is quite recovered, and that your family is well. Please remember me to them—and to Mr. Henry James if you encounter him—

Very Faithfully Yours,

Lawrence Barrett

W. D. Howells Esq.

1. Overwriting of the date in March yields three possibilities: 5, 6, and 8. Of these, 5 has a slight edge over the other two.

2. During the Philadelphia engagement, Young's *Pendragon* was to be played as well as other plays in LB's repertoire. LB had presented the play at the Fifth Avenue Theatre in New York from February 13 to 28 and followed it with *Yorick's Love* from March 1 to 4.

152. HOWELLS TO BARRETT, 24 NOVEMBER 1883, MS. (PRINCETON, 2 PP.)

4 Louisburg Square,

Boston, Nov. 24, 1883.

My dear Barrett:

I send you an outline of the new Spanish play, hastily and imperfectly done. The poetic beauty of the drama is very great, and Raimundo's is a noble part.[1]

—I saw Francesca this afternoon.[2] It is beautiful, and wonderfully well played. I found you thrilling and touching and powerfully true.

Yours ever

W. D. Howells

1. Alfred Rodriguez of the University of New Mexico has identified the Spanish play with the part of Raimundo as *Conflicto entre dos deberes* by José Echegaray (1832–1916), a physicist, mathematician, and civil engineer who received the Nobel Prize for Literature in 1904 in recognition of his popular plays of sensational situations concerned with social problems. Twelve years after writing this letter, in a *Harper's Weekly* review of Echegaray's *Mariana* (20 July 1895, p. 677), WDH would mention and summarize *Conflicto,* while forgetting its author's name:

> I should like to celebrate his exceptional excellence a little. His play is all the odder because it is in verse, and deals in the older *asonantes* with a case of conscience: that of a girl who has to choose between her father, guilty of a long-repented offence against the law, and her lover, whose office is to bring him to justice for it. I think that the play would make a strong effect in our own theatre—if we have a theatre of our own.

In the next paragraph WDH refers to "the version made for [LB] of Un Drama Nuevo," and without indicating his own part in *Yorick's Love* he calls it a "very noble tragedy" and mentions the real name of Tamayo y Baus for the pseudonym Estébanez. As late as 13 July 1916 (*SL* 6:100), when he replied to the query of a music critic, he still referred to the author by his pen name.

2. LB first presented *Francesca da Rimini,* a drama based on the story of Paolo and Francesca, in September 1882, and he continued to stage it successfully over the next several years. First produced in 1855 and then mostly forgotten, its author George Henry Boker (1823–1890) was delighted by its late recognition, though he briefly quarreled with LB about the royalty scale then customary. Though LB considered other plays by Boker, he decided not to revise or stage them as he had *Francesca.*

153. BARRETT TO HOWELLS, 4 FEBRUARY 1884, MS. (HARVARD, 3 PP.)

Monongahela House

Pittsburg[h], Pa.

Feb. 4 — 1884

My dear Howells,

I have your favor of the 31ˢᵗ Jan'y.[1] I have not forgotten our talk, and am still of the mind that "The Puritan" would be a good play, if well placed. Can you draft a Scenario? Have you got as far as that? It ought to be a type drama—full of early colonial colors[,] as the painters say, with many New England types in it.—[F]ive acts—of one scene each—love and duty—patriotism—and a happy ending after scenes of strife—I have the hero in my eye—and *you* can picture him in verse, I know. High, born of an old race, narrowly bred, pale as corn but with a volcanic soul inside his repelling exterior. His love a Catholic—a liberal—but sprightly, lively, gay and his very opposite—the great scene where he loses his balance and is swept away by passion like an avalanche, surprising to the audience as well as to the woman. All this I see, but the varied background in which all this rests, you—of course will see and find. There is a play by Sard[o]u called Daniel Rochat [*sic*]—(have you seen it[?]) which would be a good guide for you in this work.[2] I have sent for it—and if I get the Mss. you shall have it, as a study for our Puritan. Please think it over well, and there will be no trouble about the terms. I see a drama ahead, shall be here the whole of this week[,] and my next address is Columbus, O.—Then St Louis Feb. 18—to 23. I shall have heard from you before that, and will have news of Rochat [*sic*] to communicate. If I have the Scenario—I will have to see you before I sail for a long gossip over the stage part of the work which ought to furnish me for another two years— Please labor with such a purpose in mind, and it will be a delight to me to pay you well for such a work and to link my name with one which I so honor as you are in the way of duty.

Your true friend

Lawrence Barrett

1. Though WDH's letter of January 31 is no longer extant, he had clearly followed up on the undated talk mentioned by LB, realized in the "Scenario" he presents in reply in this letter.

2. Victorien Sardou (1831–1908), popular author of "well-made plays," was frequently criticized for catering to those who enjoyed sensational subjects of current interest in drama. *Daniel Rochet,* first produced in Paris in early 1880, had been played in an English version from 16 October to 14 December 1880 at the Union Square Theatre in New York. Its story line is that of a legal marriage between a French atheist and an American Christian, with the husband refusing to have a ceremony performed by a minister if it is publicized. At the wife's insistence, they are divorced in Switzerland, where religious variance in marriage is recognized as grounds for divorce.

154. BARRETT TO HOWELLS, 5 FEBRUARY 1884, MS. (HARVARD, 2 PP.)

Feby 5, 1884

Pittsburg[h]

My Dear Howells,

I found your synopsis among my papers here and forwarded at once to Mallory[1] with a line of my own.

Please do not forget my foreign cities. I open in London nine weeks from next Monday—fateful day!

Hastily yours

Lawrence Barrett

P.S. Just received your telegram—will hunt up synopsis and send to
Mallory.[2] I think it is with my papers at home. If I am long in hunting it,
[I] will notify you—

Hastily

L.B.

1. George S. Mallory (1837–1897), an Episcopalian minister, with his brother Marshall, owned and edited *The Churchman* from about 1867 until his
death. The two built the Madison Square Theatre, which opened in 1880 to
present conventional plays, a policy that was continued after they relin-
quished control in the mid-1880s.

2. WDH's telegram is not extant. LB's inconsistency between having found
the synopsis (of Echegaray's *Conflicto*) and promising in the postscript to hunt
it up has the charm of being probably the most obvious one in all his letters to
WDH.

155. HOWELLS TO BARRETT, 11 FEBRUARY 1884, MS. (PRICE, 8 PP.)

Boston, Feb. 11, 1884.

My dear Barrett:

Thanks for sending that synopsis of the Spanish play to the
Mallorys. They thought they might want it for Mr. Mantel[l].[1]

Before I draw out any careful scenario of The Puritan I wish
to know whether it would be distasteful to you to play him in
the character of a Puritan minister? The clergy were of the first
importance in the colony, but their power was just beginning
to wane in Shirley's time, when episcopacy was already
introduced.[2] We should have plenty of color in the vice-regal's
court at Province House—really a stately *mise en scene.* My
general idea is that the young minister—gifted, handsome,
idolized by his people, and betrothed to a Puritan damsel of
high birth—should attempt the conversion of the gay young
Parisian, who should be just a little of a scamp. Of course it
should never come to theology between them, but it should
come to love. The four acts would be:

Act I.

Scene: Province House.

Introduction of the subject and exhibition of the situation by action and dialogue. The clergy, magistracy and gentry in waiting for the governor and his bride who are just coming off shipboard. A brilliant colonial interior, carefully studied. A goodly number of persons introduced and characterized. Arrival of the vice-regal party. Introduction of the various dignitaries, Reverend Master Waitstill Everett among the rest, on whom Lady Shirley makes an impression at once.

Act II.

Scene: Governor Shirley's Mansion at Dorchester. The Garden.

The minister should come on his theological mission, and should be sent to Lady Shirley in the garden. Of course full preparation for the situation shall be made. But my notion is that after some preliminary passages between the governor and Everett, the whole act shall be played between Everett and the young Lady Shirley. I think I could make a great thing out of his yielding to her arch grace and capricious witchery.

Act III

Scene: House of Everett's betrothed.

A strictly puritan society makes inquest into Everett's relations to Lady Shirley. The suspicions of his betrothed are appealed to; but she will not doubt him. Lady Shirley comes to visit the girl; and they try to find each other out, the game continuing after Everett joins them.

Act IV

Scene the Garden of Province House.

Lady Shirley's appealed to in behalf of the girl by her mother, something of that kind. The play to end by her restoring Everett to reason. Perhaps it shall never come to his explicitly making love to her.

———

I see my way to something very fine and very strong in all this. The question is whether you think you would willingly appear as a Puritan minister. I shall give you plenty of passion, and plenty of ordeal, and of course you shall have the honors of action and language throughout.

Let me hear from you, and above all let me see you when

you come this way. I should like to block out the play *with* you.

I shan[']t forget the letters for England.

Yours ever

W. D. Howells

1. Robert S. Mantell (1854–1928), born in Scotland, mostly played in U.S. theaters and after 1887 almost exclusively in Shakespearean plays. He was connected with the Madison Square Theatre in 1884 at the time the Mallorys showed an interest in staging WDH's *Foregone Conclusion,* though it was given only a trial performance in 1886.

Because the Mallorys had been negotiating with WDH and Clemens since 1882 about their play *Colonel Sellers as Scientist,* WDH's thanks for LB's having sent the synopsis of Echegaray's play to them were probably less than hearty. On the same day he wrote Clemens: "Of course the widow's thirds offered us by the Mallory's were ridiculous; but it appears now that even they were not to be had" (*Mark Twain–Howells Letters,* 2:469).

2. William Shirley served two terms as governor of Massachusetts, 1741–1749 and 1753–1756. In the early years of his first term, he was generally friendly with the establishment Congregationalists, though himself an Anglican; however, his marriage to a Parisian, as young as his own daughters by his first marriage, took place between his first and second terms, so that WDH seems to have telescoped the historical record. Exactly what source WDH had beyond standard colonial histories is not known; and Waitstill Everett (see Act I) is not recorded in ministerial listings.

156. BARRETT TO HOWELLS, 24 FEBRUARY 1884, MS. (HARVARD, 3 PP.)

St. Louis, Mo.

Feb 24 — [1884]

My Dear Howells.

I am afraid of the Parson—and I want to have a *talk* with you about the Play. I have an idea of several plots, or scenes—and they ought to mix into a *money* play. I will see you in July when I return. I like the Italian Skies for a play—after the success of Francesca.[1] Look into the old plays in the next few weeks and you may run across another play like this, with color—costume and scenery—all bright and *popular,* I want to pay you a sum each year for such a play as will make you love the drama and—*one*—actor.

Drop me a line to Buffalo—March 10—and send letters of presentation.

Phillip Brooks gives me warm endorsements to the Dean of Westminster and Canon Farrar.[2]

Always Yours Faithfully

Lawrence Barrett

1. Boker's *Francesca da Rimini,* which WDH had seen on 24 November 1883.

2. Phillips Brooks (1835–1893) was the rector of the Trinity Church in Boston from 1869 to 1891 and was the bishop of Massachusetts until his death. Brooks knew both Bradley and Farrar well, having preached several times at Westminster Abbey and at St. Margaret's, Westminster; in 1885 he received the D.D. from Oxford. George C. Bradley (1821–1903) was the dean of Westminster from 1881 to 1902. Frederick W. Farrar (1831–1903) was at this time the canon and archdeacon of Westminster Abbey and later became the dean of Canterbury.

157. HOWELLS TO BARRETT, 4 MARCH 1884, MS. (PRICE, 2 PP.)

Boston, March 4, 1884.

My dear Barrett:

I send you letters to two particular friends of mine in London, who can be very pleasant and useful to you, and whom I commend to your cultivation. Gosse is the London editor of our Century Magazine, and he is also a writer in the Pall Mall Gazette.[1] Middlemore is a constant contributor to the Saturday Review. I hope they will ask you to their houses; M.'s wife is a brilliant and charming American; Gosse receives Sunday afternoons, and you see all the young literary people at his house.

I am extremely sorry that I can't come to the dinner, where I shall be in spirit, full of immortal good wishes for your prosperity and happiness.— No doubt, you're right about the Parson. I'll keep what you say in mind, and shall be prepared with a fresh design against our next meeting[.]

Yours ever

W. D. Howells

1. WDH first met Edmund Gosse (1849-1928), the well-known literary critic
and historian, during his visit to London in 1882–83. Also during that visit he
also met Gosse's friend, Samuel G. C. Chetwynd Middlemore, a writer on the
Italian Renaissance, and his wife, Maria Trinidad Howard Chetwynd
Middlemore, who wrote books on Spain.

158. BARRETT TO HOWELLS, 13 APRIL 1884, MS. (HARVARD, 1 P.)

5, Cromwell Road.

South Kensington, S.W.

April 13 — [1884]

Dear Howells,

All went well— The play was beautifully mounted—and
well received—and will merit a run for some weeks. My
reception was long and trying to my nerves and the close was
a triumph—
Thank you and

Always yours truly

Lawrence Barrett

159. HOWELLS TO BARRETT, 13 APRIL 1884, MS. (PRICE, 4 PP.)

4 Louisburg Square,

Boston, April 13, 1884.

My dear Barrett:

I was extremely gratified by your telegram of to-day,[1] and I
congratulate you with all my heart on your success, which you
will see by the enclosed scraps has already found its echo
here. But you were the first to tell of it.

We gave Henschel a dinner the other night, and there I
exchanged anxieties about you with two other friends of

yours—Rev. Mr. Houghton, and Mr. Frank Bartlett.[2] But the man who dares is usually wiser than those who fear for him, and the event has proved you right in trusting your ant to the tests of the capital of our language, if not of our race.

You may be sure of the gratification of all who know you by this triumph of yours.

I hope you may find time to write me.

Yours ever

W. D. Howells.

You ought to send a hundred pounds to the Spanish author. His pseudonym is Estebanez.[3] You could get his real name and address from the Spanish embassy in London.

1. LB's telegram is not extant.

2. George Henschel (1850–1934), conductor of the Boston Symphony Orchestra from 1881 to 1884, had composed the music for WDH's *Sea Change or Love's Stowaway,* which in spite of some interest in production by various theaters, achieved no public performance until a BBC production, probably in 1929. See Meserve, pp. 269–99, for commentary and text, the latter also a book from Ticknor and Company (1888).

George C. Houghton (1852–1923), an Episcopalian clergyman, was at this time the rector of Trinity Church in Hoboken and after 1897 the rector of "The Little Church Around the Corner" in New York. Most probably Frank Bartlett was Francis Bartlett (1836–1913), a well-known Boston lawyer and trustee of the Boston Museum of Fine Arts. The dinner was at the newly formed Tavern Club, of which WDH was the first president.

3. Whether LB paid the hundred pounds to Tamayo y Baus is not known.

160. BARRETT TO HOWELLS, 20 APRIL 1884, MS. (HARVARD, 3 PP.)

5, Cromwell Road.

South Kensington. S.W.

April 20, [1884]

Dear Howells,

We have reached the seventh performance of the "Yorick"— and I send you a few lines regarding its reception and my own— The opening night passed off with great enthusiasm—

and play and actor met only with applause—long, loud and continuous. But the papers have not sustained the public verdict, and they find fault with the original form of the drama, while praising your translation.[1] I will send you a packet of all the notices—bad and good. We take it off after three weeks run—and I play the old Cardinal till the end of my time.[2]

I fancy that where so many writers become dramatists, the foreign rival must undergo much opposition, though I cannot think I have harmed your reputation by the production, and I hope I *have* extended it—for the *translation* cannot be found fault with by anyone[.] I have been very warmly received personally by everyone—and your own personal friends have been most kind—especially the Gosses to whom we go today for a three[-]hour reception.[3]

As soon as I get all the notices together I will send them to you.

With kind regards to your wife and yourself from Mrs Barrett, I am

Very faithfully yours

Lawrence Barrett

1. Though LB had written on April 13 that the play was "well received," its reception was mixed at best. As Robert Laird Collyer reported for the *New York Herald,* "I have never been present in any London theatre when applause was thoroughly honest and given with such unconventional abandon" (29 April 1884). While LB enjoyed personal success in London, the financial rewards and press response fell below his expectations. Box receipts for *Yorick's Love* the first two nights were £152.14 and £126.15, but after the first week the revenues ran between £47 and £18.10. Miller (pp. 219–20) estimates total losses for the London engagement at about £8000. Reviewers commended LB's acting but tended to dismiss *Yorick's Love.* The *Times* praised LB's performance but panned the play for its "small variety of action" (14 April 1884, 10:4). Similarly, the *Pall Mall Gazette* dwelled "more upon the merits and defects of the play," especially its "pseudo-Elizabethanism," than upon LB's performance (15 April 1884, p. 11). The *Illustrated London News* was even more blunt: WDH's "attempt to conjure up an image of Shakspeare's England [was] not only disastrous but exasperating"; the plot of the play was "simple to baldness," though "the audience were content to forget how rubbishing much of the play was," so "thoroughly satisfactory" was LB's acting (19 April 1884, p.

370). The *Athenaeum* agreed the play was "disappointing" and occasionally
veered "dangerously near burlesque," though LB displayed "a finished method
and some genuine capacity" in his performance (19 April 1884, pp. 513–14).
Clement Scott averred he could neither "see its poetry or detect its passion"
(*Theatre*, 1 May 1884, pp. 259–60). The London *Morning Post* regretted it had
"so little to say in praise of the play" while admitting that LB "succeeded in
producing interest and even rousing excitement" with his performance
(quoted in the *New York Herald*, 5 July 1884, p. 9). Edmund Gosse wrote WDH
that his "beautiful poem . . . left upon my mind, then, the impression of *a great
popular success*. The writing told well, the situations were sharply and brightly
defined, and Barrett, though painfully nervous, was superb. The play was
received very warmly indeed and so was Barrett" (Gosse, *Transatlantic Dialogue: Selected American Correspondence,* ed. Paul F. Matthiesen and Michael
Millgate [Austin: University of Texas Press, 1965], p. 137).

2. *Richelieu,* by Bulwer-Lytton, was a longtime favorite of LB's, as it was of
many other actors of the period, including Edwin Forrest (1806–1872) and
Henry Irving (1838–1905).

3. When Gosse lectured in the United States, he and his wife stayed with
the Barretts at 1 East 28th Street from about 19 to 26 December 1884.

161. BARRETT TO HOWELLS, ca. SEPTEMBER 1884,[1] MS. (Harvard, 4 pp.)

Wednesday

My Dear Howells,

I have your valued favor. I cannot consent to the terms you
propose. No play can be said to be valuable until tested by
the public— If, then successful, the Author deserves all that
can reasonably be his in the profit. If it fails—why should the
Actor be the loser? After all my experience—the *first* night is
my only test.

I like your idea—I will give you even more than a *half* hour
daily of my dulness—and I will give you $25 per performance
forever—you and your heirs—for the Comedy if it is accepted.[2] In royalties I have paid Boker $15,000—I would like
to pay *you* more than that—but I am unable to advance
$5,000 on an untried work—even by so valued and honored a
Poet as your dear Self.

A *Partnership* is the only fair bargain between author and

Player— I will give you $25 a performance for any Play of yours which I accept—and if it succeeds it will give you a *yearly* income—a *weekly* income which will aggregate far more than the $5,000 you ask me to risk.— If it fails, we go down together, me, after my rehearsals and outlay, you after all your literary work—

Always heartily yours,

Lawrence Barrett

1. The only evidence for dating this letter is LB's remark that he has paid Boker $15,000. With the editors' perhaps too generous estimate of an average three performances a week of *Francesca* and a forty-week season starting with September 1882, Boker would have received $2,400 for the 1882–83 season and $3,600 for each succeeding season; the difference results from Boker's negotiating a raise in payment from $20 per performance the first year to $30 thereafter, with each matinee yielding $10 throughout the years. Thus, at the end of the 1883–84 season, LB would have paid Boker $6,000; anticipating the coming season in September 1884 he could have raised his estimate to $9,600, but it would have taken the 1885–86 season and half of the 1886–87 season to have reached $15,000. In view of the lack of extant LB-WDH letters dated between 3 July 1885 and 16 June 1890, the only years when we think it possible that LB could have reached the amount stated, we have ruled out the intervening years. Sometime between the letters of 20 April 1884 and 23 February 1885 (LB's last London letter and WDH's invitation to the Tavern Club) seems more reasonable. Thus, we have chosen September 1884, when LB with his financial optimism might have foreseen paying Boker a total of $15,000. As for WDH, this was the month he complained to his father that three weeks earlier he had expected *A Sea Change, Colonel Sellers as a Scientist,* and *A Foregone Conclusion* would soon be staged, but the manager of the first was killed, the Mallorys were stalling the second, and the actor of the third had delayed production until spring (*SL,* 3:111). Small wonder he had asked for an advance!

2. LB may again refer here to *Priscilla: A Comedy.*

162. HOWELLS TO BARRETT, 23 FEBRUARY 1885, MS. (PRICE, 2 PP.)

302 Beacon st.

Feb. 23, 1885.

My dear Barrett:

The Tavern Club give me, as their President, the pleasure of asking you to dine with them some night of your stay in Boston, and leaves you to fix the time, if you have any evening free.[1] If you cannot arrange a dinner, perhaps you can sup with us some Friday or Saturday night as Irving did.[2]

I have called twice to see you—once before you arrived— and if you will kindly give me an early appointment some day after 12, I will gladly come again to arrange this important business.

Yours ever

W. D. Howells.

1. A late supper was held in honor of LB on February 28, but he could not attend because of an unexpected acting engagement. The next year he was elected a member of the club.

2. Henry Irving's dinner had taken place in December 1884. Later a member recalled that at about 6 am WDH had asked, "Irving, don't you ever go home?" and Irving looked at his watch and replied, "It is getting on."

163. HOWELLS TO BARRETT, 3 JULY 1885, MS. (PRICE, 3 PP.)

302 Beacon st.

Boston, July 3, 1885.

My dear Barrett:

I got your letter at Lenox, the other day, by mere chance, for I am at Great Barrington, Mass., and am here for a few days. I wish I had time and mood to run down to see you; but I am so broken up by the uncertainty as to what is to be my publishing future that I could not give my mind [to] the comedy.[1] This is to be settled within a week[,] I believe, and I may see you soon after. I think the ideas in your letter are good.

I have partly type-written Miles Standish.[2] It is worth while
to send to you when done? If you couldn't use it, could you
help me place it? Speak from that Greek head rather than that
Irish heart of yours!

I'm glad you have your daughter with you at last.[3] With
regards to your family

Yours ever

W. D. Howells.

1. With Osgood's help, WDH had been negotiating a contract with Harper
and Brothers, while Benjamin H. Ticknor of Ticknor and Company urged
WDH to remain with his firm. The negotiations were not concluded until
October.

2. The text of *Priscilla* published in Meserve (pp. 140–204) is in manuscript,
perhaps the copy offered to Aldrich for the *Atlantic* in 1883 and evidently
declined. No typescript copy is known to exist.

3. Which of the three Barrett daughters WDH had in mind here—Mamie,
Gertrude, or Edith (also called Milly)—is unclear.

164. BARRETT TO HOWELLS, 16 JUNE 1890, MS. (HARVARD, 3 PP.)

Cohasset.

June 16 — 1890

My Dear Howells,

I am a very little man—with a great big plan—and I want a
great big Poet and Friend to help me along with it a little [.] . .
which the first letter of *his* name is Howells. I will go up to
you any day when you have an hour and are free—or I will
bring you down here for a spree in my sixty-foot Steam
Cunarder in one hour and forty-five minutes.

I will fill you with ozone and lobster and Haddock—and
some Extra Drys if you care for your sugar in that way—and
be as thankful to see you as if I really meant it[,] for I want[,]
as I said[,] a great big favor—and when a man wants that—he
will give up his dampest hammock—and go barefooted and
bareheaded in the cause.

I *can* go to you, but I will have you more at my mercy

here—and I can take advantage of you more easily here than at your own fireside. What I want won't help you a penny— but it won't hurt you a penny either, and I may as well tell you that it will be all a selfish thing on my own side of the dock. Now say, "Come" and "When"—and I go—say, "Cunarder"—and "When" and I go also, but I bring the golden Howells and fleece him. Don't think me cracked or out of joint. I am getting well, and you know that makes a fellow hilarious—even when he has never been so—Faithfully[,] Dear Howells,

Yours,

Lawrence Barrett

165. BARRETT TO HOWELLS, 18 JUNE 1890, MS. (HARVARD, 3 PP.)

Cohasset, Mass.

June 18 — 1890

My Dear Howells,

Here is my great secret, and the favor I have to ask of you. All is in confidence save to those concerned. I want to pro-duce next season but one — (91/2) Tennyson's "Becket." I can steal it and stand the pillory like many another felon, but I don't like the prison garb. I want to buy the play of the Author. I want to get the Author's cooperation and blessing for my undertaking, and I want him to make a few stage alter-ations which I think he will approve.

Now[,] I don't know Lord Tennyson—and worst of all—he don't know *me*, and it is necessary that he should be told in advance by some good American or Americans in whom he has confidence just how great and good a person I am. For if I burst upon him at once,—unpresented—unvouched for, he may fail to see in me at a glance just those qualities which it is necessary for my plan he should be made to see. He ought to know that I paid Browning for the Blot,[1] that I have done my share in giving on stage the works of modern as well as ancient Authors—don't be modest because you are one of these[,] dear Howells.—and finally—oh! Poet and truth teller, he must be told that I am the very greatest tragic Actor living or dead—the man of all men for the Canterbury Archbishop. Now[,] who will do this? Here is my favor, and you will see that it is a great one, I want you to ask Mr. Lowell, to believe your word for it—that I am as above, so that he will give me such a letter to Lord Tennyson as I can forward to ease my negotiation. Will you do this? Will Mr. Lowell hear you on such a theme? I will try not to disgrace him, if he will. Here is what I am ready to offer Lord Tennyson, for the rights (stage rights) to his play—a goodly sum down, at once, and a larger one on the success of the play. I will do it magnificently in N.Y. and it will be an honor even to me[,] so full of honors. When you have got Mr. Lowell, could you get Mr. Curtis[2] to say a word also? See what a wide[-]mouthed beggar I am. And all this to be a secret until I can give it to the press as an accomplished fact. *Now*, do you want to see me on Saturday A.M.?— Or, am I in danger of being put in chains if I touch your coat[t]ail?— Send me a wire saying "cave cavem" or "the latch string is down."

Yours ever faithfully

Lawrence Barrett

1. LB had added Robert Browning's play *A Blot in the 'Scutcheon* to his repertoire in 1884.

2. George William Curtis (1824–1892) was the author of popular sketches and preceded WDH as writer of the "Editor's Easy Chair" in *Harper's Monthly*.

166. HOWELLS TO BARRETT, 20 JUNE 1890,
MS. (PRICE, 2 PP.)

184 Commonwealth Avenue.

June 20, 1890.

My dear Barrett:

Mr. Lowell sends me this note, which he says he is "glad to give Mr. Barrett, because you (I) wish it, and because I have every reason to think well of him."[1]

Can I serve you further? You mention Curtis, but I don't believe he knows Tennyson, or that his help would add to the effect of Lowell's note.

I don't believe you need *any* help in the matter. You can't fail to write Tennyson the letter of a gentleman, a scholar and an honest man, and that will be enough in itself.[2]

Yours ever

W. D. Howells.

1. On 19 June 1890 WDH sent LB's letter of 18 June 1890 to Lowell, with a recommendation of him as "the most intellectual actor on our stage," "a generous, impulsive, faithful Irishman, true and good, and a lover of what is fine and high" (Harvard). The next day, Lowell replied to LB's request with a letter of introduction to Tennyson.

2. Tennyson accepted LB's request for the right to stage his poetic drama *Becket* (published in 1884 but written earlier), though LB died before signing the contract. For over ten years Tennyson had hoped that Irving would produce the play, but only after the poet's death in 1892 would Irving finally stage it.

167. BARRETT TO HOWELLS, 16 AUGUST
1890, MS. (HARVARD, 3 PP.)

Cohasset August 16, [1890]

Dear Howells

I have a favorable reply from Lord Tennyson, & I shall in a year or so do the Becket. I thank you for your services in the matter. Thinking it might please Mr Lowell to learn that I had been successful—I wrote him a few lines—to which he has made no reply— This coupled with your words that he had consented to oblige *you* with the letter causes me to fear that he did what he did—unwillingly—also. I am very sorry to have burdened him.

I had friends in England who would have served my purpose as well—Robert Lincoln—Frederick Locke—Canon Farrar—Dean Bradley—Lord Wolsley [*sic*], but it was a matter of pride with me to associate my work with the kindness of our own Poets.[1] Is Lowell only great behind his pen[?] If so, I am sorry to have broken a fond illusion—and I hope I misjudge him entirely. For your good self—dear Howells—you can never escape my officious love—and I give you a whole ink bottle full of it, bless you.

I am well again— I hope you are also well.— My last Daughter becomes a wife in December, & so I become childless in that sense—for they are never the same when they come back to us—all send love.[2]

Ever yours faithfully

Lawrence Barrett

1. Robert T. Lincoln (1843–1926), son of the president, served as a minister to Great Britain from 1889 to 1893. Though by this time Frederick Locke had taken the name Frederick Locker-Lampson, LB probably knew him by his earlier name from his 1884 visit to England. Locker-Lampson (1821–1895) was a distinguished writer of vers de société and had published a number of books under his earlier surname. For Canon Farrar and Dean Bradley, see note 2 to letter 156. Garnet J. Wolseley (1833–1916), first Viscount Wolseley and created baron of Cairo and Wolseley in 1885, was a well-known general who wrote frequently on military topics.

2. Milly Barrett married Marshall Lewis Perry Williams, a Boston lawyer. The daughter of this union was Edith Barrett (d. 1977), who appeared in twenty-five Broadway plays and fifteen films, from a walk-on part in Walter Hampden's *Cyrano de Bergerac* (1923) to the film *The Swan* (1956).

168. HOWELLS TO BARRETT, 20 AUGUST 1890, MS. (PRICE, 2 PP.)

Saratoga, Aug. 20, 1890.

My dear Barrett:

Don't for a moment think that of Lowell. He is no longer young, and he is feeling the weariness of his long and painful sickness.[1] You may be sure that he is glad of your letter. I was very unfortunate if I gave you the impression he acted for *me* in the matter, only.

We had heard of dear Miss Milly's engagement, and we all wish to offer our most cordial congratulations. You shall make them sympathies if you like: I quite understand how it is a loss as well as a gain.

With our love to you all,

Yours ever

W. D. Howells.

1. Lowell became severely ill in the spring of 1890 and died on 12 August 1891.

169. HOWELLS TO MOLLIE BARRETT, 22 MARCH 1891, MS. (PRICE, 2 PP.)

March 22, 1891.

184 Commonwealth Avenue.

Dear Mrs. Barrett:

I know you will not think it intrusive if I try to tell you how very deeply I sympathize with you in your great bereavement.[1] Mr. Barrett's beautiful qualities of mind and heart endeared him to everybody who knew him; and his generous enthusiasm for all good things and for all fine things was a trait of his character that fitted him for the work he constantly and ardently desired to accomplish—the work of bringing the theatre and literature together. I think it a great piece of good fortune for me to have shared the aims of such a man, and I am proud to think he was my friend.

My wife and I are both truly mourners with you. He is gone; but it is only the dead who are always with us forever, both here and hereafter.

Yours sincerely,

W. D. Howells.

1. LB had died on Friday, March 20, in New York. On the previous Wednesday he had acted through part of *Richelieu,* but he could not finish the play. After a service at the Windsor Hotel on March 24, he was buried at Cohasset.

A Counterfeit Presentment

Published serially in the *Atlantic Monthly* between August and October 1877, this three-act version of *A Counterfeit Presentment* was first acted by Lawrence Barrett's company, with Barrett in the leading role of Bartlett, in Cincinnati on 11 October 1877. It was performed a total of eight times in Cincinnati, Cleveland, Pittsburgh, Indianapolis, and Detroit over the next six weeks. Howells later added an additional act to the script to extend the length of its performance. The longer version of the play, first staged by Barrett on 1 December 1877 in Detroit, was acted nineteen times during the 1877–78 season, most triumphantly (for Howells) in Boston on 1 April 1878. The longer version was revived for three performances, albeit not by Barrett, in Boston in January 1879. Barrett performed it one more time in Boston in April 1881.

A COUNTERFEIT PRESENTMENT.

COMEDY.

IN THREE PARTS. PART FIRST.

I.

BARTLETT *and* CUMMINGS.

On a lovely day in September, at that season when the most sentimental of the young maples have begun to redden along the hidden courses of the meadow streams, and the elms, with a sudden impression of despair in their languor, betray flecks of yellow on the green of their pendulous boughs,—on such a day at noon, two young men enter the now desolate parlor of the Ponkwasset Hotel, and deposit about the legs of the piano the burdens they have been carrying: a camp-stool, namely, a field-easel, a closed box of colors, and a canvas to which, apparently, some portion of reluctant nature has just been transferred. These properties belong to one of the young men, whose general look and bearing readily identify him as their owner: he has a quick, somewhat furtive eye, a full brown beard, and hair that falls in a careless mass down his forehead, which as he dries it with his handkerchief, sweeping the hair aside, shows broad and white; his figure is firm and square, without heaviness, and in his movement as well as in his face there is something of stubbornness, with a suggestion of arrogance. The other, who had evidently borne his share of the common burdens from a sense of good comradeship, has nothing of the painter in him, nor anything of this painter's peculiar temperament: he has a very abstracted look and a dark, dreaming eye; he is pale, and does not look strong. The painter flings himself into a rocking-chair and draws a long breath.

Cummings (for that is the name of the slighter man, who remains standing as he speaks): "It's warm, isn't it?" His gentle face evinces a curious and kindly interest in his friend's sturdy demonstrations of fatigue.

Bartlett: "Yes, hot—confoundedly." He rubs his handkerchief vigorously across his forehead, and then looks down at his dusty shoes, with apparently no mind to molest them in their dustiness. "The idea of people going back to town in this weather! However, I'm glad they're such asses; it gives me free scope here. Every time I don't hear some young woman banging on that piano, I fall into transports of joy."

Cummings, smiling: "And after today you won't be bothered even with me."

Bartlett: "Oh, I shall rather miss you, you know. I like somebody to contradict."

Cummings: "You can contradict the ostler."

Bartlett: "No, I can't. They've sent him away; and I believe you're going to carry off the last of the table-girls with you in the stage to-morrow. The landlord and his wife are to run the concern themselves the rest of the fall. Poor old fellow! The hard times have made lean pickings for him this year. His house wasn't full in the height of the season, and it's been pretty empty since."

Cummings: "I wonder he doesn't shut up altogether."

Bartlett: "Well, there are a good many transients, as they call them, at this time of year,—fellows who drive over from the little hill-towns with their girls in buggies, and take dinner and supper; then there are picnics from the larger places, ten and twelve miles off, that come to the grounds on the pond, and he always gets something out of them. And as long as he can hope for anything else, my eight dollars a week are worth hanging on to. Yes, I think

I shall stay here all through October. I've got no orders, and it's cheap. Besides, I've managed to get on confidential terms with the local scenery; I thought we should like each other last summer, and I feel now that we're ready to swear eternal friendship. I shall do some fairish work here, yet. Pho!" He mops his forehead again, and springing out of his chair he goes up to the canvas, which he has faced to the wall, and turning it about retires some paces, and with a swift, worried glance at the windows falls to considering it critically.

Cummings: "You've done some fairish work already, if I'm any judge." He limps to his friend's side, as if to get his effect of the picture. "I don't believe the spirit of a graceful elm that just begins to feel the approach of autumn was ever better interpreted. There is something tremendously tragical to me in the thing. It makes me think of some lovely and charming girl, all grace and tenderness, who finds the first gray hair in her head. I should call that picture The First Gray Hair."

Bartlett, with unheeding petulance: "The whole thing's too infernally brown!—I beg your pardon, Cummings: what were you saying? Go on! I like your prattle about pictures; I do, indeed. I like to see how far you art-cultured fellows can miss all that was in a poor devil's mind when he was at work. But I'd rather you'd sentimentalize my pictures than moralize them. If there's anything that makes me limp enough to be hung over a stick, it's to have an allegory discovered in one of my poor stupid old landscapes. But The First Gray Hair isn't bad, really. And a good, senseless, sloppy name like that often sells a picture."

Cummings: "You're brutal, Bartlett. I don't believe your pictures would own you, if they had their way about it."

Bartlett: "And I wouldn't own *them* if I had *mine.* I've got about forty that I wish somebody else owned—and I had the money for them; but we seem inseparable. Glad you're going to-morrow? You *are* a good fellow, Cummings, and I *am* a brute. Come, I'll make a great concession to friendship: it struck me, too, while I was at work on that elm that it was something like an old girl!" Bartlett laughs, and catching his friend by either shoulder twists him about in his strong clutch, while he looks him merrily in the face. "I'm not a poet, old fellow; and sometimes I think I ought to have been a painter and glazier instead of a mere painter. I believe it would have paid better."

Cummings: "Bartlett, I hate to have you talk in that way."

Bartlett: "Oh, I know it's a stale kind."

Cummings: "It's worse than stale. It's destructive. A man soon talks himself out of heart with his better self in that way. You can end by really being as sordid-minded and hopeless and low-purposed as you pretend to be. It's insanity."

Bartlett: "Good! I've had my little knock on the head, you know. I don't deny being cracked. But I've a method in my madness."

Cummings: "They all have. But it's a very poor method; and I don't believe you could say just what yours is. You think because the girl on whom you set your fancy—it's nonsense to pretend it was your heart—found out that she didn't like you as well as she thought, and honestly told you so in good time, that your wisest course is to take up that rôle of misanthrope which begins with yourself and leaves people to imagine how low an opinion you have of the rest of mankind."

Bartlett: "My dear fellow, you know I always speak well of that young lady. I've invariably told you that she behaved in the handsomest manner. She even expressed the wish—I distinctly remember being struck by the novelty of the wish at the time—that we should remain friends. You misconceive"—

Cummings: "How many poor girls have been jilted who don't go about doing misanthropy, but mope at home and sorrow and sicken over their wrong in secret,—a wrong that attacks not merely their pride, but their life itself. Take the case I was telling you of: did you ever hear of anything more atrocious? And do you compare this little sting to your vanity with a death-blow like that?"

Bartlett: "It's quite impossible to compute the number of jilted girls who take the line you describe. But if it were within the scope of arithmetic, I don't know that a billion of jilted girls would comfort me or reform me. I never could regard myself in that abstract way, a mere unit on one side or other of the balance. My little personal snub goes on rankling beyond the reach of statistical consolation. But even if there were any edification in the case of the young lady in Paris, she's too far off to be an example for me. Take some jilted girl nearer home, Cummings, if you want me to go round sickening and sorrowing in secret. I don't believe you can find any. Women are much tougher about the pericardium than we give them credit for, my dear fellow,— much. I don't see why it should hurt a woman more than a man to be jilted. We shall never

truly philosophize this important matter till we regard women with
something of the fine penetration and impartiality with which they
regard each other. Look at the stabs they give and take! they would
kill men. And the graceful ferocity with which they dispatch any of
their number who happens to be down is quite unexampled in
natural history; one reads of something of the sort in those incredible stories of Russian travelers pursued by wolves. How much do
you suppose her lady friends have left of that poor girl whose case
wrings your foolish bosom all the way from Paris? I don't believe so
much as a boot-button. Why, even your correspondent—a very
lively woman, by the way—can't conceal under all her indignation
her little satisfaction that so *proud* a girl as Miss What's-her-name
should have been jilted. Of course, she doesn't say it."

Cummings, hotly: "*No,* she doesn't say it, and it's not to your
credit to imagine it."

Bartlett, with a laugh: "Oh, I don't ask any praise for the discov-
ery. You deserve praise for not making it. It does honor to your
good heart. Well, don't be vexed, old fellow. And in trying to improve me on this little point—a weak point, I'll allow, with me—do
me the justice to remember that I didn't flaunt my misanthropy, as
you call it, in your face; I didn't force my confidence upon you."

Cummings, with compunction: "I didn't mean to hurt your feel-
ings, Bartlett."

Bartlett: "Well, you haven't. It's all right."

Cummings, with anxious concern: "I wish I could think so."

Bartlett, dryly: "You have *my* leave—my request, in fact." He
takes a turn about the room, thrusting his fingers through the hair
on his forehead, and letting it fall in a heavy tangle, and then pulling at either side of his parted beard. In facing away from one of
the sofas at the end of the room, he looks back over his shoulder at
it, falters, wheels about, and picks up from it a lady's shawl and hat.
"Hallo!" He lets the shawl fall again into picturesque folds on the
sofa. "This is the spoil of no local beauty, Cummings. Look here; I
don't understand this. There has been an arrival."

Cummings, joining his friend in contemplation of the hat and
shawl: "Yes, it's an arrival beyond all question. Those are a *lady's*
things. I should think that was a Paris hat." They remain looking at
the things some moments in silence.

Bartlett: "How should a Paris hat get here? I know the landlord
wasn't expecting it. But it can't be going to stay; it's here through

some caprice. It may be a transient of quality, but it's a transient. I suppose we shall see the young woman belonging to it at dinner." He sets the hat on his fist, and holds it at arm's length from him. "What a curious thing it is about clothes"—

Cummings: "Don't, Bartlett, don't."

Bartlett: "Why?"

Cummings: "I don't know. It makes me feel as if you were offering an indignity to the young lady herself."

Bartlett: "You express my idea exactly. This frippery has not only the girl's personality but her very spirit in it. This hat looks like her; you can infer the whole woman from it, body and soul. It has a conscious air, and so has the shawl, as if they had been eavesdropping and had understood everything we were saying. They know all about my heart-break, and so will she as soon as she puts them on; she will be interested in me. The hat's in good taste, isn't it?"

Cummings, with sensitive reverence for the millinery which his friend handles so daringly: "Exquisite, it seems to me; but I don't know about such things."

Bartlett: "Neither do I; but I feel about them. Besides, a painter and glazier sees some things that are hidden from even a progressive minister. Let us interpret the lovely being from her hat. This knot of pale-blue flowers betrays her a blonde; this lace, this mass of silky, fluffy, cobwebby what-do-you-call-it, and this delicate straw fabric show that she is slight; a stout woman would kill it, or die in the attempt. And I fancy—here pure inspiration comes to my aid—that she is tallish. I'm afraid of her. No,—wait! The shawl has something to say." He takes it up and catches it across his arm, where he scans it critically. "I don't know that I understand the shawl, exactly. It proves her of a good height,—a short woman wouldn't, or had better not, wear a shawl,—but this black color: should you think it was in mourning? Have we a lovely young widow among us?"

Cummings: "I don't see how it could go with the hat, if it were."

Bartlett: "True; the hat is very reserved in tone, but it isn't mourning. This shawl's very light, it's very warm; I construct from it a pretty invalid." He lets the shawl slip down his arm to his hand, and flings it back upon the sofa. "We return from the young lady's heart to her brain—where she carries her sentiments. She has a nice taste in perfumes, Cummings: faintest violet; that goes with the blue. Of what religion is a young lady who uses violet, my reverend friend?"

Cummings: "Bartlett, you're outrageous. Put down that hat!"

Bartlett: "No, seriously. What is her little æsthetic specialty? Does she sketch? Does she scribble? Tell me, thou wicked hat, does she flirt? Come; out with the vows that you have heard poured into the shelly ear under this knot of pale-blue flowers! Where be her gibes now, her gambols, her flashes of merriment? Now get you to my lady's chamber, and tell her, let her paint an inch thick, to this favor she must come; make her laugh at that. Dost thou think, Horatio Cummings, Cleopatra looked o' this fashion? And smelt so?"—he presses the knot of artificial flowers to his mustache—"Pah!" He tosses the hat on the sofa and walks away.

Cummings: "Bartlett, this is atrocious. I protest"—

Bartlett: "Well, give me up, I tell you." He returns, and takes his friend by the shoulders, as before, and laughs. "I'm not worth your refined pains. I might be good, at a pinch, but I never could be truly lady-like."

Cummings: "You like to speak an infinite deal of nothing, don't you?"

Bartlett: "It's the only thing that makes conversation." As he releases Cummings, and turns away from him, in the doorway he confronts an elderly gentleman, whose white hair and white mustache give distinction to his handsome florid face. There is something military in his port, as he stands immovably erect upon the threshold, his left hand lodged in the breast of his frock-coat, and his head carried with an officer-like air of command. His visage grows momently redder and redder, and his blue eyes blaze upon Bartlett with a fascinated glare that briefly preludes the burst of fury with which he advances toward him.

II.

GENERAL WYATT, BARTLETT, *and* CUMMINGS.

General Wyatt: "You infernal scoundrel! What are you doing here?" He raises his stick at Bartlett, who remains motionlessly frowning in wrathful bewilderment, his strong hand knotting itself into a fist where it hangs at his side, while Cummings starts toward them in dismay, with his hand raised to interpose. "Didn't I tell you if I ever set eyes on you again, you villain—didn't I say I would shoot you if you ever crossed my path, you"— He stops with a violent self-arrest, and lets his stick drop as he throws up both his hands in amaze. "Good God! It's a mistake! I beg your pardon, sir; I do indeed." He lets fall his hands, and stands staring into Bartlett's face with his illusion apparently not fully dispelled. "A mistake, sir, a mistake. I was misled, sir, by the most prodigious resemblance."— At the sound of voices in the corridor without, he turns from Bartlett, and starts back toward the door.

A Voice, very sweet and weak, without: "I left them in here, I think."

Another Voice: "You must sit down, Constance, and let me look."

The First Voice: "Oh, they'll be here."

General Wyatt, in a loud and anxious tone: "Margaret, Margaret! Don't bring Constance in here! For God's sake, go away!" At the moment he reaches the door by which he came in, two ladies in black enter the parlor by the other door, the younger leaning weakly on the arm of the elder, and with a languidly drooping head letting her eyes rove listlessly about over the chairs and sofas. With an abrupt start at sight of Bartlett, who has mechanically turned toward them, the elder lady arrests their movement.

III.

MRS. WYATT, CONSTANCE, *and the others.*

Mrs. Wyatt: "Oh, in mercy's name!" The young lady wearily lifts her eyes; they fall upon Bartlett's face, and a low cry parts her lips as she approaches a pace or two nearer, releasing her arm from her mother's.

Constance: "Ah!" She stops; her thin hands waver before her face, as if to clear or to obstruct her vision, and all at once she sinks forward into a little slender heap upon the floor, almost at Bartlett's feet. He instantly drops upon his knees beside her, and stoops over her to lift her up.

Mrs. Wyatt: "Don't touch her, you cruel wretch! Your touch is poison; the sight of you is murder." Kneeling on the other side of her daughter, she sets both her hands against his breast and pushes him back.

General Wyatt: "Margaret, stop! Look! Look at him again! It isn't *he!*"

Mrs. Wyatt: "Not he? Don't tell me! What"— She clutches Bartlett's arm, and scans his face with dilating eyes. Then she suddenly bursts into tears. "Oh! it isn't, it isn't! But go away,—go away, all the same! You may be an innocent man, but she would perish in your presence. Keep your hands from her, sir! If your wicked heart is not yet satisfied with your wicked work— Excuse me; I *don't* know what I'm saying! But if you have any pity in your faithless soul—I—oh, *speak* for me, James, and send him—implore him to go away!" She bows her face over her daughter's pale visage, and sobs.

General Wyatt: "Sir, you must pardon us, and have the great goodness to be patient. You have a right to feel yourself aggrieved by what has happened, but no wrong is meant,—no offense. You must be so kind as to go away. I will make you all the needed apologies and explanations." He stoops over his daughter, as Bartlett, in a sort of daze, rises from his knees and retires a few steps. "I beg your pardon, sir,"—addressing himself to Cummings,— "will you help me a moment?" Cummings, with delicate sympathy and tenderness, lifts the arms of the insensible girl to her father's neck, and assists the general to rise with his burden. "Thanks! She's hardly heavier, poor child, than a ghost." The tears stand in his eyes, as he gathers her closer to him and kisses her wan cheek. "Sir,"—as he moves away he speaks to Bartlett,— "do me the favor to remain here till I can return to offer you reparation." He makes a stately effort to bow to Bartlett in leaving the room, while his wife, who follows with the young lady's hat and shawl, looks back at the painter with open abhorrence.

IV.

BARTLETT *and* CUMMINGS.

Bartlett, turning to his friend from the retreating group on which he has kept his eyes steadfastly fixed: "Where are their keepers?" He is pale with suppressed rage.

Cummings: "Their keepers?"

Bartlett, savagely: "Yes! Have they escaped from them, or is it one of the new ideas to let lunatics go about the country alone? If that old fool hadn't dropped his stick, I'd have knocked him over that table in another instant. And that other old maniac,—what did she mean by pushing me back in that way? How do you account for this thing, Cummings? What do you make of it?"

Cummings: "I don't know, upon my word. There seems to be

some mystery,—some painful mystery. But the gentleman will be back directly, I suppose, and"—

Bartlett, crushing his hat over his eyes: "I'll leave you to receive him and his mystery. I've had enough of both." He moves toward the door.

Cummings, detaining him: "Bartlett, you're surely not going away?"

Bartlett: "Yes, I am!"

Cummings: "But he'll be here in a moment. He said he would come back and satisfy the claim which you certainly have to an explanation."

Bartlett, furiously: "Claim? I've a perfect Alabama Claim to an explanation. He can't satisfy it; he shall not try. It's a little too much to expect me to be satisfied with anything he can say after what's passed. Get out of the way, Cummings, or I'll put you on top of the piano."

Cummings: "You may throw me out of the window, if you like, but not till I've done my best to keep you here. It's a shame, it's a crime to go away. You talk about lunatics: you're a raving madman, yourself. Have one glimmer of reason, do; and see what you're about. It's a mistake; it's a misunderstanding. It's his right, it's your duty, to have it cleared up. Come, you've a conscience, Bartlett, and a clean one. Don't give way to your abominable temper. What? You won't stay? Bartlett, I blush for you!"

Bartlett: "Blush unseen then!" He thrusts Cummings aside and pushes furiously from the room. Cummings looks into the corridor after him, and then returns, panting, to the piano, and mechanically rearranges the things at its feet; he walks nervously away, and takes some turns up and down the room, looking utterly bewildered, and apparently uncertain whether to go or stay. But he has decided upon the only course really open to him by sinking down into one of the arm-chairs, when General Wyatt appears at the threshold of the door on the right of the piano. Cummings rises and comes forward with great embarrassment to meet him.

V.

CUMMINGS *and* GENERAL WYATT.

General Wyatt, with a look of surprise at not seeing Bartlett: "The other gentleman"—

Cummings: "My friend has gone out. I hope he will return soon.

He has—I hardly know what to say to you, sir. He has done himself great injustice; but it was natural that under the circumstances"—

General Wyatt, with hurt pride: "Perfectly. I should have lost my temper, too; but I think I should have waited at the request—the prayer of an older man. I don't mind his temper; the other villain had *no* temper. Sir, am I right in addressing you as the Rev. Arthur Cummings?"

Cummings: "My name is Arthur Cummings. I am a minister."

General Wyatt: "I thought I was not mistaken this time. I heard you preach last Sunday in Boston; and I know your cousin, Major Cummings of the 34th Artillery. I am General Wyatt."

Cummings, with a start of painful surprise and sympathy: "General Wyatt?"

General Wyatt, keenly: "Your cousin has mentioned me to you?"

Cummings: "Yes,—oh yes, certainly; certainly, very often, General Wyatt. But"—endeavoring to recover himself—"your name is known to us all, and honored. I—I am glad to see you back; I—understood you were in Paris."

General Wyatt, with fierce defiance: "I was in Paris three weeks ago." Some moments of awkward silence ensue, during which General Wyatt does not relax his angry attitude.

Cummings, finally: "I am sorry my friend is not here to meet you. I ought to say, in justice to him, that his hasty temper does great wrong to his heart and judgment."

General Wyatt: "Why, yes, sir; so does mine,—so does mine."

Cummings, with a respectful smile lost upon the general: "And I know that he will certainly be grieved in this instance to have yielded to it."

General Wyatt, with sudden meekness: "I hope so, sir. But I am not altogether sorry that he has done it. I have not only an explanation but a request to make,—a very great and strange favor to ask,—and I am not sure that I should be able to treat him civilly enough throughout an entire interview to ask it properly." Cummings listens with an air of attentive respect, but makes, to this strange statement, no response other than a look of question, while the general pokes about on the carpet at his feet with the point of his stick for a moment before he brings it resolutely down upon the floor with a thump, and resumes, fiercely again: "Sir, your friend is the victim of an extraordinary resemblance, which is so much more painful to us than we could have made it to him that I have to struggle with my reason to believe that the apology should not come from his side rather than mine. He may feel that we have outraged him, but every look of his, every movement, every tone of his voice, is a mortal wound, a deadly insult to us. He should not live, sir, in the same solar system!" The general deals the floor another stab with his cane, while his eyes burn vindictively upon the mild brown orbs of Cummings, wide open with astonishment. He falters, with returning consciousness of his attitude: "I—I beg your pardon, sir; I am ridiculous." He closes his lips pathetically, and lets fall his head. When he lifts it again, it is to address Cummings with a singular gentleness: "I know that I speak to a gentleman."

Cummings: "I try to be a good man."

General Wyatt: "I had formed that idea of you, sir, in the pulpit. Will you do me the great kindness to answer a question, personal to myself, which I must ask?"

Cummings: "By all means."

General Wyatt: "You spoke of supposing me still in Paris. Are you aware of any circumstances—painful circumstances—connected with my presence there? Pardon my asking; I wouldn't press you if I could help."

Cummings, with reluctance: "I had just heard something about—a letter from a friend"—

General Wyatt, bitterly: "The news has traveled fast. Well, sir, a curious chance—a pitiless caprice of destiny—connects your friend with that miserable story." At Cummings's look of amaze. "Through no fault of his, sir; through no fault of his. Sir, I shall seem to obtrude my trouble unjustifiably upon you when I tell you how; you will see that it was necessary for me to speak. I am glad you already know something of the affair, and I am sure that you will regard what I have to say with the right feeling of a gentleman,— of, as you say, a good man."

Cummings: "Whatever you think necessary to say to me shall be sacred. But I hope you won't feel that it is necessary to say anything more. I am confident that when my friend has your assurance from me that what has happened is the result of a distressing association"—

General Wyatt: "I thank you, sir. But something more is due to him; how much more you shall judge. Something more is due to us: I wish to preserve the appearance of sanity, in his eyes and your own. Nevertheless"—the general's tone and bearing perceptibly stiffen—"if you are reluctant"—

Cummings, with reverent cordiality: "General Wyatt, I shall feel deeply honored by whatever confidence you repose in me. I need not say how dear your fame is to us all." General Wyatt, visibly moved, bows to the young minister. "It was only on your account that I hesitated."

General Wyatt: "Thanks. I understand. I will be explicit, but I will try to be brief. Your friend bears this striking, this painful resemblance to the man who has brought this blight upon us all; yes, sir,"—at Cummings's look of deprecation,—"to a scoundrel whom I hardly know how to characterize aright—in the presence of a clergyman. Two years ago—doubtless your correspondent has written—my wife and daughter (they were then abroad without me) met him in Paris; and he won the poor child's affection. My wife's judgment was also swayed in his favor,—against her first impulse of distrust; but when I saw him, I could not endure him. Yet I was helpless: my girl's happiness was bound up in him; all that I could do was to insist upon delay. He was an American, well related, unobjectionable by all the tests which society can apply, and I might have had to wait long for the proofs that an accident gave me against him. The man's whole soul was rotten: at the time he had wound himself into my poor girl's innocent heart, a woman was living who had the just and perhaps the legal claim of a wife upon him; he was a felon besides,—a felon shielded through pity for his friends by the man whose name he had forged; he was of course a liar and a coward: I beat him with my stick, sir. Ah! I made him confess his infamy under his own hand, and then"—the general advances defiantly upon Cummings, who unconsciously retires a pace—"and then I compelled him to break with my daughter. Do you think I did right?"

Cummings: "I don't exactly understand."

General Wyatt: "Why, sir, it happens often enough in this shabby world that a man gains a poor girl's love, and then jilts her. I chose what I thought the less terrible sorrow for my child. I could not tell her how filthily unworthy he was without bringing to her pure heart a sense of intolerable contamination; I could not endure to speak of it even to my wife. It seemed better that they should both suffer such wrong as a broken engagement might bring them than that they should know what I knew. He was master of the part, and played it well. It broke my girl's heart, but she has not had to loathe herself for his fouler shame; he showed himself to them simply a heartless scoundrel, and he remains in my power, an outcast now and a convict whenever I will. My story, as it seems to be, is well known in Paris; but the worst is unknown. I choose still that it shall be thought my girl was the victim of a dastardly slight, and I bear with her and her mother the insolent pity with which the world visits such sorrow." He pauses, and then brokenly resumes: "The affair has not turned out as I hoped, in the little I could hope from it. My trust that the blow, which must sink so deeply into her heart, would touch her pride, and that this would help her to react against it, was mistaken. In such things it appears that a woman has no pride; I did not know it; we men are different. The blow crushed her; that was all. I am afraid she is dying under it." He pauses again, and sets his lips firmly; all at once he breaks into a sob. "I—I beg your pardon, sir."

Cummings: "Don't! You wrong yourself and me. I have seen Miss Wyatt; but I hope"—

General Wyatt: "You have seen her ghost. You have not seen the radiant creature that was once alive. Well, sir; enough of this. I have told you my story and there is little left to trouble you with. We landed eight days ago, and I have since been looking about for some place in which my daughter could hide herself; I can't otherwise suggest her morbid sensitiveness, her terror of people. This region was highly commended to me for its healthfulness; but I have come upon this house by chance. I understood that it was empty, and I thought it more than probable that we might pass the autumn months here unmolested by the presence of any one belonging to our world, if not in entire seclusion. At the best, my daughter would hardly have been able to endure another change at once,—so far as anything could give her pleasure, the beauty and the wild quiet of the region had pleased her,—and she is now quite prostrated, sir,"—

Cummings, definitively: "My friend will go away at once. There is nothing else for it."

General Wyatt: "That is much to ask."

Cummings: "I won't conceal my belief that he will think so. But there can be no question with him when"—

General Wyatt: "When you tell him our story?" After a moment: "Yes, he has a right to know it—as the rest of the world knows it. You must tell him, sir."

Cummings, gently: "No, he need know nothing beyond the fact of this resemblance to some one painfully associated with your past lives. He is a man whose real tenderness of heart would revolt from knowledge that could inflict further sorrow upon you."

General Wyatt: "Sir, will you convey to this friend of yours an old man's very humble apology, and sincere prayer for his forgiveness?"

Cummings: "He will not exact anything of that sort. The evidence of misunderstanding will be clear to him at a word from me."

General Wyatt: "But he has a right to this explanation from my own lips, and—Sir, I am culpably weak. But now that I have missed seeing him here, I confess that I would willingly avoid meeting him. The mere sound of his voice, as I heard it before I saw him, in first coming upon you, was enough to madden me. Can you excuse to him my unreasonable dereliction in this respect?"

Cummings: "I will answer for him."

General Wyatt: "Thanks. It seems monstrous that I should be asking and accepting these great favors. But you are doing a deed of charity to a helpless man utterly beggared in pride." He choked with emotion, and does not speak for a moment; then he is more calm. "Your friend is also—he is not also—a clergyman?"

Cummings: "No. He is a painter."

General Wyatt: "Is he a man of note? Successful in his profession?"

Cummings: "Not yet. But that is certain to come."

General Wyatt: "He is poor?"

Cummings: "He is a young painter."

General Wyatt: "Sir, excuse me. Had he planned to remain here some time, yet?"

Cummings, reluctantly: "He has been sketching here. He had expected to stay through October."

General Wyatt: "You make the sacrifice hard to accept—I beg your pardon! But I must accept it. I am bound hand and foot."

Cummings: "I am sorry to have been obliged to tell you this."

General Wyatt: "I obliged you, sir; I obliged you. Give me your advice, sir; you know your friend. What shall I do? I am not rich. I don't belong to a branch of the government service in which people enrich themselves. But I have my pay; and if your friend could sell me the pictures he's been painting here"—

Cummings: "That's quite impossible. There is no form in which

I could propose such a thing to a man of his generous pride."

General Wyatt: "Well, then, sir, I must satisfy myself as I can to remain his debtor. Will you kindly undertake to tell him?"

An Elderly Serving-Woman, who appears timidly and anxiously at the right-hand door: "General Wyatt."

General Wyatt, with a start: "Yes, Mary! Well?"

Mary, in vanishing: "Mrs. Wyatt wishes to speak with you."

General Wyatt, going up to Cummings: "I must go, sir. I leave unsaid what I cannot even try to say." He offers his hand.

Cummings, grasping the proffered hand: "Everything is understood." But as Mr. Cummings returns from following General Wyatt to the door, his face does not confirm the entire security of his words. He looks anxious and perturbed, and when he has taken up his hat and stick, he stands pondering absent-mindedly. At last he puts on his hat and starts with a brisk limp toward the door. Before he reaches it, he encounters Bartlett, who advances abruptly into the room. "Oh! I was going to look for you."

VI.

CUMMINGS *and* BARTLETT.

Bartlett, sulkily: "Were you?" He walks, without looking at Cummings, to where his painter's paraphernalia are lying, and begins to pick them up.

Cummings: "Yes." In great embarrassment: "Bartlett, General Wyatt has been here."

Bartlett, without looking around: "Who is General Wyatt?"

Cummings: "I mean the gentleman who—whom you wouldn't wait to see."

Bartlett: "Um!" He has gathered the things into his arms, and is about to leave the room.

Cummings, in great distress: "Bartlett, Bartlett! Don't go! I implore you, if you have any regard for me whatever, to hear what I have to say. It's boyish, it's cruel, it's cowardly to behave as you're doing!"

Bartlett: "Anything more, Mr. Cummings? I give you benefit of clergy."

Cummings: "I take it—to denounce your proceeding as something that you'll always be sorry for and ashamed of."

Bartlett: "Oh! Then, if you have quite freed your mind, I think I may go."

Cummings: "No, no! You mustn't go. Don't go, my dear fellow. Forgive me! I know how insulted you feel, but upon my soul it's all a mistake,—it is, indeed. General Wyatt"—Bartlett falters a moment and stands as if irresolute whether to stay and listen or push on out of the room—"the young lady—I don't know to begin!"

Bartlett, relenting a little: "Well? I'm sorry for *you,* Cummings. I left a very awkward business to you, and it wasn't yours, either. As for General Wyatt, as he chooses to call himself:"—

Cummings, in amaze: "*Call* himself? It's his *name!*"

Bartlett: "Oh, very likely! So is King David his name, when he happens to be in a scriptural craze. Well, for all me, General Wyatt and the rest of his Bedlam-broke-loose may go to the"—

Cummings: "For shame, for shame! You outrage a terrible sorrow! You insult a trouble sore to death! You trample upon an anguish that should be sacred to your tears!"

Bartlett, resting his elbow on the corner of the piano: "What—what do you mean, Cummings?"

Cummings: "What do I mean? What you are not worthy to know! I mean that these people, against whom you vent your stupid rage, are worthy of angelic pity. I mean that by some disastrous mischance you resemble to the life, in tone, manner, and feature, the wretch who won that poor girl's heart, and then crushed it; who—Bartlett, look here! These are the people—this is the young lady—of whom my friend wrote me from Paris; do you understand?"

Bartlett, in a dull bewilderment: "No, I don't understand."

Cummings: "Why, you know what we were talking of just before they came in; you know what I told you of that cruel business."

Bartlett: "Well?"

Cummings: "Well, this is the young lady"—

Bartlett, dauntedly: "Oh, come, now! You don't expect me to believe that! It isn't a stage-play."

Cummings: "Indeed, indeed, I tell you the miserable truth."

Bartlett: "Do you mean to say that *this* is the young girl who was jilted in that way? Who—Do you mean—Do you intend to tell me—Do you suppose—Cummings"—

Cummings: "Yes, yes, yes!"

Bartlett: "Why, man, she's in Paris, according to your own showing!"

Cummings: "She was in Paris three weeks ago. They have just brought her home, to help her hide her suffering, as if it were her shame, from all who know it. They are in this house by chance, but they are here. I mean what I say. You *must* believe it, shocking and wild as it is."

Bartlett, after a prolonged silence in which he seems trying to realize the fact: "If you were a man capable of such a ghastly joke—but that's impossible." He is silent again, as before. "And I— What did you say about me? That I look like the man who"— He stops and looks into Cummings's face without speaking, as if he were trying to puzzle the mystery out; then, with fallen head, he muses in a voice of devout and reverent tenderness: "That—that— broken—lily! Oh!" With a sudden start he flings his burden upon the closed piano, whose hidden strings hum and ring with the blow, and advances upon Cummings: "And you can *tell* it? Shame on *you!* It ought to be known to no one upon earth! And you—you show that gentle creature's death-wound to teach something like human reason to a surly dog like me? Oh, it's monstrous! I *wasn't* worth it. Better have let me go, where I would, how I would. What did it matter what I thought or said? And I—I look like that devil, do I? I have his voice, his face, his movement? Cummings, you've over-avenged yourself."

Cummings: "Don't take it that way, Bartlett. It *is* hideous. But I didn't make it so, nor you. It's a fatality, it's a hateful chance. But you see now, don't you, Bartlett, how the sight of you must affect them, and how anxious her father must be to avoid you? He most humbly asked your forgiveness, and he hardly knew how to ask that you would not let her see you again. But I told him there could be no question with you; that of course you would prevent it, and at once. I know it's a great sacrifice to expect you to go"—

Bartlett: "Go? What are you talking about?" He breaks again from the daze into which he had relapsed. "If there's a hole on the face of the earth where I can hide myself from them, I want to find it. Go! Good God, man! What do you think I'm made of? Go? I ought to be shot away out of a mortar; I ought to be struck away by lightning! Oh, I can't excuse you, Cummings! The indelicacy, the brutality of telling me that! No, no,— I can't overlook it." He shakes his head and walks away from his friend; then he returns, and bends on him a look of curious inquiry. "Am I really such a ruffi-an"—he speaks very gently, almost meekly, now—"that you didn't believe anything short of that would bring me to my senses? Who told you this of her?"

Cummings: "Her father."

Bartlett: "Oh, that's too loathsome! Had the man no soul, no mercy? Did he think me such a consummate beast that nothing less would drive me away? Yes, he did! Yes, I made him think so! Oh!" He hangs his head and walks away with a shudder.

Cummings: "I don't know that he did you that injustice; but I'm afraid *I* did. I was at my wits' end."

Bartlett, very humbly: "Oh, I don't know that you were wrong."

Cummings: "I suppose that his anxiety for her life made it comparatively easy for him to speak of the hurt to her pride. She can't be long for this world."

Bartlett: "No, she had the dying look!" After a long pause, in which he has continued to wander aimlessly about the room: "Cummings, is it necessary that you should tell him you told me?"

Cummings: "You know I hate concealments of any kind, Bartlett."

Bartlett: "Oh, well; do it, then!"

Cummings: "But I don't know that we shall see him again; and even if we do, I don't see how I can tell him unless he asks. It's rather painful."

Bartlett: "Well, take that little sin on your conscience, if you can. It seems to me too ghastly that I should know what you've told me; it's indecent. Cummings,"—after another pause,—"how does a man go about such a thing? How does he contrive to tell the woman whose heart he has won that he doesn't care for her, and break the faith that she would have staked her life on? Oh, I know,— women do such things, too; but it's different, by a whole world's difference. A man comes and a man goes, but a woman *stays.* The world is before him after that happens, and we don't think him much of a man if he can't get over it. But she, she has been sought out; she has been made to believe that her smile and her looks are heaven, poor, foolish, helpless idol! her fears have been laid, all her pretty maidenly traditions, her proud reserves overcome; she takes him into her inmost soul,—to find that his love is a lie, a lie! Imagine it! She can't do anything. She can't speak. She can't move as long as she lives. She must stay where she has been left, and look and act as if nothing had happened. Oh, good Heaven! And I, *I* look like a man who could do that!" After a silence: "I feel as if there were blood on me!" He goes to the piano, and gathering up his things turns about towards Cummings again: "Come, man; I'm going. It's sacrilege to stay an instant,—to exist."

Cummings: "Don't take it in that way, Bartlett. I blame myself very much for not having spared you in what I said. I wouldn't have told you of it, if I could have supposed that an accidental resemblance of the sort would distress you so."

Bartlett, contritely: "You had to tell me. I forced you to extreme measures. I'm quite worthy to look like him. Good Lord! I suppose I should be capable of his work." He moves towards the door with his burden, but before he reaches it General Wyatt, from the corridor, meets him with an air of confused agitation. Bartlett halts awkwardly, and some of the things slip from his hold to the floor.

VII.

GENERAL WYATT, CUMMINGS, *and* BARTLETT.

General Wyatt: "Sir, I am glad to see you." He pronounces the civility with a manner evidently affected by the effort to reconcile Bartlett's offensive personal appearance with his own sense of duty. "I—I was sorry to miss you before; and now I wish— Your friend" —referring with an inquiring glance to Cummings—"has explained to you the cause of our very extraordinary behavior, and I hope you"—

Bartlett: "Mr. Cummings has told me that I have the misfortune to resemble very closely some one with whom you have painful associations. That is quite enough and entirely justifies you. I am going at once, and I trust you will forgive my rudeness in absenting myself a moment ago. I have a bad temper; but I never could forgive myself if I had forced my friend"—he turns and glares warningly at Cummings, who makes a faint pantomime of conscientious protest as Bartlett proceeds—"to hear anything more than the mere fact from you. No, no,"—as General Wyatt seems about to speak,—"it would be atrocious in me to seek to go behind it. I wish to know nothing more." Cummings gives signs of extreme unrest at being made a party to this tacit deception, and General Wyatt, striking his palms hopelessly together, walks to the other end of the room. Bartlett touches the fallen camp-stool with his foot. "Cummings, will you be kind enough to put that on top of this other rubbish?" He indicates his armful, and as Cummings complies, he says in a swift, fierce whisper: "Her secret is mine. If you dare to hint that you've told it to me, I'll—I'll assault you in your own pulpit." Then to General Wyatt, who is returning toward him: "Good morning, sir."

General Wyatt: "Oh! Ah! Stop! That is, don't go! Really, sir, I don't know what to say. I must have seemed to you like a madman a moment ago, and now I've come to play the fool." Bartlett and Cummings look their surprise and General Wyatt hurries on: "I asked your friend to beg you to go away, and now I am here to beg you to remain. It's perfectly ridiculous, sir, I know, and I can say nothing in defense of the monstrous liberties I have taken. Sir, the matter is simply this: my daughter's health is so frail that her life seems to hang by a thread, and I am powerless to do anything against her wish. It may be a culpable weakness, but I cannot help it. When I went back to her from seeing your friend, she immediately divined what my mission had been, and it had the contrary effect from what I had expected. Well, sir! Nothing would content her but that I should return and ask you to stay. She looks upon it as the sole reparation we can make you."

Bartlett, gently: "I understand that perfectly; and may I beg you to say that in going away I thanked her with all my heart, and ventured to leave her my best wishes?" He bows as if to go.

General Wyatt, detaining him: "Excuse me—thanks—but—but I am afraid she will not be satisfied with that. She will be satisfied with nothing less than your remaining. It is the whim of a sick child—sick to death I am afraid—which I must ask you to indulge. In a few days, sir, I hope we may be able to continue on our way. It would be simply unbearable pain to her to know that we had driven you away, and you must stay to show that you have forgiven the wrong we have done you."

Bartlett: "That's nothing, less than nothing. But I was thinking—I don't care for myself in the matter—that Miss Wyatt is proposing a very unnecessary annoyance for you all. My friend can remain and assure her that I have no feeling whatever about the matter, and in the mean time I can remove—the embarrassment—of my presence."

General Wyatt: "Sir, you are very considerate, very kind. I don't know what to say. My own judgment is in favor of your course, and yet"—

Cummings: "I think my friend is right, and that when he is gone"—

General Wyatt: "Well, sir! well, sir! It may be the best way. I think

it *is* the best way. We will venture upon it. Sir,"—to Bartlett,—"may
I have the honor of taking your hand?" Bartlett lays down his burden on the piano, and gives his hand. "Thank you, thank you! You
will not regret this goodness. Farewell, sir! May you always prosper."

Bartlett: "Good-by; and say to Miss Wyatt"— At these words he
pauses, arrested by an incomprehensible dismay in General Wyatt's
face, and turning about he sees Cummings transfixed at the apparition of Miss Wyatt advancing directly toward himself, while her
mother coming behind her exchanges signals of helplessness and
despair with the general. The young girl's hair, thick and bronze,
has been heaped in hasty but beautiful masses on her delicate
head; as she stands with fallen eyes before Bartlett, the heavy
lashes lie black on her pale cheeks, and the blue of her eyes shows
through their transparent lids. She has a fan with which she makes
a weak pretense of playing, and which she puts to her lips as if to
hide the low murmur that escapes from them as she raises her eyes
to Bartlett's face.

VIII.

CONSTANCE, MRS. WYATT, *and the others.*

Constance, with a phantom-like effort at hauteur: "I hope you
have been able to forgive the annoyance we caused you, and that
you won't let it drive you away." She lifts her eyes with a slow
effort, and starts with a little gasp as they fall upon his face, and
then remains trembling before him while he speaks.

Bartlett, reverently: "I am to do whatever you wish. I have no
annoyance—but the fear that—that"—

Constance, in a husky whisper: "Thanks!" As she turns from him
to go back to her mother, she moves so frailly that he involuntarily
puts out his hand.

Mrs. Wyatt, starting forward: "No!" But Constance clutches his
extended arm with one of her pale hands, and staying herself for a
moment lifts her eyes again to his, looks steadily at him with [her]
face half turned upon him, and then, making a slight, sidelong
inclination of the head, releases his arm and goes to her mother,
who supports her to one of the easy-chairs and kneels beside her
when she sinks into it. Bartlett, after an instant of hesitation, bows
silently and withdraws, Cummings having already vanished.
Constance watches him going, and then hides her face on her

mother's neck.

PART SECOND.

I.

CONSTANCE *and* MRS. WYATT.

Constance: "And he is still here? He is going to stay on, mother?" She reclines in a low folding-chair, and languidly rests her head against one of the pillows with which her mother has propped her; on the bright-colored shawl which has been thrown over her lie her pale hands loosely holding her shut fan. Her mother stands half across the room from her, and wistfully surveys her work, to see if there may not yet be some touch added for the girl's comfort.

Mrs. Wyatt: "Yes, my child. He will stay. He told your father he would stay."

Constance: "That's very kind of him. He's very good."

Mrs. Wyatt, seating herself before her daughter: "Do you really wish him to stay? Remember how weak you are, Constance. If you are taking anything upon yourself out of a mistaken sense of duty, of compunction, you are not kind to your poor father or to me. Not that I mean to reproach you."

Constance: "Oh, no. And I am not unkind to you in the way you think. I'm selfish enough in wishing him to stay. I can't help wanting to see him again and again,—it's so strange, so strange. All this past week, whenever I've caught a glimpse of him, it's been like an apparition; and whenever he has spoken, it has been like a ghost speaking. But I haven't been afraid since the first time. No, there's been a dreary comfort in it; you won't understand it; I can't understand it myself; but I know now why people are glad to see their dead in dreams. If the ghost went, there would be nothing."

Mrs. Wyatt: "Constance, you break my heart!"

Constance: "Yes, I know it. It's because I've none." She waits a little space without speaking, while she softly fingers the edges of the fan lying in her lap. "I suppose we shall become more acquainted, if he remains here?"

Mrs. Wyatt: "Why, not necessarily, dear. You need know nothing more of him than you do now. He seems very busy, and not in the least inclined to intrude upon us. Your father thinks him a little odd, but very gentlemanly."

Constance, dreamily: "I wonder what he would think if he knew that the man whom I would have given my life did not find my love worth having. I suppose it *was* worthless; but it seemed so much in the giving; it was that deceived me. He was wiser. Oh, me!" After a silence: "Mother, why was I so different from other girls?"

Mrs. Wyatt: "So different, Constance? You were only different in being lovelier and better than others."

Constance: "Ah, that's the mistake! If that were true, it could never have happened. Other girls, the poorest and plainest, are kept faith with; but I was left. There must have been something about me that made him despise me. Was I silly, mother? Was I too bold, too glad to have him care for me? I was so happy that I couldn't help showing it. May be that displeased him. I must have been dull and tiresome. And I suppose I was somehow repulsive, and at last he couldn't bear it any longer and had to break with me. Did I dress queerly? I know I looked ridiculous at times; and people laughed at me before him."

Mrs. Wyatt: "Oh, Constance, Constance! Can't you understand that it was his unworthiness alone, his wicked heartlessness?"

Constance, with gentle slowness: "No, I can't understand that. It happened after we had learned to know each other so well. If he had been fickle, it would have happened long before that. It was something odious in me that he didn't see at first. I have thought it out. It seems strange, now, that people could ever have tolerated me." Desolately: "Well, they have their revenge."

Mrs. Wyatt: "Their revenge on *you,* Constance? What harm did you ever do them, my poor child? Oh, you mustn't let these morbid fancies overcome you. Where is our Constance that used to be,— our brave, bright girl, that nothing could daunt, and nothing could sadden?"

Constance, sobbing: "Dead, dead!"

Mrs. Wyatt: "I can't understand! You are so young still, and with the world all before you. Why will you let one man's baseness blacken it all, and blight your young life so? Where is your pride, Constance?"

Constance: "Pride? What have I to do with pride? A thing like me!"

Mrs. Wyatt: "Oh, child, you're pitiless! It seems as if you took a dreadful pleasure in torturing those who love you."

Constance: "You've said it, mother. I do. I know now that I am a vampire, and that it's my hideous fate to prey upon those who are dearest to me. He must have known, he must have felt the vampire nature in me."

Mrs. Wyatt: "Constance!"

Constance: "But at least I can be kind to those who care nothing for me. Who is this stranger? He must be an odd kind of man, to forgive us. What is he, mother?—if he is anything in himself; he seems to me only a likeness, not a reality."

Mrs. Wyatt: "He is a painter, your father says." Mrs. Wyatt gives a quick sigh of relief, and makes haste to confirm the direction of the talk away from Constance: "He is painting some landscapes, here. That friend of his who went to-day is a cousin of your father's old friend, Major Cummings. He's a minister."

Constance: "What is the painter's name? Not that it matters. But I must call him something if I meet him again."

Mrs. Wyatt: "Mr. Bartlett."

Constance: "Oh, yes, I forgot." She falls into a brooding silence. "I wonder if *he* will despise me,—if he will be like in that, too?" Mrs. Wyatt sighs patiently. "Why do you mind what I say, mother? I'm not worth it. I must talk on, or else go mad with the mystery of what has been. We were so happy; he was so good to me, so kind; there was nothing but papa's not seeming to like him; and then suddenly, in an instant, he turns and strikes me down! Yes, it was like a deadly blow. If you don't let me believe that it was because he saw all at once that I was utterly unworthy, I can't believe anything."

Mrs. Wyatt: "Hush, Constance; you don't know what you're saying."

Constance: "Oh, I know too well! And now this stranger, who is so like him,—who has all his looks, who has his walk, who has his voice,—won't he have his insight, too? I had better show myself for what I am, at once,—weak, stupid, selfish, false; it'll save me the pain of being found out. Pain? Oh, I'm past hurting! Why do you cry, mother? I'm not worth your tears."

Mrs. Wyatt: "You're all the world to us, Constance; you know it, child. Your poor father" —

Constance: "Does papa really like me?"

Mrs. Wyatt: "Constance!"

Constance: "No; but why should he? He never liked *him;* and sometimes I've wondered, if it wasn't papa's not liking him that first set him against me. Of course, it was best he should find me out, but still I can't keep from thinking that if he had never *begun* to dislike me! I noticed from the first that after papa had been with us he was cold and constrained. Mamma, I had better say it: I don't believe I love papa as I ought. There's something in my heart— some hardness—against him when he's kindest to me. If he had only been kinder to *him*"—

Mrs. Wyatt: "Kinder to *him?* Constance, you drive me wild! Kind to a wolf, kind to a snake! Kind to the thief who has robbed us of all that made our lives dear; who stole your love, and then your hope, your health, your joy, your pride, your peace! And you think your father might have been kinder to *him!* Constance, you were our little girl when the war began,—the last of brothers and sisters that had died. You seemed given to our later years to console and comfort us for all that had been taken; and you were *so* bright and gay! All through those dreadful days and months and years you were our stay and hope,—mine at home, his in the field. Our letters were full of you,—like young people's with their first child; all that you did and said I had to tell him, and then he had to talk it over in his answers back. When he came home at last, after the peace— can you remember it, Constance?"

Constance: "I can remember a little girl that ran down the street and met an officer on horseback. He was all tanned and weather-beaten; he sat his horse at the head of his troop like a statue of bronze. When he saw her come running, dancing down the street, he leaped from his horse and caught her in his arms, and hugged her close and kissed her, and set her all crying and laughing in his saddle, and walked on beside her; and the men burst out with a wild yell, and the ragged flags flapped over her, and the music flashed out"— She rises in her chair with the thrill of her recollec-tion; her voice comes free and full, and her pale cheeks flush; suddenly she sinks back upon the pillows: "Was it really I, mother?"

Mrs. Wyatt: "Yes, it was you, Constance. And do you remember, all through your school-days, how proud and fond he was of you? what presents and feasts and pleasures he was always making you? I thought he would spoil you; he took you everywhere with him, and wanted to give you everything. When I saw you growing up with his pride and quick temper, I trembled, but I felt safe when I saw that you had his true and tender heart, too. You can never know what a pang it cost him to part with you when we went abroad, but you can't forget how he met you in Paris?"

Constance: "Oh, no, no! Poor papa!"

Mrs. Wyatt: "Oh, child! And I could tell you something of his bitter despair when he saw the man"—

Constance, wearily: "You needn't tell me. I knew it as soon as they met, without looking at either of them."

Mrs. Wyatt: "And when the worst that he feared came true, he was almost glad, I believe. He thought, and I thought, that your self-respect would come to your aid against such treachery."

Constance: "My self-respect? Now I know you've not been talking of me."

Mrs. Wyatt, desperately: "Oh, what shall I do?"

Mary, the serving woman, at the door: "If you please, Mrs. Wyatt, I can't open Miss Constance's hat-box."

Mrs. Wyatt, rising: "Oh, yes. There is something the matter with the lock. I'll come, Mary." She looks at Constance.

Constance: "Yes, go, mother. I'm perfectly well here. I like being alone well enough." As Mrs. Wyatt, after a moment's reluctance, goes out, the girl's heavy eyelids fall, and she lies still against her pillows, while the fan, released from her careless hold, slides slowly over the shawl, and drops with a light clash upon the floor. She starts at the sound, and utters an involuntary cry at the sight of Bartlett, who stands irresolute on the threshold on her right. He makes as if to retreat, but at a glance from her he remains.

II.

BARTLETT *and* CONSTANCE.

Bartlett, with a sort of subdued gruffness: "I'm afraid I disturbed you."

Constance, passively: "No, I think it was my fan. It fell."

Bartlett: "I'm glad I can lay the blame on the fan." He comes abruptly forward and picks it up for her. She makes no motion to receive it, and he lays it on her lap.

Constance, starting from the abstraction in which she has been gazing at him: "Oh! Thanks."

Bartlett, with constraint: "I hope you're better this morning?"

Constance: "Yes." She has again fallen into a dreamy study of him, as unconscious, apparently, as if he were a picture before her, the effect of which upon Bartlett is to reduce him to a state of immovable awkwardness. At last he tears himself loose from the spot on which he has been petrifying, and takes refuge in the business which has brought him into the room.

Bartlett: "I came to look for one of my brushes. It must have dropped out of my traps here, the other day." He goes up to the piano and looks about the floor, while Constance's gaze follows him in every attitude and movement. "Ah, here it is! I knew it would escape the broom under the landlady's relaxed régime. If you happen to drop anything in this room, Miss Wyatt, you needn't be troubled; you can always find it just where it fell." Miss Wyatt's fan again slips to the floor, and Bartlett again picks it up and restores it to her: "A case in point."

Constance, blushing faintly: "Don't do it for me. It isn't worth while."

Bartlett: "It doesn't take a great deal of time, and the exercise does one good." Constance dimly smiles, but does not relax her vigilance. "Isn't that light rather strong for you?" He goes to the glass doors opening on the balcony, and offers to draw down one of their shades.

Constance: "It doesn't make any difference."

Bartlett, bluffly: "If it's disagreeable, it makes some difference. Is it disagreeable?"

Constance: "The light's strong"—Bartlett dashes the curtain down—"but I could see the mountain." He pulls the curtain up.

Bartlett: "I beg your pardon." He again falls into statue-like discomposure under Miss Wyatt's gaze, which does not seek the distant slopes of Ponkwasset, in spite of the lifted curtain.

Constance: "What is the name? Do you know?"

Bartlett: "Whose? Oh! Ponkwasset. It's not a pretty name, but it's aboriginal. And it doesn't hurt the mountain." Recovering a partial volition, he shows signs of purpose to escape, when Miss Wyatt's next question arrests him.

Constance: "Are you painting it, Mr.—Bartlett?"

Bartlett, with a laugh: "Oh, no, I don't soar so high as mountains; I only lift my eyes to a tree here and there, and a bit of pasture, and a few of the lowlier and friendlier sort of rocks." He now so far effects his purpose as to transfer his unwieldy presence to a lateral position as regards Miss Wyatt. The girl mechanically turns her head upon the pillow and again fixes her sad eyes upon him.

Constance: "Have you ever been up it?"

Bartlett: "Yes, half a dozen times."

Constance: "Is it hard to climb—like the Swiss mountains?"

Bartlett: "*You* must speak for the Swiss mountains after you've tried Ponkwasset, Miss Wyatt. I've never been abroad."

Constance, her large eyes dilating with surprise: "Never been abroad?"

Bartlett: "I enjoy that distinction."

Constance: "Oh! I thought you had been abroad." She speaks with a slow, absent, earnest accent, regarding him, as always, with a look of wistful bewilderment.

Bartlett, struggling uneasily for his habitual lightness: "I'm sorry to disappoint you, Miss Wyatt. I will go abroad as soon as possible. I'm going out in a boat this morning to work at a bit on the point of the island yonder, and I'll take lessons in sea-faring." Bartlett, managing at last to get fairly behind Miss Wyatt's chair, indulges himself in a long, low sigh of relief, and taking out his handkerchief rubs his face with it.

Constance, with sudden, meek compunction: "I've been detaining you."

Bartlett, politely coming forward again: "Oh, no, not at all! I'm afraid I've tired *you.*"

Constance: "No, I'm glad to have you stay." In the unconscious movement necessary to follow Bartlett in his changes of position, the young girl has loosened one of the pillows that prop her head. It slowly disengages itself and drops to the floor. Bartlett, who has been crushing his brush against the ball of his thumb, gives a start of terror, and looks from Constance to the pillow, and back again to Constance in despair.

Constance: "Never mind." She tries to adjust her head to the remaining pillows, and then desists in evident discomfort.

Bartlett, in great agony of spirit. "I—I'm afraid you miss it."

Constance: "Oh, no."

Bartlett: "Shall I call your mother, Miss Wyatt?"

Constance: "No. Oh, no. She will be here presently. Thank you so much." Bartlett eyes the pillow in renewed desperation.

Bartlett: "Do you think—do you suppose I could"— Recklessly: "Miss Wyatt, let *me* put back that pillow for you!"

Constance, promptly, with a little flush: "Why, you're very good! I'm ashamed to trouble you." As she speaks, she raises her head, and lifts herself forward slightly by help of the chair-arms; two more pillows topple out, one on either side, unknown to her.

Bartlett, maddened by the fresh disaster: "Good Heaven!" He flings himself wildly upon the first pillow, and crams it into the

chair behind Miss Wyatt; then, without giving his courage time to
flag, he seizes the others, and packs them in on top of it: "Will that
do?" He stands hot and flushed, looking down upon her, as she
makes a gentle attempt to adjust herself to the mass.

Constance: "Oh, perfectly." She puts her hand behind her and
feebly endeavors to modify Bartlett's arrangement.

Bartlett: "What is it?"

Constance: "Oh, nothing. Ah—would—would you draw this
one a little—toward you? So! Thanks. And that one—out a little on
the—other side? You're very kind; that's right. And this one under
my neck—lift it up a little? Ah, thank you ever so much." Bartlett, in
a fine frenzy, obeying these instructions, Miss Wyatt at last reposes
herself against the pillows, looks up into his embarrassed face, and
deeply blushes; then she turns suddenly white, and weakly catching up her fan she passes it once or twice before her face, and lets
it fall: "I'm a little—faint." Bartlett seizes the fan, and, after a moment of silent self-dedication, kneels down beside her chair and
fans her.

Constance, after a moment: "Thanks, thanks. You are very good.
I'm better now. I'm ashamed to have troubled you. But I seem only
to live to give trouble."

Bartlett, with sudden deep tenderness: "Oh, Miss Wyatt, you
mustn't say that. I'm sure I—we all—that is— Shall I call your mother *now,* Miss Wyatt?"

Constance, after a deep breath, firmly: "No. I'm quite well, now.
She is busy. But I know I'm keeping *you* from your work," with
ever so slight a wan little smile. "I mustn't do that."

Bartlett: "Oh, you're not *keeping* me! There's no hurry. I can
work later just as well."

Constance: "Then,"—with a glance at his devout posture, of
which Bartlett has himself become quite unconscious,—"won't you
sit down, Mr. Bartlett?"

Bartlett, restored to consciousness and confusion: "Thanks; I
think it will be better." He rises, and in his embarrassment draws a
chair to the spot on which he has been kneeling, and sits down
very close to her. He keeps the fan in his hand, as he talks: "It's
rather nice out there, Miss Wyatt,—there on the island. You must be
rowed out as soon as you can stand it. The general would like it."

Constance: "Is it a large place, the island?"

Bartlett: "About two acres, devoted exclusively to golden-rod and granite. The fact is, I was going to make a little study of golden-rod and granite, there. You shall visit the Fortunate Isle in my sketch, this afternoon, and see whether you'd like to go, really. People camp out there in the summer. Who knows but if you keep on—gaining—this way you may yet feel like camping out there yourself before you go away? You do begin to feel better, don't you? Everybody cries up this air."

Constance: "It's very pleasant; it seems fine and pure. Is the island a pretty place?"

Bartlett, glancing out at it over his shoulder: "Well, you get the best of it from the parlor window, here. Not that it's so bad when you're on it; there's a surly, frugal, hard-headed kind of beauty about it,—like the local human nature,—and it has its advantages. If you were camping out there, you could almost provision yourself from the fish and wild fowl of the surrounding waters,—supposing any of your party liked to fish and shoot. Does your father like shooting?"

Constance: "No, I don't believe he cares for it."

Bartlett: "I'm glad of that. I shall be spared the painful hospitality of pointing out the best places for ducks." At an inquiring look from Constance: "I'm glad for their sakes, not mine; *I* don't want to kill them."

Constance, with grave mistrust: "Not like shooting?"

Bartlett: "No; I think it's the sneakingest sort of assassination. It's the pleasure of murder without the guilt. If you must kill, you ought to be man enough to kill something that you'll suffer remorse for. Do you consider those atrocious sentiments, Miss Wyatt? I assure you that they're entirely my own."

Constance, blankly: "I wasn't thinking—I was thinking—I supposed you liked shooting."

Bartlett: "How did you get that impression?"

Constance, evasively: "I thought all gentlemen did."

Bartlett: "They do, in this region. It's the only thing that can comfort them in affliction. The other day our ostler's brother lost his sweetheart,—she died, poor girl,—and the ostler and another friend had him over here to cheer him up. They took him to the stable, and whittled round among the stalls with him half the forenoon, and let him rub down some of the horses; they stood him out among the vegetables and allowed him to gather some of the new kind of potato-bugs; they made him sit in the office with his feet on top of the stove; they played billiards with him; but he showed no signs of resignation till they borrowed three squirrel-guns and started with him to the oak woods yonder. That seemed to 'fetch' him. You should have seen them trudging off together with their guns all aslant,—this way,—the stricken lover in the middle!" Bartlett rises to illustrate, and then at the deepening solemnity of Constance's face he desists in sudden dismay: "Miss Wyatt, I've shocked you!"

Constance: "Oh, no—no!"

Bartlett: "It *was* shocking. I wonder how I could do it! I—I thought it would amuse you."

Constance, mournfully: "It did, thank you very much." After a pause: "I didn't know you liked—joking."

Bartlett: "Ah! I don't believe I do,—all kinds. I—that is—I beg your pardon." Bartlett turns away, with an air of guilty consciousness, and goes to the window and looks out, Constance's gaze following him: "It's a wonderful day!" He comes back toward her: "What a pity you couldn't be carried out there in your chair!"

Constance: "I'm not equal to that, yet." Presently: "Then you—like—nature?"

Bartlett: "Why, that's mere shop in a landscape painter. I get my bread and butter by her. At least I ought to have some feeling of gratitude."

Constance, hastily: "Of course, of course. It's very stupid of me, asking."

Bartlett, with the desperate intention of grappling with the situation: "I see you have a passion for formulating, classifying people, Miss Wyatt. That's all very well, if one's characteristics were not so very characteristic of everybody else. But I generally find, in my moments of self-consciousness, when I've gone round priding myself that such and such traits are my peculiar property, that the first man I meet has them all and as many more, and isn't the least proud of them. I dare say you don't see anything very strange in them, so far."

Constance, musingly: "Oh, yes; very strange indeed. They're all—wrong!"

Bartlett: "Well! I don't know—I'm very sorry— Then you consider it wrong not to like shooting and to be fond of joking and nature, and"—

Constance, bewilderedly: "Wrong? Oh, no!"

Bartlett: "Oh! I'm glad to hear it. But you just said it was."

Constance, slowly recalling herself, with a painful blush, at last: "I meant—I meant I didn't expect any of those things of you."

Bartlett, with a smile: "Well, on reflection, I don't know that I did, either. I think they must have come without being expected. Upon my word, I'm tempted to propose something very ridiculous."

Constance, uneasily: "Yes? What is that?"

Bartlett: "That you'll let me try to guess *you* out. I've failed so miserably in my own case, that I feel quite encouraged."

Constance, morbidly: "I'm not worth the trouble of guessing out."

Bartlett: "That means no. You always mean no by yes, because you can't bear to say no. That is the mark of a very deep and darkling nature. I feel that I *could* go on and read your mind perfectly, but I'm afraid to do it. Let's get back to myself. I can't allow that you've failed to read my mind aright; I think you were careless about it. Will you give your intuitions one more chance?"

Constance, with an anxious smile: "Oh, yes."

Bartlett: "All those traits and tastes which we both find so unexpected in me are minor matters at the most. The great test question remains. If you answer it rightly, you prove yourself a mind-reader of wonderful power; if you miss it— The question is simply this: Do I like smoking?"

Constance, instantly, with a quick, involuntary pressure of her handkerchief to her delicate nostrils: "Oh, yes, indeed!"

Bartlett: "Miss Wyatt, you have been deluding me. You are really a mind-reader of great subtlety."

Constance: "I don't know—I can't say that it was *mind*-reading exactly"— She lifts her eyes to his, and catches the gleaming light in them; all at once she breaks into a wild, helpless laugh, and striving to recover herself with many little moans and sighs behind her handkerchief laughs on and on: "Oh, don't! I oughtn't! Oh dear, oh dear!" When at last she lies spent with her reluctant mirth, and uncovers her face, Bartlett is gone, and it is her mother who stands over her, looking down at her with affectionate misgiving.

III.

MRS. WYATT *and* CONSTANCE.

Mrs. Wyatt: "Laughing, Constance?"

Constance, with a burst of indignant tears: "Yes, yes! Isn't it shocking? It's horrible! He made me."

Mrs. Wyatt: "He?"

Constance, beginning to laugh again: "Mr. Bartlett; he's been here. Oh, I *wish* I *wouldn't* be so silly!"

Mrs. Wyatt: "Made you? How could he make *you* laugh, poor child?"

Constance: "Oh, it's a long story. It was all through my bewilderment at his resemblance. It confused me. I kept thinking it was *he,*—as if it were some dream,—and whenever this one mentioned some trait of his that totally differed from *his,* don't you know, I got more and more confused, and— Mamma"—with sudden desolation—"I know he knows all about it!"

Mrs. Wyatt: "I'm sure he doesn't. Mr. Cummings only told him that his resemblance was a painful association. He assured your father of this, and wouldn't hear a word more. I'm certain you're wrong. But what made you think he knows?!"

Constance, solemnly: "He behaved just as if he didn't."

Mrs. Wyatt: "Ah, you can't judge from that, my dear." Impressively: "Men are very different."

Constance, doubtfully: "Do you think so, mamma?"

Mrs. Wyatt: "I'm certain of it."

Constance, after a pause: "Mamma, will you help take this shawl off my feet? I'm so warm. I think I should like to walk about a little. Can you see the island from the gallery?"

Mrs. Wyatt: "Do you think you'd better try to leave your chair, Constance?"

Constance: "Yes, I'm stronger this morning. And I shall never gain, lounging about this way." She begins to loose the wraps from her feet, and [with] Mrs. Wyatt coming doubtfully to her aid[,] she is presently freed. She walks briskly toward the sofa, and sits down quite erectly in the corner of it. "There! That's pleasanter. I get so tired of being a burden." She is silent, and then she begins softly and wearily to laugh again.

Mrs. Wyatt, smiling curiously: "What is it, Constance? I don't at all understand what made you laugh."

Constance: "Why don't you know? Several times after I had been surprised that he didn't like this thing, and hadn't that habit and the other, he noticed it, and pretended that it was an attempt at mind-reading, and then all at once he turned and said I must try once more, and he asked, 'Do I like smoking?' and I said instantly, 'Oh, yes!' and then I began to laugh—so silly, so disgusting, so perfectly flat! And I thought I should *die,* it was so ridiculous! Why, it was like having a whole tobacconist's shop in the same room with you from the moment he came in; and when I said it wasn't mind-reading exactly, of course he understood, and— Oh, dear, I'm beginning again!" She hides her face in her handkerchief and leans her head on the back of the sofa: "Say something, *do* something to stop me, mother!" She stretches an imploring left hand toward the elder lady, who still remains apparently but half convinced of any reason for mirth, when General Wyatt, hastily entering, pauses in abrupt irresolution at the spectacle of Constance's passion.

IV.

GENERAL WYATT, CONSTANCE, *and* MRS. WYATT.

Constance: "*Oh,* ha, ha, ha! Oh, *ha,* ha, ha, ha!"

General Wyatt: "Margaret! Constance!" At the sound of his voice, Constance starts up with a little cry, and stiffens into an attitude of ungracious silence, without looking at her father, who turns with an expression of pain toward her mother.

Mrs. Wyatt: "Yes, James. We were laughing at something Constance had been telling me about Mr. Bartlett. Tell your father, Constance."

Constance, coldly, while she draws through her hand the handkerchief which she has been pressing to her eyes: "I don't think it would amuse papa." She passes her hand across her lap, and does not lift her heavy eyelashes.

Mrs. Wyatt, caressingly: "Oh, yes, it would; I'm sure it would."

Constance: "You can tell it then, mamma."

Mrs. Wyatt: "No; you, my dear. You tell it so funnily; and"—in a lower tone—"it's so long since your father heard you laugh."

Constance: "There was nothing funny in it. It was disgusting. I was laughing from nervousness."

Mrs. Wyatt: "Why, Constance"—

General Wyatt: "Never mind, Margaret. Another time will do." He chooses to ignore the coldness of his daughter's bearing toward himself: "I came to see if Constance were not strong enough to go out on the lake this morning. The boats are very good, and the air is so fine that I think she'll be the better for it. Mr. Bartlett is going out to the island to sketch, and"—

Constance: "I don't care to go."

Mrs. Wyatt: "Do go, my daughter! I know it will do you good."

Constance: "I don't feel strong enough."

Mrs. Wyatt: "But you said you were better, just now; and you should yield to your father's judgment."

Constance: "I will do whatever papa bids me."

General Wyatt: "I don't bid you. Margaret, I think I will go out with Mr. Bartlett. We will be back at dinner." He turns and leaves the room without looking again at Constance.

V.

CONSTANCE *and* MRS. WYATT; *then* BARTLETT.

Mrs. Wyatt: "Oh, Constance! How can you treat your father so coldly? You will suffer some day for the pain you give him!"

Constance: "Suffer? No, I'm past that. I've exhausted my power of suffering."

Mrs. Wyatt: "You haven't exhausted your power of making others suffer."

Constance, crouching listlessly down upon the sofa: "I told you that I lived only to give pain. But it's my fate, not my will. Nothing but that can excuse me."

Mrs. Wyatt, wringing her hands: "Oh, oh! Well, then, give *me* pain if you must torment somebody. But spare your father,—spare the heart that loves you so tenderly, you unhappy girl."

Constance, with hardness: "Whenever I see papa, my first thought is, If he had not been so harsh and severe, it might never have happened! What can I care for his loving me when he hated *him?* Oh, *I* will do my duty, mother; *I* will obey; I *have* obeyed, and I know how. Papa can't demand anything of me *now* that isn't easy. I have forgiven everything, and if you give me time I can forget. I *have* forgotten. I have been laughing at something so foolish, it ought to make me cry for shame."

Mrs. Wyatt: "Constance, you try me beyond all endurance! You talk of forgiving, you talk of forgetting, you talk of that wretch! Forgive *him*, forget *him*, if you can. If he had been half a man, if he had ever cared a tithe as much for you as for himself, all the hate of all the fathers in the world could not have driven him from you. You talk of obeying"—

Mary, the serving-woman, flying into the room: "Oh, please, Mrs. Wyatt! There are four men carrying somebody up the hill. And General Wyatt just went down, and I can't see him anywhere, and"—

Mrs. Wyatt: "You're crazy, Mary! He hasn't been gone a moment; there isn't time. It can't be he!" Mrs. Wyatt rushes to the gallery that overlooks the road to verify her hope or fear, and then out of one of the doors into the corridor, while Constance springs frantically to her feet and runs toward the other door.

Constance: "Oh, yes, yes! It's papa! It's my dear, good, kind papa! He's dead; he's drowned; I drove him away; I murdered him! Ah-h-h-h!" She shrinks back with a shriek at sight of Bartlett, whose excited face appears at the door: "Go! It was you, *you* who made me hate my father! You made me kill him, and now I abhor you! I"—

Bartlett: "Wait! Hold on! What is it all?"

Constance: "Oh, forgive me! I didn't mean—I didn't know it was you, sir! But where *is* he? Oh, take me to him! Is he dead?" She seizes his arm, and clings to it, trembling.

Bartlett: "Dead? No, he isn't dead. He was knocked over by a team coming behind him down the hill, and was slightly bruised. There's no cause for alarm. He sent me to tell you; they've carried him to your rooms."

Constance: "Oh, thank Heaven!" She bows her head with a sob upon his shoulder, and then lifts her tearful eyes to his: "Help me to get to him! I'm weak." She totters and Bartlett mechanically passes a supporting arm about her. "Help me, and don't—don't leave me!" She moves with him a few paces toward the door, her head drooping; but all at once she raises her face again, stares at him, stiffly releases herself, and with a long look of reproach walks proudly away to the other door, by which she vanishes without a word.

Bartlett, remaining planted, with a bewildered glance at his empty arm: "Well, I wonder who and what and where I am!"

PART THIRD.

I.

BARTLETT *and* CUMMINGS.

Bartlett: "Six weeks since you were here? I shouldn't have thought that." Bartlett's easel stands before the window, in the hotel parlor; he has laid a tint upon the canvas, and has retired a few paces for the effect, his palette and mahl-stick in hand, and his head carried at a critical angle. Cummings, who has been doing the duty of art-culture by the picture, regards it with renewed interest. Bartlett resumes his work: "Pretty good, Cummings?"

Cummings: "Capital! The blue of that distance"—

Bartlett, with a burlesque sigh: "Ah, I looked into my heart and painted, for *that!* Well, you find me still here, Cummings, and apparently more at home than ever. The landlord has devoted this parlor to the cause of art,—makes the transients use the lower parlor, now,—and we have this all to ourselves: Miss Wyatt sketches, you know. Her mother brings her sewing, and the general his bruises; he hasn't quite scrambled up, yet, from that little knockdown of his; a man doesn't, at his time of life, I believe; and we make this our family-room; and a very queer family we are! Fine old fellow, the general; he's behaved himself since his accident like a disabled angel, and hasn't sworn—well, anything worth speaking of. Yes, here I am. I suppose it's all right, but for all I know it may be all wrong." Bartlett sighs in unguarded sincerity. "*I* don't know what I'm here for. Nature began shutting up shop a fortnight ago at a pretty lively rate, and edging loafers to the door with every sign of impatience; and yet, here I am, hanging round still. I suppose this glimpse of Indian summer is some excuse just now; it's a perfect blessing to the landlord, and he's making hay—rowen crop—while the sun shines; I've been with him so long, now, I take quite an interest in his prosperity, if eight dollars a week of it *do* come out of me! What is talked of in 'art-circles' down in Boston, brother Cummings?"

Cummings: "Your picture."

Bartlett, inattentively, while he comes up to his easel, and bestows an infinitesimal portion of paint upon a destitute spot in the canvas: "Don't be sarcastic, Cummings."

Cummings: "I'm not, I assure you."

Bartlett, turning toward him incredulously: "Do you mean to say that The First Gray Hair is liked?"

Cummings: "I do. There hasn't been any picture so much talked of this season."

Bartlett: "Then it's the shameless slop of the name. I should think you'd blush for your part in that swindle. But clergymen have *no* conscience, where they've a chance to do a fellow a kindness, I've observed." He goes up to Cummings with his brush in his mouth, his palette on one hand, and his mahl-stick in the other, and contrives to lay hold of his shoulders with a few disengaged fingers. As Cummings shrinks a little from his embrace: "Oh, don't be afraid; I shan't get any paint on you. You need a whole coat of whitewash, though, you unscrupulous saint!" He returns to his easel. "So The Old Girl—that's what I shall call the picture—is a success, is she? The admiring public ought to see the original elm tree now: she hasn't got a hair, gray or green, on her head; she's perfectly bald. I say, Cummings, how would it do for me to paint a pendant, *The Last Gray Hair?* I might look up a leaf or two on the elm, somewhere,—stick it on to the point of a twig; they wouldn't know any better."

Cummings: "The leafless elm would make a good picture, whatever you called it." Bartlett throws back his shaggy head and laughs up at the ceiling. "The fact is, Bartlett, I've got a little surprise for you."

Bartlett, looking at him askance: "Somebody wanting to chromo The Old Girl? No, no; it isn't quite so bad as that!"

Cummings, in a burst: "They *did* want to chromo it. But it's sold. They've got you two hundred dollars for it." Bartlett lays down his brush, palette, and mahl-stick, dusts his fingers, puts them in his pockets, and comes and stands before Cummings, on whom, seated, he sends a curious look.

Bartlett: "And do you mean to tell me, you hardened atheist, that you don't believe in the doctrine of future punishments? What are they going to do with *you* in the next world? And that picture dealer? And *me?* Two hund— It's an outrage! It's— The picture wasn't worth fifty, by a stretch of the most charitable imagination! Two hundred d— Why, Cummings, I'll paint no end of Old Girls, First and Last Gray Hairs— I'll flood the market! Two— Good Lord!" Bartlett goes back to his easel and silently resumes his work. After a while: "Who's been offered up?"

Cummings: "What?"

Bartlett: "Who's the victim? My patron? The noble and discriminating and munificent purchaser of The Old Girl?"

Cummings: "Oh! Mrs. Bellingham. She's going to send it out to her daughter in Omaha."

Bartlett: "Ah! Mrs. Blake wishes to found an art-museum with that curiosity out there? Sorry for the Omaha-has." Cummings makes a gesture of impatience. "Well, well; I won't, then, old fellow! I'm truly obliged to you. I accept my good fortune with compunction, but with all the gratitude imaginable. I say, Cummings!"

Cummings: "Well?"

Bartlett: "What do you think of my taking to high art,—mountains twelve hundred feet above the sea, like this portrait of Ponkwasset?"

Cummings: "I've always told you that you had only to give yourself scope,—attempt something worthy of your powers"—

Bartlett: "Ah, I thought so. Then you believe that a good big canvas and a good big subject would be the making of me? Well, I've come round to that idea myself. I used to think that if there was any greatness in me, I could get it into a small picture, like Meissonier or Corot. But I can't. I must have room, like the Yellowstone and Yo-Semite fellows. Don't you think Miss Wyatt is looking wonderfully improved?"

Cummings: "Wonderfully! And how beautiful she is! She looked lovely that first day, in spite of her ghostliness; but now"—

Bartlett: "Yes; a *phantom* of delight is good enough in its way, but a *well woman* is the prettiest, after all. Miss Wyatt sketches, I think I told you."

Cummings: "Yes, you mentioned it."

Bartlett: "Of course. Otherwise, I couldn't possibly have thought of her while I was at work on a great picture like this. She sketches"—Bartlett puts his nose almost on the canvas in the process of bestowing a delicate touch—"she sketches about as badly as any woman I ever saw, and *that's* saying a good deal. But she looks uncommonly well while she's at it. The fact is, Cummings,"—Bartlett retires some feet from the canvas and squints at it,—"this very picture which you approve of so highly is—Miss Wyatt's. *I* couldn't attempt anything of the size of Ponkwasset! But she allows me to paint at it a little when she's away." Bartlett steals a look of joy at his friend's vexation, and then continues seriously: "I've been having a curious time, Cummings." The other remains silent. "Don't you want to ask me about it?"

Cummings: "I don't know that I do."

Bartlett: "Why, my dear old fellow, you're hurt! It *was* a silly joke, and I honestly ask your pardon." He lays down his brush and palette, and leaves the easel. "Cummings, I don't know what to do. I'm in a perfect deuce of a state. I'm hit—awfully hard; and I don't know what to do about it. I wish I had gone at once—the first day. But I had to stay—I had to stay." He turns and walks away from Cummings, whose eyes follow him with pardon and sympathy.

Cummings: "Do you really mean it, Bartlett? I didn't dream of such a thing. I thought you were still brooding over that affair with Miss Harlan."

Bartlett: "Oh, child's play! A prehistoric illusion! A solar myth! The thing never was." He rejects the obsolete superstition with a wave of his left hand. "I'm in love with this girl, and I feel like a sneak and a brute about it. At the very best it would be preposterous. Who am I, a poor devil of a painter, the particular pet of Poverty, to think of a young lady whose family and position could command her the best? But putting that aside,—putting that insuperable obstacle lightly aside, as a mere trifle,—the think remains an atrocity. It's enormously indelicate to think of loving a woman who would never have looked twice at me if I hadn't resembled an infernal scoundrel who tried to break her heart; and I've nothing else to commend me. I've the perfect certainty that she doesn't and can't care anything for me in myself; and it grinds me into the dust to realize on what terms she tolerates me. I could carry it off as a joke, at first; but when it became serious, I had to look it in the face; and that's what it amounts to, and if you know of any more hopeless and humiliating tangle, *I* don't." Bartlett, who has approached his friend during this speech, walks away again; and there is an interval of silence.

Cummings, at last, musingly: "*You* in love with Miss Wyatt? I can't imagine it!"

Bartlett, fiercely: "You can't imagine it? What's the reason you can't imagine it? Don't be offensive, Cummings!" He stops in his walk and lowers upon his friend. "Why shouldn't I be in love with Miss Wyatt?"

Cummings: "Oh, nothing. Only you were saying"—

Bartlett: "I was saying! Don't tell me what *I* was saying. Say something yourself."

Cummings: "Really, Bartlett, you can't expect me to stand this sort of thing. You're preposterous."

Bartlett: "I know it! But don't blame me! I beg your pardon.Is it because of the circumstances that you can't imagine my being in love with her?"

Cummings: "Oh, no; I wasn't thinking of the circumstances; but it seemed so out of character for you"—

Bartlett, impatiently: "Oh, love is always out of character, just as it's always out of reason. I admit freely that I'm an ass. And then?"

Cummings: "Well, then, I don't believe you have any more reason to be in despair than you have to be in love. If she tolerates you, as you say, it *can't* be because you look like the man who jilted her."

Bartlett: "Ah! But if she still loves *him?*"

Cummings: "You don't know that. That strikes me as a craze of jealousy. What makes you think she tolerates you for that reason or no-reason?"

Bartlett: "What makes me think it? From the very first she interpreted *me* by what she knew of *him.* She expected me to be this and not to be that; to have one habit and not another; and I could see that every time the fact was different, it was a miserable disappointment to her, a sort of shock. Every little difference between me and that other rascal gave her a start; and whenever I looked up I found her wistful eyes on me as if they were trying to puzzle me out; they used to follow me round the room like the eyes of a family portrait. You wouldn't have liked it yourself, Cummings. For the first three weeks I simply existed on false pretenses,—involuntary false pretenses, at that. I wanted to explode; I wanted to roar out, 'If you think I'm at all like that abandoned scoundrel of yours in anything but looks, I'm *not!* But I was bound by everything that was sacred, by everything that was decent, to hold my tongue, and let my soul be rasped out of me in silence and apparent unconsciousness. That was *your* fault. If you hadn't told me all about the thing I could have done something outrageous and stopped it. But I was tied hand and foot by what I knew. I had to let it go on."

Cummings: "I'm very sorry, Bartlett; but"—

Bartlett: "Oh, I dare say you wouldn't have done it if you hadn't had a wild ass of the desert to deal with. Well, the old people got used to some little individuality in me, by and by, and beyond a suppressed whoop or two from the mother when I came suddenly into the room, they didn't do anything to annoy me directly. But they were anxious every minute for the effect on *her;* and it worried me as much to have them watching her as to have *her* watching *me.* Of course I knew that she talked this confounded resemblance over with her mother every time I left them, and avoided talking it over with her father."

Cummings: "But you say the trouble's over, now."

Bartlett: "Oh, *over!* No; it isn't over. When she's with me a while she comes to see that I'm not a mere *doppelgänger.* She respites me to that extent. But I have still some small rags of self-esteem dangling about me; and now suppose I should presume to set up for somebody on my own account; the first hint of my caring for her as I do, if she could conceive of anything so atrocious, would tear open all the old sorrows— Ah! I can't think of it. Besides, I tell you, it isn't all over. It's only not so bad as it was. She's subject to relapses, when it's much worse than ever. Why"—Bartlett stands facing his friend, with a half-whimsical, half-desperate smile, as if about to illustrate his point, when Constance and her mother enter the parlor.

II.

CONSTANCE, MRS. WYATT, BARTLETT, *and* CUMMINGS.

Constance, with a quick, violent arrest: "Ah! Oh!"

Mrs. Wyatt: "Constance, Constance, darling! What's the matter?"

Constance: "Oh, nothing,—nothing!" She laughs, nervously. "I thought there was nobody—here; and it—startled me. How do you do, Mr. Cummings?" She goes quickly up to that gentleman, and gives him her hand. "Don't you think it wonderful to find such a day as this, up here, at this time of year?" She struggles to control the panting breath in which she speaks.

Cummings: "Yes; I supposed I had come quite too late for anything of the sort. You must make haste with your Ponkwasset, Miss Wyatt, or you'll have to paint him with his winter cap on."

Constance: "Ah, yes! My picture. Mr. Bartlett has been telling you." Her eyes have already wandered away from Cummings, and they now dwell, with a furtive light of reparation and imploring upon Bartlett's disheartened patience: "Good *morning.*" It is a delicately tentative salutation, in a low voice, still fluttered by her nervous agitation.

Bartlett, in dull despair: "*Good* morning."

Constance: "How is the light on the mountain this morning?" She drifts deprecatingly up to the picture, near which Bartlett has stolidly kept his place.

Bartlett, in apathetic inattention: "Oh, very well, very well indeed, thank you."

Constance, after a hesitating glance at him: "Did you like what I had done on it yesterday?"

Bartlett, very much as before: "Oh, yes; why not?"

Constance, with meek subtlety: "I was afraid I had vexed you—by it." She bends an appealing glance upon him, to which Bartlett remains impervious, and she drops her eyes with a faint sigh. Then she lifts them again: "I was afraid I had—made the distance too blue."

Bartlett: "Oh, no; not at all."

Constance: "Do you think I had better try to finish it?"

Bartlett: "Oh, certainly. Why not? If it amuses you!"

Constance, perplexedly: "Of course." Then with a sad significance: "But I know I am trying your patience too far. You have been so kind, so good, I can't forgive myself for annoying you."

Bartlett: "It doesn't annoy me. I'm very glad to be useful to you."

Constance, demurely: "I didn't mean painting; I meant—screaming." She lifts her eyes to Bartlett's face, with a pathetic, inquiring attempt at lightness, the slightest imaginable experimental archness in her self-reproach, which dies out as Bartlett frowns and bites the corner of his mustache in unresponsive silence. "I ought to be well enough now to stop it; I'm quite well enough to be ashamed of it." She breaks off a miserable little laugh.

Bartlett, with cold indifference: "There's no reason why you should stop it—if it amuses you." She looks at him in surprise at this rudeness. "Do you wish to try your hand at Ponkwasset this morning?"

Constance, with a flash of resentment: "No; thanks." Then with a lapse into her morbid self-abasement: "I shall not touch it again. Mamma!"

Mrs. Wyatt: "Yes, Constance." Mrs. Wyatt and Cummings, both intent on Bartlett and Constance, have been heroically feigning a polite interest in each other, from which pretense they now eagerly release themselves.

Constance: "Oh,—nothing. I can get it of Mary. I won't trouble you." She goes toward the door.

Mrs. Wyatt: "Mary isn't up from her breakfast, yet. If you want anything, let me go with you, dear." She turns to follow Constance. "Good morning, Mr. Cummings; we shall see you at dinner. Good morning,"—with an inquiring glance at Bartlett. Constance slightly inclines towards the two gentlemen without looking at them, in going out with her mother; and Cummings moves away to the piano, and affects to examine the sheet-music scattered over it. Bartlett remains in his place near the easel.

III.

BARTLETT *and* CUMMINGS.

Bartlett, harshly, after a certain silence which his friend is apparently resolved not to break: "Sail in, Cummings!"

Cummings: "Oh, I've got nothing to say."

Bartlett: "Yes, you have. You think I'm a greater fool and a greater brute than you ever supposed in your most sanguine moments. Well, I am! What then?"

Cummings, turning about from the music at which he has been pretending to look, and facing Bartlett, with a slight shrug: "If you choose to characterize your own behavior that way, I shall not dispute you, at any rate."

Bartlett: "Go on!"

Cummings: "Go on? You saw yourself, I suppose, how she hung upon every syllable you spoke, every look, every gesture?"

Bartlett: "Yes, I saw it."

Cummings: "You saw how completely crushed she was by your tone and manner. You're not blind. Upon my word, Bartlett, if I didn't know what a good, kind-hearted fellow you are, I should say you were the greatest ruffian alive."

Bartlett, with a groan: "Go on! That is something like."

Cummings: "I couldn't hear what was going on—I'll own I tried—but I could see; and to see the delicate *amende* she was trying to offer you, in such a way that it should not seem an *amende,*—a perfect study of a woman's gracious, unconscious art,—and then to see your sour refusal of it all, it made me sick."

Bartlett, with a desperate clutch at his face, like a man oppressed by some stifling vapor: "Yes, yes! I saw it all, too! And if it had been for *me,* I would have given anything for such happiness. Oh, gracious powers! How dear she is! I would rather have suffered any anguish than give her pain, and yet I gave her pain! I knew how it entered her heart: I felt it in my own. But what could I do? If I am to be myself, if I am not to steal the tenderness meant for another man, the *love* she shows to me because I'm like somebody else, I *must* play the brute. But have a little mercy on me. At least I'm a *baited* brute. I don't know which way to turn, I don't know what to do. She's so dear to me,—so dear in every tone of her voice, every look of her eyes, every aspiration or desire of her transparent soul,—that it seems to me my whole being is nothing but a thought of her. I loved her helplessness, her pallor, her sorrow; judge how I adore her return to something like life! Oh, you blame me! You simplify this infernal perplexity of mine and label it brutality, and scold me for it. Great Heaven! And yet you saw, you heard how she entered this room. In that instant the old illusion was back on her, and *I* was nothing. All that I had been striving and longing to be to her, and hoping and despairing to seem, was swept out of existence; I was reduced to a body without a soul, to a shadow, a counterfeit! You think I resented it? Poor girl, I *pitied* her so; and my own heart all the time like lead in my breast—a dull lump of ache! I swear, I wonder I don't go mad. I suppose—why, I suppose I *am* insane. No man in his senses was ever bedeviled by such a maniacal hallucination. Look here, Cummings: tell me that this damnable coil isn't simply a matter of my own fancy. It'll be some little relief to know that it's *real*."

Cummings: "It's real enough, my dear fellow. And it *is* a trial,—more than I could have believed such a fantastic thing could be."

Bartlett: "Trial? Ordeal by fire! Torment! I can't stand it any longer."

Cummings, musingly: "She *is* beautiful, isn't she, with that faint dawn of red in her cheeks,—not a color, but a colored light like the light that hangs round a rose-tree's boughs in the early spring! And what a magnificent movement, what a stately grace! The girl must have been a goddess!"

Bartlett: "And now she's a saint for sweetness and patience! You think she's had nothing to bear before from me? You know me better! Well, I'm going away."

Cummings: "Perhaps it will be the best. You can go back with me to-morrow."

Bartlett: "To-morrow? Go back with you to-morrow? What are you talking about, man?" Cummings smiles. "I can't go to-morrow. I can't leave her hating me."

Cummings: "I knew you never meant to go. Well, what will you do?"

Bartlett: "Don't be so cold-blooded! What would *you* do?"

Cummings: "I would have it out, somehow."

Bartlett: "Oh you talk! How?"

Cummings: "I am not in love with Miss Wyatt."

Bartlett: "Oh, don't try to play the cynic with me! It doesn't become you. I know I've used you badly at times, Cummings. I behaved abominably in leaving you to take the brunt of meeting General Wyatt that first day; I said so then, and I shall always say it. But I thought you had forgiven that."

Cummings, with a laugh: "You make it hard to treat you seriously, Bartlett. What do you want me to do? Do you want me to go to Miss Wyatt, and explain your case to her?"

Bartlett, angrily: "No!"

Cummings: "Perhaps to Mrs. Wyatt?"

Bartlett, infuriate: "No!"

Cummings: "To the general?"

Bartlett, with sudden quiet: "You had better go away from here, Cummings—while you can."

Cummings: "I see you don't wish me to do anything, and you're quite right. Nobody *can* do anything but yourself."

Bartlett: "And what would you advise me to do?"

Cummings: "I've told you that I would have it out. You can't make matters worse. You can't go on in this way indefinitely. It's just possible you might find yourself mistaken,—that Miss Wyatt cared for you in your own proper identity."

Bartlett: "For shame!"

Cummings: "Oh, if you like!"

Bartlett, after a pause: "Would you—would you see the general?"

Cummings: "If I wanted to marry the general. Come, Bartlett; don't be ridiculous. You know you don't want my advice, and I haven't any to give. I must go to my room a moment."

Bartlett: "Well go! You're of no advantage here. You'd have it out, would you? Well, then, *I* wouldn't. I'm a brute, I know, and a fool, but I'm not such a brute and fool as that!" Cummings listens with smiling patience, and then goes without reply, while Bartlett drops into the chair near the easel, and sulkily glares at the picture. Through the window at his back shows the mellow Indian summer landscape. The trees have all dropped their leaves, save the oaks, which show their dark crimson banners, among the deep green of the pines and hemlocks on the hills; the meadows, verdant as in June, slope away toward the fringe of birches and young maples along the borders of the pond; the low blackberry trails like a running fire over the long grass limp from the first frosts, which have silenced all the insect voices. No sound of sylvan life is heard but

the harsh challenge of a jay, answered from many trees of the
nearest wood-lot. The far-off hill-tops are molten in the soft azure
haze of the season; the nearer slopes and crests sleep under a
grayer and thinner veil. It is to this scene that the painter turns from
the easel, with the sullen unconsciousness in which he has dwelt
upon the picture. Its beauty seems at last to penetrate his mood; he
rises and looks upon it; then he goes out on the gallery, and, hidden by the fall of one of the curtains, stands leaning upon the rail
and rapt in the common revery of the dreaming world. While he
lingers there, Cummings appears at the door, and looks in; then
with an air of some surprise, as if wondering not to see Bartlett,
vanishes again, to give place to General Wyatt, who after a like
research retires silently and apparently disconcerted. A few moments later Mrs. Wyatt comes to the threshold, and calling gently
into the room, "Constance!" waits briefly and goes away. At last, the
young girl herself appears, and falters in the doorway an instant,
but finally comes forward and drifts softly and indirectly up to the
picture, at which she glances with a little sigh. At the same moment
Bartlett's voice, trolling a snatch of song, comes from the gallery
without:—

ROMANCE.

I.

HERE apart our paths, then, lie:
This way you wend, that way I;
Speak one word before you go:
Do not, do not leave me so!

II.

What is it that I should say?
Tell me quick; I cannot stay;
Quick! I am not good at guessing;
Night is near, and time is pressing.

III.

Nay, then, go! But were I you,
I will tell you what I'd do:

> Rather than be baffled so,
> I would never, never go!

As the song ends, Bartlett reappears at the gallery door giving into the parlor and encounters Constance turning at his tread from the picture on which she has been pensively gazing while he sang. He puts up a hand on either side of the door.

IV.

BARTLETT *and* CONSTANCE.

Bartlett: "I didn't know you were here."

Constance: "Neither did I—know you were, till I heard you singing."

Bartlett, smiling ironically: "Oh, you didn't suppose I sang!"

Constance, confusedly: "I—I don't know"—

Bartlett: "Ah, you thought I did! I don't. I was indulging in a sort of modulated howling which I flatter myself is at least one peculiarity that's entirely my own. I was baying the landscape merely for my private amusement, and I'd not have done it, if I'd known you were in hearing. However, if it's helped to settle the fact one way or other, concerning any little idiosyncrasy of mine, I shan't regret it. I hope not to disappoint you in anything, by and by." He drops his hands from the door-posts and steps into the room, while Constance, in shrinking abeyance, stands trembling at his harshness.

Constance, in faltering reproach: "Mr. Bartlett!"

Bartlett: "Constance!"

Constance, struggling to assert herself, but breaking feebly in her attempt at hauteur: "Constance? What does this mean, Mr. Bartlett?"

Bartlett, with a sudden burst: "What does it mean? It means that I'm sick of this nightmare masquerade! It means that I want to be something to you—all the world to you—in and for myself. It means that I can't play another man's part any longer and live. It means that I love you, love you, love you, Constance!" He starts involuntarily toward her with outstretched arms, from which she recoils with a convulsive cry.

Constance: "You love me? *Me?* Oh, no, no! How can you be so merciless as to talk to me of love?" She drops her glowing face into her hands.

Bartlett: "Because I'm a man. Because love is more than mercy,—better, higher, wiser. Listen to me, Constance!—yes, I will call you so now, if never again: you are so dear to me that I must say it at last if it killed you. If loving you is cruel, I'm pitiless! Give me some hope, tell me to breathe, my girl!"

Constance: "Oh go, while I can still forgive you."

Bartlett: "I won't go; I won't have your forgiveness; I will have all or nothing; I want your love!"

Constance, uncovering her face and turning its desolation upon him: "My love? I have no love to give. My heart is dead."

Bartlett: "No, no! That's part of the ugly trance that we've both been living in so long. Look! You're better now than when you came here; you're stronger, braver, more beautiful. My angel, you're turned into a woman again! Oh, you can love me if you will; and you will! Look at me, darling!" He takes her listless right hand in his left, and gently draws her toward him.

Constance, starting away: "You're wrong, you're all wrong! You don't understand; you don't know— Oh, listen to me!"

Bartlett, still holding her cold hand fast: "Yes, a thousand years. But you must tell me first that I may love you. That first!"

Constance: "No! That never! And since you speak to me of love, listen to what it's my right you should hear."

Bartlett, releasing her: "I don't care to hear. Nothing can ever change me. But if you bid me, I will go!"

Constance: "You shall not go now till you know what despised and hated and forsaken thing you've offered your love to."

Bartlett, beseechingly: "Constance, let me go while I can forgive myself. Nothing you can say will make me love you less; remember that; but I implore you to spare yourself. Don't speak, my love."

Constance: "Spare myself? Not speak? Not speak what has been on my tongue and heart and brain, a burning fire, so long?— Oh, I was a happy girl once! The days were not long enough for my happiness,—I woke at night to think of it. I was proud in my happiness and believed myself, poor fool, one to favor those I smiled on; and I had my vain and crazy dreams of being the happiness of some one who should come to ask for—what you ask now. Some one came. At first I didn't care for him, but he knew how to make me. He knew how to make my thoughts of him part of my happiness and pride and vanity till he was all in all, and I had no wish, no hope, no life but him; and then he—left me!" She buries her face in her hands again, and breaks into a low, piteous sobbing.

Bartlett, with a groan of helpless fury and compassion: "The fool, the sot, the slave! Constance, I knew all this,—I knew it from the first."

Constance, recoiling in wild reproach: "You *knew* it?"

Bartlett, desperately: "Yes, I knew it—in spite of myself, through my own stubborn fury I knew it, that first day, when I had obliged my friend to tell me what your father had told him, before I would hear reason. I would have given anything not to have known it then, when it was too late, for I had at least the grace to feel the wrong, the outrage of my knowing it. You can never pardon it, I see; but you must feel what a hateful burden I had to bear, when I found that I had somehow purloined the presence, the looks, the voice of another man—a man whom I would have joyfully changed myself to any monstrous shape *not* to resemble, though I knew that my likeness of him, bewildering you in continual dream of him, was all that ever made you look at me or think of me. I lived in the hope—Heaven only knows why I should have had the hope!—that I might yet be myself to you; that you might wake from your dream of him and look on me in the daylight, and see that I was at least an honest man, and pity me and may be love me at last, as I loved you at first, from the moment I saw your dear, pale face, and heard your dear, sad voice." He follows up her slow retreat, and again possesses himself of her hand: "Don't cast me off! It was monstrous, out of all decency, to know your sorrow; but I never tried to know it; I tried *not* to know it." He keeps fast hold of her hand, while she remains with averted head. "I love you, Constance; I loved you; and when once you had bidden me stay, I was help-less to go away, or I would never be here now to offend you with the confession of that shameful knowledge. Do you think it was no trial to me? It gave me the conscience of an eavesdropper and a spy; but all I knew was sacred to me."

Constance, turning and looking steadfastly into his face: "And you could care for so poor a creature as I—so abject, so obtuse as never to know what had made her intolerable to the man that cast her off?"

Bartlett: "Man? He was *no* man! He"—

Constance, suddenly: "Oh, wait! I—I love him yet."

Bartlett, dropping her hand: "You"—

Constance: "Yes, yes! As much as I live, I love him! But when he left me, I seemed to die; and now it's as if I were some wretched ghost clinging for all existence to the thought of my lost happiness. If that slips from me, then I cease to be."

Bartlett: "Why, this is still your dream. But I won't despair. You'll wake yet, and care for me; I know you will."

Constance, tenderly: "Oh, poor soul, I'm not dreaming now. I know that you are not he. You are everything that is kind and good, and some day you will be very happy."

Bartlett, desolately: "I shall never be happy without your love." After a pause: "It will be a barren, bitter comfort, but let me have it if you can: if *I* had met you first, could you have loved *me?*"

Constance: "I might have loved you if—I had—lived." She turns from him again, and moves softly toward the door; his hollow voice arrests her.

Bartlett: "If you are dead, then I have lived too long. Your loss takes the smile out of life for me." A moment later: "You are cruel, Constance."

Constance, abruptly facing him: "I cruel? To *you?*"

Bartlett: "Yes; you have put me to shame before myself. You might have spared me! A treacherous villain is false in time to save you from a life of betrayal, and you say your heart is dead. But that isn't enough. You tell me that you cannot care for me because you love that treacherous villain still. That's my disgrace, that's my humiliation, that's my killing shame. I could have borne all else. You might have cast me off however you would, driven me away with any scorn, whipped me from you with the sharpest rebuke that such presumption as mine could merit; but to drag a decent man's self-respect through such mire as that poor rascals' memory for six long weeks, and then tell him that you prefer the mire"—

Constance: "Oh, hush! I can't let you reproach him! He was pitilessly false to me, but I will be true to him forever. How do I know—I *must* find some reason for that, or there is no reason in anything!—how do I know that he did not break his word to me at my father's bidding? My father never liked him."

Bartlett, shaking his head with a melancholy smile: "Ah, Constance, do you think *I* would break my word to you at your father's bidding?"

Constance, in abject despair: "Well, then I go back to what I always knew: I was too slight, too foolish, too tiresome for his lifelong love. He saw it in time. I don't blame him. You would see it, too."

Bartlett: "What devil's vantage enabled that infernal scoundrel to blight your spirit with his treason? Constance, is this my last answer?"

Constance: "Yes, go! I am so sorry for you,—sorrier than I ever thought I could be for anything again."

Bartlett: "Then if you pity me, give me a little hope that sometime, somehow—"

Constance: "Oh, I have no hope, for you, for me, for any one. Good-by, good, kind friend! Try—you won't have to try hard—to forget me. Unless some miracle should happen to show me that it was all his fault and none of mine, we are parting now forever. It has been a strange dream, and nothing is so strange as that it should be ending so. Are you the ghost, or I, I wonder! It confuses me as it did at first; but if you are he, or only you— Ah, don't look at me so, or I must believe he has never left me, and implore you to stay!"

Bartlett, quietly: "Thanks. I would not stay a moment longer in his disguise, if you begged me on your knees. I shall always love you, Constance, but if the world is wide enough, please Heaven, I will never see you again. There are some things dearer to me than your presence. No, I won't take your hand; it can't heal the hurt your words have made, and nothing can help me, now I know from your own lips that but for my likeness to *him* I would never have been anything to you. Good-by!"

Constance: "Oh!" She sinks with a long cry into the arm-chair beside the table, and drops her head into her arms upon it. At the door toward which he turns Bartlett meets General Wyatt, and a moment later Mrs. Wyatt enters by the other. Bartlett recoils under the concentrated reproach and inquiry of their gaze.

V.

GENERAL WYATT, MRS. WYATT, CONSTANCE, *and* BARTLETT.

Mrs. Wyatt, hastening to bow herself over Constance's fallen head: "Oh, what is it, Constance?" As Constance makes no reply, she lifts her eyes again to Bartlett's face.

General Wyatt, peremptorily: "Well, sir!"

Bartlett, with bitter desperation: "Oh, you shall know!"

Constance, interposing: "I will tell! You shall be spared that at least." She has risen, and with her face still hidden in her handkerchief she seeks her father with an outstretched hand. He tenderly gathers her to his arms, and she droops a moment upon his shoulder; then with an electrical revolt against her own weakness she lifts her head and dries her tears with a passionate energy. "He— Oh, speak *for* me!" Her head falls again on her father's shoulder.

Bartlett, with grave irony and self-scorn: "It's a simple matter, sir. I have been telling Miss Wyatt that I love her, and offering to share with her my obscurity and poverty. I"—

General Wyatt, impatiently: "Curse your poverty, sir! I'm poor myself. Well!"

Bartlett: "Oh, that's merely the beginning; I have had the indecency to do this, knowing that what alone rendered me sufferable to her it was a cruel shame for me to know, and an atrocity for me to presume upon. I"—

General Wyatt: "I authorized this knowledge on your part when I spoke to your friend, and before he went away he told me all he had said to you."

Bartlett, in the first stages of petrifaction: "Cummings?"

General Wyatt: "Yes."

Bartlett: "Told you that I knew whom I was like?"

General Wyatt: "Yes."

Bartlett, very gently: "Then I think that man will be lost for keeping his conscience *too* clean. Cummings has invented a new sin."

Mrs. Wyatt: "James, James! You told me that Mr. Bartlett didn't know."

General Wyatt, contritely: "I did, Margaret; I didn't know what else to do."

Mrs. Wyatt: "Oh, James!"

Constance: "Oh, papa!" She turns with bowed head from her father's arms, and takes refuge in her mother's embrace. General Wyatt, released, fetches a compass round about the parlor, with a face of intense dismay. He pauses in front of his wife.

General Wyatt: "Margaret, you must know the worst, now."

Mrs. Wyatt, in gentle reproach, while she softly caresses Constance's hair: "Oh, is there anything *worse,* James?"

General Wyatt, hopelessly: "Yes; I'm afraid I have been to blame."

Bartlett: "General Wyatt, let me retire. I"—

General Wyatt: "No, sir. This concerns you, too, now. Your destiny has entangled you with our sad fortunes, and now you must know them all."

Constance, from her mother's shoulder: "Yes, stay,—whatever it is. If you care for me, nothing can hurt you any more, now."

General Wyatt: "Margaret,—Constance! If I have been mistaken in what I have done, you must try somehow to forgive me; it was my tenderness for you both misled me, if I erred. Sir, let me address my defense to you. You can see the whole matter with clearer eyes than we." At an imploring gesture from Bartlett, he turns again to Mrs. Wyatt. "Perhaps you are right, sir. Margaret, when I had made up my mind that the wretch who had stolen our child's heart was utterly unfit and unworthy"—

Constance, starting away from her mother with a cry: "Ah, you *did* drive him from me, then! I knew, I knew it! And after all these days and weeks and months that seem years and centuries of agony, you tell me that it was *you* [who] broke my heart! No, no, I never *will* forgive you, father! Where is he? Tell me that! Where is my husband—the husband you robbed me of? Did you kill him, when you chose to crush my life? Is he dead? If he's living I will find him wherever he is. No distance and no danger shall keep me from him. I'll find him and fall down before him, and implore *him* to forgive you, for I never can! Was this your tenderness for me—to drive him away, and leave me to the pitiless confusion and humiliation of believing myself deserted? Oh, great tenderness!"

General Wyatt, confronting her storm with perfect quiet: "No, I will give you better proof of my tenderness than that." He takes from his pocket-book a folded paper which he hands to his wife: "Margaret, do you know that writing?"

Mrs. Wyatt, glancing at the superscription: "Oh, too well! This is to you, James."

General Wyatt: "It's for you, now. Read it."

Mrs. Wyatt, wonderingly unfolding the paper and then reading: "'*I confess myself guilty of forging Major Cummings's signature, and in consideration of his and your own forbearance I promise never to see Miss Wyatt again. I shall always be grateful for your mercy; and'*—James, James! It isn't possible!"

Constance, who has crept nearer and nearer while her mother has been reading, as if drawn by a resistless fascination: "No, it isn't possible! It's false; it's a fraud! I *will* see it!" She swiftly possesses herself of the paper and scans it with a fierce intentness. Then she flings it wildly away. "Yes, yes, it's true! It's his hand. It's true; it's the only true thing in this world of lies!" She totters away toward the sofa. Bartlett makes a movement to support her, but she repulses him and throws herself upon the cushions.

General Wyatt: "Sir, I am sorry to make you the victim of a scene. It has been your fate, and no part of my intention. Will you look at this paper? You don't know all that is in it yet." He touches it with his foot.

Bartlett, in dull dejection: "No, I won't look at it. If it were a radiant message from heaven, I don't see how it could help me now."

Mrs. Wyatt: "I'm afraid you've made a terrible mistake, James."

General Wyatt: "Margaret! Don't say that!"

Mrs. Wyatt: "Yes, it would have been better to show us this paper at once,—better than to keep us all these days in this terrible suffering."

General Wyatt: "I was afraid of greater suffering for you both. I chose sorrow for Constance rather than the ignominy of knowing that she had set her heart on so base a scoundrel. When he crawled in the dust there before me, and whined for pity, I revolted from telling you or her how vile he was; the thought of it seemed to dishonor you; and I had hoped something, everything, from my girl's self-respect, her obedience, her faith in me. I never dreamed that it must come to this."

Mrs. Wyatt, sadly shaking her head: "I know how well you meant; but oh, it was a fatal mistake!"

Constance, abandoning her refuge among the cushions, and coming forward to her father: "No, mamma, it was no mistake! I see now how wise and kind and merciful you have been, papa. You can never love me again, I've behaved so badly, but if you'll let me, I will try to live my gratitude for your mercy at a time when the whole truth would have killed me. Oh, papa! What shall I say, what shall I do, to show how sorry and ashamed I am? Let me go down on my knees to thank you." Her father catches her to his heart, and fondly kisses her again and again. "I don't deserve it, papa! You ought to hate me, and drive me from you, and never let me see your dear face again." She starts away from him as if to execute upon herself this terrible doom, when her eye falls upon the letter where she had thrown it on the floor. "To think how long I have been the fool, the slave, of that felon!" She stoops upon the paper with a hawk-like fierceness; she tears it into shreds, and strews the fragments about the room. "Oh, if I could only tear out of my heart all thoughts of him, all memory, all likeness!" In her wild scorn she has whirled unheedingly away toward Bartlett, whom, suddenly confronting, she apparently addresses in this aspiration; he opens wide his folded arms.

Bartlett: "And what would you do, then, with this extraordinary resemblance?" The closing circle of his arms involves her and clasps her to his heart, from which beneficent shelter she presently exiles herself a pace or two and stands with either hand pressed against his breast, while her eyes dwell with rapture on his face.

Constance: "Oh, *you're* not like him, and you *never* were!"

Bartlett, with light irony: "Ah!"

Constance: "If I had not been blind, blind, blind, I never could have seen the slightest similarity. Like *him?* Never!"

Bartlett: "Ah! Then perhaps the resemblance which we have noticed from time to time, and which has been the cause of some annoyance and embarrassment all round, was simply a disguise which I had assumed for the time being to accomplish a purpose of my own?"

Constance: "Oh, don't jest it away! It's your soul that I see now, your true and brave and generous heart; and if you pardoned me for mistaking you a single moment for one who had neither soul nor heart, I could never look you in the face again!"

Bartlett: "You seem to be taking a good provisional glare at me beforehand, then, Miss Wyatt; I've never been so nearly looked out of countenance in my life. But you needn't be afraid; I shall not pardon your crime." Constance abruptly drops her head upon his breast, and again instantly repels herself.

Constance: "No, you must not if you could. But you can't—you can't care for me after hearing what I could say to my father"—

Bartlett: "That was in a moment of great excitement."

Constance: "After hearing me rave about a man so unworthy of—any one—you cared for. No, your self-respect—everything—demands that you should cast me off."

Bartlett: "It does. But I am inexorable,—you must have observed the trait before. In this case I will not yield even to my own colossal self-respect." Earnestly: "Ah, Constance, do you think I could love you the less because your heart was too true to swerve even from a traitor till he was proved as false to honor as to you?" Lightly again: "Come, I like your fidelity to worthless people; I'm rather a deep and darkling villain myself."

Constance, devoutly: "You? Oh, you are as nobly frank and open as—as—as papa!"

Bartlett: "No, Constance, you are wrong, for once. Hear my dreadful secret: I'm not what I seem,—the light and joyous creature I look,—I'm an emotional wreck. Three short years ago I was frightfully jilted"—they all turn upon him in surprise—"by a young person who, I'm sorry to say, hasn't yet consoled me by turning out a scamp."

Constance, drifting to his side with a radiant smile: "Oh, I'm *so* glad."

Bartlett, with affected dryness: "Are you? I didn't know it was such a laughing matter. I was always disposed to take those things seriously."

Constance: "Yes, yes! But don't you see? It places us on more of an equality." She looks at him with a smile of rapture and logic exquisitely compact.

Bartlett: "Does it? But you're not half as happy as I am."

Constance: "Oh yes, I am! Twice!"

Bartlett: "Then that makes us just even, for so am I." They stand ridiculously blest, holding each other's hand a moment, and then Constance, still clinging to one of his hands, goes and rests her other arm upon her mother's shoulder.

Constance: "Mamma, how wretched I have made you, all these months!"

Mrs. Wyatt: "If your trouble's over now, my child,"—she tenderly kisses her cheek,—"there's no trouble for your mother in the world."

Constance: "But I'm not happy, mamma. I can't be happy, thinking how wickedly unhappy I've been. No, no! I had better go back to the old wretched state again; it's all I'm fit for. I'm *so* ashamed of myself. Send him away!" She renews her hold upon his hand.

Bartlett: "Nothing of the kind. I was requested to remain here six weeks ago, by a young lady. Besides, this is a public house. Come, I haven't finished the catalogue of my disagreeable qualities, yet: I'm jealous. I want you to put that arm on *my* shoulder." He gently effects the desired transfer, and then, chancing to look up, he discovers the Rev. Arthur Cummings on the threshold in the act of modestly retreating. He detains him with a great melodramatic start. "Hah! A clergyman! This is indeed ominous!"

A New Play

W. D. Howells' original translation of *Un drama nuevo* by Manuel Tamayo y Baus ("Joaquin Estébanez") consists of 150 pages in Howells' hand. This script, mailed to Lawrence Barrett act by act in September 1878, was first performed with minor revisions under the title *A New Play* in Cleveland on 25 October 1878. It was staged by Barrett's company, with Barrett in the role of Yorick, forty-eight times during the 1878–79 season. The original manuscript, hitherto lost to scholarship, is located in the V. B. Price Collection in Albuquerque.

Act I

A room in the house of Yorick; on the right a small table; on the left a bench; lateral doors, and another at the bottom.

Scene I

Enter Woodford and Thomas at rise.

Woodford (flushed and troubled, pulling himself together): By my word, methinks this fellow does not like the part.

Thomas: What fellow? Which part?

Woodford: This Master Edmund of yours, whom they have given the part of Manfredo in my new play—a play that Shakespear himself hath taken for his theatre. They tell me he would fain have refused my tragedy but he is a manager as well as an author, and if his Richards, his Hamlets, and his Othellos and his other blackamoors and lunatics and hunchbacks please no longer, faith he must turn to new talents for succor.

Thomas: Truly. Master Woodford, you are right.

Woodford: Dost thou think so? And yet see how he hath slashed my play. (*Showing MS.*) A speech of fifty lines gone here; a whole scene crossed out at this place; sentences blotted every where; exclamations and epithets quenched by the hundred! I hardly know my own work!

Thomas: All the better for it when it comes before the public. Thou canst say, when they hiss it—

Woodford: Hiss it? Hath not Shakespeare passed upon it?

Thomas: Oh aye, aye! But you said that Shakespear had grown out of favor—

223

Woodford: Nonsense! He is still a good critic of others' work. But I will not be bearded by this boy Edmund. He is cast for the part, and he must play it.

Thomas: I cannot understand why he should not like it.

Woodford: 'Tis a part that gives him wider scope than ever he has had before. He is the character that makes love to the young wife of his benefactor, and wins her heart from her husband— (Thomas gives a start.) Eh?

Thomas: Nothing, nothing!

Woodford: I have always liked his playing, and I had him in my eye when I imagined this character.—

Thomas: Master Edmund? Did you think— Had you heard—

Woodford: I told him he was the original of Manfredo, thinking to please him, and he took me by the throat!

Thomas aghast: You told him—

Enter an old Servant of Yorick

Scene II

The Same, and Servant, then Shakespear.

Servant, to Thomas: Mistress Alice will see thee now.

Thomas bewildered: Mistress Alice— O, aye! I remember. (To Woodford:) And you told Master Edmund that you had him in mind when— O, ha, ha, ha! Oh, ha, ha, ha! (Exit.)

Woodford: What can the boy mean? What did he find to laugh at in that? Did he laugh at *me*? By my faith, one would think so! (To Servant:) Prythee, friend, wilt thou answer me civilly a civil question?

Servant: Oh, sir! You are in my master's house. You shall command my best will and endeavor.

Woodford: What is so strange, then, in my telling yonder rattle-pate boy that I thought of Edmund when I wrote the part of a young man who betrays his old friend's wife? Why should he laugh at that?

Servant, with a start of terror, which he subdues: Truly, he should rather weep at it!

Woodford: Why yes, if it be matter for either the one or the other! With me, 'tis but a matter of business. (Pompously.) We grow used to these things, in writing for the stage. Here is my play, which Shakespear bade me leave with thee for [him]. Guard it as if it were the Golden Fleece, and thou a dragon breathing fire and smoke.

Servant: It shall be done, sir.

Woodford: Look that it leave thy hand only for Shakespear's; and as to thy young master Edmund, tell him that if he do not maltreat my Manfredo, he may misuse *me* all he will. First an author, then a man! There is no hurt he hath done me for which his apt performance of the part shall not atone. (exit)

Servant: Rest you will, sir. (Alone.) His apt performance of a traitor's part! Oh, oh, oh!

Enter Shakespear.

Welcome, welcome, good Master!

Shakespear: Why, what now, Gregory? What sorrowful thing hath befallen thee? Did our new author read you his play?

Servant: Oh, aye; his play!

Shakespear: O, come! Not so bad as that!

Servant: Nay, he did not read it me. He left it with me for you, Master. (Give the MS. to Shakespear.)

Shakespear: Well! But wherefore this cloudy front, good Gregory? Where is the cheerful winter sunshine of thy face?

Servant: The sun hath set for me, and for my master. The night is coming—all the sadder and drearer that he sees no shadow yet.

Shakespear: Oh, no, no, no! All will be well, yet. I know thy fears, and I have shared them. But I will not think the harm inevitable. I have watched it, and I will grapple with it in time. Is Edmund here?

Servant: Aye.

Shakespear: And Yorick's wife, fair Mistress Alice?

Servant: Aye.

Shakespear: Where are they?

Servant: Together—in her room. *They are studying their parts in the new tragedy.* (Very significantly.)

Shakespear: No, no, Gregory. Not that tone, yet, good friend. Courage! (After a painful pause.) Where is Yorick[?]

Servant: He is not at home. He bade me pray you stay his return. I would you had not to stay it long!

Shakespear: Why so would I! Where dost think he is?

Yorick, entering with a burst: Here, here, here! (Opens his arms to Shakespear.) Crying thee mercy for his absence, and bewailing every moment he hath lost of thy presence.

Shakespear (after their embrace): Well, well; may I know now why thou hast sent for me to thy house?

Yorick: Does it grieve thee to be here?

Shakespear: That is not the question. Thou knowest whether it vexes me or no.

Yorick: Then what is the reason of thy disquiet?

Shakespear: Disquiet? Why, man, dost thou not know whom we are keeping waiting at my house—eminent personages who have come all the way from the other world, merely for the pleasure of seeing me?

Yorick: Let me make amends to your guests with certain flasks of Spanish wine, which I thought of sending you to-day. 'Tis a wine to wake the dead, and it will be a brave sight to see our English kings assembled in your room, coming to life and arming against each other to contend for the throne. Prythee, whom else hath thy pen lately recalled to this world?

Shakespear: Nay, Yorick; what wilt thou with me?

Yorick: What but the happiness of boasting that the famous poet, the great Shakespear, the pride and glory of England, hath been under this roof and in these arms? (He casts his arms around Shakespear's neck.)

Shakespear: (Ironically) Ah! Farewell, thou incomparable comedian, delightful Yorick, ornament and rapture of the theatre: I have no time to waste in flatteries and pretty phrases.

Yorick: But thou must not go!

Shakespear: Absolutely? Well, then, I must stay.

Yorick: Ay, stay! And sit thee down.

Shakespear: Done! Now I shall really know what thou wilt with me. (He seats himself near the table, and lays a manuscript upon it.)

Yorick: Honestly, what think you of this drama that you are going to play? (He seats himself at the other side of the table and, as he talks, turns over the leaves of the MS.)

Shakespear: Honestly, then, I like it very much.

Yorick: And is it the youngster's first play?

Shakespear: His first.[1]

---

1. WDH added a line in pencil to this speech, perhaps a later gloss on the manuscript, which does not appear in LB's transcription of the play: "'Tis a continual marvel to me that so vain a coxcomb could have written it. But these things happen. 'Tis a good play."

Yorick: I think it very well too; but I notice some little blemishes in it.

Shakespear: O let the envious find the blemishes; we will look only at the beauties.

Yorick: Ay, thou who hast never felt the sting of envy; thou who hast nought to envy others—

Shakespear: You are too daring in your flatteries to-day; and you know that what you are saying now is not true. The envious never lack for something to envy. Envy sets enchanted spectacles upon the nose, that make everything of one's own look mean and ugly, and everything else beautiful and grand. You shall find the wretches who wear these spectacles envying not only those who have more, but those who have less than themselves, and people's curses as well as their blessings. I know a certain gentleman who is so unhappy as to have a neighbor too miserable to be envied: consequently he envies him the only remarkable thing he has, the hump that loads the poor devil's shoulders.

Yorick: I should know something of envy, in such a hot-bed of envy as the theatre. Did you ever see a lot of greater rogues than players are?

Shakespear: Present company excepted?

Yorick: Oh, as to that—the devil take the hindmost! How they snarl at one another! How each desires his fellow's defeat rather than his own success! How every one thinks himself sovereign and singular upon the scene!

Shakespear: Ay, rivalry brings ruin, but men achieve the impossible through its force. Let it grovel in the dust; for there are times when it mounts to the sky.

Yorick: But thou hast done well to lay down the actor's part, and keep only the poet's.

Shakespear: Nay, there are noble exceptions to the rule thou hast established.

Yorick: Surely! My wife and Edmund are living proof of that. God has blessed me with the great happiness of seeing in this life the reward of whatever good I have done. Because I have striven to be faithful and generous, He has given me in Alice a wife of angelic truth, and in Edmund a friend—a friend?—a son, full of the noblest qualities. And what talent, what genius they have! How they play Romeo and Juliet together! The lovers to whom thy imagination gave being are marvellous creations, but how wonderful they are when Alice and Edmund lend them human form and soul! What gestures, what glances, what passionate embodiment of love! 'Tis the very truth of nature!

Shakespear: (aside) Alas! poor Yorick! (To Yorick) And now, may I retire.

Yorick: Nay, not yet; not yet till I have said a word to the manager of our theatre, to the laureled poet, to—

Shakespear: By Heaven, these sugared endearments cloy me! I might have known thou hadst something to ask of me, and wast striving to pay me for the favor in advance.

Yorick: Yes, truly, I have a favor to ask.

Shakespear: Ask it, then.

Yorick: That is what I would like to do, if only I knew how.

Shakespear: Why, man, speak out!

Yorick: Tell me honestly your opinion of my merit as an actor!

Shakespear: As if thou didst not know it! There is no medicine for sick and sorrowing spirits, so potent as thy presence on the boards.

Yorick: And thou thinkest that I can do nothing but make people laugh?

Shakespear: I think that is glory enough for thee.

Yorick: When is this play to be given?

Shakespear: As soon as possible.

Yorick: And whom do you give the part of Count Octavio?

Shakespear: It is a great part, full of tragic excellence. It goes to Walton, who is incomparable in that way.

Yorick: I knew it! To whom should any great part go, except to Walton? What luck the bitter rascal has!

Shakespear: The green fruit perishes if the frost touches it in ripening; the heart perishes when freezing treachery greets its opening. Walton was very unhappy in his youth: he should have your pity. For the third and last time, farewell! (Rising)

Yorick (rising also): But if I have not yet said—

Shakespear: Say on, then!

Yorick: I would like—I would like— But you are not to mock at me, now—

Shakespear: By heaven if you do not speak—

Yorick: I would like—

Shakespear: What? Speak, or I vanish through the trap!

Yorick: I would like to have that part!

Shakespear: What part?

Yorick: That in the new play.

Shakespear: But which?

Yorick: Which but that of Count Octavio?

Shakespear: That of the husband?

Yorick: That.

Shakespear: Thou?

Yorick: I.

Shakespear: Good Heavens! Take physic, Yorick, for thou art perilously ill.

Yorick: Why so the fools talk! And I, talking like a fool that knew only thy tragedies would have said thou wert incapable of writing comedy. Because I have till now done nothing but interpret jests and merriment, must I be condemned never to leave the beaten path?

Shakespear: To leave it for the unknown mountain-top? Why, thou hast been so long the very type and arch-conceit of mirth, that when I cast about me for some name by which the sweetest and dearest wit should be known—the jester who enthralled the memory of my melancholy Dane with tenderness and delight, I could not but make free with thine, and call him—*Yorick.* If Hamlet live to aftertime—and sometimes I think the poor prince may survive us both, in spite of Laertes' venomed point,—thou shalt go down with him, the bright foil of his dark sadness to remotest fame!

Yorick: Thanks for immortality for which I shall be none the happier. But grant me now the favor of a present triumph.

Shakespear: Yorick, Yorick! Till now, thou hast tried to make people laugh, and they have laughed. Woe to thee when thou triest to make them weep, and they continue to laugh!

Yorick: Ungrateful! Deny so slight a favor to one who was ever your loyal friend, who held you precious as the apple of his eye! Very well; give the count's part then to another; but we, we are no longer friends, and next year I quit your theatre. And with me goes Alice . . . and Edmund, too. We shall see which of the two is the greater loser. (*Greatly moved.*)

Shakespeare: What a formidable array of words!

Yorick: But do not imagine they are the words, words, words of Hamlet.

Shakespear: And there is really no one in the world contented with his lot!

Yorick: Must one be forever amused with the business of amusing others?

Shakespear: Didst thou speak seriously? Couldst thou in truth abandon me?

Yorick: Abandon thee! I said it, and thou believest me not? (Weeping) When thou didst doubt my talent, nothing more was wanting but that thou shouldst doubt my heart! No, I will not abandon thee! Yorick may not know how to feign that he feels, but he knows how to feel. Thou woundest him, thou puttest him to shame, and he—look!—he opens thee his arms!

Shakespear: Good heavens! Weeping?

Yorick: I weep because it is not Walton alone who holds me for a gross buffoon, fit only to make fools burst into stupid laughter! Because I see that thou, too—and this is the crushed hurt—that thou—God help me! What an unhappy wretch I am!

Shakespear: Oh, devil take thee! Dost thou wish the part of the husband? 'Tis thine, then; and much good may it do thee.

Yorick: Truly? Thou speakest truly? (*With great delight; and suddenly ceasing to weep.*)

Shakespear: Ay, glut this cursed fancy, from which I have vainly endeavored to persuade thee!

Yorick: And if I should succeed in the part?—

Shakespear: And if they strike you dead with hisses?—

Yorick: Nothing ventured nothing gained. . . . I should like to do it well if only in thy despite!

Shakespear: I hope thou wilt not do it ill in thine own.

Yorick: Go, friend, and take the air!

Shakespear: I desire nothing so much. (Taking his hat and turning toward the door.)

Yorick, with an air of comic menace: And thou wilt have me the part written out? (Detaining him)

Shakespear: Nay, dost thou doubt it?

Yorick: Make haste, then; make all speed!

Shakespear: Go to! Why not?

Yorick: In good truth, Shakespear, if they should applaud me in this part—

Shakespear: Well?

Yorick very earnestly: My joy would be very great!

Shakespear: And mine no less, Yorick! (With sincerity and tenderness, offering him his hand. Yorick presses it, greatly moved, and suddenly embraces S., who goes out.)

Scene III

Edmund and Yorick.

Yorick: Ah, is it thou, Edmund! "Tremble, ingrate!"

Edmund, abashed: Tremble, sir?

Yorick: Aye—in the new play! But not thou—at least not thou, first. It is Alice who is to tremble, when I speak. Dost thou know, Edmund, that I am to have a great part in the new play—a part in which I shall win laurels that none but Walton has worn till now? "Oh, it is easy to make people laugh," he said to his friends the other night. They shall see that with this part of Count Octavio, I know how to make men weep, when there is need; they shalt see, and they shalt rage to see, that as I have hitherto poured mirth, I can pour pity and terror into every heart. (*He takes the MS. from the table.*) But I must go carefully; this part of Count Octavio has its little difficulties, Edmund, and at the slightest miss-step I should fall and break my neck.

["]Tremble, unfaithful woman, tremble." (*Reading MS.* During this speech Edmund betrays a painful consciousness.) Ah here is the best of it: Thou must know that a certain Rodolfo, or Pandolfo—Landolfo, Landolfo's the name—a famous rogue and a familiar of the Count, delivers him a letter, in which he declares that Manfredo, to whom Octavio has been like a father, is in love with his wife, the fascinating Beatrice. Octavio has been suspecting everybody under the sun, except this pretty gentleman, and when this thunderclap comes, he takes it with mouth wide open, and as if the world was tumbling about his ears.

> Tremble, unfaithful woman, tremble ingrate,
> Who robb'st me of mine honor and my peace.
> Vain all thy subtlety; here stands thy guilt
> Revealed.

To begin with, he opens the letter—

"My blood is frozen in my veins."

And without daring to read it—

"Nay, let it burn with wrath. Woe to the wretch
"For whose vile sake thou puttest me to
    shame.
"Oh! What do I behold? Merciful God!"

Of course! "He fixes his eye upon the letter, gives a terrible cry, and falls into his chair as if struck by lightning." (*From "Tremble unfaithful woman," up to this point, he has been reading the MS., giving both verses and stage directions.*) Very good. Let us see now how I can do that terrible cry. (*He takes an attitude of burlesque tragedy, folds the MS. to serve for the letter, and declaims the lines with ludicrous intonations.*)

"Woe to the wretch
"For whose vile sake thou puttest me to
    shame!
"Oh! What do I behold!"

(*He gives a discordant cry.*) No . . . that will not do. Again: "Oh!" (*He gives a worse cry than before.*) Bad, very bad! That is the cry of a man when you tread upon his toes. Once more: "Oh!" That is not a human cry: it is the shriek of a parrot. Bah! Now for the thick of the situation:

"Thou art the villain, then,"—

Very feeble.

"Thou art the villain, then,"—

Villain and idiot I, to attempt at my time of life to go counter to my natural inclination and inveterate usage! But perhaps it is not altogether my fault—it may be that the author—authors are so apt to write nonsense—

"Thou art the villain, then,"—

How the devil to do that properly! If Shakespear's foreboding should come true—if they should hiss me—I won['']t think of it; I should die of shame. Down, fear! Forward! (*He reads the MS. in a low voice, with gestures and contorsions*) Ah, now I begin to get it. It comes out very well, when I say it under my breath! Oh, if I could only do it as I feel it! Well, what dost think, Edmund?

Edmund: Think, sir?

Yorick: Aye—of the new play—of my performance.

Edmund: Ah—very good, very good, sir, indeed. (Abstractedly.)

Yorick, laughing: Nay, nay! Very bad!

Edmund: Bad, sir?

Yorick, with sudden earnestness: Edmund, for some time past thou called me *sir* instead of father, and I have reprehended thee in vain. "Tremble unfaithful woman!" Is it for some fault of mine that thou denyest me the dearer name?

Edmund: I am not worthy to pronounce that name.

Yorick: Since when? Ah, Edmund thou art losing the old tenderness that thou hadst for me!

Edmund: Oh no! What has made you fancy that?

Yorick: Thou wouldst be less reserved with me if thou didst love me still.

Edmund: And how am I reserved with you?

Yorick: In not telling me the cause of thy sadness.

Edmund: I sad?

Yorick: Sad, and full of disquiet. Can it be that thou art in love?

Edmund: In love? I! Do you think—?

Yorick: Do I think? It would seem that I have accused thee of a crime! (Smiling; then with sudden seriousness.) Ah! Love may be a crime. Dost thou love a wife?

Edmund, changing color: Oh!

Yorick: Thou growest pale—thy hand trembles—

Edmund: Yes,—surely; you looked at me in such a way—

Yorick: Infirm must be thy conscience when a look can startle thee. Consider well: he who steals a man's money does him no such harm as the thief who steals his honor; nor he who wounds his body as the assassin who strikes at his soul! Edmund, do not do this: ah, my son, for the love of God, forbear!

Edmund: You suspect me without cause, I do assure you.

Yorick: I believe thee; thou canst not deceive me. Is it not droll that Alice should be going to play the guilty wife, and thou the gay seducer, in this new drama?

Edmund, trying to dissemble: Yes?

Yorick, with comic emphasis: And I—I am going to do the injured husband!

Edmund, transported by his emotion: *You!*

Yorick: Yes, I. Does it surprise thee?

Edmund, striving to recover himself: No—

Yorick, angrily: What wert thou thinking of but now when I read that passage of the play to thee? That was the speech of Count Octavio, and I told thee I was to play the part. Where were thy wits? Dist thou not understand—

Edmund: I understand—yes, yes. But I did not realize—I did not imagine—

Yorick, with severity: Art thou too one of those who think I cannot play a serious part?

Edmund: No, sir,—no! Unless—that is—

Yorick, lightly again: Faith, I have no slight task before me. In the first place, no part could suit me less than a jealous husband's, for I have not the least idea what kind of animal a jealous man is. Always hard at work since I can remember, and so unmoved of fame that I found my sole content in her, my head was already whitening when by a rare and happy chance I found myself young at heart.[2] And Alice, as thou knowest well, has never caused me a pang of jealousy and never will as long as I live. It is not possible to doubt so high and pure a creature?

Edmund: No, sir; it is not possible—

Yorick: Thou speakest coldly. Edmund, thou dost ill to try to hide what I have now sometimes noted.

Edmund: Have you noted anything? What—what have you noted?

Yorick: That while Alice is no less thy friend than ever, thou sometimes lookest on her with aversion.

Edmund: You have noted that—

Yorick: And I understand the reason. Thou didst reign alone in my heart before Alice became my wife, and it vexes thee to share thy empire with her. Egotist! Promise me to make thy peace with her this very day. And here after thou must call her simply, Alice. It were even better thou shouldst call her mother; and if not mother, because she is too young for that, then sister; for brother and sister you should be since you have both the same father. (*Embracing him.*)

Edmund, aside: What misery!

Yorick: Thou weepest? Nay, nay; do not weep, unless thou wouldst that I wept too. (*Drying his tears upon his hands.*) Dost thou know what I think? If thou art so jealous as a son, thou

---

2. This sentence in the original manuscript was struck, probably by WDH. LB did not copy it in his "stage version."

wouldst be something terrible as a jealous lover! They say that there is no passion so potent as this same jealousy; that it dominates the whole soul, and makes one forget everything else.

Edmund: Everything, sir! Aye, everything!

Yorick: Of whom hast thou been jealous and for what woman's sake? This pleases me! Why, thou canst study this part of the jealous husband with me, and explain how this passion, unknown to me, unfolds itself, what kind of torments it occasions, and by what outward signs it may be recognized—all, in fine, that thou hast felt and known. Begin by reading me this scene, here. (*Giving him the MS.*) From this point. (*Showing a certain place.*) Go on!

Edmund: "Wert thou the villain, then—?["]

Yorick: This is what I am to say to thee.

Edmund, changing countenance, and continuing to read in a dull dismay: "Wert thou the cunning and perfidious knave—["]

Yorick: My lad, thou couldst not possibly have done that worse! More spirit! More vehemence!

Edmund: "The infamous seducer thou, that durst"—

Yorick: More soul! More life!

Edmund: "Pierce thus the bosom of thine ancient friend?["]

Yorick: Thou art not in the mood for it to-day. (Taking the MS.) Listen!

"Wert thou the villain, then,
Wert thou the cunning and perfidious knave,
The infamous seducer, thou—["]

Scene IV

Walton, Yorick, and Edmund.

Walton, from the door in the background: Who is raving here?

Yorick, shutting up the MS.: Walton!

Walton: Wert thou quarreling with Edmund?

Yorick: I was quarreling with no one.

Walton: Methought as I came in—

Yorick, aside: He knows about it already, and is seeking some cause for dispute.

Walton: It seems to me thou dost not receive me with pleasure.

Yorick: I divine thy intentions.

Walton: Truly, it is divination.

Yorick: Let us leave idle words: what brings thee here?

Walton: As thou hast already divined it, why should I tell thee?

But (speaking as another to himself) what dost thou on foot, Master Walton? Here is a chair. (Taking a chair, and placing it in the centre of the stage.) Thanks! (Sitting down.)

Yorick: Dost thou gird at me with a mock of civilities that pertain to me? If thou seekest to annoy me—

Walton: Oh! This is a pleasant greeting! Why, he has the spirit of a tiger. Eh, Edmund?

Edmund: Eh?

Yorick, to Walton: Dost thou make a jest of me?

Edmund: Make a jest of you?

Walton: 'Tis well that thou shouldst defend thy friend Yorick, thy protector, thy second father. (To Yorick) This boy is a jewel. How pleasant it is to meet such agreeable people!

Edmund, with a threatening air: Walton!

Walton: My compliments incommode you?

Yorick: What is thy intent?

Walton: You are both out of temper to-day. Fare you well. (Rising) But thou art the loser. (To Y.)

Yorick: I loser—I—

Walton: I came here to seek a friend; I find a fool, and I am going away.

Yorick: Dost thou call me fool?

Walton: I would not if I could think of a better word.

Yorick: Hast thou seen Shakespeare?

Walton: No, only the author of the new play.

Yorick: Well?

Walton: Shakespeare met him by chance as he came away from you, and told him that you were to do the part of the husband.

Yorick: Ah, now we understand each other!

Walton: He left the author like a man in a dream.

Yorick: 'Twas not an evil dream!

Walton: The author came to me in a great rage, to beg that I should reclaim a part that fitted me, and—

Yorick: And thou—well!—thou—

Walton, as if doing violence to himself: I? I wish you to know the truth. At first I was furious; then I saw that I was wrong, and I said to the author— But, (making some paces towards the door) why should I trouble myself to tell you?

Yorick, seizing his hand, and dragging him back: No—listen! Come! What didst thou say to him?

Walton: I told him that you were my friend; that an actor of your merit and experience could do well any part that he attempted, if he would but throw himself into it; that I would play the part of the confidant, which is difficult though detestable; that I would aid you with my advice if you would accept it, and—Farewell. (He tries to go.)

Yorick, detaining him, and pulling toward the front again: Nay, come hither, man; come hither! Didst thou say that?

Walton: And when I come, very well pleased with myself, I am received with a presence of vinegar and words of gall. By my word, I must pay you back in the same coin. I have mistaken— (Making towards the door again.)

Yorick, detaining him as before: No, thou shalt not go! This is all very strange, this thing that thou hast told me!

Walton: And why is it so strange? Come, let us hear!

Yorick: It would seem more natural thou shouldst be vexed to lose the occasion of a new triumph; to see me—

Walton: Tut, tut! The temple of fame is so vast that it never yet was filled, and never will be filled.

Yorick: Ay, but that bitter humor of thine—

Walton: You think me bitter because I know not how to feign or lie!

Yorick: And thou art not piqued that I should have the part of Count Octavio?

Walton: I have told you, no!

Yorick: And thou wilt play the confidant?

Walton: I have told you, yes!

Yorick: And thou wilt study the part for me?

Walton: You insult me with your doubts.

Yorick: Edmund, dost thou hear this?

Walton: Let us see if for once I shall be justly appreciated.

Yorick: To be frank with thee, I have always held thee till now a subtle rogue.

Walton: So the world judges men!

Yorick: Confession is the beginning of repentance. If thou art in the humor now to give me half a dozen honest thumps about the head—

Walton: Faith, I owe thee as many!

Yorick: Begin, then! And I pray thee in charity let them be well laid on.

Walton: Enough of this.

Yorick: Then give me thy hand.

Walton: Ay, that will I. (They clasp hands.)

Yorick: And I—I could have sworn— Hast thou aught to do at present?

Walton: Nothing.

Yorick: I would fain hear thee read the part before I begin to study it!

Walton: Why, if thou wilt—

Yorick: If I will? Have I not good reason to wish it? I wish nothing so much. Thou hast astounded me by thy unmeasured goodness and nobleness. Who would have imagined that thou—

Walton, angrily: Wilt thy return to thy insults?

Yorick: No, no—on the contrary—I meant— But come with me to my closet; we will lock ourselves in, and— Frankly, the part of outraged husband seems to me rather difficult—

Walton: Thou art deceived. The part of outraged husband is played without the least difficulty. What does Edmund think?

Edmund: I— (*Aside:* What does this man mean?)

Yorick: It will be easy to me with thy instructions. And wilt thou teach me something of those inflections of voice with which thou makest such effect?

Walton: Assuredly.

Yorick: And some of those sudden transitions that every one applauds?

Walton: Without doubt.

Yorick: And that trick of feigning tears that makes the public weep?

Walton: Yes, man, yes: everything that thou wilt[.]

Yorick: And thinkest thou that I shall succeed?

Walton: Thou wilt triumph.

Yorick, rubbing his hands with delight: Truly?

Walton: Thou dost not thyself know what thou canst do.

Yorick: But—but (*With rapture that scarcely permits him to speak.*)

Walton: O, I plume myself upon knowing actors.

Yorick: I could fly for joy! Come in, come in! (*He turns with Walton toward the door on the right, where the latter waits while Yorick runs back to Edmund.*) But, Edmund! Is it possible that seeing me mad with joy thou art not joyful? Rejoice with me, in Heaven's name! I would have the whole world glad!

        "Wert thou the villain, then"—

Walton: Come, come! We are losing time.

Yorick: Yes, let us go, and not lose time, since I have lost my wits for joy. Hist! Dost thou hear, Edmund? Walton is going over the part with me, but I depend upon thee too, boy. I must have thy help, thy counsel, thy criticism, aye, even thy derision when I go wrong. (*Going to the centre of the scene, and pointing to Edmund and Walton:*) With two such masters—and Shakespeare in addition—And I am no fool!

    "Tremble, unfaithful woman, tremble in-
      grate"—

Without question, I shall do it divinely! I could dance like a child!

Walton: But thou dost not come!

Yorick: Yes, yes—I come! (Exeunt Y. & W. by R. door.)

Scene V.

Edmund, and then, Alice

Edmund: What to think? What to believe? Does Walton know my secret? God forbid! Did he speak without malice, without evil insinuation? O, this perpetual concealment, this perpetual terror! What hideous unrest is guilt! And what a life the sinner leads! (*He seats himself at the table, and lets his head fall upon his arms. Alice appears at the left-hand door, and at [the] sight of his attitude, starts and runs swiftly to him.*)

Alice: What is the matter, Edmund? What has happened to thee? What is it?

Edmund: Thou too, poor child, dost thou tremble too?

Alice: And why should I not tremble? One does not defy one's conscience without terror.

Edmund: And must we always live thus? Tell me in pity: is this life?

Alice: Dost thou ask *me*? It is possible to number the moments of a day, but not to count the pangs and agonies I suffer in a day. If any one looks at me, I say "He knows it!" If any one accosts my husband, I say, "He is going to tell it him." In every face I see a threat; the simplest word strikes like a menace on my heart. The light makes me afraid lest it reveal my evil conscience; the dark frightens me: in the night my guilt shows all the blacker. At times I seem to feel a brand of shame upon my face; it is as if I touch it

with my hand, and my mirror scarce can bid the stubborn illusion
vanish. My strength forsakes me; my sore heart scarcely beats, and
the blessed hour of rest comes only with new horrors for me. I
dread to sleep, but I shall dream of thee, lest thy name shall escape
my lips, lest I shall say I love thee! And if worn out with misery I
sleep at last, then am I most unhappy, for then the vague terrors of
the day take on a hideous embodiment. And again the morning
comes; and the bitterness of today ever surpasses the bitterness of
yesterday that seemed insurpassable, and the bitterness of another
morrow when it comes, even surpasses that of to-day. Tears?
Groans? There are no tears or groans of all I spend that bring relief
to me! When thou comest to me, what anguish, what unrest till
thou art gone! When thou goest, what agony, what longing till thou
art returned! And thou returnest, and when I speak to thee alone,
as I speak now, my words seem to fill the world: the buzzing of a
fly sends all the blood to my heart; all ears seem to listen, all eyes
to look; and I know not where to turn my own. (*Starting in terror,
and glancing away*) And—oh! (*With a cry.*)

Edmund, leaping to his feet, and gazing in the same direction:
What? Speak!

Alice: Nothing. My shadow—my shadow, that seemed to me an
accusing witness. And thou askest me if this is life! What is it to be
alive, Edmund? No, this is not life; it is perpetual death.

Edmund: Calm thyself, Alice; if thou wert more guilty thou
wouldst think thyself less so. Sin never seems so foul as when
virtue shines beside it.

Alice: Do not talk to me of virtue! In loving thee I violate all
duties, I offend heavens and earth. Save me, save me, as a strong
man may save a weak woman.

Edmund: O, yes! We must needs save each other; but how? See
and not speak to thee; speak to thee and not tell thee that I love
thee; cease to love thee, having loved thee once! What folly! What
madness! I pass my days in forming good purposes with no intention to fulfill them: a thing to make the Devil laugh. I do as every
one has done in such a case: I dream of turning love into friendship. And love, striving to decrease itself, only grows the more.
Love cannot turn to friendship, though it may turn to hate as fierce
and deep. The thought of loving thee less than I love thee, affronts,
infuriates me. Love thee to delirium, or abhor thee to frenzy—there
is no middle course. Tell me, teach me, how shall I abhor thee?

Alice: And I, I too pass whole days imagining means to over-come the passion that enslaves me. Sometimes I think if thou shouldst love some other woman, all would be well; but when I think of thee beside some other woman, I tremble with hate; and there is no other pang that is not bliss to the agony I suffer. I kneel down to pray God that thou mayst forget me, and I find myself asking him for thy love. It is vain to struggle longer. I know my ingratitude to the best of men: I love thee! I know my baseness: I love thee! I bade thee save me. My safety is not loving thee. Thou canst not save me. I love thee!

Edmund: Alice, Alice, my soul!

Alice: Edmund! (They rush to embrace each other, but arrest themselves at a noise in the corridor.) O, fly!

Scene VI

The Same, and Shakespear; then Yorick & Walton.

Shakespear: Thank God, I find you alone. I came to look for you.

Edmund, suspiciously: Whom? Me?

Shakespear: For thee and her.

Alice: Both?

Shakespear: Both.

Edmund, aside: Heavens!

Alice, aside: My God!

Shakespear: Can I speak here without fear of being overheard?

Edmund: Is what you have to say so secret?

Shakespear: So secret that I would that I myself might not hear it.

Edmund: Speak, but look to what you say.

Shakespear, transfixing him with a glance: Look thou to what thou sayst.

Edmund: I will not suffer you—

Shakespear, imperiously: Cease, and listen!

Edmund: Oh! (He drops his head, subdued by S's tone and bear-ing.)

Shakespear: Time was when I should have taken voluntarily, the step to which necessity now forces me. I was a coward. Cursed be the pitying weakness that makes a coward of an honest man! I hesitate no longer. Edmund, thou lovest this woman.

Edmund: I?

Shakespear: Alice, thou lovest this man.

Alice, with amaze and anguish: Ah!

Edmund: By what right do you accuse us?—

Shakespear: By the right of a friend to the husband of Alice, the benefactor of Edmund.

Edmund: But if it is not true—if you have been deceived—

Alice: O do not doubt it—you have been deceived!

Shakespear: Hypocrisy and guilt are twin sisters. Come hither. (He takes Alice by the hand, and draws her toward him.) Come hither. (He takes Edmund's hand, and confronts him with Alice.) Lift thy head, Edmund. And lift thou thine. Look each other in the face with the color of innocence. (He raises the head of each.) Look! Oh, you were white a moment since, and now what makes you so sad? You wore the color of remorse, you wear the hue of shame!

Alice: Mercy!

Edmund, in agony: Enough!

Alice: We have struggled hard—

Edmund: I will tell you the truth—

Alice: Oh yes! He loves me; I love him.

Edmund: Be merciful, be generous!

Alice: Have pity on two hapless wretches!

Edmund: Do not add to our misery!

Alice: Save us, defend us from ourselves!

Shakespear: Courage, my children.

Alice: His children? Didst thou hear him?

Edmund: O let us fall at your feet[.]

Alice, kneeling: Yes!

Shakespear: You were better in my arms. (Opening his arms.)

Edmund, hesitating in confusion: Shakespeare!

Alice: Can it be?

Shakespear: Come!

Edmund: Save us! (He throws himself into Shakespear's [arms.])

Alice, with the same action: Save us, for mercy's sake!

Shakespear: Yes, I will save you with the help of God. (A pause, in which are heard the sobs of Edmund and Alice.)

Alice: Edmund, heaven hast sent us a protector. And we would have deceived him! How blind is misery! O, happiness! I breathe again— Ay, Edmund, this is life!

Shakespear: There is no time to lose. Speak. I must know all.

Edmund, after a pause: Alice came to our theatre two years ago. I saw her then for the first time. Oh, if I had never seen her!

Alice: Oh, if we had never met.

Edmund: I saw her; a mysterious power drew me to her side. I looked, I saw nothing; I spoke, I knew not what I said; I trembled, I loved her!

Alice: And I loved him!

Edmund: Love, even when lawful, seeks to hide itself in the inmost heart. The days passed—I wished to tell my love—impossible!

Alice: Yorick had already shown his regard for me.

Edmund: My rival was the man to whom I owed everything.

Alice: My mother fell sick; we had no one to help us; Yorick seemed a friend sent from heaven. "Alice," my mother said one day, "I must leave thee soon; wed Yorick: he loves thee so much, and is so kind."

Edmund: Yorick had taken me naked and starving from the street, to give me love and shelter and fortune, and a place in the world.

Alice: Yorick crowned with peace my mother's last days on earth.

Edmund: To have destroyed the happiness of such a man would have been a villainy without parallel.

Alice: My mother besought me on her death bed.

Edmund: I did what he who adds reverence to gratitude must do.

Alice: I answered as one must answer a dying mother's prayer.

Edmund: I swore in my heart to forget her.

Alice: I strove to love him less—and loved him more.

Edmund: The struggle was vain.

Alice: Yet I said, Edmund is Yorick's son.

Edmund: Yorick is my father, I said.

Alice: And when I marry Yorick, my love for Edmund will cease.

Edmund: And I believed that when she became Yorick's wife, my love for her would end.

Alice: And at last the hour came—

Edmund: They were married!

Alice: And in that hour of its despair, love instead of dying in our hearts—

Edmund: Rose mightier than ever, inexorable, resistless—

Alice: And yet we did not speak!

Edmund: In spite of Yorick's tears and prayers, I refused to live under his roof; yet I must often come to him; he exacted that.

Alice: We saw each other daily; yet we did not speak.

Edmund: We passed whole hours together; yet we did not speak.

Alice: At last one night, as we were playing Romeo and Juliet—

Edmund: Moved by the beautiful story—

Alice: Blent in its passionate fire, the fire of truth—

Edmund: When all eyes were fixed upon us—

Alice: When all ears waited on our words—

Edmund: Then tongue, mind, heart, asked in the same low whisper, "Dost thou love me?"

Alice: And tongue, mind, heart responded faintly, "Yes."

Edmund: That was our sin!

Alice: Our punishment has been to fear every one and suspect every thing.

Edmund: Inappeasable remorse!

Alice: Comfort? None.

Edmund: Refuge? One only.

Alice: Death!

Edmund: And our sole crime is to have spoken.

Alice: We swear it.

Edmund: By Yorick's life!

Alice: By his life!

Edmund: This is all.

Alice: All.

Shakespear: Poor humanity! The noble impulse lacking force of accomplishment turns to a source of crimes. Poor humanity! Daunted by a mole-hill and ready to leap a mountain. You love; it is necessary that you should not love.[3]

---

3. The following dialogue in the original manuscript was struck, probably by WDH. LB did not copy it in his "stage version":

Edmund: He who tells us this knows not that the soul enslaved by passion cannot liberate itself.

Shakespeare: He who tells you this knows that the Soul is free, as the daughter of God.

Alice: But in pity tell me what shall one do who loves and would not love?

Shakespear: Will not to love.

Edmund: To will is not enough.

Shakespear: Enough unless the will is feigned.

Alice: How can you be sure of that?

Shakespear: By unimpeachable witness.

Edmund: What witness[?]

Shakespear: Your own conscience. If you were not responsible for your wrong, why these terrors, these tears, this remorse? You must part with Alice forever.

Edmund: I have thought of that a thousand times. But we cannot accomplish impossibilities.

Shakespear: In the process of every crime, there is a moment to recede or to advance.[4]

Alice: Edmund will obey you. With you for our protector, you will see how truth and strength will spring up in us again.

Edmund: O yes; with your help nothing will be impossible.

Shakespear: I confide in the promise of a man (giving one hand to Edmund) and of a wife (giving the other hand to Alice.)

Edmund & Alice: Yes!

Shakespear: Then till the day comes that Edmund goes, never be alone together, never exchange a glance in the presence of others. Duty, necessity demands it. I had vainly fancied myself the sole possessor of your secret. I was a fool! Love can never be hid.

Alice: What say you?

Edmund: Speak!

Shakespear: This horrible secret is known to a man from whom some villainy is deeply to be feared.

Edmund: What man?

Shakespear: On account of the distribution of the parts in a new play, Walton is furious against Yorick.

Edmund, in terror: Walton!

---

4. The following dialogue in the original manuscript was struck, probably by WDH. LB did not copy it in his "stage version":

Edmund: Would you send me away by force?

Shakespear: When there is no other way, one must do good by force.

Shakespear: I know it from the author of the play, who came to me from Walton, and repeated the talk that they had had together.[5]

Edmund, despairingly: Alice, we are lost—lost beyond all hope!

Shakespear: Not yet. I am going to look for him, and when I find him, you will have nothing to fear. (Turns towards the door.)

Edmund: Alice, Alice! (Going to her and wringing his hands.)

Alice: What is the matter? Why art thou so afflicted?

Shakespear: (from the door,) Courage, Edmund. I will come again presently to calm your fears.

Edmund: For God's sake do not leave us! Do not go!

Shakespear: Not go? Wherefore?

Edmund: Walton is not at home.

Shakespear, returning to Edmund: How knowest thou?

Alice: O save me from this horrible suspense!

Shakespear: Where is the man?

Edmund: Here.

Shakespear: Heavens!

Alice: With him?

Edmund: With him.

Shakespear: Thou hast seen him, doubtless.

Edmund: He began to disclose his purpose in my very presence.

Alice: Oh, what shall we do now? My God, what shall we do?

Shakespear: What a fatality!

Alice: Do not abandon us! Defend us, save us!

Edmund: In pity, find us some way, some hope—

Shakespear: Let us keep our wits about us. Be calm—be quiet— (Yorick appears at the door on the left, followed by Walton, to whom he gives the comedy he carries in his hand, and with a joyful face makes him a sign of silence, putting his finger to his lip. Then he rapidly approaches his wife on tip-toe.[)]

---

5. The following dialogue in the original manuscript was struck, probably by WDH. LB did not copy it in his "stage version":

Shakespear: . . . Walton used words or phrases that the author did not understand, like these: "The part of outraged husband fits Yorick marvellously—it cannot be denied."

Alice: Merciful heaven!

Shakespear: ["]If he should fail, through carelessness or blindness[,] to note the excellencies of so fine a part, I will open his eyes for him."

Alice: Oh, there can be no doubt! This man is a wretch, and will destroy u

Edmund, anxiously to Shakespear: What have you decided[?]

Alice: Tell us!

Yorick, seizing his wife by the arm, in an attitude of affected tragedy, and declaiming with burlesque emphasis:

"Tremble, thou faithless woman, tremble"—

Alice, in frantic terror: God! Mercy! (She falls senseless.)

Yorick: Mercy? What did she—

Edmund, launching himself towards Walton: Villain!

Shakespear, in a low voice to Edmund, detaining him: Mad man!

Yorick, turning confused and stupefied, to Shakespear: She cried me *mercy*! Why should she cry me *mercy*?

Shakespear, whom he detained from lifting Alice: Oh, away, Yorick, away! Seest thou not how delicate and slight she is—how any sudden noise convulses her?

Yorick, as before: Oh, aye! But—mercy: what need had *she* of mercy? Why should she cry *me* mercy?

Shakespear: This is intolerable! Let me come to her, Yorick! Thou stealest upon her with that villainous yell; and startled by the sudden accusation—accused she knows [not] how or why—her mind mechanically yields to the impulse—

Yorick: Aye, so. But—*mercy*?

Walton, ironically: A singular accident.

Yorick, still striving to understand what has happened, while S succors Alice: Mercy?

End of Act I.

Act II The Scene is in Yorick's house as before.

Scene I

Walton, alone.

Walton, speaking as if to some one within: I will wait till he returns. (To himself) He passes more than three hours with me at rehearsal, and then he comes to my house to look for me. What can he want with me? And I[,] what do I want with him? The thing we hate attracts us like the thing we love. To-night they give the new play; to-night Yorick plays the part that he has vilely robbed me of. Will he do it well? To let him try, to encourage him in attempting impossible things, to play an inferior part beside him better than his own—this seemed to me the best means of assuring the keenest shame for him, the most satisfactory revenge for me. But now I fear I have erred. Every one expects him to fail—except myself! Moreover, the vulgar applaud from habit—Yorick is their idol—even the fact of his exchanging the comic for the tragic mask will commend him— And my enemies will not lose the occasion to injure me! O, fame—my only hope and comfort since my heart received the wound that will never be healed—thou comest with leaden feet, thou hast eagle-wings for flight! We suffer when we desire thee, more when we enjoy thee, more yet a thousand times when we lose thee! How often does thy worshipper stifle in his heart the voice of honor and of truth! . . .

When Yorick sought to wrong me, I resolved to strike him dead with the knowledge of his shame. The quickest and the surest vengeance is the best. And there is no doubt but Yorick is jealous. He strives to hide it in his heart, but jealousy always mounts to the eyes. Accident has done for me in part what I would have done, and this barbed suspicion once fixed in his soul, he cannot rest till he puts his hand upon the truth. And who knows but the actor in his feigned jealousy may be inspired by the real jealousy of the man? It lacked but this: that the miseries of my enemy should recoil upon my head! (Changing tone at Yorick's appearance:) Ah, is it thou?

Scene II

Yorick and Walton.

Yorick: Thou here?

Walton: I knew thou wast at my house after rehearsal, and I came to see how I could serve thee.

Yorick: It is true, I was there. I thank thee for thy courtesy.

Walton: Bah! Between friends and comrades—Say, what wilt thou?

Yorick, restlessly: I merely wished— I will tell thee—

Walton, aside: What can it be?

Yorick: I have walked far, and I am half dead with fatigue. (Sinking into a chair.)

Walton: Well, rest thee, then.

Yorick: I thought to find relief in the open air of the fields, but I found none.

Walton, with irrepressible joy: Thou art not well? Thou art—
Yorick: Restless,—ill,—
Walton, touching his hands and forehead: Thou art heated. Methinks thou art feverish!
Yorick: 'Tis possible.
Walton: And why dost thou not send word to Shakespear?
Yorick, rising promptly, and in an accent of annoyance: To Shakespear? Wherefore?
Walton, with affected anxiety: Perhaps thou wilt not be able to play to-night; perhaps the performances should be postponed—
Yorick: 'Tis not so bad as that.
Walton, making some paces towards the door: Come, come! I will go to Shakespear myself, and—
Yorick, vehemently: I tell thee that I will not see him. I tell thee that I will play.
Walton, with ironical solicitude: But how canst thou hope for a triumph to-night if—
Yorick, as if thinking of something else: A triumph—yes, a triumph. Walton!
Walton, with harshness: Well?
Yorick: Walton.
Walton: That is my name.
Yorick, disconcertedly: Nay, do not jest at me!
Walton: By my faith, I think thou art mad.
Yorick: I have a failing that I must correct.
Walton: Only one? Happy thou!
Yorick: I am a slave to curiosity.
Walton: Adam and Eve were the parents of mankind.
Yorick: This morning thou wast speaking with Shakespear in private at the theatre, and as I passed near by accident, I heard thee say—
Walton: What?
Yorick, aside: He changes countenance. *To Walton:* I heard thee say: "I have not broken my promise. Yorick knows nothing from me."
Walton: And what else didst thou hear?
Yorick: Only what I have told thee.
Walton: Well?
Yorick: And as I am so curious, I long to know what thing it was that Shakespear made thee promise not to tell me.

Walton: On my word, thou art curious indeed.

Yorick: I began by confessing that.

Walton: Thou hast another little foible.

Yorick: What?

Walton: That of dreaming in broad day.

Yorick: What dost thou mean?

Walton: Thou thinkest thou hast heard me speak words that never passed my lips.

Yorick: No?

Walton: No.

Yorick: This is sorcery.

Walton, taking up his hat, and turning toward the door: If thou hast no other commands—

Yorick, aside: I cannot believe him. *To W.:* Walton.

Walton, returning some paces, hat in hand: Thou callest me?

Yorick: To wish thee joy.

Walton: Of what?

Yorick: Of lying very ill.

Walton: Neither ill nor well: I do not lie!

Yorick, in sudden fury: Thou liest!

Walton: Yorick!

Yorick: Thou liest![6]

Walton: Art thou beside thyself?

Yorick: It seems not[,] since I see that thou hast lied.

Walton: I will give thee another proof of my regard by turning my back upon thee.

Yorick: Thou shalt not go till thou hast told me what thou didst promise to conceal.

Walton: Why, fool, if I promised to conceal it, how should I tell it thee?

Yorick: Ah! Then I did not dream! Then in truth I did hear the words that thou hast just denied!

Walton: Leave me in peace. Farewell!

Yorick: Walton, in pity, speak!

Walton: Yorick, in pity I will not speak.

---

6. WDH noted in pencil on the original manuscript, "Use either thou or you. I prefer thou for now. If Yorick changes from thou to you, Walton must, also."

Yorick: Is it some misfortune that thou hidest from me?

Walton: If thou couldst but know how foolish is thy persistence and how generous my silence—

Yorick: By my soul thou shalt speak!

Walton: By thy soul, I will not speak.

Yorick: Speak.

Walton, as if yielding to Yorick: Ah! (Then as if resolving to keep silent) No!

Yorick: No?

Walton, coldly: No.

Yorick: I give thee an hour to think of it.

Walton: Dost thou threaten me?

Yorick: Ay, methinks.

Walton: Listen!

Yorick: Within an hour I will seek thee to know thy last decision.

Walton: And if thou dost not find me?

Yorick: I shall say thou art afraid.

Walton: Of whom? Of thee?

Yorick: Of me.

Walton: I will be here within an hour!

Yorick: Thou wilt come?

Walton: Be sure of it.

Yorick: To tell me what thou dost now refuse?

Walton: No: to see what thou wilt do when I refuse again.

Yorick: 'Tis ill playing with fire, Walton: worse a thousand times to jest with the misery of a desperate man.

Walton: Art thou a desperate man?

Yorick: I know not. Leave me!

Walton: Farewell, then. Do we part friends[?]

Yorick: No—yes—

Walton: Yes, or no?

Yorick: No.

Walton: Then I will not offer thee my hand.

Yorick: We were friends for life, didst thou change thy purpose.

Walton: Within an hour, Yorick.

Yorick: Walton, within an hour.

Walton, seeing Edmund, who enters: Good morrow, Edmund.

Edmund: Good morrow.

Walton, aside: Since he is resolved to know it, 'twill be the easier for me to keep silence. (*Exit*)

Scene III

Edmund and Yorick

Yorick, pacing back and forth in great agitation: Ah, Master Edmund, by what miracle do I see thee here at last?

Edmund: This morning you reproached me for not coming—

Yorick: And thou art come because I reproached thee? Because of that alone?

Edmund, disconcerted: No—I meant to say—

Yorick: Do not weary thyself in contriving an excuse.

Edmund: You seem preoccupied—disturbed. Doubtless the rehearsal of the play—(As if seeking something to say.)

Yorick: The rehearsal of the play—certainly—that is—(He speaks mechanically and absently, walking hither and thither, now swiftly, now slowly; pausing at times and sitting down in the nearest chair, and showing in all his actions the agitation that masters him.)

Edmund: As regards you, there is nothing to be feared. The public loves you blindly—to-night it will recognize your talent, as it always does, and—(Seeing that Yorick does not listen, he ceases, drops into a chair, and anxiously watches Yorick as he paces the room. A pause.)

Yorick, without stopping: What wert thou saying? Speak. I hear thee.

Edmund, aside: He must know everything at last. There is no help!

Yorick: Thou dost not speak?

Edmund: Yes, sir; I was saying that the play to-night—

Yorick, stopping abruptly in front of Edmund: Thou hast not asked for Alice. Why hast thou not asked for Alice?

Edmund: Having seen her at the rehearsal this morning—

Yorick, walking away: Yes, it is true—

Edmund, aside: His doubts grow momently; they have reached their height!

Yorick: And the play to-night?

Edmund: It will please, I think. It has interest and movement; the author is unknown and therefore unenvied—

Yorick, speaking to himself and stamping his foot: It shall not be!

Edmund, rising suddenly: Ah!

Yorick: What? Did I say anything? Words escape me without my knowing. I am not well, these days. (Touching his forehead.)

Edmund, affectionately approaching: You are ill? What is the matter?

Yorick: A long and difficult part—the rehearsals—excessive study— But there is nothing serious. It will pass. It has passed. Let us talk here together awhile. (Sitting at the table.) We were talk-ing—of what? Ah yes, of the new play. Yes, thou wilt do thy part wonderfully. And Alice, how dost thou find her in the part of dis-loyal wife?

Edmund: Good,—very good—

Yorick, impetuously, leaping to his feet: Good?

Edmund: Yes, sir: I think—

Yorick, restraining himself and dissimulating: And thou seest how happy I am that thou—(Taking a sudden resolution and draw-ing close to him.)

Edmund, come hither. Hast thou ever felt a furious tempest bursting in thy heart? Couldst thou long hide the blaze of its lightnings, the voice of its thunders, the impetus of its blasts? Is it not true that pain can tear pitiful groans from the bravest and strongest heart? And is sorrow wise to let an irresistible burden crush it down before turning to friendship for help? And thou, art thou not my son, the son of my heart?

Edmund, come hither:
There is a furious tempest of the
      heart
Whose lurid lightnings and
      whose thunder-peals,
Whose wild tornado-blasts, the
      heart in vain
Struggles to hide and hush. Yes,
      there is torment,
That from the stoutest and the
      bravest breast
Can drag forth pitiful groans.
      And there is sorrow
Whose burden is so great that if
      it find not
Help in the heart of some
      compassionate friend,
It grows intolerable. Edmund,
      methinks
That thou shouldst be my
      friend—even more than
      friend.

Edmund, embracing him: O yes, I am your son!

Yorick:

Love thy father, then! Alas, I have dire need of some one to love me now! For thou must know, Edmund, that Alice— O how my lips abhor the words! And if I might but utter them without hearing them— Alice loves me not!

Love me a little, then, my son! For I,—

I have dire need of some one's love, now. Edmund— Thou must know, Edmund, that—that Alice— Oh! How my tongue shrinks from uttering the words That I abhor to hear even more than speak!— She loves me not.

Edmund: Heavens!

Yorick:

Thou seest the vastness of my misery! Could there be greater? It seems impossible. Yet listen: Alice loves another! Ay, there is greater misery, there is greater misery in that!

Thou seest the greatness of my misery! Could there be greater? Ay, there can be greater: Vaster than mind can measure! She loves another!

(Greatly moved.)

Edmund: But surely you deceive yourself. How do you know that your wife—(Then with rising fury) Who has persuaded you to believe—

Yorick: Hearing me call her faithless wife, in the words of that accursed play, that seemed my own, she was so stricken that she swooned away.

Edmund: Is it strange, she being so delicate and sensitive that the lightest sudden noise, startles and convulses her? Did not Shakespeare say—

Yorick, with irony: Aye, he said so. Alice, in her dismay, prayed for mercy.[7]

Edmund: Startled by the sudden accusation her mind followed the impulse received like a blind machine. Did not Shakespeare tell you—

---

7. WDH added a penciled note on the original manuscript: "I have had Shakespear say this at end of Act I. Be sure to keep the repetition here, please."

Yorick, as before: He told me that also, in effect.

But it left a little thorn in my heart; it has waxed since, and now it is a red-hot bolt. I had seen nothing, I had suspected nothing; the light of happiness dazzles like the light of the sun. But the heaven of my bliss once overcast, I saw everything clear and distinct. I remembered one *yes* as ardent as love, another *yes* tepid as gratitude; only with love can love unite in an indissoluble bond. I remembered tears I untimely shed, tremors and fears without reason. She seemed to me younger and lovelier than ever; I found myself suddenly ugly and old. At every moment my suspicions find new aliment; Alice does not attempt to feign or to deceive; the weight of her guilt palsies her will. When I look at her she is so moved and agitated, she shows such distress that I come to wonder if my glances have some supernatural power upon her, and pierce her like arrows. She never speaks to me but her trembling lip betrays the tremor of her conscience. When a rebellious tear sometimes springs to her eyes, she struggles to lock it within again, and it is anguish to watch it growing under the lid that imprisons it. If she laughs, her laughter is sadder than her tears. Yes, I would	It left a barb to rankle in my heart, A little barb that has waxed greater since, Till now it is a red-hot bolt! O, Edmund, I had seen nothing, had suspected nothing: The light of happiness dazzles like the sun! But the sweet heaven of my bliss o'ercast, I saw all things, so vaguely fair before, Distinct and terrible within the shadow! Then I remembered tears ˈ untimely shed, Then I remembered groundless fears and tremors! I saw her younger, lovelier than ever— Myself grown suddenly hideous and old! And Alice seeks not to deceive, or feign: The burden of her guilt palsies her will! She shows Such anguish when I chance to look upon her; She is so moved and stricken that I marvel If my regards have supernatural power To pierce her inmost soul. Her trembling lip Betrays the tumult of her conscience when She speaks to me. Sometimes, rebellious tears Spring to her eyes, and grow

swear it before God: Alice is hiding some foul secret in her heart. I have learnt to believe it at last with terror: with such terror as one should feel who saw the blue heavens open, and darkness and the fires of hell within the rift! Who is the thief that stole my peace? Who is the thief that stole her innocence? Speak, I say! Do not tell me that thou dost no know; that were idle; I would not believe thee. Who is it? Thou dost not speak? Thou wilt not speak? My God! What a world is this where guilt finds so many accomplices!

beneath the lids
That vainly struggle to imprison
  them:
It wrings my heart! And if she
  ever laugh,
Her laughter is sadder than her
  tears to me.
Yes, I would swear before God
  in Heaven:
Alice is hiding in her soul, once
  pure,
A secret foul as sin! Oh, I have
  learned
To know it with such terror as
  the wretch
Should feel who saw the blue
  heavens rent asunder,
And in the rift the lurid fires of
  hell!
Who is the thief that robbed me
  of my peace?
Who is the thief that stole her
  innocence?
Speak! Do not tell me that thou
  dost not know!
'Twere idle; I would not believe
  thee; speak!
Thou dost not speak? Thou wilt
  not speak? My God!
Is all the world in league with
  guilt against me?

Edmund: To see you suffer such bitter anguish leaves me almost powerless to open my lips. But I repeat that your suspicions are unfounded; that I know nothing—

Yorick: Why hast thou ever been so disdainful of Alice? Why hast thou ceased to frequent this house? Because thou knowest this woman has betrayed thy more than friend; because thou wouldst not countenance my shame with thy presence.

Edmund: Oh, do not believe it! It is a hideous illusion.

Yorick: I tell thee that my eyes are purged, and that my brain is clear at last. Dost thou know my rival? Help me to discover him! Is it, haply, Walton?

Edmund, indignantly: How could you imagine it?

Yorick: Enough, enough! It is not Walton; decidedly it is not Walton. Is it Lord Stanley?

Edmund: Lord Stanley? Because the other night he spoke to her a moment—

Yorick: Peace! Tis as little he as Walton. I imagined so. Is it the earl of Southampton, the friend of—Shakespear? (He pronounces the last name with difficulty.)

Edmund: Impossible! the earl of Southampton loves a great court lady.

Yorick: Then, who is it? It must be he whom least I would it were. The treachery of my wife is not enough; I must weep the treachery of a friend as well.

Edmund: Suspect no one; this rival does not exist; Alice is guiltless.

Yorick: I will solve my doubts this instant. I am going to know whether she be guilty or no. (Turning toward the door on the left.)

Edmund: What do you mean?

Yorick, turning to Edmund: Nothing: the most natural thing in the world; to ask *her* the question.

Edmund, horrified: No, no! In mercy, no!

Yorick: And wherefore no? Can I do less than trust her word?

Edmund: But if you accuse her without cause? If she is innocent?

Yorick: If she is innocent, why should she tremble? Why should I tremble? Why shouldst thou tremble?

Edmund: Time will solve all your doubts!

Yorick:

Time, that seems to fly so fast, pauses now and then, and appals the soul with an image of eternity. For some days past, time has stood still with me: I would fain exist again.	Ay, Time that seems to fly so swiftly, pauses At terrible moments, and appals the soul With th' image of an eternity of pain. For some days past Time has stood still with me; I would fain live again.

Edmund: Wait for another day! Wait one day more! (Seizing his hand.)

Yorick, struggling to free himself: Not a day more, not an hour more, not an instant more! Off!

Edmund: Oh, consider what you are doing!

Yorick, still struggling: Insufferable obstinacy! The boy is stubborn.

Edmund: Listen!

Yorick: And a fool, to boot! Away! (He frees himself by a violent effort.)

Edmund: Oh!

Yorick, furiously: There is no help. I must know all.

Edmund: Mercy!

Yorick, changing tone, and in a tearful voice: As if I would not have mercy! (Exit by the door on the left.)

Scene IV

Edmund and Alice

Edmund: My God! Oh! (On seeing Alice appear through the hangings of the left-hand door, with her face pale and gaunt, and with signs of consternation. A brief pause, and the[n] E. runs to A., who has remained motionless, and leads her forward.) Didst thou hear?

Alice: Yes.

Edmund, speaking rapidly in a low voice: To-morrow a ship sails at day-break; the captain is my friend: let us escape!

Alice: No.

Edmund: By night, everything could be ready for our flight.

Alice: No.

Edmund: If there be no other means to reach thee, thou wilt receive a letter to-night at the theatre, telling thee what I have done, and what we have both to do.

Alice: No.

Edmund: Thy husband will soon know all.

Alice: God's will be done!

Edmund: And what will become of thee?

Alice: Why should I care?

Edmund: What will become of us both?

Alice: Fly, thou.

Edmund: Alone? Never.

Alice: Fly.

Edmund: With thee.

Alice: No, a thousand times!

Yorick, calling within: Alice! Alice! (She starts.)

Edmund: Dost thou hear? Already thou art faint and breathless.

Alice, in terror: He is looking for me.

Edmund: To ask thee if thou art guilty. What wilt thou say?

Alice: What will I say? *Yes!*

Edmund: And then?

Alice: And then? Oh dost thou think he will kill me? (As if animated by a joyous hope.)

Edmund: His fury or thine own anguish will be thy death.

Alice: Oh, rapture!

Edmund: Thou seekest not thy death alone, but mine as well.

Alice, with a start of pain: Thine!

Yorick, within but nearer: Alice!

Edmund: He comes.

Alice: I will be silent, I will lie to him. I cannot be more unhappy, but do not fear: I can be more despicable.

Yorick: Alice!

Alice: Here; I am here! (Yorick enters by left door.)

Scene V

The same, and Yorick.

Yorick, starting at sight of Alice: Ah!

Alice, smiling and affecting serenity: You were looking for me, and I for you, and it seems we were running from each other.

Yorick, aside: This woman is cheerful? *To Edmund:* I wish to speak with Alice alone for a moment. Wait for me in my room.

Edmund, aside: At least I shall be at hand. (Exit by right door.)

Scene VI

Yorick and Alice

Yorick, contemplating Alice for a moment in silence and then sitting down upon a bench: Come hither, Alice. (She makes some paces toward him.) Nearer, Alice. (She draws nearer.) Sit here beside me. Art thou afraid of me?

Alice Sitting: Afraid! Wherefore? What do you wish with me?

Yorick, rising and aside: She tranquil, I perturbed! Alice, there is a guilty conscience here: is it thine or mine?

Alice: A guilty conscience? Thine—or—

Yorick:

Alice, a man commonly awakes to love in the first dawn of youth; he runs heedlessly in pursuit of the pleasure he sees before him, and involves himself in one passion after another, fertile or shameful, leaving in each, along the thorny way of life, a piece of his heart. Mine was entire and pure when I saw thee and loved thee; and O how potent is the love felt in the autumnal years, when one has never loved before, and it is not possible to love again! Thus I loved thee, Alice. Dost thou love me as thou shouldst love me? Speak!

Alice, men commonly awake to love
In the first dawn of youth, and recklessly
Press in pursuit of the divine allure
Shining before them, and involve themselves
In passion after passion, foul or futile,
Leaving along life's thorny labarynth [*sic*],
Bits of their hearts on every briar. My heart
Was whole and virgin when I saw and loved thee.
And oh, how potent is the love felt first
In the autumnal years to which can come
No second love! Thus, Alice, I loved *thee*!
Dost thou love *me*, as thou shouldst love me? Speak!

Alice: I—surely—I owe you so much for the benefits—

Yorick: Benefits! Who spoke of benefits? Dost thou love me?

Alice: Love you? Am I not your wife?

Yorick: Dost thou love me?

Alice: Yes, sir; yes, I love you.

Yorick, rapturously: In very truth? Yes? Shall I believe it? For God's sake, tell me the truth! Dost thou love none but me? None?

Alice, confused and rising: What is it you ask me?

Yorick, energetically and detaining her: Dost thou love another?

Alice: No, sir—no—

Yorick: I think that thou deceivest me. Ah! (as if with a flattering hope:)

Perhaps thou lovest another
and hast not yet told thy love!
If this be true, do not fear to
confess it to me. Humbly will
I accept the penalty of having
taken for my wife one who
might have been my daugh-
ter; not with the harshness of
a husband, but with the
tenderness of a father will I
hear thy confession; I will
teach thee to see the difference between the adulterous
love that makes hell rejoice
and that conjugal love for
which heaven reserves a
crown and palm; I will
redouble all my arts and
devotion for thee, and show
thee my affection with every
sweetest and most potent
charm; I will not cease to
supplicate thy guardian angel
that he keep thee in his hand;
and do not doubt, my life, my
love!—do not doubt, Alice,
my soul!—but I shall overcome my rival at last, and win
all thy heart, and turn thee
again into the path of duty
and happiness: for thou art
good; thy heart is noble and
generous; thou couldst sin
through error, but not
through wilfulness; and when
thou hadst seen the ugliness
of sin thou wouldst fly from it
in horror; and when thou
hadst known all my tenderness— Ah, believe it, child:
some little love is due to him
who loves so much!

I think—I fear—thou art deceiv-
ing me.
Perchance thou lovest another
and hast not
Yet told thy love. Alice, if this be
true,
Fear not to own thy secret
before me.
Humbly will I accept the penalty
Of taking for my wife a child
who might
Have been my daughter. Tender-
ly, like a father,
Not harshly like a husband, will I
listen
To thy confession; I will make
thee see
The difference betwixt the
adulterous love
That makes hell laugh, and that
pure wedded love
For which heaven keeps its
crowns and palms. For thee
I will redouble all my arts and
worship,
And I will never cease to suppli-
cate
Thy guardian angel that he hold
thee safe
Within his hand! And do not
doubt, my love,
Alice, my soul!—but I shall yet
prevail
Against my rival, and shall win
thy heart
And lead thee once again in the
path
Of duty and happiness! For thou
art good;
Thy heart is noble and generous.
Thou couldst sin
Through error, but not through
wilfulness; and when

Thou hadst not seen the ugliness
of sin
Must fly it in horror! And when
thou hadst known
All of my tenderness— Ah,
believe me, child,
Some little love is surely due to
him
Who loves so much!

Alice, aside: This air chokes me! Oh, if I could die!
Yorick:

Thou answerest nothing? Thou art silent? Thou lovest, and thy love is known? Then thou shouldst as little hide it from me! Thou knowest well that so black a sin could not remain unpunished. Destroy a family, and drag a husband's honor through the mire— And if that husband's sole care were to save his wife from every slightest sorrow; if he had no joy but in adoring her, no life but what he received from her; if for this unhappy wretch in losing her love must perish in despair; and she knew it, and doomed him to the pangs of hell in this world and the next—oh, then the iniquity were so great that the mind could not grasp it, so great that it would seem a lie! No, I will not believe that thou— Such infamy with me? That thou hast been— No, no! I do not believe it, I cannot, I will not believe it. (He covers his face with his hands, and sobs aloud. Alice while Yorick speaks gives signs of greater	Thou answerest nothing? Thou art silent still? Thou lovest another, and thy love is known? As little shouldst thou hide it from me, then! For wilt thou knowest that so black a sin Could not remain unpunished. Sully thy name, And drag thy husband's honor through the mire— And if that husband's only care had been To save his wife from every slightest sorrow, His only happiness in adoring her; And if he had no life but hers; no hope Of heaven but in her love, and losing that, Only despair and death: And if she knew it, All this and doomed him to the pangs of hell In this world and the next, then were her guilt Too great for thought to grasp; and though as proved As holy writ, it needs must seem a lie!

and greater anguish; she tries to rise, but he prevents her; overcome by emotion she sinks slowly to her knees before him. When Yorick uncovers his eyes, and sees her, he starts back in fury.) Kneeling! (Alice lets fall her face upon the bench, with her back to the spectators.) Kneeling! If she were inno- cent she would not kneel! Then I have not deceived myself! Infamous! (He rushes threateningly upon her, but seeing that she does not move, he falters, and then stops over (approaches) her with an entirely contrary expression.) What is it? What hast thou— (Raising her head, gazing at her, and putting his hand upon her forehead.) Speak—weep— Art thou dying? But what am I doing? (checking his tender- ness.) What does it matter to me whether or no she dies? (Then retiring from her with renewed indignation.) Her anguish may be feigned— Yes, all is foulness and deceit! The woman knows not even the name of truth!

Incredible! I will not think that thou— Such treachery with me—That thou hast been— No, no; I do not, cannot, will not, think it— Kneeling? Ah—kneeling! Were she innocent She would not kneel! Infamous woman! Then, I have not been deceived! What is it? What— What hast thou? Speak! Weep! Art thou dying? Oh, What is't to me, whether she die or live? Her suffering may be feigned— All is deceit And vileness in her. Nay, the woman knows not Even the name of truth!

Alice: Oh! (With a deep sigh, she falls heavily forward upon the bench.)

Yorick, again running toward her: Alice! Tis over—calm thy- self— To-morrow we shall see what is to be done; to-day we must think of other things. The play to-night— Alice, for God's sake rouse thyself. (Shakespear appears at the door in the background; Yorick throws himself before his wife.) Ho! Who is it? Who is there? Who dares to enter here?

Scene VII

The Same, and Shakespear.

Shakespear: So blind that thou dost not know me?

Yorick: Shakespear! Thou!

Shakespear, approaching her: Rise, Alice.

Yorick: Do not touch her!

Shakespear, lifting Alice, who supports herself upon him: Since thou hast taken this fancy for tragedy, thou art grown insufferable.

Yorick, approaching his wife: Did I not bid thee to touch her not?

Shakespear, repelling him with an outstretched arm: Stand aside.

Yorick: Am I dreaming?

Shakespear: I could swear thou wast; or else drunk, or mad. Come to thy chamber, Alice. (He moves slowly with her toward the left door.)

Yorick, following them: What! Thou?

Shakespear, stopping him: Wait a moment. I would speak with thee.

Yorick, recovering his strength, and attempting to separate his wife from Shakespear: I tell thee Alice must not leave me! (Shakespear seizes his hand with impressive quiet, and draws him towards the front, looking him steadily in the eye.)

Shakespear: I tell thee to wait a little! (He returns to Alice, and giving her his arm leads her to the door, without lifting his eyes from Yorick, who remains stupefied and motionless.[)]

Scene VIII

Yorick, alone.

Yorick, after a brief pause, pressing his hand to his forehead, and looking round him like one roused from sleep: What is it? Has the reality of my life turned to some fantastic drama whose end cannot be foreseen? Am I the sport of some black sorcery? Shakespear? Yes, there is no doubt— No! Impossible! What misery to live forever in this darkness! Light, light, eternal God!— He went with her—they are together! Damnation! *I* will part them! (Rushing toward the door through wh[ich] Sh. and A. passed.)

Scene IX

Yorick and Walton.

Walton, from the door in the background: The hour is past, and here I am.

Yorick, with great apparent joviality: O, it is Walton. Welcome, Walton, thrice welcome! This is really keeping one's promise.

Walton: I always keep my promises.

Yorick: And thou art come to tell me thou wilt not satisfy my curiosity?

Walton: Precisely.

Yorick: Since I threatened thee, thou wilt show me that thou dost not fear me?

Walton: Even so.

Yorick: Why, I like that! There shall be no quarrel between us. (Placing his hand on W's shoulder.) Away with those punctilios!

Walton: As thou wilt. But in good faith, I had not hoped to find thee so reasonable.

Yorick: Ay, there is no need that thou shouldst tell me anything. On the contrary, I have an amusing story for thee.

Walton: For me?

Yorick: There was once a youngster, all vehemence, all fire. He fell furiously in love with a lady nearly twice his age, but of irresistible beauty. (Walton starts.) His love was returned—what rapture! They were married—bliss beyond measure!

Walton, greatly moved: Wilt thou cease?

Yorick: These loving turtles had passed the honeymoon in peace, when one night the youngster[,] returning home unexpectedly, found his wife—

Walton: It is false! It is a lie!

Yorick: Found his wife in the arms of another man.

Walton: I swear to heaven—

Yorick: O *he* swore to heaven, too! And fancy what he must have said when he found that this man, a gentleman of lofty lineage, was an old lover with whom she had often—

Walton: It is a lie! Peace!

Yorick: He resolved to take vengeance on his wife, and his wife disappeared as if by magic.

Walton: Wilt thou be silent?

Yorick: He resolved to take vengeance on the lord, and the lord had him well cudgeled by his lackeys.

Walton, blind with fury, seizing Y. by the arm and shaking him violently: Wilt thou *cease?*

Yorick, in the same tone, and shaking W.: Wilt thou *begin?* Ha, ha, ha! The little story amuses thee! Ha, ha, ha! (Laughing still more jovially.) Well, thou must know that twenty years after, the cudgeled husband, under another name, and far from the scene of the event, which he believed buried in oblivion— But, look you, he deceived himself: he was known to bear a false name, that he might hide the dishonor of his own—(speaking with renewed energy.)

Walton: What art thou doing, Yorick?

Yorick: And there were not wanting those who pointed their fingers at him—

Walton: O fury!

Yorick: And when they saw him pass, cried: "There goes a poltroon." For the outraged husband who does not avenge himself, is infamous!

Walton, with a burst: Then, who more infamous than thou?

Yorick: Ah! ah! Thou wilt speak at last! Go on—tell—speak!

Walton: I at least discovered the intrigue.

Yorick: Speak!

Walton: I at least *tried* to avenge myself.

Yorick: And I? Speak! And I?

Walton: Thou art blind.

Yorick: Speak!

Walton: Thou livest in peace with thy dishonor.

Yorick: Speak!

Walton: Thy wife—

Yorick: My wife? Speak!—Nay, cease, or by living God, I tear thy tongue from thy throat!

Walton: Ah, thou seest now? Thou art more infamous than I!

Yorick: My wife?—

Walton: Has betrayed thee.

Yorick: Betrayed me? Prove it! Give me evident proofs, proofs clearer than the sun in heaven! Thou dost not launch this horrible accusal without the power to make good thy words. Then give me thy proofs! Give them— Why dost thou delay? Thou shouldst have them! Thou hast them not! I knew it! This man tells me that an angel is a demon, and expects me to believe it on his word!

Walton: I say that Alice is unfaithful to thee.

Yorick: I say that thou shalt prove it. (Approaching him closely.) And if thou canst not prove it now upon the instant, confess that thou hast lied: say that Alice is an honored wife; say that she loves none but me; say that the world reveres and worships her; say that [the] heavens rejoice to look down upon her! Say it! If thou wilt not—

Walton: I say that Alice has a lover.

Yorick: Thou sayest it?

Walton: Yes.

Yorick: And provest it not? Villain[,] thou shalt never say it more! (Flings himself at W's. throat.)

Walton: Yorick!

Scene X

The Same, Shakespear, Alice and Edmund.
S. & A from the left. E. from the right.

Edmund*:*   Ah! ⎫
Alice*:*   Ah! ⎭

Shakespear, throwing himself between Y. and W.: Hold!

Walton, confounded at seeing him: Shakespear!

Shakespear, in low voice to W.: To break a promise is the basest villainy!

Walton, stricken by the reproach, and turning to the door in the background: Oh! (To Yorick.) Thou shalt weep tears of blood for what thou hast done. (Exit.)

Shakespear: What has that man said to thee?

Yorick: What I knew already: that my wife has a lover. Thou art he!

Shakespear, with indignant surprise: I!

Alice: Merciful heaven—

Edmund, approaching to speak to Yorick: Oh!

Shakespear, angrily: I? Fool! Ha! Ha! Ha! By heaven, thou makest me laugh.

Yorick: Thou art not he? It is not he! (With tender emotion.) It is not my friend who puts me to shame and death! Then have I yet some comfort in my misery! I feared two treasons, and but one exists. Forgive me, Shakespeare; I am so unhappy!

Shakespeare, greatly moved: If thou art unhappy, come hither to a faithful heart!

Yorick, falling into his arms: My friend, my friend! (He sobs aloud.)

Edmund, in a low voice full of terror: Alice?

Alice, desperately: Yes!

Edmund, rapidly: To-morrow!

Alice: To-morrow! [( ] Edmund exit in background; Alice by right door. S. leads Y. away.)

End of Act II.

Act III

Part I.

Room of Yorick and Alice at the theatre. Large table with cover, two small mirrors, theatrical properties, and lights; two deep cornices from which hang ample curtains that reach the ground, half concealing the dresses heaped behind them; some chairs; door on the right, leading to the stage.

Scene I

Woodford & Thomas

Both enter from the door on the right; the Scene-shifter with an open MS.

Thomas: There ought to be some water here for Mrs. Alice.

Woodford: Yes: I see a bottle. (Indicates it upon the table.)

Thomas: Take some. (Pours from the bottle into a goblet. Author drinks.)

Woodf.: Ah! I breathe again! I had my heart all doubled up in a knot. I thought they were going to— So many emotions! Such joy! Oof! (Takes a paper from the table and fans himself.) Well, Master Thomas, what think you of my play, now?

Thos.: What do I think? Come! Mighty pretty! And this last act in my opinion is going to please as much as the others.

Woodf.: Certainly, if one were at all vain— Some men in my place would fancy that they rivaled Shakspear. I do not; out of sheer modesty I go about doing him homage. But, poor soul!— I pity him, to-night; for he must feel that the new author is bearding him. But how can it be helped? He cannot expect to be always the first!

Scene II

The Same, and Edmund, as Manfred.

Edmund: Tell me, Thomas, does Alice come off the stage before I go on?

Thos., turning the pages of the play: No, sir.

Edmund: And I am on the stage till the end?

Thos.: Did not you know it? (as before.)

Edmund, aside: The play over, it will be impossible to reach her. What a fatality! (Turning to the door.)

Woodf.: Master Edmund, in that challenge scene— To tell the truth, I thought you— Well, you were better at the rehearsals. Ah?

Edmund: Yes, sir, yes. (Exit, with an absent-minded air.)

Scene III

Woodf. and Thomas; then Walton as Landolfo.

Woodf.: He scarcely deigned to answer me! I rack my brains making plays like this, in order that an impertinent little actor—

Walton: Edmund has just gone? (To Thos.)

Thos.: Yes, sir.

Walton: What did he want?

Thos.: Nothing: to know when Mistress Alice came off.

Woodf.: Master Walton, do you not think that Edmund is playing pretty badly to-night?

Thos.: Something must have happened to him.

Woodf.: Twice, when I went to his room I found him talking with Dervil in a low voice, and when they saw me they changed the subject of their conversation. Actors should not be allowed to receive visits behind the scenes.

Walton: And this Dervil, who is he?

Woodf.: The captain of a ship that sails to-morrow.

Thos.: As soon as the captain went away, Edmund asked me for ink, and wrote a letter.

Woodf.: Writing letters during the representation of a play!

Walton, aside: A letter! A ship that sails to-morrow!

Thos.: And talking of letters: here is the one you are to take with you on the stage, and give to Count Octavio. (*Giving him a paper folded in the form of a letter.*)

Walton: Well. (*He puts it in the pocket of his costume. The sound of cheers and applause heard without. Walton starts.*)

Woodford: What's that? Whom is that for?

Thos.: Whom? Whom else but Yorick? (*Exit running*)

Scene IV

Walton and Woodford.

Woodf.: How that man is playing to-night! Why when they told me he was to do the Count, I was ready to dash my head against the wall. But so it goes! Who would have imagined that an actor used only to the part of buffoon— Why, he has left all the actors in the world behind him. Why, he does better than you!

Walton, ironically: Really?

Woodf.: Much better!

Walton: And if that is your opinion, does it seem civil or prudent to tell it me, face to face? (*He lays hold upon him, and furiously drags him forward.*)

Woodf.: Pardon— I thought— The glory of a fellow actor—

Walton, contemptuously releasing him: You are a fool!

Woodf.: How? What? A fool,—I?

Scene V

The Same and Thomas.

Thos.: It was just as I said. The applause was for Yorick.

Woodf., aside: Walton is consumed with envy! (*Aloud:*) Bravo, Yorick, bravo! *Aside:* Digest that, thou sour-stomached ruffian! (Exit.)

Thos.: And what think you of Yorick?

Walton: Thou art a good lad, Thomas. Look well to thy duty, and I will make Shakespeare increase thy wages.

Thos.: Oh, if I do not! I will be greatly beholden to you!

Walton: Thou askest me what I think of Yorick?

Thos.: Yes, sir.

Walton, hopefully: Well, what thinkest thou?

Thos.: I?

Walton: Yes; tell me. This morning thou saidst he would do very badly.

Thos.: How often I said so!

Walton, joyously: And now thou thinkest—

Thos.: I do not think; I am sure—

Walton: What?

Thos.: That I talked nonsense.

Walton: Ah!

Thos.: He has played us all a fine trick. In the first act, you know, he was—well, somewhat embarrassed, but he soon— Ay faith! he came mighty well out of some scenes, even then! I stood there gaping and staring at him till I forgot to call Mistress Alice, and if the author had not given me a good pinch to bring me to my senses, the play would have ended there! Look you, Master Walton: when I saw you play Macbeth, I thought that nothing could be better; but now—

Walton: Come, come! Don't fall into a new blunder!

Thos., startled, and shuffling the MS.: Eh? No; this scene is very long. We may be sure after this that as long as Yorick is in the company, no one else will have the first parts. Who could rival him in them?

Walton: Faith, thou art a chatterer.

Thos.: Enthusiasm was always a great talker; and I am enthusiastic for Yorick. Every one is. The principal actors grumble under their breath; but 'tis envy, pure envy!

Walton: Wilt thou leave me in peace?

Thos., aside: What a gesture! What a look! O, what a fool I am! Hold thy tongue, my good friend, Thomas!

Walton: What art thou muttering?

Thos.: Nay, I did not mutter. On the contrary—

Walton: Away with thee, or I swear—

Thos.: Going, going! (Walton drops into a chair, vexed and annoyed. Thos. continues, aside:) Rage, rage, rage, and eat thy bitter heart! (Exit, with gestures and grimaces unseen by Walton.)

Scene VI

Walton, alone.

Walton, after a thoughtful silence: Yes! Yorick applauded with enthusiasm. What a triumph! What glory! Greater than mine, a thousand times greater! If I could not pardon him the injury he did me before, how could I pardon him this! I will have revenge equal to the offense; revenge— (Shouts without.) More applause! (He goes to the right door) Ah! For Alice! (Calming himself.) She is coming off; Edmund is going on by the same side. They exchange glances— Yes! without question— The act was quick as thought, but I saw it: Edmund gave her something as he passed. What could it be? Perhaps that letter— The proof that Yorick demanded? If it were only a letter! If fate should favor me! Hither she comes— Ah! (He hides behind one of the curtains.)

Scene VII

Walton, and Alice as Beatrice

Alice enters by the right-hand door; after looking round she closes it slowly without noise; with signs of intense excitement she approaches the middle of the stage, stops irresolute, then opens her left hand, and looks at the paper in it.

Walton, joyously, and thrusting his head from the curtain: Yes, it is Edmund's letter! [(]Alice rapidly draws near the lights on the table. She glances at the door, and then with visible commotion reads the letter.[)]

Alice: "Till now I did not know with certainty that we could fly to-morrow. But all is ready.— At five in the morning, I will await thee in the street.— We will never part— My love will last my life— Fly with me; there is no other hope; fly, Alice, my soul, and"— Fly! Abandon my unhappy husband? Make my wrong irremediable, an eternal shame? Never! Death were better! (She puts the letter in the flame to burn it. Walton, stealthily approaching, seizes her arm.) Oh! (She swiftly changes the letter to her other hand.) Walton! (Shrinking away.)

Walton: Ay, Walton.

Alice: Where were you?

Walton: Behind the curtain.

Alice: What is your purpose here?

Walton: I want Edmund's letter which you hold in your hand there[.]

Alice, staying herself by the table: Mercy!

Walton: Give it me.

Alice: Do not come near me!

Walton: Why should I not?

Alice: I will cry out.

Walton: Oh, very well! That will serve my purpose even better.

Alice: Oh, what *is* your purpose?

Walton: You will see.

Alice: Would you betray him to my husband?

Walton: Perchance.

Alice: To-night! Here! During the play! But that were infamous, base beyond example! There is no name for such a horrible deed!— Oh, be merciful! A little mercy for him, for him alone. I implore you! Whom do you love? What words will soonest touch your heart? Tell me what I must do to move you!

Walton: You can do nothing. I must be revenged.

Alice: And why should you not be revenged? But must you be revenged to-night? To-morrow I will give you the paper I crush in my hand: believe me; I swear it. To-morrow my husband shall know the truth. You shall be present; you shall slake your thirst for vengeance with his agony and mine; it will not vex you then to have waited till to-morrow! Leave me—I hear him coming. On my knees I pray you. (She kneels to him.) Look; I am at your feet! You will grant me the favor that I ask? You will grant it, will you? Why should [it] be so hard to say yes?

Walton: No, and a thousand times, no!

Alice, springing to her feet, full of indignation: Ah! I took him for a man, and he is a demon!

Walton: I am a man—a man with a wrong to be avenged.

Alice: Oh! (She sees Yorick enter from the right; she puts behind her the hand in which she holds the letter, and remains as if frozen with terror.)

Scene VIII

The Same, and Yorick as Count Octavio.

Yorick, quietly to Walton: What dost thou here? It were well we did not meet to-night, except upon the stage.

Walton: Truly, thou art right; but when thou knowest what has happened—

Yorick: I would know nothing. (Sinks wearily into a chair.) To-night we belong to the public. Go!

Walton: Is the greed of glory so great in thee that thou forgettest all else?

Yorick, with sad irony: Greed of glory—? Prithee, go!

Walton: As thou didst once ask me for a certain proof—

Yorick: What? What sayest thou? (Rising and approaching Walton.)

Alice, aside, as she awakens from her stupor: Can this be reality?

Yorick: Walton—(Restraining himself.) See, she is here! Beware thou defame her not in her presence. (Then losing his self-control:) A proof? Can it be? Where is it[?]

Walton: Bid thy wife show thee her hands.

Alice: Do not heed him!

Yorick, to Walton: Go; leave us!

Walton: In one of her hands she holds a paper.

Alice: He is a villain!

Yorick: A paper? (Starting toward his wife, and checking himself with difficulty.) Go! (To Walton.)

Walton: That paper is a letter from her lover.

Alice: Ah! (She crushes the paper in her hand.)

Yorick: Ah! (Runs towards her.) Give me that letter, Alice! (Checks himself again.)

Alice: It is not a letter. Did he say it was a letter? He lies. Do not believe him—

Yorick: He accuses thee; justify thyself! If this paper be not a letter, thou canst easily confound the slanderer. Do it!

Alice: It is— I will tell you— This letter—

Yorick: I must see it.

Alice: It is impossible! (Desperately.)

Yorick, yielding to his fury: Impossible? Give it me! (Rudely seizing her hand, and struggling with her for the letter.)

Alice: Ah! (By a violent effort she disengages herself from Yorick, and runs to the door; he intercepts her and locks it.)

Yorick: What wouldst thou do? Wouldst thou make my dishonor public?

Alice: Pity me, thou Mother of the Friendless!

Walton: Resistance is useless. You had better yield at once.

Alice: And who authorizes *you* to counsel me?

> Yorick, Bid this man hold his peace. *You*
> Shall use me as you will. You are my husband;
> You have the right to do me wrong. But *this*
>   man,
> Do not let *him* insult me; do not let him
> Speak to me; do not let him look upon me!

No woman, not the vilest, most degraded,
Merits the ignominy of the glance
Of such a man!

[Walton continues to regard her with a smile of triumph.]

I have told thee not to look
At me. Yorick!

(Knocking at the door.)

Yorick to Alice: Dost thou hear? I am called; I must go on the stage.

Alice: Go, go! For God's sake!

Thos., without: Yorick, Yorick!

Yorick: Do not force me to use violence with a woman!

Thomas: Yorick! You are keeping the scene waiting.

Yorick: Dost thou not hear them?

Alice: I shall go mad!

Yorick: Dost thou despise my threats?

Woodford, without: Open, open! The stage is all prepared.

Yorick: Oh, let us make an end of this! (He flings himself upon his wife, and tries to force the letter from her hand.)

Alice, struggling with him: Mercy! Mercy!

Yorick: The letter! The letter!

Alice: No! Have pity on me!

Shakespear, knocking on the door without: Will you open here, I say?

Alice: Shakespear! Shakespear!

Yorick: The letter!

Alice: No, my life first! (Walton seizes the hand in which she holds the letter.) Ah!

Walton, securing the letter: Here it is!

Yorick: Give it me!

Woodford, Shakespear and Thomas, without: Yorick! Yorick!

Walton, as if struck by a sudden idea: Ah, not yet! (He puts the letter in his pocket.)

Yorick: You will not?

Alice: What does he say?

Scene IX

The Same, with Shakespear, Woodford, and Thomas, who, battering down the door, enter tumultuously. Cries and stamping heard without.

Shakespear: Walton!

Woodford, with comic desperation: You have ruined me!

Thomas: The stage has been waiting two minutes.

Yorick, sotto voce to Walton: That letter!

Walton: I have told you, not now.

Woodford: What are you doing? (Cries and stamping, without.) Do n't you hear?

Thomas, prompting Yorick from the play:

> "Heaven helps me at last,
> And now I burst the prison of my doubt!"

Yorick, to Walton as before: His name, at least his name!

Walton: Presently.

Shakespear: The public is waiting, Yorick.

Thomas: The public is furious!

Woodford: O my poor play! (These then push Yorick towards the door.)

Yorick: Let me go! I am not an actor, now; I am a man—a man who suffers unto death. (Frees himself and runs to Walton.) Wilt thou give it me?

Walton: It shall not leave my hands except for thine.

Woodford, seizing Yorick again: Come!

Thomas, prompting: "Heaven helps me at last."

Shakespear: Duty before everything.

Yorick: A curse upon duty! A curse on me! (Exit precipitately. Alice whispers with Shakespear.)

Thomas, to Alice: You, now.

Alice, sotto voce to Shakespear: A letter from Edmund—

Woodford, in despair: And she won't go on, either!

Alice, to S, as before: If my husband sees it—

Shakespear to A: He shall not see it.

Woodford: Madam!

Alice: Support me! Lead me! (Exit, leaning on Woodford.)

Thomas to Walton: Did I hand you the letter you are to give the Count[?]

Walton: Yes!

Thomas: I don't know whether I'm standing on my head or my feet! (Exit.)

Scene X

Shakespear and Walton; then Woodford and Thomas.

Shakespear: Walton, this paper does not belong to thee.

Walton: Nor to thee.

Shakespear: The owner has charged me to reclaim it from thee.

Walton: Let me see then how thou wilt reclaim it.

Shakespear: How? (Angrily at first; then he recovers himself.) Walton, brave and generous hearts feel only compassion for the misfortunes of others. Have pity on Yorick; have pity on Alice! Save her, if it be possible. Her fault is not so grave as thou thinkest, and can be easily repaired. Let us destroy that paper.

Walton: Yorick has wrong[ed] me.

Shakespear: Yorick has wronged thee? Then take thy revenge; but take it nobly. Thou canst not heal thy honor by committing a villainy. If Alice has offended thee in nothing, why shouldst thou make her the victim of thy resentment? To wound at the same stroke the innocent and the guilty, is the act of a savage or a madman. And even if this unhappy woman had done thee wrong, thou couldst not avenge thyself on her without cowardice. Men avenge themselves on men; not on women.

Walton: Ask me whatever you will, so you do not ask me for that letter.

Shakespear: Do not think me ignorant of the cause of thy hate for Yorick. Thou hatest him not because he has wronged thee, but because thou enviest him.

Walton, with violent emotion: What? Darest thou say—

Shakespear: I have called thee villain and coward; thou art worse yet: thou art envious.

Walton: I envious? Nothing could pain me so much as that.

Shakespear: Because thou most deservest it. Yes, Envy holds thy soul within her clutch; envy that laughs at others' evil and bewails their good; envy, the most pitiable of afflictions if it were not the most repulsive of vices; envy, the shame and dishonor of the mind, the leprosy of the heart! (Applause without.)

Walton, turning away: Duty calls me: as thou saidst to Yorick, duty before everything.

Shakespear: They are applauding *him.* Hear them! Dost thou tremble to hear them? There is no sound in the world so deadly to the envious soul as the applause a rival wins.

Woodford, entering jubilant: Hurrah! Hurrah! The public is ours again! They could not choose but applaud when they heard those verses:

"We wait with anxious eagerness the good
That sends its brightness from afar before it;
But not with such impatience as we wait
The evil that appals us with its coming."

The verses certainly are not bad, but how Yorick spoke them! What gestures! What intonations! (Sounds without.) More applause,—more! Admirable! Divine! (Clapping his hands.)

Walton, starting to go: I shall be late, if you keep me here.

Shakespear, putting himself before him: Give me the letter first!

Woodford: What is the matter with every body to-night?[8]

Shakespear, violently arresting him: Stop, I say!

Woodford and Thomas, astonished: Oh!

Shakespear: I will tear it from thee with thy life, if needs must.

Woodford, to Shakespear: Do you want to ruin my play? Ah, now I understand you!

Walton, as if taking a sudden resolution: Oh!

Shakespear: Well?

Woodford, looking at his comedy: Only five verses more.

Walton: Duty is stronger than will. Take it. (He draws a letter from his pocket, and gives it to Shakespear.)

Shakespear: At last! (He seizes the letter eagerly. Walton goes out by the right door.)

Woodford, following him: Run!

Thomas, prompting him: "My Lord, behold me here!" [(Exeunt all but Shakespear and Woodford.)]

Scene XI

Shakespear, tremulously opening the letter: A piece of blank paper. Ah! (With a terrible cry.) The one he was to give Yorick in the play! And the other! The other! Great God! (He runs

---

8. The following dialogue in the original manuscript was struck, probably by WDH. LB did not copy it in his "stage version":
Thomas, entering: Come, (to Walton) you are to go on in a moment.
Walton, to Shakespear: You see? (To Thomas.) Go; I am coming.

furiously towards the door on the right; there he suddenly stops, looking out.) He is on the stage! (A supplementary curtain falls. The wait between this and the second part of the act should be almost momentary.)

Part Second.

Magnificent hall in the palace of Count Octavio. Table and arm chair on the right. Hangings, with armor, on each side of the scene.

Yorick as Octavio; Edmund as Manfred; Alice as Beatrice; Walton as Landolfo; the Prompter in his place. (A half-umbrella shaped thing in the floor of the stage.) At the end of the action, Shakespear, Woodford, Thomas and other actors and employees of the theatre.

The Count and Landolfo speak together without being heard by Beatrice and Manfred, who are at the other side of the scene, their attitudes and faces betraying dismay and sorrow.

Yorick as the Count:

> Landolfo, though a deep anxiety
> Preyed on my heart when thou wert absent,
>> yet
> Thy presence causes me still greater sorrow:
> Prythee, if thou hast that letter still
> Give it me now, and end at least my doubt.

Walton as Landolfo, giving him Edmund's letter: Take it.

Y. as the C., receiving it with emotion: Oh!

Walton: (I am avenged!)

Y. as the C.: Go, Landolfo. (Landolfo bows and retires. As Walton reaches the left door he looks back at Yorick with malicious joy.)

Alice as Beatrice, in a low, agitated tone: Manfred!

Edmund as Manfred: Beatrice!

A. as B.: The hour has come!

Y. as the C., to Beatrice:

> Now, I shall know at last thy lover's name!
> Tremble, unfaithful woman, tremble ingrate,
> Who hast robbed me of my honor and my
>> peace.
> Vain all thy cunning, for here stands revealed
> Thy guilt.

(He opens the letter, and draws near the table where there are lights.)

My blood is frozen in my veins!
(Without looking at the letter.)
Now let it burn like fire! Woe to the wretch
For whose vile sake thou bring'st this shame
upon me!
(He fixes his eyes on the paper and starts violently.) How! What!
(Overwhelmed with amazement Yorick forgets the play and speaks
in his own tone. Edmund and Alice look at him in dismay.)

The Prompter: "Oh, what do I behold!" (He prompts Yorick loudly, and slaps the MS. on the floor to attract his attention, thinking he
has forgotten himself.)

Yorick: What is this?

Prompter: O Lord, no! "What do I behold!" (He thrusts his head
from his conch-shell, and prompts still more loudly.)[9]

Yorick: Ah! Merciful God! (He utters these words of the play as if
they were the expressions of his own anguish. He drops helpless
into the armchair near the table, and hides his face in his hands. A
pause. Yorick looks round slowly at Edmund and Alice, and then at
the audience, and so remains motionless without knowing what to
do, supporting himself by the table. Then he mechanically declaims the words of the play:)
Here, there is no escape in doubt: the truth
Imprisons me! Come.
(To Alice and Edmund, who tremulously approach.)
Look!
(With reviving energy, showing them the letter.)

Edmund and Alice:
Oh!
(They give a real cry at [the] sight of the letter, and shrink back in
terror.)

Yorick as the Count:
Would the earth
Might swallow us!
(He drops again into the chair, and stares at the letter, and then,
as with desperate resolve, flings himself threateningly towards

9. WDH added a penciled note on the original manuscript: "(On the continental stage the prompter has a little roof in the floor of the stage that hides
him from the audience.)"

Edmund, but checks himself, and looks at the audience giving
them to understand the tumult of emotions in his soul. He turns his
eyes away, and they fall upon Alice; he rushes towards her, but
again checks himself, and goes up the middle of the stage, pressing
his hands alternately to his forehead and his heart. Edmund and
Alice look on in terror.)

The Prompter:
      "Wert thou the villain, then"—
(In a loud voice, and slapping the floor with his MS.)
      "Wert thou the villain, then"—
(Yorick, yielding to the circumstances, and unable to master his
fury, makes the situation of the play his own, and speaks to
Edmund in the words of the person he represents. From this point
the dramatic fiction is converted into vivid reality, and Alice,
Edmund and Yorick all lose themselves in its characters.)[10]
      Why, what accursed coil is this, thou knave?
      Thou mockst me with a mimic misery
      So apt with that which eats into my soul,
      That I could well believe you[r] poet made
      My wretchedness the mirror of his art
      His words spring to my lips; they speak my
        hate,
      My fury, my despair! Thou painted count,
      Thou poor unreal thing, thou effigy,
      Yorick and thou are one in wretchedness:
      Let us be one in language, and speak thou
      For me that else were speechless in amaze
      Before this Devil's miracle of falsehood!
      I make thy griefs my own and from this point,
      I'll be no longer Yorick, but Octavio;
      And oh, let them beware, whose guilt has
        turned
      This shadow of sorrow into living shame
      When Yorick and Octavio unite
      To right their wrongs!

10. WDH added a penciled note on the original manuscript: "(In order to
make this intention of the dramatist clear, and to put the audience fully in
possession of it, I have written the following lines, which I think should be
here introduced.)"

(To the prompter:)
>   What was the word thou gavest?
Prompter: "Wert thou the villain"
Yorick: "Aye, well!"
(He now turns fiercely on Edmund, and speaks as the Count.)
Yorick as the Count:

>   Wert thou the villain, then, thy faithless wretch,
>   The infamous seducer, thou, whose hand
>   Could strike his benefactor to the heart?
>   Thou, hapless orphan, that didst owe my pity
>   Succour and home, and foundst at once in me
>   Father and friend? And art thou then the thief
>   That robbed me of my wife? And wert thou he
>   That put this mark of shame upon my brow,
>   To make me, while I live, the mock of men,
>   A hissing and a by-word? O, the serpent
>   Henceforth should hide himself, to be outdone
>   By one that wears the semblance of a man!
>   My God! Is this the recompence he earns
>   Who pities and who trusts the friendless? No!
>   Even as I am, wounded and shamed to death,
>   I still rejoice that I had pity on thee,
>   That I did trust thee! No, on the betrayer
>   Fall the dishonor and disgrace! To the betrayed
>   Be all respect!

Edmund as Manfred: Oh, father!
Y. as C.:   Do I dream?

>   Thy father, I? Then may a father's curse
>   Be evermore on such a son as thou!

E. as M.: O no, no, no! What hast thou said?
Y. as C.: (to A. as B.)   And thou,
>   Unhappy woman, what shall I say to thee?
(With a slow and measured accent.)

>   Thou standest there so breathless and so mute,
>   So all immovable, with thy gaze so fixed,
>   That I could swear thou wert carved out of
>   marble
>   But that I hear the violent palpitation
>   With which thy heart responds to mine. Oh,
>   where,

Where is the light that in a fatal hour
Shone on me from those beautiful eyes of
    thine,
Whose timorous softness shamed the evening-
    star?
Where is that face divine, wher[e]in together
The red-rose and the orange blossom glowed?
And is there nought of all those fair allures
Left now to paint thy visage gaunt and white?
How suddenly sin can make us hideous!
—I saw thee first—would I had never seen
    thee!
When sad and wayworn I drew near the
    bounds
Of middle-life, and unto me thou wast
A ray of sunshine from a clouded heaven!
My sadness turned to rapture, I adored thee
With all my whole soul, as men look up to
    angels!
Who could have dreamt thy loveliness was the
    mask,
The white sepulchre, of a rotten heart?
But now that o'er the blackness of the pit
The beauteous lie can throne itself no more,
Now I can see that thou wert false as fair,
And I can hate thee—Nay, I do not know
Whether I hate or love thee! Woe to thee,
For love turned madness knows not how to
    pardon.
(*He seizes her hand, and continues violently.*)
And if thou wouldst I should not strike thee
    dead,
Look at me, face to face, and die of shame!
(*He dashes her to her knees.*)
Alice as B.: O, Mercy!
Y. as the C.: In vain thy criest me mercy.
Thou shalt have none!
E. as M.: And yet she merits it.
Y. as the C.: Nor she, nor thou!
A. as B.: My life belongs to thee:

O have a little pity, and kill me quickly!

E. as M.: I alone wronged you, and on me alone
Let your wrath fall.

Y. as the C.: The guilt belongs to both,
And both of you shall render me account.

E. as M.: She too? And will you kill her with your hand?

Y. as the C.: Fool! for such guilt as hers could I do less
Than kill her?

A. as B.: Ay, I do but ask to die,
For life is nothing if not innocent.
My blood can give him back his name, unstained.
My blood alone can wash away his shame!

Y. as the C.: Oh, thou wouldst die content if *he* were spared!
But his blood shall be shed as well as thine,
And his blood first. (*He snatches two swords from the wall.*)

E. as M.: O fatal night!

A. as B.: O heaven!

Y. as the C.: (presenting the swords.)
Choose thy sword.

E as M: Yes, to sheath it in my breast.
(*He seizes a sword, and turns the point on himself.*)

Y. as the C.: (turning his on Alice.)
And I will sheath mine in thy paramour's!

E. as M.: Oh! (He flings himself before her.)

Y. as the C.: Then defend her! And remember well
It is the hand of vengeance threatens her!

A. as B.: No! In the name of pity let me die!

E. as M., transported by his love:
As long as I have life thou shalt not die!

Y. as the C.: Then thou art ready to defend her? Thou
Wilt fight with me?

E. as M.: I will.

Y. as the C.: In very earnest?
Regardless who I am and who thou art?

E. as M.: Yes!

Y. as the C.: And thou'lt do thy best to kill me?

E. as M.: Yes! By heaven, I will!

A. as B. to Edmund: Oh, stay!

E. as M.: No, never!

A. as B.: Listen—

E. as M., beside himself with fury: This man's thy enemy!

A. as B.: Eternal God!

Yorick as the C.: Good, then; we fight this quarrel to the death!

E. as M.: Crime cries for crime, and hell is all too good
For such as thine! (*They fight furiously.*)

A. as B., clinging to E: Oh, Hold!

E. as M.: Unhand me!

A. as B.: Wait!

Y. as the C.: Thou makest him lose heart.

A. as B., clinging to Yorick: Then listen, you!
Be merciful!

Y. as the C.: Thou aidest him against me?

A. as B., shrinking from him: O, cruel!

(The fight is renewed.)

E. as M., feeling himself wounded: Heavens!
 (He drops his sword and falls heavily.)

Y. as the C., to Alice: Look!

(He points at E. with his sword.)

A. as B.: Ah!

E. as M. dying: God, forgive me!

(Alice runs to him, bends over him, and after touching him gives
a terrible cry, and springs to her feet staring at her hands.)

Alice: Blood!— Edmund! Blood! Help! Mercy!

Yorick: Silence! (He drops on his knees beside Edmund.)

Shakespear, coming from the left hand door: Yorick, what hast
thou done? (He looks at E. and touches him. Woodford, Thomas,
and all the actors and employees crowd round with expressions of
amaze and horror. Some kneel, some stand, and hide the sight from
the audience.)

Alice: Blood—blood on every hand! A sea of blood that I am
drowning in!

Yorick: Silence!

Shakespear, turning to the audience: Gentlemen, the play cannot
go on. Carried away by his part, the comedian Yorick, has actually
wounded the actor who was playing Manfred. Nor is this the only
misfortune. The famous tragedian Walton—

Yorick and Alice: Walton!

Shakespeare to the audience: —has just been found in the street,
stabbed through the heart.

(Here the supplementary curtain falls, and then follows the end.)

Yorick, starting up from Edmund's body, with sudden energy:[11]
>
>> Stabbed? Walton stabbed? Why, then, he
>>> stabbed himself!
>> I had not thought Walton had so much cour-
>>> age!
>> Brave fellow! Stabbed himself! Oh, well, well,
>>> well!
>> I drop a tear to Walton. But unless
>> I could weep blood I have no tears for this.

(He drops on his knees beside Edmund, and passing his arm tenderly under his neck looks down into his face.)

>> My boy, my boy, my boy! (To Shakespear:)
>> Why, look you, Master,
>> He was a little lad when first I saw him,
>> Tattered, and wan with hunger, with such eyes,
>> Full of such silent histories of sorrow,
>> Of orphanage, and all the world's unkindness,
>> They went straight to my heart. I took him
>>> thither
>> And there I have kept him ever since; nor love
>> Nor hate, nor even murder, could
>> Dislodge him. There he lieth dead, within
>> My heart. O I could tell you things, of how
>> I used to watch him in the night, and rise
>> And creep and kneel beside his little bed
>> Where we had prayed together ere he slept
>> And listen to his breathing, feel his pulse,
>> To know if any sickness threatened him.
>> If he were hurt, I suffered more than he;
>> His childish joys made me a happy child.
>> You all can hear me witness how I loved him:
>> My love has made me many a time the laugh
>> Of all of you. You can remember how
>> I used to look for him when he came from
>>> school,
>> Running to meet me— O me, methinks I
>>> dream;

11. WDH added a penciled note on the original manuscript: "These are the lines which W.D.H. supplies to close the tragedy."

And am not I or was not what I was!
And when he grew a man, he grew a man
After my heart, so generous, true and bold,
So faithful and so loving— Oh, well, well!
This hand to which thy little hand so oft
Clung in the dark for safety, this red hand
That took thy life away, did only snatch
My darling from the ruin that offered
His soul to Hell! Oh, would that some kind
      hand
Had been as good to me before I saw
You hapless creature whom my love was
      doomed
To doom to such black sorrow. Alice, child,
Get thee away from England; seek abroad
Some convent's shelter, and there spend thy
      life,
Thy poor, spoiled life, in prayer for all of us,
For him, and for thyself, and most for me!
(He rises from Edmund's body.)
And Walton stabbed himself! Why, good for
      Walton!
Stabbed through the heart? Why, then, he had
      a heart.
O yes; I know he had a heart: I wrung it
With torture here, one day—poor soul, poor
      Walton!
(To Shakespear.) Master, how ill a thing it is to
      be
Revenged! Ay, vengeance is too much
For us weak mortals—the blood makes us
      drunk,
It makes us mad! Ay, vengeance is the Lord's:
"Vengeance is mine; I will repay," He said.
He will repay; He will repay, He said.
Canst thou imagine how I could kill my boy?
It must have been an accident, methinks;
A slip o' the foot, an error of the hand
That did so often bless him. I would fain

Know how it chanced. Lend me thy sword
   good master.
Since *he* hath worn my point within his heart,
   I—cannot touch it.
(Shakespear shrinks back, but Yorick snatches his sword from its sheath.)

Why, be not afraid!
You are thinking of that blackamoor of Venice;
And surely not of this poor, merry Yorick,
That never yet was apt for tragedy.
I shall not harm myself: I am past all harm!
I[t] must have happened thus.
(As he turns the point on his breast, they start towards him; he laughs and removes it.)

Nay, do not fear:
If I should pass this rapier through my breast,
It would not hurt me; I am dead within.
Shakespear: Seize him; stay him! He's mad!
Yorick: no; *was* mad.
(Kneeling beside Edmund.)

Kiss me once more, my boy: thy lips are yet
Warm with the life shall redden them no more.
O, Edmund, Edmund, Edmund! Oh my son!
My hope, my pride, my hero among men!
My good sweet boy, my little loving lad!
(Kisses him)

Here, Shakespear, take thy sword! It tempts
   me.
(He suddenly thrusts it into his breast; then withdraws it and flings it to Sh. He falls on Edmund's body.)

Alice, dropping on her knees beside them: Mercy!

Curtain

Excerpt from *A New Play*

This altered opening scene of *A New Play,* to judge from a penciled headnote, was written by William Seymour, an actor in Lawrence Barrett's company, in July 1879. It was revised by W. D. Howells in August 1879, and it remained the version of the first scene performed by Barrett's company to the end of his career. Howells' alterations to Seymour's text are printed in bold-face. By this point in the evolution of the play, the character named Shakespeare in the early draft has been renamed Heywood. This manuscript, with its interpolations in Howells' handwriting and familiar blue ink, is also located in the V. B. Price Collection in Albuquerque.

A New Play.

Act I.

Scene: A room in Yorick's house. Enter Gregory L.2.E. preceding two servants. One of them bears Alice's portrait, heavily framed, the other an easel.

Gregory.

Hither! Hither! this way, I say! Look that you mar it not, or woe upon your lives. 'Twere the same in my master's eyes, as if you offered wrong to Mistress Alice herself.

1ˢᵗ Servant (with easel.)

Nay, we know our parts. Master Warrener hath given us our charges. (*Placing, and arranging Easel R.H. near window R.2.E.*) Here, brother, set it here.

Gregory. (regarding Easel)

And what manner of strange, three-legged beast is that, prythee?

2ᵈ Servant

(*setting picture upon the Easel.*) Ay, a beast, indeed. Well said, goodman Gregory. For it['ls called by the Frenchman "a little horse"; and by your Italian "a pony," and by your high Dutchman "an ass"—the more ass he! "It will not kick, it will not shy," quoth our master— "Fear not! 'twill bear you safely":—said he not so, brother?

1ˢᵗ Serv.

Ay, that he did. And then we laughed—"ha, ha!"— We know how to laugh at this saying—he gave us each sixpence, and bade us go drink a mug of ale to his good health.

2ᵈ Serv. (significantly to Gregory.)

Aye—he gave us sixpence each—

1ˢᵗ Serv.

And bade us go drink—

2ᵈ Serv.

Aye—to your fair mistress' health.

1ˢᵗ Serv.

He gave us—

2ᵈ Serv.

Truly, 'twas sixpence each, no less!

Gregory.

Oh! a plague o' you! Think you that ye should leave Yorick's roof without remembrance, on Yorick's birthday? There! There—ye varlets! (*Gives them money.*) Get ye gone!

2ᵈ Serv.

Save you, goodman Gregory!

1ˢᵗ Serv.

My service to you, master.

{*Exeunt L.2.E.*}

Gregory.

Master!— Well—well—'tis a good lad! He meant no harm, though I am but Yorick's poor old serving man. "Master!" Aye, he meant no ill. 'Twas a good face: I like not the other with his bold "goodmans" and his "Gregories"!

{*Enter Dorothy R.2.E.*}

Dorothy: What art thou mopping and mowing about now, Gregory?

Gregory. A saucy knave, I say, to call me goodman!

Dorothy. A saucy knave indeed! I would never call thou Goodman. 'Twere the same as I should say husband, and that were too bold.

Gregory, *flattered*. Not in thee, sweet Dorothy; not in thy mouth.

Dorothy. Nay, nay, I know the respect that should be paid to age and its infirmities: I would call thee *Gaffer*. Ha, ha, ha!

(*As Gregory moves indignantly down the stage, carrying the easel before him:*) What has thou there, Gaffer Gregory, that I partly spy between the ribs of thy skeleton?

Gregory, *setting it down:* Never ask aught of me, thou jade. Look for thyself if thou may'st face the effigy of one that is a daily reproof to all lightness and folly.

Dorothy. Oh, Mistress Alice's picture sent home! I care not for Mistress Alice's picture.

Gregory. And why, Mistress Malapert?

Dorothy. Because I care not for the moonlight when the sun shines, or for a death's-head when thou art by. (*Coaxingly*.) Wilt thou marry me, Gaffer Gregory? 'Tis the fashion of the house for old men to mate with young wives, and I would mourn for thee truly when thou madest me a widow. (*A knocking*.) There, thou art called. Stay not to woo! Fly, fly, thou spectre! Ha, ha, ha! Is the picture for Master Edmund?

Gregory. No, chatterer, for Master Yorick.

Dorothy. Oh, methought Master Edmund might at least have the shadow. Poor Master Edmund! He should be an old man.

Gregory, What dost thou mean, thou— (*Knocking again*)

Dorothy. Dost thou stay, yet? Why[,] thou wilt linger when Death knocks for thee. Run—limp—crawl! (*Exits.*) (*To the portrait*) O dost thou think *I* am blind, Mistress? Thou a reproof to folly!

{*Re-Enter Gregory ushering in Heywood.*}
Gregory.

Good Master Heywood, you are come upon the instant. {*Dor. curtseys to him*}

Hey.

For what, Gregory, for what?

Greg. (*indicating the portrait.*)

To welcome Mistress Alice home.

Hey.

So! Master Warrener hath finished his work in time. (*to Dorothy.*) **Let thy mistress know my coming, pretty Dorothy.**

(*Dor. curtseys & exits.*) (*Hey. turning lightly away and laughing.*} Well, 'tis a quaint fancy and like Yorick, to make himself a gift of his wife's portrait on his birthday.

Greg.

'Tis all his love of her. 'Tis like father and daughter to see them together. His hair just touched with frost, and her's all sunshine! 'Tis like April and October—I can think of nothing else.

Hey. (absently.)

And Yorick is five and forty to-day!

Greg.

Truly—truly. You are right, Master Heywood. And Mistress Alice is a good child—a good child—and she hath never turned to look at any of the fine court gallants that go mad of her beauty, and write themselves blind upon her eyebrows.

Alice.

(*who has entered unknown to Gregory R.3.E.*) Thanks, good Gregory. But defend me not to every one, or thou wilt make the world suspect me.

Greg.

Nay, never fear for me, Mistress Alice. I am no fool.

Alice. (laughing)

Well, well! Go now, and make ready against thy master's coming. He will be here anon.

Greg.

Ay, mistress. (*As he goes, aside*) Where is Master Edmund? He never failed before to be the first to welcome Yorick on his birthday. Why does he stay away—why? (*Exits mumbling L.2.E.*)

Alice.

I have made you wait, Master Heywood. Cry you mercy! (*Drops a curtsey in mock humility.*)

Hey.

(*indicating the portrait with exaggerated compliment.*) Nay, you have been here ever since I came, only I marvel you did not speak before.

Alice. (archly.)

Was it too long for a woman to keep silence? You think the picture is not like, then?

Hey.

Like? Oh—a good map!

Alice.

Map, do you call it? That's a phrase for Master Warrener the Limner. When I shall tell him **the terms of Master Heywood's praise**, you shall see the painter's pencil to a rapier turn—his palette to a buckler **and woe to thee when you encounter**! Come, now, some kinder word. Is it not alive? Doth it not breathe? Doth it not follow you with its eyes about the room? (*She moves playfully about from one corner to another.*) Is there not somewhat of Appelles here? Oh, Appelles at the very least! You cannot say *less* than Appelles.

Hey.

Well, well, say Appelles, and all the other masters of antiquity to boot. Truly, if Warrener was not inspired—he should have been.

Alice.

What should have been our painter's inspiration?

Hey.

Not wholly thy fair look, though thou shoulds't know
By this time that thy looks are fair indeed.
Thy goodness, child, that shines through every word, glance, act of thine, transfiguring all thy life—**might well have touched his brush with heavenly light.** (*As he speaks, Alice droops[,] sighs[,] turns away*) There, I have made thee blush!

Alice (evasively)

I am sorry Yorick is not here!

Hey.

Nay, my errand was half to you. I came to wish you joy—both you and Yorick—of this happy day.

Alice (trying to recover herself.)

Only to wish us joy?

Hey.

Oh, aye! And to temper his raptures a little with some talk of affairs.

Alice.

I might have known it. Atlas is ever bearing up the globe. You have come to talk of the new play, I warrant me. Cannot you leave us poor **fictions** of your stage one little day of real life? I was trying to feign myself the happy wife of a happy husband— in and for myself—not in any play, but in very truth, and here you come—

Hey.

Is it so difficult a fancy, then, that you cannot resume it afterwards, when we have spoken of the play?

Alice.

(*with a touch of consciousness*) Difficult? What mean you, Master Heywood?

Hey.

I? I meant nothing—nothing!

(*Yorick, bursting in upon them L.2.E.*)

Yorick.

Nothing, whatever, I will dare be sworn! What was he saying? {*Embraces Heywood, while he speaks to Alice.*)

Alice (*embarrassed*)

Oh, nothing, nothing!

Yorick.

Why, so I said!

Hey.

Yorick, I came to wish you many happy days,
Like this, but happier, and brighter each,
Till your round century makes you last of us.

Yorick.

Oh! do not wish me to outlive my friends.
For I have but a weak and doting heart,
And were a sorry centenarian—
No gayer than a youngster crossed in love!—
Without the kindness that hath filled my life.
But I'll live on another fifty years
In friendly memories, if thou wilt, as one
That made men laugh, till not one bitter drop
Lurked in his blood for any soul on earth.

Hey.

Not even Walton?

Yorick.

Nay, not even Walton.

Hey.

Well, I believe it, and die when thou wilt
I will write down these words thy epitaph.
There's nothing that I should enjoy so much—
As writing Yorick's epitaph.

Yorick. (*laughing*)

Why, this
Is like a friend indeed.

Alice.

Oh, do not talk
Of epitaphs on such a day as this! (**On Yorick's coming
into the room she has placed herself before the
portrait as if to hide it.**)

Yorick.

Nay, thou says't well! Our talk should be of—what?
(*He looks about the room in feigned inquiry.*)

Our talk should be, methinks, of lofty themes:
Of beauty taught to be immortal, of sweet eyes
Bidden shine with fadeless lustre after ours
Are dim with dust! Our talk should be of—painting!
Our talk should be of fine arts—of the art
The limner hath to image of Loveliness,
And the art of Loveliness to hide herself!

(He runs suddenly upon Alice, and pulls her away from before the portrait.)

Ah, thou rogue! What art can equal thine?
Except my own! Always except my own!
And did'st thou think that I should not have known
This masterpiece was present, though the clouds
Of damnest night involved it from mine eyes?
This is a work appeals to *all* the senses!
Hast seen it, Heywood?

Heywood. Aye, I have seen it, Yorick.

Yorick. But you should know how it came to be here. You
should have heard the pretty encounter of our wit when I
thought to have it done. She would fain have made me some
other gift for my birthday. "Nay[,] give me your self," quoth I.
"Me you have already," quoth she. "I would have you more
and more," quoth I. "I am but one, and that one you have,"
said she. "Be two!" said I. "Sit for Master Warrener, the limner,
and let him paint me your face, that in your absence it may
look on me, and seem to smile and say: She hath you in her
heart, as you have her in yours, and grieves to be with you.

Alice, putting her hand over his mouth, Nay, then, sir, this
passes patience. Wilt thou have done?

Yorick, kissing the hand on his mouth, before he takes it
down, and holds it in his: Forever, on these terms! *To*

Heywood. Well, what dost thou think of the picture?
> *Alice.*
> Oh, you should have heard him only now,
> Lauding it with fine phrases; bidding me
> Tell Master Warrener 'twas a good *map.*
> > *Yorick (gaily.)*
> Map? And, why, sweetheart—so it is a map.
> It is the world! The world in which I live:—
> The pleasantest country where my soul abides!

(*Putting his arm around her waist, and leading her up to the picture.*)
> Map's not so ill, and yet a better word,
> Methinks he might have chosen—say, a landscape.
> Here are your golden harvest fields of hair—
> Here your white brow—a buckwheat field in bloom—
> And here those lovely blue twin lakes—your eyes—
> From which, like rounded shores, do rise your cheeks
> A wilderness of roses and of lilies:—
> And here your lips—and here your lips—And here your
> lips—
> > *Alice (laughing)*
> Oh, come, come, come!
> Come get you to my lips!
> > *Yorick (kissing her.)*
> Why, so I will!
> > *Alice (pulling away from him.)*
> Nay, then, I meant not that.
> You shall not cheat me of the proper phrase.
> Come, now, begin again. My hair is like
> A wheat field, or a haystack, and my brow
> As brown as buckwheat meal— oh! And my eyes
> Pale watery green, like two dull pools: my cheeks
> Purple as thistles, and my lips—my lips—
> > *Yorick (rapturously.)*
> The praise of them is inarticulate.
> A bird might chirp out something like the sound.
> > *Alice.*
> Or a door creak it!
> > *Yorick.*

(*Clasps Alice's waist, and drawing her to him, fondly, addresses Heywood.*)

Heywood, you have not wished me half the joy
That is my due, this day.

     Hey.

Then take the rest
With all my heart!

     Yorick.

And didst thou not remember
My birthday also was our wedding day?

     Hey.

I do remember now, but on my word
I had forgotten. I wish you joy again.

     Yorick.

Three years ago, a fair and trusting girl
Laid her dear hand in mine, who might have been
Her father, but that the youth within my love
Made me the youngest husband in the land.
If I should tell how she hath blessed my life,
T'would seem such profanation, as if I
Should boast of Heaven—and I will not speak.

     Alice.

Oh, Yorick!

     Yorick.

There is no speck, flaw in my content!
I am so wholly, absolutely happy,—
Except—except— Why is not Edmund here,
On this my birthday morn? Heywood, I know not
What I should think of Edmund's waywardness.
Is it my fancy that I find him cold?
This is his home, **and Edmund is** my son;
And yet I rarely **see** him at my board,
And never **more** a night beneath my roof.

     Hey.

The boy is steeped in study. **I never see him but with**
book in hand, lacklustre eyes, and lost to all his
friends.

     Alice.

Yes, Yorick, 'tis his study—do not think of it. (Knocking
L.2.E.) Why, that's his knock!

     Yorick (starts)

The time hath been he hath not staid to knock.

(*Enter Gregory L.2.E.*)
Greg.

Master Yorick—

Yorick (quickly.)

Is Edmund there?

Greg.

Master Yorick!

Yorick.

Does he **wait** to be announced? Ha! ha! ha! Let me go usher in this
Sir Punctill[i]o! {*Starts toward the door, and runs into the arms of
Woodford, who is entering.*}

Greg.

There! there! I told you it was not Master Edmund.

Yorick.

You might have told me in the course of time.
But never mind. (*To Woodford.*)
You, sir, whom I have taken so warmly to my heart,
You shall not say I drove you from my door.
Welcome!

Hey. (coming forward.)

This is the author of our new play;
Brave Master Woodford, whom a fortnight hence
I shall not need to name to anyone.

{*Woodford and Yorick salute each other, then Yorick takes him by
the hand and leads him up to Alice's portrait.*}

Yorick.

And this is Mistress Alice, Yorick's wife. {*Woodford stops, and stares
round confusedly.*}

Hey. (laughing.)

Yorick! Yorick! What a mad wag thou art!

Yorick.

(*Keeping hold of Woodford's arm and leading him gravely up to
Alice.*) And this is her picture, painted in oils, after the new Venice
fashion, and but now sent home by Master Warrener the limner. Is
it not like, sir? How cunningly the painter hath counterfeited nature
in these eyes, that seem to move and to have speculation in them.
See this smiling mouth that might any moment break in laughter—

Alice (laughing and hiding her face.)

For shame, Yorick, for shame! {*She continues to laugh. Yorick looks
round with affected surprise; he runs back to portrait, then returns*}

to Alice, as if in doubt which is which. Then he bows very low to Woodford.)

Yorick.

Good sir, I do entreat your pardon for my error, for which the painter's skill is much to blame. I see more clearly now, and I do assure you that yonder is the portrait and this is the lady. Trust me, 'tis so—'tis so. This—*this* is Mistress Alice.

Woodford.

The heroine, I hope, of my new play!

Alice.

Why that shall be as Master Heywood will.
We are but puppets in his sovereign hands.
We rage, we languish, burn with hate, or love.
Kiss—kill—weep, bleed, live, die, or walk as ghosts.
Just as he chooses to appoint our parts.
He is a pitiless tyrant to us players—
I hope his poets find him merciful.

Wood.

Why, truly, Madam, I have nothing to lament in Master Heywood's usage. My play coming to him as it hath, with Master Shakespeare's praise—'tis not as if it were unfriended, and 'tis not as if I approached him without authority.

Yorick.

Hath Master Shakespeare praised it? Then, I warrant me, he hath not indulged his envious wont of striking all the good things from your page.

Wood.

Why, truly, as to that, good Master Yorick, we have not agreed, as I could wish, on certain passages. At his insistence I have greatly reduced the speeches—

Yorick.

Oh, shameful!

Wood.

And several scenes I have suppressed.

Alice.

Oh, cruel!

Wood.

And some of the highest languaged encounters, where I had spent my very best on verse, I have, at his instance, resolved to their native prose.

Alice.

Why, this is sacrilege—

Hey.

Good Mistress Alice, if you embroil me with this poet again, whom, after dire endeavor, I have brought to know his place—under the manager's feet—I swear you shall play his whole tragedy yourself.

Wood.

Ha, ha! Very good. I' faith, very good. Good, by'r lady! If Mistress Alice *might* but play it all—

Hey.

See to what a pass you have flattered him already. Yorick, will you not use a husband's authority?

Yorick.

Nay. She does my pleasure, whatever she may do. But let us hear Master Woodford expound the argument of his play, **for I fancy he hath honored us in seeking you to talk after distribution of the parts.** How runs it, sir?

Wood.

The manner of my tragedy is this. The Count Octavio hath a young wife, and his son loves her. This is known to all—

Alice. (with sensation.)

What!

Wood.

That the young man loves his adoptive father's wife. This is known to all—to all but the Count Octavio, of course—it ever befalls so— ha! ha!

Yorick.

'Tis true. 'tis a good point. 'Tis nature. {*Puts his arm around Alice.*}

Wood.

Then the Count hath a familiar, one Landolfo, who, by means of a letter, acquaints him with the guilt of his son and wife—

Alice.

Horrible!

Wood.

Aye! 'Tis strong—and so they fight, and the young man is slain.

Alice.

Oh, slain!

Wood.

By his father's hand. I had a touch there that Shakespeare pronounced the best in the whole play. (*Fumbles with his ms. as if to seek it*)

Yorick.

'Tis a good argument—and these are the chief persons. The Count and his son—what call you him?

Wood.

Manfredo—'tis in Spanish taste.

Yorick.

Aye—and the wife?

Wood.

Beatrice.

Yorick.

Very good--and then this villain Landolfo. Master Heywood, of whom think you for the part of Beatrice?

Hey.

Mistress Alice, with your leave.

Yorick.

Excellent! and whom have you chosen for Manfredo?—Edmund?

Hey.

You have guessed.

Yorick.

I could not have erred. There are no such lovers as they to be found in any theatre. Excellent well! And the villain goes to Walton.

Hey.

Why, there I have been given pause. Walton is a good villain—

Yorick.

Nature framed him so!

Hey.

Nay—you said but now you had no unkindness even for Walton.

Yorick.

Said I so?—I lied! I did but wish I had none.

Hey.

Well—here comes the rub. Walton is our first player, and the Count Octavio is the principal part. If I give him the villain, who will play Octavio?

Yorick.

Ah! (*after a pause.*) Is there no part in our new play for me, Master Woodford?

Wood. (bowing)

Sir, you know me past all deserving. But my poor play is a *tragedy.*

Yorick. (*ironically.*)

Aye, so! And yet, methinks—or am I wrong to think it?—
Shakespeare writ tragedy.

Wood.

The highest!

Yorick.

And still he put some light-heart jester in.

Wood.

Oh! there, by your leave, I have thought Master Shakespeare out of
taste.

Yorick. (*musingly.*)

I do remember me that once the Master
Would have me walk with him in London streets,
Where oft he loved to note the passing crowd,
And make his studies from the life. It chanced
That as we went we talked of tragedy:—
"And, pray thee, what is tragedy," I cried.
We had stopped to hear a strolling mountebank,
Making the crowd roar with his cap and bells,
When on a sudden there arose a shriek,
And a wild mother caught her dead child up
From under flying wheels. The fool, who knew not,
Capered and babbled on! And the great master
Seized on my arm, and pointed—"There, there, there!"
'Twas all he said.

Wood.

Grant you that. But we do not copy life. We but choose—banish
and reject.

Yorick.

Aye, so? Well, I would fain see your play, though I be elected,
chosen, banished, or rejected out of it— Hist! what step is that
upon the stairs. That's my lad! That's my boy Edmund— (*goes to
door L.2.E. and listens.*) No—no—**it was** not he! He **doth** not
come. (*back to C.*) Have you children, Master Woodford?

Wood.

Three lovely boys—I cannot call them less.

Yorick.

Nor should you. And they love you, these three boys?

Wood.

As dearly, I do think, as I love them.

> *Yorick.*
> You have not noticed that, as they grew older,
> They waxed indifferent and cold to you?
> > *Wood.*

No.

> > *Yorick.*
Nor seemed to seek your absence?
> > *Wood.*

No, indeed.

> > *Yorick.*
Nor distraught and silent in your presence?
> > *Wood.*

Surely, no.

> > *Yorick.*
Why, this is strange! My Edmund— (*after a pause, with a sigh.*) I give you joy of them! If **Edmund** comes not I shall feel **that** I have been neither born or married! (**As if a thought had struck him.**) **Married! Why we must marry Edmund! Tis the only means to reclaim this runagate, and bring him back to the friends he shuns. Alice!**

Alice, starting: **Sir?**

Yorick: **Thou must help me find a wife for Edmund. What think'st thou of Mistress Rosabel?**

Alice painfully: **For Edmund?**

Yorick: **Aye, for Edmund. Not for Heywood, nor for Master Woodford, nor even for me. For Edmund.**

Alice, distractedly: **Oh—she—she— She is fair, very fair; and she is quick of wit, and gay; and dances well; and plays passingly upon the spinnet [*sic*]; and—**

Yorick. **Well, well?**

Alice. **I fear she is fickle.**

Yorick. **Then she will never do, for Edmund is so absent of mind that he will forget his wife, and she must needs remember herself. What of pretty Mistress Celia? Is she not constant?**

Alice. **She is true, and she is good. She hath not all the graces, but she is very learned; and—**

Yorick: **Well?**

Alice. **Methinks she is but sober company.**

Yorick. Away with her! Edmund is dull enough. And Mistress Viola?

Alice: **Perfect.**

Yorick. Well?

Alice, demurely: **She hath one shoulder a little fatter.**

Yorick. Ha, ha, ha! I see that in thy eyes there is no one good enough for Edmund, and we must try otherwise to reclaim him. You will stay dinner with us, Master Woodford?

Wood.

Good **Master** Yorick, **hold me excused!**—for on a day of private merry making I must not stay. Pray, Madam, let me commend to your special kindness the part you are to bear in my tragedy. Without your interest in Beatrice, the best Octavio and Landolfo in the world cannot save it: fall it must! And though it be so opposite, madam, to your natural frame, to play the part of a lady who loves not her lord, let it not displease **you,** for at the worst she is innocent and doth hate—

Alice (hysterically.)

Enough—Enough— I understand!

Wood.

You shall see the delicacy with which I have endeavored it. A lawless and unhappy love so treated—the son to love his benefactor's wife—

Alice.

It is too terrible—

Wood.

And yet loving her not willingly—

Alice. (rising.)

No more—no more!

Wood.

Ah! It kindles your fancy. I'm glad of that. And for Master Edmund—he will not *play* his part—with his talent, he will *live* it.

Alice.

Merciful Heaven!

Wood.

There is a scene where the lovers are together and the husband comes suddenly upon them—

Alice.

(*in great excitement, appears faint. Yorick supports her*) Prithee, no more!

Wood.

'Tis the very action! 'Tis marvellous fine! If you can do it so in my play, they shall **clap** you to the skies. 'Tis no acting—'tis the very truth of nature.

Yorick.

Truth! (*Tenderly and seriously*) You do well to praise her in that word. The secret of her art—the secret of her life is—truth!

Alice, (distractedly,) O—aye—truth—better death than false-hood— Yorick, Yorick!

Yorick: O, my child!

Alice, No, no. 'Tis naught—a giddiness. (Commanding herself, and smiling) Good Master, you see how the mere argument of your tragedy plays upon a weak woman's nerves! Think what havoc it shall work upon the scene!

Woodford, with flattered and joyous effusion: O, could I but hope for such effect—

Alice, seriously: Write comedy hereafter. Though this tragic story comes from your brain, oh believe me, master poet, it shall go to many a stricken heart in them that hear it! Remember that even guilt may claim some pity, and the next time, be merrier and—mercifuller! Write comedy hereafter!

Dorothy, at the door: Mistress Alice, the cook hath sent me—

Alice: Aye, aye. Master Woodford, the truth muse calls me. 'Tis a man-muse, this truth, and weareth a white cap and apron, and his symbol is a basting spoon, and his votive bird a goose, stuffed! Fare you well! (She curtsies in mock ceremony, and Heywood gaily kisses his hand to her as she goes out.)

Heywood: By my soul, she is in herself all the muses in one—ten or ten thousand.

Woodford, enchantedly: How prettily she mocked away the effect of my tragedy!

Yorick: Yet not the less her soul abhorred the guilty case. I could see that it sank deep. But you shall see how her very recoil from it shall be the backward step with which the runner renders the greater leap. Her loathing of the treachery will teach her how to paint it best.

Woodford: If she but paint it to the world as she now colored it for us, she will make me immortal. But she shall not make you wish my death now in defect of my absence. Farewell, Master Yorick—

Yorick: And will you not stay my birthday feast?

Woodford, in going: Nay, nay! I will not be your skeleton. You shall feast in peace. Master Heywood, *will* you not think of Walton for the part of Octavio?

Heywood: I cannot think of any other. Stay, Master Woodford: I will go with you *now* to Walton.

Yorick. What, thou? Master Woodford, will you let me [be] robbed of *both* my guests? This is a sorry return. Nay, nay! (Detaining Heywood) Thou shalt not go! A thought has struck me. Thou shalt wait and see if it prove serious—or be at hand to call a physician.

Woodford: Ha, ha! Very good. Very excellent good. Well, then, Master Heywood, I will wait you at the Mitre when you have seen Master Yorick out of danger. We will go together to Master Walton's. Give you good day, gentlemen.

Yorick: Save you, Master Woodford, to write many tragedies. (Exit W.[)]

Heywood: Now, Yorick, what is thy thought? Or is it some new jest?

Yorick: Not unless thou make'st a jest of it, old friend.

Excerpt from *Civil Death*

W. D. Howells translated Paolo Giacometti's *La morte civile* for Lawrence Barrett in August 1880. Barrett ultimately chose not to perform the play, and the text of Howells' translation was subsequently lost to scholarship. The holograph fragment printed below, about half of the manuscript Howells completed (though apparently all that survives), is located in the V. B. Price Collection in Albuquerque.

CIVIL DEATH.

Act I

Parlor in the house of Dr. Palmieri, comfortably and pleasantly furnished. The ingress is in the center, other doors at the sides open into the garden, the library and the chambers.

Don Fernando and Agatha.

Fernando. So you would have known me at once?

Agatha. Instantly! One doesn't easily forget the face of a baby that one has suckled.

Fern. Even when it is equipped with a pair of cavalry moustaches? I was fourteen years old at least when you saw me last, and when my uncle, the syndic, sent me to school at Catania—

Ag. Ah! A great while ago! Don't you see, my dear little Fernando, how old I have grown? But you are as young as ever!

Fern. And was that the reason why, when you had looked me thoroughly over, you welcomed me with that cry of *Always the same?*

Agatha. Oh, no! I merely meant, always the same featherhead!

Fern. O many thanks! When you had hoped [manuscript torn—word missing] to see me serious, with brow knit in thought, and—

Ag. Ah, I had so often prayed the Lord th[at] you might turn out a great lawyer!

Fern. And a pretty turn you did me! with your praying!

Ag. I? How?

Fern. If one takes up a trade without liking, one never prospers in it.

Ag. And you call the law a trade?

Fern. Very often it becomes a trade. I yielded to my uncle's will with a bad grace, as you knew when he sent me to the university of Bologna, to study the law. But it was all a mistake: I studied little, I enjoyed much, and I came away with less sense than ever, and a great many debts.

Ag. And I suppose you expect your poor uncle to pay them?

Fern. Why, no, to tell the truth—well, not immediately: I expect his heir to pay them!

Ag. His heir? You?

Fern. I am the next of kin, and we are the last of our race. Come, Agatha, make me your compliment. As a good Italian you must admire me in the king's uniform. When Garibaldi came our way with his redshirts, there was no thinking of the law. I joined them, and went about with him helping to topple over all the little thrones in our neighborhood, and when we reached Naples and Garibaldi handed over the kingdom—as if it had been a pomegranate—to Victor Emmanuel, I passed into his majesty's service, and so I wear the jacket of one of his hussars. It is rather becoming, isn't it, Agatha?

Ag. Oh, mercy upon us! And this is the babe that I brought up so religiously, so piously, on my own milk. A Garibaldino. Oh, poor me! Think how furious his honor the syndic would be if he heard such things from you! Be careful with him, Fernando!

Fernando. I have been and I shall be. One must cherish even the foibles of a rich uncle, who has no other nephew. Why, to appease him, I have promised to do a little business for him in my old way—the way of the law. I have come here to-day to hold an inquest!

Ag. An inquest!

Fern. An inquest, or an inquisition. It is very pleasant and very innocent business: it is [an] inquest upon a lady!

Ag. A lady! Ah, I think I know; but it doesn't seem an affair for you[,] exactly. However, if his worship the syndic has sent you—But I thought you had come to see Dr. Palmieri, your old playmate, and to embrace me!

Fern. And you were partly right. I have already embraced you with considerable pleasure, and I shall be glad to see Arrigo again.— But this mysterious lady, whom the doctor, from what my uncle says, has brought with him from Catania, and is now concealing in these Calabrian shades—it is she who chiefly interests me. Who is she? What is her name?

Ag. Who is she? I don't know. What's her name? Rosalia.

Fern. There are many Rosalias in Sicily—I have known several, myself. But this particular Rosalia—is she a young girl?

Ag. Who knows?

Fern. Married?

Ag. Who knows?

Fern. Widow?

Ag. Who knows?

Fern. No one knows! Well, is she pretty?

Ag. (shrugging her shoulders) Hum!

Fern. Really, I shouldn't have asked you that last question.

Ag. Why?

Fern. Because an old woman never answers it: she always shrugs her shoulders as you did. No matter; I can decide for myself. As I understand, the case is this: My uncle, in his quality of syndic[,] is obliged to foster the local morality, eradicate abuses, and suppress evil example; and this fair unknown is at present wringing his virtuous spirit, rousing deleterious conjecture, and contaminating the consciences of the neighboring peasantry, by her equivocal position in this house.

Ag. Exactly. The scandal is terrible. And the evil example— When I go about this house I feel my feet burn as if I were walking on live coals!

Fern. Oh, poor old dove! Why not fly away?

Ag. Fly? If I only could! But what can I do? I was put here with the doctor by his worship the syndic himself, who has always been so kind to me—

Fern. That's very odd! Perhaps my uncle has had some cause to dislike the doctor?

Ag. I don't know.

Fern. And what is this cause?

Ag. Oh, Don Fernando, it can't be explained; it's too great an offense against morality.

Fern. Ah! Humph! Then, as I understand, my uncle is as great a friend of morality as ever?

Ag. Oh quite.

Fern. And of religion?

Ag. More.

Fern. And is still that pleasing mixture of bigot and hypocrite?

Ag. Your uncle is too good a man not to be grieved at such a nephew!

Fern. Very good, Agatha! Ha, ha! But then why has my scrupulous uncle placed you in this wicked house? Perhaps to stand guard, and report—

Ag. Oh—how should I know?

Fern. [*Sotto voce.*] (I shouldn't like it if they had planted a spy in my old friend's house.)

Ag. Excuse me, Don Fernando, but I must be looking after my work, now.

Fern. Wait. I wish to ask you one question more, and I don't want you to answer me with a shrug of the shoulders. Wasn't the doctor married?

Ag. He certainly was, but his wife died many years ago.

Fern. And where did she die?

Ag. In this very house, just two years before Dr. Arrigo went to Catania with his little Emma.

Fern. To Catania? It must have been after I came away, or we should have met. But has he never married since?

Ag. Who knows?

Fern. Oh, have done with your Who-knows!

Ag. What should I say?

Fern. Say anything else! Is it suspected that he married again?

Ag. Humph!

Fern. Secretly? With the mysterious Rosalia?

Ag. Well!

Fern. Humph! and Well! You make me [more] curious than a governess!

Ag. And I am not at all curious. (*Seeing Rosalia approach.*) Do you wish to see this unknown lady? (Pointing to the left.) Yonder she is.

Fern. I can't make out, precisely— She has a young girl with her— Who is it? Her daughter? The doctor's?

Ag. I don't know!

Fern. This is amusing! I like mysteries, and if I can find out—

Ag. Oh, but you can't!

Fern. Who knows? Stop! They're coming this way. Let us get back a little— (They withdraw to the bottom of the stage.)

Rosalia and Emma, and the others.

Rosalia. (*holding Emma's hand*) Shall we go down into the garden for some flowers, my dear?

Emma. O yes; and make a bouquet to give papa when he comes home from his sick people. Oughtn't I to give him flowers to pay him for the good he is always doing? I give him flowers, and he gives me kisses, and I have the best of the bargain, haven't I?

Rosalia. Yes, a parent's kisses are holy, as I know who shall never feel them any more.

Emma (*sadly*). Ah, and I only have them from him!

Ros. (quickly) Come, come, let us go into the garden. (*She starts to go, when Fernando, who has softly approached, encounters her.*)

Fern. Pardon me, if—

Em. (*aside to Ros.*) A gentleman? Who can it be?

Ros. (*after hav[ing] looked at Fern.*) I think I have seen him before, but—

Fern. I was looking—mere curiosity— (*To Agatha*) I think I knew her.

Ag. Really?

Ros. (*glancing at Fern., and speaking to herself.*) Yes, it is he— I knew it— But how to escape him? (To Fern.) Excuse me, sir, we are waited for—

Ag. By whom?

Fern. One moment, pray. Now that I recollect, I am sure that I am not mistaken.— We have met before—at Catania?

Ros. I do not remember it, sir.

Fern. Do not you remember that Don Fernando, who used to come to your father's, and was the friend of—

Ros. (*quickly in order to interrupt him.*) It may be— Indeed, I think— But it was so many years ago—

Fern. Some ten years.

Ag. Yes, ten years.

Ag. (*aside*) They know each other. Now we shall learn something.

Fern. What a lucky chance! And this charming little lady is your daughter?

Em. Ah, no, sir! I never knew my mother. She died when I was born—

Fern. Poor child!

Em. But if this dear Rosalia were only my mother!

Ag. (*aside*) As she probably is!

Em. I should have nothing to ask in this world, with such a father as mine—so good, so loving—

Fern. Then you are Palmieri's daughter—the daughter of my old friend and playfellow?

Ros. Your friend?

Ag. aside. She seems not to like it!

Em. Ah, you know my father? You love him? Is he not an angel?

Ag. aside. With that smell of sulphur about him!

Fern. Yes, Arrigo Palmieri is one of those rare men whom God creates now and then for the relief of their suffering fellow-men. He deserved a reward here upon earth, and I see that he has received it. I remember very well that he had a child—

Ag. What did I tell you, Don Fernando? A child born in this very place. But greatly changed in growing up, particularly in the eyes which turned from black to blue—at least according to what her nurse says, and as I know from experience, nurses are not apt to be mistaken.

Ros. What are you talking about, Agatha?

Ag. Nothing, nothing. I only say what I have heard said a hundred times.

Ros. Be careful of your stories. At present we have had enough of them, and I think you had better go about your work—

Ag. Do you order me? You are not master here?

Ros. There is but one master here.

Ag. Oh, indeed!

Em. Wicked Agatha! You are always quarreling! What nonsense is that you have been talking about blue eyes and black? If the Lord made my eyes, he can change them. And I can't bear to see you so spiteful with my dear Rosalia, who has always been like a mother to me, and whom I love like a mother.

Ag. Ay, ay!

Em. Go away! I don't love you any more.

Ag. (*going*) Very well, I will go. (*Aside*) What airs these children of sinful love take on!

Fern.(*looking after her*) What hags these old bigots are!

Ros. (*aside*) I must bear it!

Fern. Tell me of your family, Signora Rosalia—

Ros. (*motioning him to be silent*) Emma[,] I wish to speak with this gentleman. Wouldn't you like to run down into the garden yourself?

Emma. Yes, indeed. I will get the flowers ready for papa before he comes back. Good-bye, Rosalia! Good-day, Don Fernando!

Fern. Good bye, my pretty angel! (*Emma exit.*) The little one could have remained perfectly well. I was merely going to ask you about yourself since we last met.

Ros. The child knows nothing of my history, and it has been so full of misery that my answers to your questions would have wrung her tender heart—for the poor thing

[The editorial interpolations that follow are based on other English translations of *La morte civile*. In a part of WDH's translation that has been lost, Rosalia explains that after she separated from her husband, she was saved from utter destitution by the physician Palmieri. She adds that although Don Gioacchino, Fernando's uncle, has spread slander about her, she lives quite innocently in the doctor's home. Don Gioacchino urges Palmieri to send Rosalia back to her husband for the sake of her reputation, but Palmieri refuses as Act I ends.

Act II opens as Don Gioacchino, at his country estate, resolves to rid the neighborhood of Rosalia, if necessary by finding her husband. At this point Gaetano announces that a stranger has appeared at the estate.]

and if I hear aught again, I shall know better than to repeat it. But I thought I had better tell your worship that an unknown man, whom I had never seen before, has got into the court of the chateau, perhaps through the chapel—

Don G. At this hour? Hast thou not questioned him?

Gaet. Yes, though to tell your worship the truth, that strange figure crouching in the dusk[,] at the base of one [of] the pillars, didn't inspire me with a great deal of confidence at first. But at the sound of my steps, the man sprang to his feet, and stared at me in such dismay that I took courage. I understood[,] from his few broken words, that he was a traveler who had lost his way in our mountains, and that he wished to see your worship; perhaps to ask shelter—

Don G. Shelter we deny to none. But there are still brigands in the mountains—

Gaet. He seemed unarmed, and unless he carried concealed weapons—

Don G. How was he dressed?

Gaet. Very much like our mountaineers. He looked very pale, and he had large eyes and a heavy beard.

Don G. How old, did he seem?

Gaet. Well, as to that—perhaps forty or more. He is a very strange looking creature, in fact. When I had seen him better by the light of the lantern, I could not tell whether his face expressed more fury and hate, or more sorrow and remorse, or all at once. He may be one of the brigands, but in that case he is very ill, for he breathed painfully, and he trembles on his feet,—perhaps from fatigue. If your worship wishes to question him—

Don G. I not only wish to do so, but in virtue of my office, I must. Thou hast not told him who I was?

Gaet. No, indeed!

Don G. So much the better. Bring him in, then, at once. But have some of my people ready so that—

Gaet. Of course, your worship. (*exit.*)

Don G. A brigand. It is scarcely possible. But there is nothing to be afraid of, in any case. I am really anxious to see him, and ask him— But here they come.

Enter Gaetano and Corrado.

Gaet. Here is the master.

Don G. Come forward, my good man. There is nothing to fear. You seem tired. Gaetano, give him a chair.

Cor. (*sitting*) Thanks. Thanks to you too. (To Gaetano.)

Don G. Leave us, Gaetano. (*Aside.*) But watch! (*Exit Gaet. Don G. examines Corrado attentively.*) Gaetano was right: he has a very strange face. Well, speak, my friend. What do you wish to ask of me?

Corrado. Nothing but shelter for the night, and a little rest. I have been walking all day, and the sunset overtook me on the slope of the mountain in sight of your towers. The melancholy sound of a

bell that rang the knell of the dying day woke old memories in my
heart, and I felt a longing to enter the chapel which I saw before
me. The door was open, and I dragged myself in. For the first time
in many years I was able to pray.

Don G. In many years? That was not well. However, if you felt
repentance at last—

Corrado (*suspiciously*) Repentance? Why should I repent? Do
you take me for—

Don G. Nay, do not be alarmed! Trust in me. Whatever you are,
hospitality is sacred.

Cor. So much the better. I ask a night's rest and shelter. Do you
grant it or not?

Don G. Yes, my friend. I see in you a sufferer rather than a
sinner, and you interest me greatly. From your appearance I judge
that you have not always been in the humble condition which your
dress indicates.

Cor. No, I am not one of your mountaineers, unhappily. I was
not rich, but once I exercised a noble art.

Don G. You were—?

Cor. A painter.

Don G. You are a Sicilian?

Cor. Yes.

Don G. Have you a family?

Cor. I had.

Don G. And you are alone, now?

Cor. Alone? Oh, my God, if— Enough[,] sir! I have one hope
still—let me keep it. You examine me like a magistrate. I ask you
for a little rest for my body; but I never granted you the right to rack
my soul! What more does it concern you to know? Come[,] sir: I ask
you for a heap of straw, a crust of bread, and a jug of water, to
quench this fire in my blood. I need nothing more.

Don G. Nay, you shall be treated as your condition requires. I
wish to be of use to you, and if you will permit [me] to inquire
which way you are going—

Cor. Towards Etna—towards Catania.

Don G. If I knew some particulars concerning you, I might—

Cor. Thanks!

Don G. Have you ever been in Catania?

Cor. I was born there.

Don G. Indeed? Then, one question more, and the last. Did you ever know there a young man named Fernando Morrano?

Cor. I think I remember the name. But it was a long time ago. Was he studying law at the university?

Don G. Precisely.

Cor. Yes, we were acquainted; we were friends, even.

Don G. Friends? Then I can serve you in spite of yourself. Don Fernando is my nephew, and is now with me in this very house.

Cor. (*surprised and displeased*) Here? But what matter? I want rest. It is the third time I have asked it. Show me to the kennel, and let me sleep with your dogs.

Don G. Have a little patience; my nephew will be glad to see you. I will call him.

Cor. I will not see him; I will not be questioned further; your examination has been enough, sir.

Don G. Let me use this little violence with you. (*Rings a bell. Enter Gaetano.*) Ask my nephew to come here a moment; tell him that an old friend of his from Catania wishes to see him.

Gaet. (*aside*) An old friend? Then we shall know who he is! (*Exit*)

Cor. Sir, your mercy is cruel! My former position is known to you, you see me in this miserable shape, and yet you wish to put me to shame before a man who knew me in other days! You make me pay dearly for your pity; and as I see that I have stumbled upon an inquisitor, I will go at once. (*He rises painfully*)

Don G. Pray, do not go! If you had not told me you were born at the foot of Etna I should know it from your fiery temperament. Be careful, my friend, for such natures easily fall into error, and often into crime—

Cor. Crime? (*Grows calmer, and rests his arm on the back of the chair.*) Yes, it is true!

Don G. (*aside[,] observing him.*) That quieted him! Ah, perhaps— (*rising*) Well[,] I will leave you with my nephew, whom I hear coming.

Cor. (*with drooping head*) As you will, sir.

Don G. You will feel more confidence with an old friend. (*Aside*) And I shall know whether presentiments are to be trusted. (*exit R.*)

Cor. (*slowly lifting his head*) There are winds that freeze! What shall I say to this man? What will he say to me? Ah, perhaps he can give me some hint— If those two are living yet, I will keep on till I have found them. If they are dead, I shall stir no more forever.

Enter Fernando.

Fern. (*To Gaetano as they enter*) Where is my uncle?

Gaet. He must have gone out so as to leave you alone with this stranger, who says he is an old friend of yours. There he is.

Fern. (*surprised at Corrado's dress.*) He?

Gaet. Exactly. I will retire. If you need me, you can ring.

Fern. A mountaineer[.] (*advances and looks at Corrado*) I don't remember him. Friend, where have we met?

Cor. At Catania.

Fern. Many years ago?

Cor. Yes, many years.

Fern. I have a dim recollection— It seems to me—

Cor. Ah, a truce to this! I am Corrado.

Fern. Corrado? Yes, it is! But it's as if I saw you in a dream— You? How greatly you are changed!

Cor. You are not. You have not suffered.

Fern. It may be. Your dress is somewhat peculiar; and how does it happen—

Cor. By many terrible chances—

Fern. I know— I have heard—

Cor. (*with quick suspicion*) What have you heard?

Fern. Nothing— I know that you have suffered— I should know it from looking at you— (*Aside*) I don't want to make any blunder here. What is he after? We must find out.

Cor. What are you thinking?

Fern. I was thinking how very remarkable it was that I should find you here at my uncle's, to whom I don't think I ever mentioned you—and here at the foot of the Appen[n]ines, in the neighborhood of a place where— But tell me something about yourself! Where have you been all this time? Where have you come from?

Cor. I do not know.

Fern. That is even stranger than your looks. Excuse me. I remember very well that when I left Catania to go to the University of Bologna, you were just married.

Cor. I was.

Fern. And if I remember rightly your wife was good, beautiful—

Cor. Very beautiful!

Fern. Where is she now? Dead—?

Cor. (*quickly*) I hope not!

Fern. You hope? Perhaps you have quarreled—separated—

Cor. Yes, separated.

Fern. And for what reason?

Cor. Horrible!—

[In the next gap in the manu-
script, Fernando informs Corrado that Rosalia lives nearby and in-
troduces Corrado to his uncle as her husband. Corrado explains
that he killed Rosalia's brother Alonzo in a fit of anger. Sentenced
to life in prison, he has escaped after several years' imprisonment
to seek out his wife and child, if possible.]

Fern. And bravely done!

Don G. I can imagine how you must have felt when you found
yourself free.

Cor. No[,] you cannot imagine it. Unless you had been buried
alive for ten years, and counted those years month by month, week
by week, day by day, hour by hour, longing for liberty, friends, air,
sun!—you could not imagine it. I felt well, strong, happy. My brow
was cool, my lungs dilated in the atmosphere sweetened by the
breath of the earth's manifold life! A good peasant of the Abruzzi
gave me these clothes, another a little money, and so I dragged
myself along the Appen[n]ines till I reached your door.

Don G. Heaven has befriended you: it has brought you to your
wife.

Fern. Courage, then; have courage!

Cor. I have had courage. I will have courage. But since you tell
me that my little Ada is not living with her mother in the house of
this physician—

Don G. Your little Ada?— Wait! From what I have understood,
the child must be about eleven years old?

Cor. Yes.

Don G. Very nearly the age of the little girl whom the doctor has
placed in Rosalia's charge. And as Dr. Palmieri's legitimate daughter
died a long time ago—

Fern. What!

Don G. (*going to a writing-desk*). I have here the certificate of
her death, and I have already left a copy with the doctor; so—

Cor. (*with sudden passion.*) Who, then, is the mother of this
child?

Don G. Who knows?

Cor. Speak! What is it you mean?

Don G. How you let that hot southern fancy of yours hurry you away! I am not so ready to imagine evil, and I was merely supposing that your little Ada might be living in this pretended daughter of Palmieri.

Cor. Ada!

Fern. O, the devil! This is impossible!

Don G. Who can say? Among the different constructions which may be put upon the mystery—

Cor. My Ada believes another man her father? Love him?— Then these hell-born dreams of mine—

Fern. Hell-born, you may be sure of it, and devil-inspired now!

Don G. You will have some means of identifying your daughter?

Cor. Ah, me! What means? Did I not tell you she was only a year old when I saw her last?

Don G. That is true! But what means does a father need? The voice of nature—

Cor. Yes, yes, my heart will speak. But what will it tell me after these ten years?

Don G. Then ask Rosalia! The mother will answer for the daughter, the wife for herself.

Cor. For herself?

Don G. You have a right to know—

Cor. A right? I do not know, sir: I can only tell you that I have longed so much, and suffered so much to see my wife again, and now I tremble, and would be glad to escape to my prison!

Don G. But why, my friend?

Cor. I do not know!

Fern. Come, Corrado; you are over-excited, and you are very weak. What you want now is a hearty supper and a good bed.

Don G. And you shall have both, immediately. Say, to-morrow— Take courage; the mercy of the Lord is great.

Cor. But his justice! Which led me here? To-morrow, to-morrow, to-morrow! (*Exit with Fernando.*)

Don G. To-morrow, the lion will have recovered his strength, and then, my good doctor, we will resume the thread of our discourse.

End of Act II.

Act III.

Same Scene as First Act.

Don Gioacchino and Agatha.

Don G. And the doctor is not at home to-day, either?

Ag. No, your worship. This is the usual time for his visits, and he does not get home very promptly, for he plays the philanthropist as well as the physician, you know. So if your worship will consent to wait to-day, too—

Don G. No, I will not. Call me that woman.

Ag. Immediately. And when is this scandal to stop?

Don G. Very soon.

Ag. I hope so! (*exit*)

Don G. The scandal *may* continue, worse than ever. That depends upon Rosalia's answer to me. It is a play that can end, or that can begin over again. We shall see.

Enter Rosalia.

Ros. Your worship has sent for me; but did you wish to speak with me or with Dr. Palmieri[?]

Don G. I talked enough with the doctor yesterday.

Ros. Too much!

Don G. That may be; but don't disturb yourself; I am not going to administer any reproof; your stay in this house is about to cease.

Ros. Yes, I have heard that your worship has had the goodness to charge my benefactor to drive me from his door. I might claim the protection of the law against your persecutions; but I shall not do so. We know each other, and I shall have you in greater anxiety than I shall carry with me. That is enough. I am ready to go.

Don G. You can go, if you please, but you will not go alone.

Ros. And who will go with me?

Don G. Your husband.

Ros. Your worship cares to make a *jest* of me, too?

Don G. Quite the contrary, my dear.

Ros. But you must know where the man who was my husband is now?

Don G. Was? He is and always has been your husband, and in his longing to see you once more, he has broken his chains and prison bars, and since last night he has found shelter under my roof.

Ros. (*Amazed*) Under your roof? Corrado? You are deceiving me! It cannot be!

Don G. Do you think I could deceive you in so serious a matter?

Ros. Corrado here? Escaped, and in hiding at your house?

Don G. You reproach me for my generosity! Do you not know that I have incurred a great risk, which might cost me dear?

Ros. But why has he come? What does he want here?

Don G. His family.

Ros. He has none any longer.

Don G. If you are not jesting I must tell you that I am greatly surprised at your receiving in this manner the news which I so gladly hastened to bring you. Any other wife would have thrown herself on her knees to thank me.

Ros. You are right: any other wife but me!

Don G. Think well of what you are saying.

Ros. And you, sir, think well of what you are doing.

Don G. I have thought of it.

Ros. Then know, before you judge me—

Don G. I know that Corrado had the misfortune to kill your brother, but—

Ros. And after that you dare to say that such a man has a family? That I am his wife? That I should follow him?

Don G. Yes, I say all this. But I fully understand the difficulty of the position in which this poor man, more to be pitied than blamed, finds himself. He returns to the world after ten years of oblivion, and suddenly—too suddenly—comes upon his wife, still young and beautiful, who has consoled herself— So, it is not a pleasant surprise either for him or for her! But patience! It is better to go with any sort of husband than alone.

Ros. No, I would rather go alone.

Don G. You have no choice. You forget the jealous, violent nature of Corrado.

Ros. Will he force me—?

Don G. No, he means to use no harsh measures. But you must not whet the scythe if you fear the sparks. Do not wait for him to come, but go to him: I will lead you to his arms!

Ros. His arms? I?

Don G. Listen. As yet your husband has nothing to fear. No one knows him here, no one will find him under my roof. I have promised to procure him a safe conduct, and in some other land you can still be happy. Do I return good for evil? Be advised by me, and come!

Ros. (*after reflection.*) I cannot!

Don G. (*aside*) So much the better. (*Aloud*) Remember, he will come to you, then. He is not far from here!

Ros. Here? He? No!

Don G. And you will have to answer his questions—he will have many to ask you. For instance[,] you must tell him whose child this mysterious young girl is—and what has become of his little Ada.

Ros. (*alarmed*) Ada?

Don G. Yes. He remembers her, he demands her, he will have her. Well, at any rate I have given you warning. You have a little time yet to prepare yourself for an interview which will certainly be painful, and may assume the shape of judgment and condemnation. Good-morning, madam.

Ros. And what will you say to him meantime?

Don G. That you are impatiently waiting to see him.

Ros. No, no! Tell him not to come! Tell him to respect my helplessness! Tell him to have mercy on me!

Don G. What, goad the lion when I have heard his roar? No, consider, my dear, and prepare to receive him kindly. (*Aside*) The blow cannot fail! (*Exit.*)

Ros. Corrado! See Corrado again? It must be a dream from which I cannot rouse myself! After that horrible night, after so many years—see him once more, speak with him? Now, here! I shall not have the strength, the words will fail me, I shall not dare to look at him! . . . This man was right: he will have many questions to ask that I must answer—and how shall I answer them? Tell him, what shall I tell him of Ada? Nothing? Everything?— Doctor Palmieri is not at home; and I cannot advise with him. If I could escape, or hide myself—but that might be worse. . . . And him, have I the right to shun him, repulse him, deny him the comfort he comes to seek? Did I not love him once? Did I [not] fly with him from my father's house? Ah[,] yes, yes! Our love has borne its fruit of crime! And Corrado is coming now to rob me of everything, to snatch from me . . . (*She sees Emma approaching, and stops in visible agitation.*)

Enter Emma.

Emma. (*noticing her agitation*) Dear Rosalia, what is the matter[?]

Ros. Nothing, dear.

Em. Nothing? Truly? But you seem so sad, and I don't like that. Haven't you a little hug for me? Don't I deserve one?

Ros. (*embracing her.*) You!

Em. Yes, but I want a kiss, too; or else I shall think that I have been naughty. (*Rosalia kisses her*) Why[,] you have drenched me with tears! Look! (*She puts her finger to her face, and shows it to Rosali[a], as if she had gathered a tear upon the point*) What are you crying for? Why do you look at me so sorrowfully? Am I pale? Do I look sick?

Ros. No . . .

Em. But why . . . Oh, and papa has lost his good humor, too, these last two days. He neglects me; he forgets to kiss me when I give him his flowers. He stays away so much, and when he comes home he is so solemn and silent; and he doesn't notice me when I creep up on tiptoe to play a trick on him. What is the matter with him? Is he angry with me? Have I offended him?

Ros. You? Poor child! And how?

Em. Is he afraid of something dreadful happening? Oh, if you know of anything, do tell me!

Ros. Something dreadful? No . . . You love your father dearly, Emma?

Em. I love him more than I can tell. You know that already. Don't you remember when he tried sending me to school at Naples? How long did I stay? Six months! And then he had to come and get me because I couldn't live among strangers, and should have died because I couldn't run into his study every morning, and hug him and kiss him! Why, if girls have to leave their fathers when they get married I shall never marry! I can't understand how a girl can bear to leave her father, and go off with some man she has scarcely seen. What a bad daughter! . . . Why, what is the matter, Rosalia? Why are you frowning so? Have I said something wrong?

Ros. Oh, no, my child!

Em. I like to hear you say that—your child! The word sounds so sweet when you say it! I want to tell you something, and you won't scold me, will you? One night—yes, and several nights—I dreamed that you were really and truly papa's wife, and, of course, my mother. I was sitting between you, and I was tying you together with a string of roses. I was *so* happy! When I woke in the morning, I ran into papa's study— He was alone! I cried in his arms!

Ros. Ah! (*Deeply moved, and unable to speak, she wildly embraces and kisses Emma, then to hide her emotion she runs from the room.*)

Em. She runs away from me; but she kissed me as she never did before. Her lips trembled— Ah, that dream of mine! I've not only dreamed it, I've thought of it so much! Perhaps I've done wrong; perhaps I oughtn't to think of it. It was my fault; but that sad story that I read with such delight affected me so— These two poor young things that married secretly, and no one knew of it; if they could— If it were true— But no, it couldn't be! My mother died when I was born! (*She sits down, and hides her face in her hands.*)
Enter Corrado.

Cor. (*at the door*) Where is she? Refuse to see me? (*He enters impetuously and sees Emma.*) A child? It may be— (*He softly approaches, and as he cannot well see her face, he touches her hand to take it away.*)

Em. (*Starting to her feet she sees Corrado, and shrinks back in alarm.*) A man! Who are you? What do you want? My father?

Cor. (*quickly*) Who is your father?

Em. Doctor Arrigo Palmieri.

Cor. Palmieri? (It is my child!)

Emma. Yes, do you know him?

Cor. I would like to know him.

Em. (*still retreating*) Then—

Cor. (*following her up*) Then—

Em. Oh, don't come so near!

Cor. (*gazing intently at her*) Why?

Em. Because your eyes are like burning coals. Don't look at me! They scorch my face!

Cor. But I must look at you.

Em. Must? (*offers to hide her face again*)

Cor. (beseechingly) Let me look at you! I thought I saw in your face the likeness of my own little girl . . .

Em. Have you a little girl? Then I will not be so much afraid, for a father can never be bad.

Cor. Yes. And I could be good if I had my child!

Em. Have you lost her?

Cor. Yes, but I shall find her if she is in this world. Let me look at you. (*He studies her intently, as if striving to recall something, and says, sadly and bitterly*) I am a fool! What is it that I wish to recall? What is your name?

Em. Emma.

Cor. Emma?

Em. Don't you like my name?

Cor. I would rather you were called Ada.

Em. And why Ada[?]

Cor. Because that is my daughter. Has no one ever mentioned her to you?

Em. No one.

Cor. Not even your mother?

Em. My mother is in heaven.

Cor. And she was this doctor's wife?

Em. Certainly. She died when I was born.

Cor. (*Aside*) A lie! Here comes the horrible suspicion: if my Ada be dead, and the child of Palmieri's wife be dead, whose child is this? Shall I take her to my heart, or shall I— (*He advances threateningly upon her.*)

Em. (terrified) Oh, do not hurt me!

Cor. (*recovering himself.*) No, no, my child; do not be afraid.

Em. But your eyes are burning me again!

Cor. It is not always fire that comes from my eyes. They have their looks of love—and their tears! I like to look at you. You are so fair and sweet, that looking on you, I seem to grow young and pure and calm— Oh, look at me!

Em. Oh, dear! When you are gentle with me it frightens me more than when you are angry.

Cor. (*impetuously*) Frightened? Always frightened! (*More gently*) Didn't you say that a father could never be wicked? I will call you Ada, and you shall call me father— I will be your father. (*approaching*)

Em. (*retiring*) You my father?

Cor. (*furiously*) Woe to you if I am not your father!

Em. Mercy! O help, some one, help!

Enter Rosalia.

Ros. (*frightened by Emma's cry, and without having seen Corrado.*) What is it, Emma? (*She sees him, and after a moment's observation, recognizes him with a cry of surprise and terror; then as if struck speechless she locks Emma in her arms, and so pushes her out through the open door, and remains on the threshold, motionless, with downcast head.*)

Cor. (*profoundly agitated at Rosalia's appearance, nervous from the shock, and after having in vain awaited a word from his wife, moves towards her.)* Rosalia! (*She hides her face in her hands and slightly turns from him.*) Am I a ghost that I frighten you so much? You should have been prepared for my apparition here when you would not come to me! I cannot understand you. I cannot tell whether the mere sight of me has struck terror to your heart, or whether finding me here with a child whom I believe to be our daughter—

Ros. Ada? You are mad! Did not the child say her name was Emma?

Cor. Aye, she said so!

Ros. That she was the daughter of Dr. Palmieri?

Cor. Aye, she said that, too. Do you repeat it?

Ros. I repeat it.

Cor. So much the worse. For if it is true that this girl is Palmieri's daughter it is no less true that his only legitimate child—his wife's child—died many years ago. Who is the mother of this little one whom you made such haste to remove from your husband's ferocity?

Ros. Who is her mother? I do not know. When I was taken starving into this house, I thought myself excused from asking to see her certificate of baptism. Ask her father!

Cor. Oh, I will ask him! But now I will ask you to answer me another question, and beware of lying! Where is my Ada? What have you done with her?

Ros. What have I done with her? She is dead.

Cor. Ada is dead?

Ros. Yes; the famished, outcast wife of a convict could not nourish her child, and it died of hunger at her breast.

Cor. My Ada? And you coldly announce her death to me? You, to me? Where is the proof of her death?

Ros. Go to Catania and ask it! They will answer you there that a murderer, escaped from prison, has no right to ask any account of his family—that he has forfeited that right.

Cor. I forfeited that right? I? (*With rising agitation.*) Then how have I lived to bear my chain for these ten years? How could I have bowed body and soul to that terrible load, without falling crushed like a beast of burden? Why did I not die under the lash? What kept me alive but the hope of once more taking my wife to my heart, of seeing my child once more? Why did I break and gnaw the bars of my dungeon away? Why, with a price set upon my head, did I drag myself on, through rocks and brambles, with bleeding feet, on limbs wasted by the shackles, breathless, panting? Whither was I going, but to the house where I had left Rosalia, the only woman I had ever loved, my first love, lost so soon? Ah, Rosalia, to see what I have suffered in dragging myself to your knees,—look at me and forgive me! (*Kneels to her.*)

Ros. Forgive the murderer of my—

Cor. (*quickly, as he struggles to rise*) Do not speak the name which since that fatal hour has never ceased to ring in my heart! which has made me shudder, and wail and blaspheme— Not hate, not murder; no, love and jealousy armed my hand—thou knowest it! Alonzo would have taken all from me; I took all from him. It was a reprisal; it was a terrible crime, but terribly have I expiated my crime.

Ros. You believe it? I will not deny it. But is the infamy of your crime effaced by penalties and anguish? It remains ineffaceable, and becomes a heritage on which the innocent must enter. When the sentence of the law is fulfilled, the punishment of society begins, inexorable, perpetual? Because I took your name when it was pure and honored, you cannot, and no one can, force me to wear it when it is stained [with] shame and blood.

Cor. No, Rosalia, no human or divine law demands it. Only, the heart is a merciful and natural law. If the opinion of the world dismays you, we can elude the world. Thou wilt not bear my name? Thou shalt not bear it. I will change it. We will hide ourselves in other lands, far from this—where thou wilt— Take what is thine and come with me.

Ros. And will you change your nature with your name? And shall I forget? Will not two spectres always rise between us?—Yes, that of my mother, too, who died of sorrow? Be just, and let this wretched meeting end. Ah, go!

Cor. Go without you? Leave you in this house? Rosalia, that cannot be. You too must own it. If you fear the dishonor that has fallen on my name, you should fear no less the shame that may fall on yours.

Ros. What do you mean?

Cor. I mean what I have not said before, because I would gladly have deceived myself. If you persist in remaining here, I shall think that I have been a fool to break the stone of my sepulchre; I shall feel that I am indeed a ghost come to surprise your secrets, to trouble your joys, to interrupt your happiness—

Ros. My joys? My happiness?

Cor. I shall believe that this house is fairer and more delightful to you than the house I destroyed, because it shelters your new lover, your new daughter—

Ros. Believe that, then; believe everything! Calumny has followed me in a thousand forms because of you. No one has trusted the virtue, the self-sacrifice of a woman, young, poor, divided from her husband! And now you join these fools, my slanderers. You too fling your handful of mud in my face.

Cor. I would shake it from your garments. In the name of mercy, come with me before I meet this man! Save me! Save him!

Ros. Are you ready for a second crime?

Cor. Who plays with fire? Who puts hand upon the asp? God knows I would not commit a crime, that I would fain risk myself. But my blood will not always obey. (*Desperately.*) Rosalia, come!

Ros. (frightened) Have mercy on me! (*She sees Palmieri at the door, and gives a cry of terror.*) Ah, he!

Enter Palmieri.

Cor. (*at Rosalia's cry turns and sees him.*) He? Is it he? Palmieri[?]

Pal. It is I. Who are you?

Cor. A man come to claim his wife.

Pal. (*astounded*) Corrado!

Cor. Corrado, who will judge you both.

Pal. You shall do it.

End of Act III

[Act IV opens on the same scene as Act III. Fernando interrogates Corrado regarding his meeting with Rosalia.]

Cor. Whose child?

Fern. That is just what I wished to know. Did you question her?

Cor. Yes.

Fern. And what was your impression?

Cor. How explain certain impressions? I longed to kiss her, to kill her!

Fern. At the same time?

Cor. Precisely.

Fern. Therefore, darkness visible?

Cor. I am waiting for light from this doctor, who is very long in coming; I am waiting anxiously, feverishly. We are to meet here; that is the reason I have asked you to leave me. I ask you the third time. Do not stay for the fourth!

Fern. I will not stay. But I wish to leave you calmer, to beg you to consider your position which may become still more precarious. I saw some mounted gendarmes going towards my uncle's house—

Cor. To arrest me? So much the better! When one has no longer anything to live for, would not one do well to die?

Fern. Oh come, my friend! Die! That is such a frightful conundrum! But remember in any case that you have not the right to punish, much less to avenge.

Cor. But he doesn't come! Why doesn't the man come?

Fern. He is only too sure to come, and I tremble for the consequences of your meeting. If Arrigo has the generous imprudence to confess— My God, what will you do?

Cor. What will I do? Does the murderous ball know where it shall strike before it leaves the cannon's mouth? Go, go! I wish to think before speaking with this doctor—

Fern. Yes, think, and consider well. Courage, my poor friend! (*presses his hand, and exit.*)

Cor. I have not the right to punish, much less to avenge— He said it as if he had been my judge, and his words did not fall into the void: they cut into my heart, with those of Rosalia. I have no right— I can be just enough to grant it. Rosalia, flung by one to the brink of the abyss, without a guide, weak, alone, might have slipped, fallen— Who can deny it? But there are strong souls, generous hearts, capable of sublime self-sacrifice. The wife of the prisoner who resigns herself to solitude in memory of her love; the woman who comes and crouches under the prison gate, watching her chance to throw the poor convict a crust of white bread—that woman is holy. But Rosalia did not come. I hoped it, but should I have hoped it? No, it was pride, conceit, idiocy. She must have longed for my death; she must have waited for it from day to day as for good news, that would make her free, happy, and— But this doctor does not come! What keeps him so? He is advising with her how he may best cheat me— Woe to them if they confess, woe! (*Sees Palmieri coming.*) Here he comes at last! Now God keep us!

Enter Palmieri.

Pal. I am with you. Excuse me for keeping you; but I had to prepare myself for this interview, I had to consider what I was to say to you.

Cor. So I had imagined.

Pal. The conclusion was easy in my case, for one quickly takes counsel with the uprightness of one's own purpose. But I had to consult another's will.

Cor. Rosalia's?

Pal. Precisely, and I have done so. And our decision, the hopes that we have formed, rest upon one principle: that when a man has committed the gravest errors, he should be willing to repair them even at the cost of his own life.

Cor. Is this your confession?

Pal. I have not finished. I was speaking of you.

Cor. Of me? First of all, show me the certificate of your daughter's birth!

Pal. You ask what is impossible. I have no daughter.

Cor. No daughter? But that little girl—

Pal. That angelic child, who believes herself, and whom all believe to be, Emma, is Ada.

Cor. (*with a cry*) Ada?

Pal. Your daughter.

Cor. Ada living? Here? And I saw her? It was she? (*He trembles.*)

Pal. Ah! You seem weak,—you are trembling—

Cor. Should I not tremble for joy? Sir, there are raptures that kill— But I shall live— I have not lived till now. My pretty Ada!— But why does she believe you are her father? Why does she love you?— No, I do not wish to know. You give her back to me and that is enough. I forgive you the rest; I forgive all to all. Ah let me run and tell her—

Pal. Wait.

Cor. I tell you it is enough.

Pal. But I must know if you are worthy of Ada.

Cor. I have not been; I will be.

Pal. That is what I hoped; that is what we shall see. Calm your spirit; silence your heart, that your mind may clearly understand and weigh all that I shall tell you; for as yet I have told you little. We had better sit down.

Cor. (folding his arms on his breast) Speak.

Pal. I need not explain by what providential means I met

Rosalia. It was some months after your imprisonment. I found her afflicted, crushed, destitute, without friends, without a home, repulsed even by her dying mother, who had fallen heart-broken on the grave of her son. Her misery appealed to my heart, and I believed that it was not by chance that God had brought me to that unhappy creature. I was unhappy, too, for I had lately lost my wife and my little Emma; it would not have been possible for me to feel a guilty passion. Yet I will confess that if Rosalia had been free, I would have given her my name to rehabilitate her. But the poor soul was shackled with your chain! I was anxious from the first about your little Ada, who slightly resembled my Emma, and who grew strangely fonder of me day by day, perhaps because I overwhelmed her with caresses. She was scarcely more than two years old, but I saw from her features, her pallor, and above all from the conformation of her brain, that with her growth she would develop one of these natures, sensitive and essentially nervous, on which the lightest impressions of joy or sorrow fall with force, almost with violence. I was sure that with the passage of time, the knowledge of her situation and the sense of infamy would undermine her health and bring her to an early death. I said to myself, Poor child! When thou comest to the age [of] reason, and askest for thy father, what will thy mother answer thee? what will others tell thee? One shameful, fixed idea will mingle with all thy joys, and all thy afflictions, and darken all thy dreams; and later, at the age of happy illusions, when the virgin soul feels the need of love, who will offer it to thee, who will give his name to the convict's daughter? These reflections led me to think of a remedy. I determined, as far as she was concern[ed], to baffle the inveterate prejudices; and one day I said to Rosalia, 'Good mother, if you will allow it, I will make the world respect this child. If I cannot rehabilitate the mother, I can rehabilitate the daughter, and give her an unspotted name—my own. I will imagine that I have had an evil dream, and in your Ada I will embrace my Emma again: I shall have [an] angel in heaven and a child on earth.'— So it fell out; and now judge me, you!

Cor. Without doubt there was generosity in what you did—the more, if no one rewarded you.

Pal. I expect you to reward me.

Cor. Me?— But I tell you that there is no merit in a good deed if one usurps another's rights in doing it. Sir, that child had a father.

Pal. I could not realize this because of a principle that forbade me to distinguish between a prison and the grave, between the man who dies by a physical law, and the man who dies by a civil law. At any rate, if I usurped a right, I did it for no bad end, and if I committed an error, it was at least a noble and compassionate error.

Cor. Which you will repair at any cost— I appeal to your words.

Pal. My words, I told you, referred solely to your errors, graver far than mine; from *you* reparation is due. Rosalia, who has been and remains your victim, offers you a signal example of fortitude; for you will easily understand that to credit our deception the world must believe my Emma was not dead, and that Rosalia has had to renounce her rights and her happiness as a mother.

Cor. What? Rosalia resigned herself?— But you will see that *I* cannot and will not resign myself.

Palm. You will resign yourself because you must.

Cor. Must?

Pal. And why not? I do not know where you would find the words to tell this child whose frail and delicate constitution has verified all my for[e]bodings—to say to her: Listen, my child, they have cheated thee. The honest man whom thou hast loved and honored with so much ardor is not thy father. I, still stained with the blood of an innocent man, thy uncle; I who show thee these wrists festering from the manacles; I who have borne my penalty for ten years, and have not yet fulfilled it; I who am an escaped convict, and may any day, any hour, be taken and dragged back to my prison, I[,] *I* am thy father! Die of shame and heart-break, what does it matter, so that I have held thee in my arms!

Cor. Oh, in the name of God, forbear!

Pal. I will forbear. But I wished your heart to speak.

Cor. You bade me silence it.

Pal. But now—

Cor. Now that you have rent it in twain you bid it speak.

Pal. Let us end this, then. (*Goes to the right, and beckons to some one within.*)

Cor. What is that?

Pal. You shall see. I have done my duty, you shall do yours. Judge, absolve, punish, as you will. You wish to destroy my work of redemption? The law empowers you to do it, I permit it; I grant you the right to kill your child. Look, there she comes, and it is her poor magnanimous mother who is leading her to judgment. Up, then! Courage! With one word you can pierce two hearts; I will stay to see it done.

Cor. What torture is this!

Enter Rosalia and Emma.

Em. (*runs to Palmieri without noticing Corrado.*) I have found thee at last, thou naughty papa! I could not bear it any longer without seeing thee, when dear Rosalia came to tell me thou wast waiting for me. Well, so much the better. Hast thou a kiss for me?

Pal. I was going to tell thee something— But now I was talking with this man—

Em. (*fearfully noticing Corrado.*) Here yet?

Pal. Does he frighten thee?

Em. Very much. I saw him once before, and Rosalia came just in time to save me from him.

Cor. But I was then— (*Rosalia keeps her eyes fixed on him in the greatest anxiety.*)

Em. What had I done to you? Imagine, papa! He pretended that my name was Ada—

Cor. Because— (*he meets Rosalia's eye and stops.*)

Em. Because your daughter was named

[Rosalia agrees to go away with Corrado, leaving Ada with the doctor as his daughter Emma. However, Don Gioacchino insists that Rosalia has been unfaithful to Corrado, and in effect he withdraws the safe conduct he has promised Corrado.

In Act V, Rosalia admits to Corrado that she and the doctor have fallen in love but resisted the temptation to become lovers, and she offers to leave with him at once. Emma/Ada appears and is reconciled to her father, who tells her that Rosalia is indeed her mother. The stress is too much for Corrado, however, and he falls suddenly and violently ill. On the last page of the play, he blesses Rosalia and the doctor and attempts to kiss Emma/Ada farewell, but he dies as they are about to embrace.]

Index

338

WITHDRAWN

ALBERTSON COLLEGE OF IDAHO

3 5556 0012 8920 6